Queer Bloomsbury

Edited by
Brenda Helt and Madelyn Detloff

EDINBURGH
University Press

Edinburgh University Press is one of the leading university presses in the UK.
We publish academic books and journals in our selected subject areas across the
humanities and social sciences, combining cutting-edge scholarship with high
editorial and production values to produce academic works of lasting importance.
For more information visit our website: www.edinburghuniversitypress.com

© editorial matter and organisation Brenda Helt and Madelyn Detloff, 2016
© the chapters their several authors, 2016

Edinburgh University Press Ltd
The Tun – Holyrood Road, 12(2f) Jackson's Entry, Edinburgh EH8 8PJ

Typeset in Bembo
by R. J. Footring Ltd, Derby, and
printed and bound in Great Britain by
CPI Group (UK) Ltd, Croydon CR0 4YY

A CIP record for this book is available from the British Library

ISBN 978 1 4744 0169 2 (hardback)
ISBN 978 1 4744 0171 5 (webready PDF)
ISBN 978 1 4744 0170 8 (paperback)
ISBN 978 1 4744 0172 2 (epub)

The right of Brenda Helt and Madelyn Detloff to be identified as the editors of this
work has been asserted in accordance with the Copyright, Designs and Patents Act
1988, and the Copyright and Related Rights Regulations 2003 (SI No. 2498).

Published with the support of the Edinburgh University Scholarly Publishing
Initiatives Fund.

Contents

List of Images   v

Acknowledgements   vii

List of Contributors   ix

Introduction   1
   Madelyn Detloff and Brenda Helt

Part One: Ground-Breaking Essays

Introduction to Carolyn Heilbrun's 'The Bloomsbury Group', 1968   15
   Brenda R. Silver

The Bloomsbury Group   23
   Carolyn G. Heilbrun

Bloomsbury Bashing: Homophobia and the Politics of Criticism in the Eighties   36
   Christopher Reed

Camp Sites: Forster and the Biographies of Queer Bloomsbury   64
   George Piggford

Redecorating the International Economy: Keynes, Grant and the Queering of Bretton Woods   89
   Bill Maurer

Passionate Debates on 'Odious Subjects': Bisexuality and Woolf's Opposition to Theories of Androgyny and Sexual Identity   114
   Brenda Helt

Part Two: New Essays

The Bloomsbury Love Triangle   135
  Regina Marler

Duncan Grant and Charleston's Queer Arcadia   152
  Darren Clarke

Nailed: Lytton Strachey's Jesus Camp   172
  Todd Avery

'[T]here were so many things I wanted to do & didn't': The Queer
Potential of Carrington's Life and Art   189
  Gretchen Holbrook Gerzina

Making Sense of Wittgenstein's Bloomsbury and Bloomsbury's
Wittgenstein   210
  Gaile Pohlhaus, Jr and Madelyn Detloff

Deviant Desires and the Queering of Leonard Woolf   223
  Elyse Blankley

Clive Bell, 'a fathead and a voluptuary': Conscientious Objection
and British Masculinity   240
  Mark Hussey

'I didn't know there could be such writing': The Aesthetic Intimacy
of E. M. Forster and T. E. Lawrence   258
  Jodie Medd

Virginia Woolf's Queer Time and Place: Wartime London and a
World Aslant   276
  Kimberly Engdahl Coates

Index   294

Images

Figure 1. Charleston. Courtesy of the Charleston Trust. © Penelope Fewster   154

Figure 2. Duncan Grant, *Bathing*, 1911, oil on canvas, © Tate, London, 2015   161

Figure 3. Duncan Grant, *Bathers by the Pond*, 1920–21, oil on canvas, Pallant House Gallery, Chichester. © 2015 DACS, London   164

Figure 4. Duncan Grant, *Study for The Bathers*, c.1920–21, gouache on paper, courtesy of the Charleston Trust. © 2015 DACS, London   165

Figure 5. Duncan Grant, *Erotic Study*, c.1950, pen and gouache on paper, courtesy of the Charleston Trust. © 2015 DACS, London   168

Figure 6. Carrington, Ralph Partridge, Lytton Strachey, Oliver Strachey, Frances Marshall (later Partridge). Photograph by Lady Ottoline Morrell, 1923. © National Portrait Gallery, London   198

Figure 7. Carrington, *Reclining Nude with Dove in a Mountainous Landscape* (portrait of Henrietta Bingham), c.1924. Private collection   202

Figure 8: Carrington, Drawing of Henrietta Bingham in heels, c.1924. © Devonshire Collection, Chatsworth. Reproduced by permission of Chatsworth Settlement Trustees   203

Figure 9. Carrington, Drawing in undated letter to Poppet John. © Dora Carrington. Reproduced by permission of the Estate of Dora Carrington, c/o Rogers, Coleridge & White Ltd, London. Used with permission of the Harry Ransom Center, University of Texas, Austin   206

Figure 10. Carrington, Drawing in undated letter to Poppet John. © Dora Carrington. Reproduced by permission of the Estate of Dora Carrington, c/o Rogers, Coleridge & White Ltd, London. Used with permission of the Harry Ransom Center, University of Texas, Austin   206

Figure 11. Carrington and Poppet John. Private collection   207

Figure 12. Leonard Raven-Hill, 'A Voluptuary', *Pick-Me-Up* 12.288 (1894): 233   242

Figure 13. Archibald English, 'The Conscientious Objector at the Front!', 1916 postcard   244

Acknowledgements

First and foremost we want to thank our contributors to this volume. Two of them are not academics, so the publication is nothing on their curricula vitae. Many others are now so established in their careers that this publication is for them primarily a labour of love. We believe that writing for *Queer Bloomsbury* was a labour of love for *all* our contributors, and we offer our gratitude and love in return.

We don't know what this collection would have been without the groundbreaking contributions of scholars who did difficult and often thankless work in more fraught times. And so we want to thank Emily Heilbrun, Margaret Heilbrun and Robert Heilbrun for permission to reprint Carolyn Heilbrun's 'The Bloomsbury Group'. For permission to republish Christopher Reed's 'Bloomsbury Bashing', we thank the University of Texas Press, Journals Division. Our thanks also to the University of Chicago Press for permission to reprint George Piggford's 'Camp Sites'. We thank NYU Press for permission to abridge Bill Maurer's 'Redecorating the International Economy'. And we thank *Twentieth-Century Literature* for permission to print an abridged version of Brenda Helt's 'Passionate Debates on "Odious Subjects"', a quite recent work, but one that came out of and addressed fraught times, nonetheless.

We would both like to thank the editorial staff at EUP, especially Jackie Jones, who had faith in this project, as well as Adela Rauchova for her attentiveness to our queries. We also thank Rebecca Mackenzie for support professional and Puckish.

Madelyn would like to acknowledge Gaile Pohlhaus, Jr, for her wisdom and patience throughout the process and, most importantly, Brenda Helt for conceiving of *Queer Bloomsbury* and for lending her prodigious energy and talent to its successful completion.

Brenda would like to thank Madelyn for her expertise, good sense and cool-headedness. Both Mark Hussey and Chris Reed have been staunch supporters of the project since its conception in 2009, and have continued to offer advice, friendship and snarkiness through it all. Bonnie Kime Scott's positive outlook has been a source of strength, as has her friendship and advice in all things collection-editing. Ann Grugel helped me to keep important life-work in perspective and Jermaine Singleton has been the supportive baby-brother-I-chose. Most important has been the constant, unflinching support of Jon Helt – words cannot characterise his role nor express my gratitude.

Contributors

Todd Avery is Associate Professor of English at the University of Massachusetts, Lowell. His publications include *Radio Modernism: Literature, Ethics, and the BBC, 1922–1938* (2006); *Desmond and Molly MacCarthy: Bloomsberries* (2010); (as editor) *Unpublished Works of Lytton Strachey: Early Papers* (2011); and *Saxon Sydney-Turner: The Ghost of Bloomsbury* (2015). His current research explores aspects of Bloomsbury's engagements with religion.

Elyse Blankley is Professor of English and Women's Studies at California State University, Long Beach. She has published essays on Stein, Forster and Renee Vivien and also writes on and reviews contemporary women's fiction. Her current long project is a study of Virginia Woolf and Lytton Strachey.

Darren Clarke is Curator at Charleston. He recently completed an AHRC-sponsored PhD in collaboration with the University of Sussex and the Charleston Trust. He has been involved with the Charleston Trust since 2003 and has lectured extensively on Bell and Grant and Bloomsbury's queer heritage. He has also curated several exhibitions, including 'Fragments: Textile Designs by Duncan Grant and Vanessa Bell' (2009) and 'Naked – Representations of the Body by Duncan Grant and Vanessa Bell' (2011), both for the Charleston Trust. In 2011, he was assistant curator for 'Radical Bloomsbury: The Art of Duncan Grant and Vanessa Bell, 1905-1925', at Brighton Museum.

Kimberly Engdahl Coates is Associate Professor of English at Bowling Green State University in Ohio. She has Affiliate Faculty status in Women's, Gender, and Sexuality Studies as well as American Culture Studies. Her work on Virginia Woolf has appeared in *Literature and Medicine*, *Woolf Studies Annual* and in several issues of the *Selected Papers from the International Conference on*

Virginia Woolf. She is currently working on an article on Emily Holmes Coleman's novel *The Shutter of Snow* and a book project titled '*Come See My War*': *Female Bodies and the Politics of Perception*.

Madelyn Detloff is Associate Professor of English and Global and Intercultural Studies at Miami University in Oxford, Ohio. Her publications include *The Value of Woolf* (2016), *The Persistence of Modernism: Loss and Mourning in the 20th Century* (2009), *Virginia Woolf: Art, Education and Internationalism* (co-edited with Diana Royer), and essays on queer theory, modernism, pedagogy, feminist studies, crip theory, and trauma.

Gretchen Holbrook Gerzina is Dean of the Commonwealth Honors College at the University of Massachusetts, Amherst. She was the Kathe Tappe Vernon Professor in Biography at Dartmouth College, where she was the first woman to chair the English Department and the first African American woman to chair an Ivy League English Department. She has published essays on Bloomsbury and art, empire, and race, and is author or editor of seven books: *Carrington: A Life* (1989); *Black England* (1995; US title *Black London*); *Black Victorians/Black Victoriana* (2003); a biography of Frances Hodgson Burnett (2004) and two editions of *The Secret Garden* (2006, 2007); and *Mr. and Mrs. Prince* (2009), the true story of two eighteenth-century former slaves who were among the earliest settlers of Vermont. She has held two NEH fellowships, and was Fulbright Distinguished Scholar to Great Britain, and George Eastman Professor to Oxford in 2009–10.

Carolyn Heilbrun (1926–2003) was the first woman to receive tenure in the English Department at Columbia University, where she taught from 1960 to 1992. She was the author of several academic books and, under the pseudonym Amanda Cross, several bestselling mystery novels. Her academic publications include *The Garnett Family* (1961), *Toward a Recognition of Androgyny* (1973), *Reinventing Womanhood* (1979), *Writing a Woman's Life* (1988), *The Education of a Woman: The Life of Gloria Steinem* (1995), *The Last Gift of Time: Life Beyond Sixty* (1997) and *When Men Were the Only Models We Had: My Teachers Barzun, Fadiman, Trilling* (2002).

Brenda Helt holds a PhD in English and Feminist Studies from the University of Minnesota. She has taught courses in English and Queer Studies at The Ohio State University, the University of Minnesota and Metropolitan State University, St Paul, Minnesota. Her recent publications include an award-winning essay on Woolf in *Twentieth-Century Literature* and an essay in *The Cambridge Companion to H.D.* She co-edited (with Madelyn Detloff) a special issue of the *Virginia Woolf Miscellany* titled 'Queering Woolf'. She is now a full-time fine artist in San Diego, where she not only sells her paintings (www.brendahelt.com) but also painted the cover for *Queer Bloomsbury*.

Mark Hussey is Distinguished Professor of English at Pace University in New York. He is general editor of the Harcourt annotated editions of Woolf's works, for which he edited *To the Lighthouse*, and is on the editorial board of the Cambridge University Press edition of Woolf's works, for which he edited *Between the Acts*. Hussey is founding editor of *Woolf Studies Annual* and has written or edited several books and articles on Woolf, including *The Singing of the Real World: The Philosophy of Virginia Woolf's Fiction* (1986), *Virginia Woolf and War: Fiction, Reality and Myth* (1991) and *Virginia Woolf A to Z* (1995). His *Major Authors on CD-ROM: Virginia Woolf* (1996) received a *Choice* Magazine Outstanding Academic Book award. He is coordinator of scholarly content for the NEH-supported Woolfonline.com. His *Modernism's Print Cultures*, co-authored with Faye Hammill, is forthcoming in 2016. He is currently working on a biography of Clive Bell.

Regina Marler has written for the *New York Times Book Review*, *Times Literary Supplement*, *Los Angeles Times*, *San Francisco Chronicle*, *The Advocate*, and elsewhere. She was chosen by the Estate of Vanessa Bell to edit her letters while still in graduate school (*Selected Letters of Vanessa Bell*, 1993). She is also the author of the social history *Bloomsbury Pie: The Making of the Bloomsbury Boom* (1996) and the editor of the collection *Queer Beats* (2004). She recently contributed an essay to *The Cambridge Companion to Bloomsbury* (2014).

Bill Maurer is Dean of Social Sciences and Professor of Anthropology and Law, University of California, Irvine. His work explores the technological infrastructures and social relations of exchange and payment, from cowries to credit cards. He is the author or editor of eight books and numerous other publications on money, alternative economies and the economic imagination.

Jodie Medd is Associate Professor of English at Carleton University in Ottawa, Canada. She is author of *Lesbian Scandal and the Culture of Modernism* (2012) and editor of *The Cambridge Companion to Lesbian Literature* (forthcoming).

George Piggford is Associate Professor of English and Director of the Moreau Honors Program at Stonehill College, Easton, Massachusetts. He is editor of E. M. Forster's *The Feminine Note in Literature* (2001) and co-editor, with Robert K. Martin, of *Queer Forster* (1997). He has published essays on Woolf's *Orlando*, on Forster's *A Passage to India* and on a variety of topics in modern and contemporary literature. Piggford has taught courses on the Bloomsbury Group, the history of gender and sexuality, and critical theory at the University of Montreal, Tufts University and Stonehill College.

Gaile Pohlhaus, Jr is Associate Professor of Philosophy and Affiliate Faculty in Women's, Gender, and Sexuality Studies at Miami University. Her work focuses on the relations between knowledge, agency and social position, as well as the later work of Wittgenstein. She has published in *Hypatia*, *Political Theory*, *Social Epistemology* and *Feminist Epistemology and Philosophy of Science: Power in Knowledge*. She is currently completing her manuscript *Knowing (with) Others*, which develops a social epistemology focusing on the role of intersubjectivity in knowing.

Christopher Reed is Professor of English and Visual Culture at the Pennsylvania State University. His most recent book is the co-authored *If Memory Serves: AIDS, Gay Men, and the Promise of the Queer Past* (2012). His other books include *Art and Homosexuality: A History of Ideas* (2011), *The Chrysanthème Papers: The Pink Notebook of Madame Chrysanthème and Other Documents of French Japonisme* (2010), *Bloomsbury Rooms: Modernism, Subculture, and Domesticity* (2004), *A Roger Fry Reader* (1996) and the anthology *Not at Home: The Suppression of Domesticity in Modern Art and Architecture* (1996). He co-curated (with Nancy E. Green) the travelling exhibition 'A Room of Their Own: The Bloomsbury Artists in American Collections' (2008–10) and co-edited the exhibition catalogue of the same title (published by Cornell University, 2008). *Bachelor Japanists: Japanese Aesthetics and Western Masculinities* is forthcoming from Columbia University Press.

Brenda R. Silver is Mary Brinsmead Wheelock Professor Emerita at Dartmouth College and Adjunct Professor of English at Trinity College Dublin. Her books include *Virginia Woolf Icon* (1999), *Virginia Woolf's Reading Notebooks* (1983) and *Rape and Representation* (1991, edited with Lynn A. Higgins). She has published articles on Woolf, Charlotte Brontë, E. M. Forster, John le Carré, the politics of anger, hypertext, Bloomsbury and psychoanalysis, the digital public sphere, and popular culture in the digital age. She is currently researching an essay on *Between the Acts* and *The Waste Land*.

Dedicated with love to Jon and to Gaile

Introduction

Madelyn Detloff and Brenda Helt

There has been an upsurge in critical and popular attention to the Bloomsbury Group in recent years. However, with a few important exceptions, such as the work of those who write for this volume, that attention has been curiously bifurcated – either focused on the personal lives and artistic and erotic entanglements of a core set of 'Bloomsberries' (Thoby Stephen, Adrian Stephen, Virginia Woolf, Vanessa Bell, Duncan Grant, Roger Fry, Leonard Woolf, Lytton Strachey, Desmond MacCarthy, Clive Bell, Maynard Keynes, E. M. Forster and Saxon Sydney-Turner) or focused on core philosophical and aesthetic principles, following G. E. Moore's theories on the inter-relation of the beautiful and the good, for example, or Roger Fry's promotion of post-impressionist aesthetics (Rosner 3). Even Victoria Rosner's laudable attempt to bring these two perspectives together merely places the two approaches alongside each other.[1]

By distinction, *Queer Bloomsbury* demonstrates the importance of reading the elements of culture routinely relegated to personal life and those routinely elevated to an allegedly higher status – art, politics, philosophy – as more than intertwined, but, rather, inseparable aspects of the same phenomenon. In this way *Queer Bloomsbury* honours not only the Bloomsbury Group's belief that 'the public and private worlds are inseparably connected', but also the fruitfulness of *conviviality* – a term repurposed by Paul Gilroy to describe the 'processes of cohabitation and interaction that have made multiculture an ordinary feature of social life in Britain's urban areas' (Woolf, *Three Guineas* 168; Gilroy 15). Gilroy sees conviviality as a post-imperial phenomenon, one that has the virtue of taking shared space into account and prioritising the importance of *being together* (or more aptly, *being thrown together*) over the ontological condition of being that we more colloquially call 'identity'.

While identity is important, especially as a strategic way of understanding one's position within social hierarchies, as an analytic tool it has the unfortunate side-effect of fixing one's objects of study into relatively static categories or characteristics of *being* at the expense of *becoming*, of co-evolving, or (a phenomenon that has special resonance for the Bloomsbury Group) of *becoming together*. Becoming together captures both the contingency and the generativity of inhabiting space *beside* one another, to invoke Eve Sedgwick's potent theorisation of the power of contiguity. Sedgwick, for example, explains the spatial and tactile insights that are illuminated by theorising what lies 'beside' rather than 'beneath', 'behind' or 'beyond' any given phenomenon:

> *Beside* is an interesting preposition also because there's nothing very dualistic about it; a number of elements may lie alongside one another, though not an infinity of them…. Its interest does not, however, depend on a fantasy of metonymically egalitarian or even pacific relations, as any child knows who's shared a bed with siblings. *Beside* comprises a wide range of desiring, identifying, representing, repelling, paralleling, differentiating, rivaling, leaning, twisting, mimicking, withdrawing, attracting, aggressing, warping, and other relations.
> (*Touching Feeling* 8)

One major premise of *Queer Bloomsbury* is that there is nothing remotely dualistic about Bloomsbury, and therefore we have chosen an editorial approach that elucidates how various elements of Bloomsbury touch each other, inhabit space beside each other and, to evoke Judith Butler's notion of being '*beside ourselves*', transform each other through the boundary-exceeding intensity of 'sexual passion, or emotional grief, or political rage' (20).

Although this volume covers the first half of the twentieth century, when Britain's empire was relatively intact, if gradually corroding, Bloomsbury – an urban geographical location as well as a signifier for a group of people living, thinking and creating together – provides a rich example of how conviviality works to shape and reshape culture. 'Conviviality' – derived from the Latin term describing those who feast together, via the Old French *convivere* (to live together) – resonates with Bloomsbury in a number of registers. Certainly the circle of friends that came to be known as the Bloomsbury Group feasted together (a custom delightfully described in Jans Ondaatje Rolls' culinary history *The Bloomsbury Cookbook*), enjoying in the process life and love, sex and friendship, art and argument together. Many also lived together in intimate, sometimes sexual, and domestic relationships. The intimacy of everyday living (something that is difficult to measure, yet remiss to ignore) produces what geographers Kath Browne, Jason Lim and Gavin Brown describe as the sexualisation of space: 'how, in various ways, everyday spaces are produced through embodied social practices … it is often through these practices that the norms regulating such spaces – and the sexualised relations between bodies, selves and others that constitute these spaces – become enacted' (2). We take from this insight that the 'queer' of Queer Bloomsbury was 'produced through embodied social practice' that was dynamic and generative of new norms that the members of the group took to the other spaces in which they lived and worked (Richmond, Cambridge, Charleston, Rodmell, Dewas, Cassis).

The house at 46 Gordon Square, where Thoby, Vanessa, Virginia and Adrian Stephen moved after the death of their father (their mother having died years earlier), is one site of Bloomsbury conviviality. As several contributors to this volume note, the conversations that took place during the Stephens' 'Thursday Evenings' cultivated an ethos of free and frank discussion of sexual, philosophical and aesthetic matters (Woolf, 'Old Bloomsbury' 194–5). Pushing beyond the boundaries of family as the unit of cohabitation, Adrian and Virginia Stephen, who moved to 38 Brunswick Square in 1911, shared their home with Duncan Grant (who had been their neighbour in Fitzroy Square), Maynard Keynes and Leonard Woolf. This practice of cohabiting with friends was repeated at Charleston Farmhouse, where Grant and Vanessa Bell set up house along with Vanessa and Clive's two sons (Julian and Quentin Bell) and Vanessa and Duncan's daughter, Angelica, as well as (at various times) Clive Bell, David Garnett and Keynes.

Conviviality – living together, feasting together, thinking and debating together, and developing lasting intimate friendships – thus forms a core value of Bloomsbury life and culture. Sexual intimacy between friends of either gender was not only accepted, but understood as a rich source of intellectual, artistic and philosophical affinity among the group. Convivial practices or, more aptly, arts of living are not inconsequential, as many of the essays in this volume attest. The value placed on such arts coincides with the philosophical importance of *doing* (a less fancy way of denoting queer theory's focus on the 'performative') in evaluating what it means to live a good life (both an ethical life and a life worth living).[2] One could say that contemporary philosophical and political theory has returned to the insights cultivated by the Bloomsbury Group, but only if that return is characterised as a recognition of what Queer Bloomsbury has always held out to us when understood holistically, as a way of living sexually, intellectually, artistically, ethically and intimately, rather than in parts – whether those parts are imagined as triangles or, as in recent popular culture depictions of Bloomsbury, squares.

The Peculiar Reception of Bloomsbury

Quentin Bell remarked that 'Success is never, in itself, an endearing quality, and in the 1920s Bloomsbury was unforgivably successful' (85). And so

Bloomsbury had its detractors before it even had a convenient label to which criticism might be appended. Further, so diverse and 'amorphous' were the opinions and the work of its individual members that what Quentin Bell found true in 1968 is still true today – it is still 'possible to criticise Bloomsbury as one pleases so long as one defines it in a convenient way' (Bell 12–13). Indeed, in Britain it no longer seems necessary to define Bloomsbury at all; one might fire at will, the less information offered the better.[3] It is striking (and yes, admittedly irritating) to find that mainstream stereotypes of Bloomsbury as a group of elite and snobbish dilettantes, perceptions shaped by early personally and ideologically motivated detractors such as Queenie and F. R. Leavis, D. H. Lawrence, Ezra Pound and Wyndham Lewis, have had such staying power despite the decades of careful and committed research that has provided ample evidence to the contrary.[4]

The motives of Bloomsbury detractors, however, have come under scrutiny for homophobia, misogyny, misunderstanding of class and social relations, misinformation and anti-intellectualism since the Leavis's 'Scrutineers' penned their vitriolic critiques. In his 1991 'Bloomsbury Bashing' (reprinted in this collection), Christopher Reed brilliantly exposes the role homophobia has played in Bloomsbury detractions from some surprising sources: art critics of Duncan Grant and feminist Virginia Woolf scholars, for example. Mark Hussey has revealed the uses of Bloomsbury bashing for conservative British politicians complicit with 'Thatcher's anti-intellectualism'; in this rhetoric, 'homophobia joins with class hatred to condemn a *tone*; it is the voice of an outraged masculinity that ... fears the feminized man' (25). If anything has changed since the late 1960s, when Heilbrun published her essay on 'The Bloomsbury Group' (reprinted in this collection), or the early 1990s, when Reed coined the term 'Bloomsbury bashing', it is that the more explicit homophobia and fear of male effeminacy betrayed by early critiques of Bloomsbury now manifest themselves within a more generalised erotophobia (apparently it is now socially acceptable to be gay if one is properly coupled off in a state-sanctioned union) and what can be described as a neoliberal valorisation of (repro)productivity. There have always been more ways to constitute networks of support and sustenance than monogamous marriage, as Bloomsbury, H.D. and Bryher's Kenwin, and, more recently, Patti Smith's abiding friendship with Robert Mapplethorpe, among other artistic chosen families, attest.

The 'elitist dilettantes' label still often applied to Bloomsbury in Britain implies that the Bloomsbury Group members were wealthy (they were all middle class) and not properly productive. This labelling says more about the ideological assumptions of the group's detractors than the group itself, however, as the artistic, intellectual, political and aesthetic labour of the group, whose work ethic was prodigious to a person, often served as a critique of the more blatant excesses of commodity capitalism. Now, a century or so after the Bloomsbury Group coalesced, when citizens of neoliberal states are being persuaded to think of themselves as 'self-investing human capital' in the words of Wendy Brown, Bloomsbury's emphasis on small-scale 'making', as opposed to large-scale production, is a stark reminder that 'making' (*poiesis* in Ancient Greek) entails more than making money (48). Making is creative. It involves working together to create a good life (in the ethical and aesthetic meanings of the word), a beautiful life, a philosophically 'happy' life.[5] It is no small wonder, then, that conservatives and Thatcherites fostered disdain for the group.

Bloomsbury's Queer Legacy

The very phrase 'queer Bloomsbury' is in its way redundant, implying that there could somehow be a neutral or 'unqueer' Bloomsbury. We think such a separation impossible. But, does the term 'queer' still have cultural currency in the twenty-first century, when marriage equality and, to a lesser extent, trans rights are garnering mainstream attention and, by and large, social acceptance? Dennis Allen, in a contribution ('The Queer Debt Crisis') to an essay cluster titled, aptly, 'How Queer Is Now?', suggests that 'queer' may have lost its practical usefulness in a historical moment when (according to Allen) 'the LGBT community itself has largely abandoned both this [queer] identity and this practice, focusing instead on recognition by the dominant culture, including, pre-eminently, an insistence on the right to "marriage equality", a concept that would have been anathema to any self-respecting 1990s queer' (106). While the uptake of the term 'queer' as an identity marker (synonymous with Lesbian, Gay, Bisexual and, to a lesser extent, Trans identity categories) in the 1990s does present a paradox if one presumes that the meaning of 'queer' in 'queer theory' or 'queer studies' or, more to our purposes, 'Queer Bloomsbury' derives from that colloquial usage of 'queer' as an umbrella identity category. This apparent paradox dissolves if we turn the equation around and derive 'queer' from Bloomsbury, or at least the 'wide range of desiring, identifying, representing, repelling, paralleling, differentiating, rivalling, leaning, twisting, mimicking, withdrawing, attracting, aggressing, [and] warping' (to quote Sedgwick, above), that Bloomsbury made possible. That is, Bloomsbury's habits of intimate, sensual, artistic and philosophical conviviality intentionally resist the heteronormative 'logic of cultural intelligibility' that underpins western neoliberal ideals for social and familial organisation.[6]

Contributors to this volume neither shrink from nor capitalise on sexual details, but are primarily interested in how group members' queer perspectives enabled their thinking and the products of that thinking. For example, although Lytton Strachey's sado-masochistic crucifixion fantasy is of interest to Todd Avery, it is so within the context of the atheist Strachey's ruminations on religion and its relevance to queer politics. What we know, or think we know, about other Bloomsbury members' sexual practices is complicated by how very little we know about how other people in general conduct their sexual lives. That is, we may know that X and Y (or X, Y and Z) are lovers, but rarely do we find that X and Y (or Z) have left documentary or physical evidence of what, exactly, they did together when they were together. There has been much speculation about Virginia and Leonard Woolf's sex life, for instance, but they did not leave clear statements or evidence to support those speculations. To belabour the obvious, one rarely divulges to one's nephew (or sister, or other family members) the exact details of how one touches one's lover, where, with what body parts, what intensity and duration, et cetera. Moreover, we are all different, as Sedgwick noted (also restating the obvious), and an act that to one person may be exquisitely sexual to another may be utterly unremarkable, and to yet another may be unbearably unpleasant (*Epistemology* 25–6). What matters to us – the editors of and contributors to *Queer Bloomsbury* – more than the generally unknowable details, is that Bloomsbury carved out a space where its members' differences were not forced into a single, heteronormative mould, but could proliferate, grow, evolve, and thus contribute to the intellectual creativity that marked and enabled their extraordinary lives and careers.

What we do know about the members of the Bloomsbury Group is that they arranged their intimate lives and kinship networks in ways that reinforced their ethical commitments. These commitments have garnered new appreciation from thinkers and artists across a range of disciplines represented here, from Art History, Cultural Anthropology, Literary Studies, Cultural Studies, Biography, Women's, Gender and Sexuality Studies, Philosophy, and the Fine Arts. We shall let these approaches speak for themselves in this volume, but in general we see the resurgence of scholarly interest in Bloomsbury to be consonant with the expansion of interdisciplinary approaches to culture. To consider Bloomsbury as an interdisciplinary field – inhabited by artists, authors, philosophers, economists, political activists, art critics, journalists and biographers – enriches our understanding of early twentieth-century cultures in ways that single-author or single-artist studies (as important as they are) cannot do.

The Design of *Queer Bloomsbury*

This book brings together previously published paradigm-shifting essays which had become hard to find with new essays written specifically for this volume by Bloomsbury scholars. Our aim is to make these essays easier to access, but also to underscore the ways the new work draws on the older work.[7] As teachers, we both found that our students (not to mention our colleagues) had a difficult time procuring carefully researched scholarship on queer (as opposed to gay or lesbian) Bloomsbury. We repeatedly felt ourselves wishing for a single volume drawing together important early essays (the ones we most often forwarded to colleagues and students) with exciting new work that builds from this foundation to produce an even more capacious and subtle understanding of Bloomsbury's contributions to culture.

And so we begin with the essay Bloomsbury scholars generally cite as foundational and ground-breaking: Carolyn Heilbrun's 1968 'The Bloomsbury Group', republished here in its entirety, and with a new introduction to that essay by Brenda Silver. Heilbrun argues that the 'profound hostility' directed at Bloomsbury stemmed from discomfort with members of the Bloomsbury Group's acceptance of – even delight in – homosexuality and disruption of normative expectations for masculine and feminine behaviour. *Queer Bloomsbury* begins with this essay not only to honour Heilbrun's important contributions to later scholars' understanding of Bloomsbury, but because it validates sexual dissidence as an important source of Bloomsbury's creative and intellectual energy and ethos. For several decades, until the 1991 publication of Christopher Reed's 'Bloomsbury Bashing', critical work on Bloomsbury largely ignored (at best) or deprecated what we might now call Bloomsbury's queer sensibility. For this reason, Heilbrun's essay should be regarded as an even more courageous and ground-breaking assessment of the importance of sexual dissidence to the group's conceptualisation. Brenda Silver draws on her personal experience in her introduction to Heilbrun's essay to clarify not only the importance of the essay to early Bloomsbury scholars, but that of Carolyn Heilbrun herself to other women and feminist scholars throughout her career.

The second full-length essay in the book is that mentioned above, Christopher Reed's 'Bloomsbury Bashing: Homophobia and the Politics of Criticism in the Eighties', republished here in its entirety and with a new introduction by Reed for this collection. Written twenty-three years after Heilbrun's essay, Reed's essay explored the way citations of homosexuality were used by critics of divergent ideological stripes in strikingly similar ways. Neo-conservative, Marxist and feminist critics, united in little else, were similar in using homosexuality to totalise the meaning of Bloomsbury as the manifestation of what they were against. Homosexuality, in these arguments, signified, respectively, left-wing degeneracy, bourgeois privilege and patriarchal power. The essay makes sense of this paradox by arguing that, for all these critics, the spectre of the feminised man served as a powerful image of disorder, the ultimate taboo. Totalising Bloomsbury as homosexuality, and homosexuality as male effeminacy, these critics fell into errors of both fact and logic. Many of these errors continue to be replayed in Bloomsbury criticism today, most commonly the citation of the phrase 'the Higher Sodomy' as Bloomsbury's sobriquet for its own ideology (in fact, this was the term they applied mockingly to an older generation of Aesthetes).

In 'Camp Sites: Forster and the Biographies of Queer Bloomsbury' (1997), George Piggford argues that camp style permeated the Stracheyesque biographies of the Bloomsbury Group: Virginia Woolf's *Orlando* and *Flush*, Clive Bell's *Old Friends* and E. M. Forster's early non-fiction sketches and his biographies of Goldsworthy Lowes Dickinson and Marianne Thornton. Though Piggford is most interested here in Forster, whose work is not usually thought of as participating in camp, he shows that the Stracheyesque camp of Bloomsbury biography provides a common quality and arguably queers readers' expectations of modernist literary practices. As with the pervasive irregularity of their sexual practices, such textual play might readily be understood as liberatory and subversive.

Like Piggford's, Bill Maurer's 2002 essay (in an abridged version) shows how the ideas of one member of the Bloomsbury Group influenced the work of another. This particular essay is extraordinary, however, because the intellectual cross-pollination occurred between two very different careers, from fine art into economics. It might also surprise some to find that the renowned economist John Maynard Keynes adapted for his economic theories ideas that originated with his intimate and sexual partner of six years and his lifetime friend, the artist Duncan Grant. Maurer provides what many will find fascinating: the precise details that substantiate his claim.

Brenda Helt's 2010 essay (abridged here) shows that Woolf neither understood herself as lesbian nor promoted the concept of androgyny – two axioms of feminist, modernist, Bloomsbury and Woolf scholarship that have become unquestionable. Helt argues that Woolf's reasons for disputing both were conceptually consistent, and consistently Woolfian and Bloomsburian – they were what we today would term 'queer reasons'. Far from arguing that Woolf did not have sex with women, Helt argues that Virginia and Vita Sackville-West's mutual attraction was partly due to their enjoyment of 'passionate debate' – and they did not agree about sexual and gender typing: the lesbian, the sapphist, the invert, the androgyne or androgynous genius.

Queer Bloomsbury's section of new essays begins with two queer historical essays. First, Regina Marler's essay 'The Bloomsbury Triangle', which one might characterise as a romp through Bloomsbury's triangulated and quadrangulated, mutable yet enduring relationships. For those not already conversant with the ins and outs and in-agains of Bloomsbury relationships, Marler provides a fun and irreverent but also historically well-informed summary. At base, however, Marler's point is that Bloomsbury's approach to intimate and sexual relationships privileged friendship and honesty above all else, and so their relationships proved remarkably resilient. Next, Charleston curator Darren Clarke offers a queer historical and biographical essay – one enriched with images of rough studies not previously published, together with two fairly well-known masterpieces. Clarke focuses on the ways Duncan Grant used his art and design aesthetic to create a queer Eden or queer Arcadia at Charleston. Like Marler's, Clarke's essay is approachable for the non-expert at the same time that it offers new insights (and images) even for highly specialised art historians.

Todd Avery's essay on Lytton Strachey might seem hair-raising to some, as it draws on information fairly recently exposed regarding Strachey's sado-masochistic fantasies played out with his lover Roger Senhouse. However, what Avery shows is that Strachey was far more, and far more seriously, interested in religion and spirituality than is commonly thought. Though his interest was secular, it appears to have been a prime interest in his life and career, and one he, being Strachey, most definitely queered.

Gretchen Holbrook Gerzina draws on new work on Henrietta Bingham and new archival research of her own to add biographical and psychological elements of Carrington's love of women (as well as her hatred of her own female body) to her earlier work published in *Carrington: A Life*. Several previously unpublished drawings and a painting make of this essay a nicely illustrated biographical primer for all things queer Carrington.

Another figure who is 'Bloomsbury' by association is treated by Gaile Pohlhaus, Jr and Madelyn Detloff, who bring a philosophical outlier into Bloomsbury's scope. Ludwig Wittgenstein, who influenced Keynes and had an ambivalent relationship with the 'Apostles' of Cambridge, shares more affinities with Bloomsbury ethics and ethos than may have been previously acknowledged.

Both Elyse Blankley and Mark Hussey describe the critically queer attitudes of the two most prominent 'straight' men in the group. Blankley explores how Leonard Woolf incorporated the group's queer attitudes into his early thinking about gendered relations and Britain's anti-Semitism in *The Wise Virgins*. Mark Hussey shows how Clive Bell's conscientious objector politics were upheld by a critical attitude towards the national construction of a heteronormative masculinity used to promote war and military service before and during World War I.

Jodie Medd brings to our attention the epistolary eroticism between T. E. Lawrence and Forster, highlighting the potential intimacy and eros of textual exchange, something also characteristic of Virginia Woolf's relationships with a number of female friends.

We end with Kimberley Engdahl Coates on Woolf, arguably the anchor of Bloomsbury literary thought. Coates draws on theories of queer phenomenology proposed by Judith Halberstam and Sara Ahmed to explore not only how Woolf depicts war as queering London, but also what new narratives and alternative relations to time and space are opened up by the 'queer' angles from which Woolf's characters in her war novels ask us to see London, effectively providing a queered political analysis of wartime London worthy of new scholarly attention.

∆ ∆ ∆

The conviviality and friendship so important to the Bloomsbury Group is in some ways matched by the group of scholars who have written for *Queer Bloomsbury*, as it is a work conceptualised, edited and written by friends – friends working to make sense together. Doing this scholarship has not always been easy for most of us, but we have been supported by each other and by what seems sometimes almost a religious belief that the Bloomsbury Group *qua* group really had the right idea, in short. The right idea was a leftist idea, of course, and a queer idea. What we hope is that this is only the beginning of a conversation about the ways critically queer attitudes prevalent in the Bloomsbury Group a century ago are now being understood by modernist scholarship generally, as well as by left-thinking folks generally, as central and formative. We also hope our readers will find these essays as brilliant and as much fun as we the editors have found them.

Notes

1. See Rosner, Introduction.
2. On the notion of 'liveable' lives, see Butler 4–8.
3. Bloomsbury bashing remains great sport in the UK, as evidenced by media responses to the 2015 BBC2 television series *Life in Squares*, primarily focused (sometimes accurately, sometimes not) on Vanessa Bell's life at Charleston. See, for example, Ellen E. Jones' review in *The Independent* (27 July 2015), '*Life in Squares*, BBC2 – TV review: Self-indulgent and over-sexed, the Bloomsbury set were hard to take seriously'. See also Christopher Stevens on the website of the *Daily Mail*, 27 July 2015: 'Clever and romantic? No, these foppish failures were just awful: Christopher Stevens reviews last night's TV'. Stevens opines: '*Life In Squares* conveyed the impression that these upper-class Edwardian rebels were destined to change the world, rather than remain a pack of self-indulgent failures' (n. pag.).
4. On the role of the Leavises in forming and propagating Bloomsbury bashing

trends in Britain, see Hussey 14–15; on the role of Lewis and his champions (including, infamously, Hugh Kenner) as well as of Leavis and his students, see Silver 154–6 and Marler 9–14.

5. For more on Woolf's philosophy of making happiness, see Detloff, *The Value of Woolf* chapter 1.
6. For a fuller description of the Butlerian concept of the 'logic of cultural intelligibility', see Detloff, 'Woolf and Lesbian Culture' (346–7).
7. Where authors of new essays and introductions written for *Queer Bloomsbury* quote the original ground-breaking essays, in order to facilitate accessibility, the parenthetical citations refer to the identical passage in the essay reprinted here in *Queer Bloomsbury*.

Works Cited

Allen, Dennis, Judith Roof and Alanna Beroiza. 'The Queer Debt Crisis'. *Journal of the Midwest Modern Language Association* 46.2 (2013): 99–110.

Bell, Quentin. *Bloomsbury*. 1968. New ed. London: Weidenfeld and Nicolson, 1986.

Brown, Wendy. *Undoing the Demos: Neoliberalism's Stealth Revolution*. New York: Zone, 2015.

Browne, Kath, Jason Lim and Gavin Brown. 'Introduction'. *Geographies of Sexualities: Theory, Practices and Politics*. Burlington: Ashgate, 2012.

Butler, Judith. *Undoing Gender*. New York: Routledge, 2004.

Detloff, Madelyn. 'Woolf and Lesbian Culture: Queering Woolf Queering'. *Virginia Woolf in Context*. Ed. Bryony Randall and Jane Goldman. New York: Cambridge University Press, 2012. 342–52.

—. *The Value of Woolf*. New York: Cambridge University Press, 2016.

Gilroy, Paul. *Postcolonial Melancholia*. New York: Columbia University Press, 2004.

Hussey, Mark. 'Mrs. Thatcher and Mrs. Woolf'. *Modern Fiction Studies* 50.1 (2004): 8–30.

Marler, Regina. *Bloomsbury Pie: The Making of the Bloomsbury Boom*. New York: Holt, 1997.

Reed, Christopher. 'Bloomsbury Bashing: Homophobia and the Politics of Criticism in the Eighties'. *Genders* 11 (1991): 58–80. Rpt. in *Queer Bloomsbury*. Ed. Brenda Helt and Madelyn Detloff. Edinburgh: Edinburgh University Press, 2016. 36–63.

Rolls, Jans Ondaatje. *The Bloomsbury Cookbook*. New York: Thames and Hudson, 2014.

Rosner, Victoria. 'Introduction'. *The Cambridge Companion to Bloomsbury*. Cambridge: Cambridge University Press, 2014. 1–15.

Sedgwick, Eve Kosofsky. *Epistemology of the Closet*. Berkeley: University of California Press, 1990.

—. *Touching Feeling: Affect, Pedagogy, Performativity*. Durham: Duke University Press, 2003.

Silver, Brenda R. *Virginia Woolf Icon*. Chicago: University of Chicago Press, 1999.

Woolf, Virginia. 'Old Bloomsbury'. *Moments of Being*. Ed. Jeanne Schulkind. 2nd ed. San Diego: Harcourt, 1985. 179–201.
—. *Three Guineas*. 1938. Ed. Jane Marcus. New York: Harcourt, 2006.

Part One: Ground-Breaking Essays

Introduction to Carolyn Heilbrun's 'The Bloomsbury Group', 1968

Brenda R. Silver

'A key figure in the Bloomsbury revival'; 'Carol created Bloomsbury' (Pollitt; Grigoriadis). These comments, found in articles marking Carolyn Heilbrun's death in 2003, affirm what those of us who lived through the days when Bloomsbury was not considered serious or seriously know well: Heilbrun's immense influence in establishing it as a legitimate field of study, one that valued the work as much as the lives and recognised the significance of both to the contemporary world. Heilbrun herself would probably have demurred at the second comment, noting, as she does in the 1968 essay reprinted here, her debt to Michael Holroyd's 'recent monumental biography of Lytton Strachey' and the debates it had evoked (35n1). Nevertheless, her willingness to take risks when it came to championing Bloomsbury cannot be overstated. This is true whether her topic was Bloomsbury as a group, the individuals who comprised it, their rebellious defiance of sexual and intellectual conventions and taboos, or those scholars who in 1968 were just beginning to write about them. Nor can her contributions be separated from her acute awareness that she wrote as a woman in a scholarly world where women were just beginning to be accepted as colleagues. This awareness of gender deeply informs her emphasis on what she famously termed Bloomsbury's androgyny: their rejection of 'the Victorian stereotypes of masculine and feminine in favour of an androgynous ideal' in which, 'for the first time, masculinity was infused, actually merged, with femininity' (25). Heilbrun, to borrow the title of one of her books, may have wanted to 'reinvent womanhood', but she wanted to reinvent manhood and gender roles as well, imagining a world where the gender of the scholar or the subject did not prevent anyone from participating fully and equally in the intellectual and academic realms.

Risk is the term that jumped out at me while reading descriptions of Heilbrun by those who worked with her during the years that she taught at

Columbia University, mentored students and faculty, and started the organisations that made Bloomsbury, Virginia Woolf, and women's and gender studies legitimate fields of enquiry: the risks she took; the risks she encouraged her students to take. To some extent both her interest in Bloomsbury and her distinct perspective on it are apparent in her first book, *The Garnett Family* (1961). The book charts the lives and work of three generations of what she describes as 'a literary family' and places squarely in the 'intellectual aristocracy' that

> arose in the beginning of the nineteenth century, when members
> of families of intellectual distinction – families like the Darwins,
> the Wedgwoods, the Trevelyans, the Macaulays, the Stephens, the
> Stracheys, to name only a few – began to intermarry and to produce
> outstanding scholars, teachers, artists, and civil servants. (15)

We are already in what is today familiar Bloomsbury territory. The study covers Richard, his son Edward, Edward's son David, and Edward's wife Constance, and this, one might say, is where risk enters the story: Heilbrun's decision to bypass the conventional father–son story by including a long chapter on Constance, not only a brilliant translator of Russian texts but also one of the 'first generation of women that received an education comparable to a man's, and, shaping its life according to its own, rather than society's, or parental, decision, remained in a very real sense in control of its own destiny' (163). Her decision to include Constance, she explained in her book on her male intellectual role models, *When Men Were the Only Models We Had*, seemed only natural to her: 'she simply belonged there, with her group of guys' (2). Heilbrun's biographer Susan Kress reads this assumption as an indication of Heilbrun's nascent feminism and her lifelong concern that women be considered the intellectual equals of men: that work and intellectual fulfilment and independence should be rightfully theirs. Looking back to Heilbrun's earlier essay, 'The Character of Hamlet's Mother', where she had 'championed a mother's right to a life beyond mothering', Kress describes Heilbrun's portrait of Constance as one of respect: respect for her ability 'to combine the roles of mother and successful translator' (65). Constance represented a woman for whom, in Heilbrun's words, 'personal independence was her highest ideal for human life' (*Garnett* 167).

The more specific Bloomsbury connection, and with it questions of gender and sexuality, comes into play in the figure of the third generation of Garnetts, David, or Bunny as he was known. Heilbrun uses him in her 'Introduction' as an exemplum of the intellectual aristocracy: 'David Garnett's second marriage … is a case in point. Angelica Bell Garnett is the daughter of Vanessa Bell, the granddaughter of Leslie Stephen, and the niece of Virginia Woolf' (*Garnett*

15). What she doesn't say is that Bunny had lived with the Bloomsbury pacifists during World War I and had been Duncan Grant's lover. In 1961 there was still no good way to write about Bloomsbury sexuality and, as she knew, even without the homosexuality, '"Bloomsbury"' often 'arouses violent antagonism' (197). Taking her cue from David's own extensive memoirs, *The Golden Echo*, which had begun life as talks given among his Bloomsbury contemporaries in the Memoir Club, she describes it 'as complete and frank a story of his life as is likely to be written. Where reticence has restrained him it must, for many years, restrain others' (196).

But reticence was no longer necessary in 1968 when, post-Holroyd, she published 'The Bloomsbury Group', which begins with an anecdote of a student locating his 'loathing' of the group in part in their 'being, many of them, homosexual' (24). The essay appeared in *Midway: A Magazine of Discovery in the Arts and Sciences*, published by the University of Chicago. *Midway* described itself as a 'journal presenting innovations in thought at the highest level of professional achievement, but published for an audience not limited to the authors' professional colleagues', a 'forum in which the specialist may speak in his own voice to specialists in other areas' (*Midway* n. pag.). In the essay, Heilbrun's voice, explicitly not the generic 'his', was clearly on the side of the 'rebellious youth' who in 1968 were 'so busy casting off the artificial signs of sexual difference' and for whom homosexuality was no longer a taboo subject (23, 27). This is just one way in which, Christopher Reed writes, the essay 'stands as a milestone in American scholarship on Bloomsbury' and was prescient of so much of the subsequent reception (67). For one thing, her opening gambit of reassessing 'Bloomsbury in relation to the social and intellectual ferment of the 1960s', perhaps the 'first' work to do so (67), anticipated a trend that Regina Marler, in her history of Bloomsbury's reception, evokes in tracking the impact of Holroyd's Strachey biography: that one of the 'immediate effects' of the biography 'on the critical and popular perception of Bloomsbury was that it managed to make the Group seem revolutionary again', referencing Heilbrun's 1968 article as an example (93). For another, Heilbrun was not afraid in her reading of Bloomsbury to speak 'as a woman', a stance, she explains in *When Men Were the Only Models We Had*, that would not have been thinkable or feasible earlier in her career. Here, she speaks 'as a woman' to declare her identification with Virginia Woolf, making her, Reed notes, one of the 'first feminist scholars who explicitly acknowledged their identification with Woolf' (67).

And, of course, Heilbrun's essay stands out, becomes prescient, in her declaration that what, perhaps more than anything, defined the Bloomsbury Group was its androgyny. Depicting its 'androgynous ideal', its infusion or merging of masculinity with femininity, as the source of the 'ascendancy of reason which excludes violence but not passion' endemic to the group, she also identifies its 'androgynous nature' as its 'most threatening and most distinguishing characteristic. Their celebration of the feminine principle', she continues, 'is connected with their pacifism, as well as with the particular quality of their individual geniuses and their openness before new concepts of art' (25–6). All of this, she asserts, stands in sharp contrast not only to the excessive masculinity of writers such as 'Kipling, Galsworthy, Wells, and Bennett' – not to mention D. H. Lawrence and his many admirers – but also to the 'age of manliness' currently under attack in the late 1960s (26).

As it turned out, antagonism to the concept, if not to Bloomsbury per se, was not, as one might have expected, limited to men. From the beginning of its currency in the 1960s and 1970s, *androgyny* has provoked arguments that radiated outwards, encompassing broader issues of gender, sexuality, culture, politics, literary criticism and more. When Heilbrun published her 'pioneering feminist text' (Reed 67) *Toward a Recognition of Androgyny* in 1973, which included an expanded version of the 1968 essay, reactions were decidedly mixed. Two reviews in the *New York Times* illustrate this response in the literary press. In one, predictably negative, Anatole Broyard assures us that he is sympathetic to the idea of androgyny and asks, rhetorically, 'haven't quite a few of us been' borrowing from the other sex 'all the while?' But Heilbrun's book, he continues, made him '*less* sympathetic'. Like all women who write on the topic, he declares, she seems unable 'to write without hyperbole on this subject', despite the fact that she's 'no furious militant ... but a Professor of literature at Columbia University'. Nor does he like her critique of contemporary male writers. 'If', he concludes, 'this is the voice of androgyny, I can't see it luring the guys out of the locker room'. Joyce Carol Oates, in the second review, expresses far more admiration for the book's 'frank, passionate plea for us to move "away from sexual polarization"' towards freely chosen roles and behaviour, describing it as 'an interesting, lively, and valuable general introduction to a new way of perceiving our Western cultural tradition'; but she also balks at Heilbrun's critique of male writers such as D. H. Lawrence and expresses her puzzlement that 'Heilbrun totally neglects a number of very important contemporary novelists', male and female alike, 'who would have supported her thesis and who have written near-masterpieces'. This last phrase indicates what ultimately bothers her: that androgyny, and with it the political discussion of novels, isn't what matters; what matters is the art.

Not surprisingly, many of the academic arguments about androgyny have focused on Woolf, whose comments about the writer and androgyny in *A Room of One's Own* constitute a recurring refrain; in this sense Heilbrun's early introduction of the concept radiated outwards into a debate about the term that charts many of the larger conflicts within Woolf criticism and feminist criticism in subsequent years. To get a sense of the scope and nature of these debates, you need only turn to the entry on androgyny in Mark Hussey's *Virginia Woolf A to Z*, which takes up almost three full pages and is the longest entry on a 'term' in the book (3–6).[1] Kress, charting the response to Heilbrun's book, notes that 'Feminists within the academy clearly regarded the topic as an important one', pointing to the conferences and special editions of journals in the year the book was published; but she also notes that many feminists rejected the idea. As the debates about androgyny became 'a debate about who would speak for feminism' and grew more contentious, she continues, Heilbrun's more idealistic imagining of a liberation from gender constraints and her 'nuanced and modulated tones' were pushed to the background (105–6). Heilbrun herself, we know, turned to other topics more directly related to women. Still, in what one of her PhD students, Margaret Vandenburg, describes as an emblematic Heilbrun moment, she came to its defence:

> By the time I completed my dissertation on 'The Androgyny Crisis in Modernism', twenty-three years after Carolyn's publication of *Toward a Recognition of Androgyny*, I was perhaps the only person left in the academy who still believed in the theoretical viability of androgyny. I am not convinced even she still stood behind the thesis of her earlier work. Nevertheless, at my defence, Carolyn deflected an examiner's question as to whether or not this model, along with Cixous's 'other bisexuality', was not outdated, if not outright counterproductive. With characteristic authority, gloriously dismissive in this case, Carolyn said, 'That question is hardly relevant here. The dissertation speaks for itself'.... I have never felt so supported and protected and vindicated in my life, before or since, as though an army of Amazons (with buns) had just vanquished every last hostile force in the field of gender studies. If I were to psychoanalyze the almost embarrassing fact that I continue to believe that the androgynous syzygy dismantles dualistic hierarchies, and still read Jung and Cixous with my students, I might say that I am unwilling to let go of that moment of *jouissance*, when the feminist mentor of us all defended me at my defence. (N. pag.)[2]

Vandenburg made these comments at the 2005 conference at Columbia University, 'Writing a Feminist's Life: Academics and Their Memoirs', held to commemorate and explore Heilbrun's life and work, including her influence on her colleagues, her students and women trying to write honestly about their lives. The conference was sponsored by the Institute for Research on Women and Gender at Columbia, founded by Heilbrun, as several of the speakers noted, in 1987 (Miller and Rosner). Here, we come to yet another way that Heilbrun was instrumental in establishing Bloomsbury studies, Woolf studies and gender studies as legitimate areas of academic research and teaching: her founding role in so many of the societies and institutes where the new scholarship could be shared with colleagues at the highest professional levels. As Joan Ferrante tells the story, the Institute at Columbia

> was created ... with a small endowment. Carol was its first director and had to raise money to do what she wanted with it, but it brought women to the university [in] other departments and created an intellectual community. (N. pag.)

Jean Howard concurs, attributing 'one of the very happiest and most productive aspects of my own life at Columbia' to

> the existence of the Institute ... that Carolyn founded in the mid-1980s. She herself only ran it a year or two, but the crucial step was simply to create it, to make it possible, and leave it for others to use. The Institute has grown and flourished, and it has become a crucial meeting place and site of work.... (N. pag.)

The story of Heilbrun's 'pivotal' role in the formation and success of what became the International Virginia Woolf Society brings together once again Woolf, Bloomsbury, David Garnett, androgyny and Heilbrun's intellectual independence. The story comes from Morris Beja, who, with Madeline Hummel Moore and James Naremore, wrote to Heilbrun in 1975 asking about 'the possibility and desirability of forming a scholarly "foundation" devoted to Virginia Woolf, or perhaps to the Bloomsbury Group in general' (Beja). Heilbrun's reply was not encouraging:

> My first response is that I really could not bear another scholarly group. Is it a sign of age, or the particular point we have reached in the semester, that I feel as the scholarship industry increases, the life of literature somehow fails? Probably this is just a bad month. All of which amounts to this: if I can help, I shall, but the thought of such enterprise does not fill me with enthusiasm. Why does there seem to me something especially ironic about an institution devoted to Bloomsbury, a 'group' of individuals outstanding above all for their intolerance of institutions? Should I, like Virginia Woolf at another occasion, simply say I have nothing to wear? Joyce, on the other hand, obviously dreamed of this sort of attention. (Beja)

Nevertheless, when Beja wrote again in 1976 to ask if Heilbrun would serve as the first President of the Society, adducing as one argument the organisers' desire to have a woman as the first President, in particular 'someone as widely respected as you', who 'would set a tone – and provide an image', Heilbrun agreed. In part, Beja notes, she was amused by his honesty in saying that while Quentin Bell, John Lehmann and Nigel Nicolson supported the idea, David Garnett did not: '"I wrote a book, long ago'", she told him, '"about the Garnett family, which appealed to me precisely because they never had anything to do with societies'". In what Beja describes as her 'elegant and eloquent inaugural speech, she remarked that she had been asked to be the first President because she was "a woman". She then stated, however, that she wasn't a woman: "I'm androgynous"' (Beja).

Heilbrun may not have 'created Bloomsbury', but she did open the door for scholars and general readers to hear the Bloomsbury Group speak in their individual voices, voices that in the latter part of the twentieth century spoke so directly to those just beginning to resist, as Bloomsbury had, the conventions that restricted their work as well as their sexuality. Equally important, her own voice made it possible for those who were not part of the traditional academic scene, who were excluded from the 'we' that constituted the male intellectual world she had entered in the 1950s, to imagine and create a 'we' inclusive of those who spoke in a different voice. In her 'Foreword' to *The Poetics of Gender*, a collection of essays first given as talks at the 1984 conference of that name at Columbia University, Heilbrun addressed this directly. Noting that at the conference 'none felt excluded, all felt stimulated, provoked, enabled. Ours was the right to walk upon the patriarchal lawn', she ends with a challenge that still resonates today. The work of deconstructing the power of pronouns, of transforming them is not yet over, she declares; '"We" must do that' (ix).[3]

Notes

1. For a detailed history of the concept of androgyny in relation to Bloomsbury and Woolf, see Helt.
2. In their 'Introduction' to *Writing a Feminist's Life*, Nancy K. Miller and Victoria Rosner describe the importance of Heilbrun's friendship and mentoring and her influence on their own work; in Rosner's case this included their shared 'passion' for Bloomsbury.
3. For Heilbrun's discussion of Lionel Trilling's 'we', see Heilbrun, *When* 8.

Works Cited

Beja, Morris. 'Carolyn Heilbrun and the Creation of the [International] Virginia Woolf Society'. International Virginia Woolf Society Annual Conference. Senate House, University of London, London. June 2004. Panel presentation.

Broyard, Anatole. 'The Androgynous Ideal'. *New York Times* 24 Mar. 1973: 31. Web. 1 Sept. 2014.
Ferrante, Joan. 'Carol and Columbia'. In Miller and Rosner. Web. 1 Sept. 2014.
Grigoriadis, Vanessa. 'A Death of One's Own'. *New York Magazine* 1 Dec. 2003. Web. 1 Sept. 2014.
Heilbrun, Carolyn G. 'The Bloomsbury Group'. *Midway* 9.2 (1968): 71–85. Rpt. in *Queer Bloomsbury*. Ed. Brenda S. Helt and Madelyn Detloff. Edinburgh: Edinburgh University Press, 2016. 23–35.
—. 'Foreword'. *The Poetics of Gender*. Ed. Nancy K. Miller. New York: Columbia University Press, 1986. vii–ix.
—. *The Garnett Family*. London: Allen, 1961.
—. *When Men Were the Only Models We Had: My Teachers Barzun, Fadiman, Trilling*. Philadelphia: University of Pennsylvania Press, 2002.
Helt, Brenda S. 'Passionate Debates on "Odious Subjects": Bisexuality and Woolf's Opposition to Theories of Androgyny and Sexual Identity'. *Twentieth-Century Literature* 56.2 (2010): 131–62. Abridged and rpt. in *Queer Bloomsbury*. Ed. Brenda S. Helt and Madelyn Detloff. Edinburgh: Edinburgh University Press, 2016. 114–31.
Howard, Jean E. 'Opening Remarks for the Carolyn Heilbrun Conference'. Miller and Rosner. Web. 1 Sept. 2014.
Hussey, Mark. *Virginia Woolf A to Z*. New York: Facts on File, 1995.
Kress, Susan. *Carolyn G. Heilbrun: Feminist in a Tenured Position*. Charlottesville: University of Virginia Press, 1997.
Marler, Regina. *Bloomsbury Pie: The Making of the Bloomsbury Boom*. New York: Holt, 1997.
Midway 9.2 (1968): n. pag.
Miller, Nancy K., and Victoria Rosner, eds. *Writing a Feminist's Life: The Legacy of Carolyn G. Heilbrun*. The Scholar and Feminist Online 4.2 (2006). Web. 1 Sept. 2014.
Oates, Joyce Carol. Rev. of Carolyn G. Heilbrun, *Toward a Recognition of Androgyny* and Nancy Topping Bazin, *Virginia Woolf and the Androgynous Vision*. *New York Times* 15 Apr. 1973: 374. Web. 1 Sept. 2014.
Pollitt, Katha. 'The Lives They Lived; Choosing Death'. *New York Times* 28 Dec. 2003. Web. 1 Sept. 2014.
Reed, Christopher. 'Only Collect: Bloomsbury Art in North America'. *A Room of Their Own: The Bloomsbury Artists in American Collections*. Ed. Nancy E. Green and Christopher Reed. Ithaca: Herbert F. Johnson Museum of Art, Cornell University, 2008. 58–87.
Vandenburg, Margaret. 'The Life of the Author'. Miller and Rosner. Web. 1 Sept. 2014.

Take timelines

The Bloomsbury Group

Carolyn G. Heilbrun

It is tempting to begin by pointing out how like they were, when young, to the rebellious youth of today. 'Is there no possibility', Strachey asked in a speech to the Apostles at Cambridge, 'of a break-up so general and so complete that the entire reorganisation of society would be a necessary sequence? Personally, I welcome every endeavour, conscious or unconscious, to bring about such an end. I welcome thieves, I welcome murderers, above all I welcome anarchists. I prefer anarchy to the Chinese Empire. For out of anarchy good may come, out of the Chinese Empire nothing'.[1]

No longer as young as that, the members of the Bloomsbury Group and men like Bertrand Russell, then closely associated with it, were almost the only people in England to fight against the patriotic butchery of World War I and the nationalistic fervour which accompanied it. Even the usually iconoclastic Wells called the war an affair of honour, not of reason. D. H. Lawrence, who hated the war, nonetheless wrote: 'I am mad with rage myself. I would like to kill a million Germans – two millions'. Meanwhile Strachey, whose long locks and golden pirate earrings had already scandalised several English country towns, went to his trial as a conscientious objector (though bad health quite precluded his serving in even the most desperate army) rigged in an outfit designed to infuriate the self-righteous court and preceded by his brother

---

'The Bloomsbury Group' by Carolyn Heilbrun was first published in *Midway* 9.2 (1968): 71–85. It was originally published without source information for quoted material. Reprinted here in its entirety with the kind permission of the Heilbrun estate. Copyright © 1968 Carolyn Heilbrun.

carrying an air cushion for him to sit upon. As Maynard Keynes was to write years later, 'our beliefs influenced our behaviour, a characteristic of the young which it is easy for the middle-aged to forget'. Through the war Keynes had believed that 'it was for the individual to decide whether the question at issue was worth killing and dying for'.

This sounds quite up to date, yet Bloomsbury nevertheless arouses profound hostility in the young. Considerable animus was expressed to me this past year by a seminar at Columbia to which I lightly exposed the Bloomsbury Group. The spokesman for the general contempt felt by the seminar was a very bright young Englishman who tried heroically to enunciate the reasons for his loathing. Having accused them all of being shrill, arty, escapist, aristocratic and insufficiently talented (was *Mrs. Dalloway*, after all, as great a book as *Ulysses*?) he finally attacked them, with passion, for being, many of them, homosexual. This truly astonished me, for he was at that time engaged in a study of another Englishman, greatly admired by both of us, who is also homosexual. 'That', my student announced, 'is different. He admits it'. Ignoring the fact that he had not 'admitted' it in any document I had read, I pointed to the evidence in Holroyd's biography of Strachey's eagerness to 'admit it'. 'Oh, well', my young Englishman said, 'the truth is I just can't bear them'. I approved the bluntness of this statement and sensed in it an honourable challenge.

Those who have defended Bloomsbury have been members of the group, or friends of its members, and have tried, with a plaintiveness not unmixed with humour, to set the record straight. Quentin Bell's new study of Bloomsbury is certainly the most measured, and successful, example of this. Bloomsbury, Bell has said, was prepared to sacrifice the heroic virtues in order to avoid the heroic vices, among which violence was the chief. They recognised reason as always and unquestionably superior to unleashed violence, but they are notable not because they honoured reason but because they came as near as any group of people has to allowing it sway in their lives.

Holroyd records that Strachey, like his friends, refused to accede any rights or claims to jealousy. This is not easy – it is certainly less easy than the violent expression of jealousy – but it did lead to humane and sophisticated relationships. However irregular their lives by conventional standards – for they believed that where passion is, lovemaking should follow – they held, through the fluctuations of passion, to the sacredness of friendship. If attacks were launched on them by inconstant friends, they outraged their opponents by refusing to fight back. For themselves, they regretted not the attack but the lost friendship. 'How wretched all those quarrels and fatigues are', Strachey wrote. 'Such opportunities for delightful intercourse ruined by sheer absurdities! It is too stupid. "My children, love one another" – didn't Somebody, once upon a time, say that?'

It is ironic that though scorning Christianity as identical with its institutions, the group should carry about them some aura of the Gospels. Commenting on *Principia Ethica*, Keynes said, 'the New Testament is a handbook for politicians compared with the unworldliness of Moore's chapter on "The Ideal"', and he noted, concerning his friends, that 'of beauty, and knowledge, and truth and love, love came a long way first'. It is not altogether clear that Bloomsbury's encompassing definition of love was less holy than that of the churches, but such a statement would have shocked them if anything could. Strachey was amused, during the war, to hear himself echoing, in his pacifism, the words of Jesus. Imagine, he wrote, finding oneself on the same side as that fellow. Never inclined to grapple, as their parents had, with the arduous demands of agnosticism, they shed religion as easily as convention and with as little regret.

The ascendancy of reason which excludes violence but not passion was possible to the Bloomsbury Group, I believe, because within it, perhaps for the first time, masculinity was infused, actually merged, with femininity. I have avoided the word feminism, with its inevitable odour of militancy. Nothing could have been further from the quality I wish to identify as uniquely a part of Bloomsbury, although several of Strachey's sisters were, in fact, militant fighters for women's rights. Rather, Bloomsbury insisted on rejecting the Victorian stereotypes of masculine and feminine in favour of an androgynous ideal. Indeed, the very model of Victorian manhood was Sir Leslie Stephen himself, the father of Bloomsbury's Virginia Woolf and Vanessa Bell. There was as yet no Freudianism to deter Sir Leslie's intrepid masculinity, with its outspoken admiration of the virile and its horror of the effeminate.

Sir Leslie's attitude toward women was one of benevolent despotism, and toward his daughters a despotism, encouraged by self-pity, which was often less than benevolent. From this masculinity the Bloomsbury Group, homosexual or not, were consciously to detach themselves. It is the quality about them, apparently, most difficult of appreciation, at least by Americans in recent times. So broadminded and liberal an imagination as Lionel Trilling's, for example, cannot encompass a world in which the 'sacred' fathers and mothers, manliness and womanliness, are not always and forever absolutely distinguishable. It is perhaps because men like F. R. Leavis and Trilling so admired Lawrence as opposed to Bloomsbury that they were unable to perceive in Lawrence's masculine chauvinism a peculiarly virulent homosexual jealousy which, rather than any confrontation with Bloomsbury ideas, was, as Bell clearly shows, the cause of his violent antagonism toward some members of the group. 'Ottoline', Lawrence said, in a statement typical of him, 'has moved men's imaginations and that's perhaps the most a woman can do'. It would not have occurred to any member of the Bloomsbury Group to make so Victorian a statement.

When one has mentioned the androgynous nature of the group – a factor which must not, of course, be confused with the homosexuality of many of its members – one has, perhaps, identified at once its most threatening and most distinguishing characteristic. Their celebration of the feminine principle is connected with their pacifism, as well as with the particular quality of their individual geniuses and their openness before new concepts of art. It is not possible to examine the Edwardian period without recognising that the new literary forms – created by Joyce and Lawrence and James, as well as by members of the Bloomsbury Group – were in direct opposition to the world of Kipling, Galsworthy, Wells and Bennett, whose views Virginia Woolf identified as unremittingly masculine: 'The emotions with which these books are permeated are to a woman incomprehensible. One blushes ... as if one had been caught eavesdropping at some purely masculine orgy'. There is probably no question but that the wave of hostility toward Virginia Woolf which followed her death had its origin exactly in such an observation. We have been in, and are now perhaps just leaving, an age of manliness.

Have I enunciated a contradiction? The Bloomsbury Group, I have said, extolled reason above violence, finding in the use of reason one of man's ideals. Yet at the same time they eschewed the purely masculine virtues of which, surely, reason is the chief. But while reason is an ideal of masculinity, convention and the violent defence of convention have been, in fact, its practice. Any reader of Strachey's essay on Florence Nightingale, for example, must soon discover that the masculine defenders of the status quo in the Crimean War could scarcely be said, by any standard, to have had reason on their side. Later, Miss Nightingale herself, defending the medical principles she had discovered in the Crimea, did not, when applying them to different climates, have reason on her side either. Reason, in fact, belongs exclusively to neither sex. Strachey saw this when he accused Thomas Arnold of having tried to institutionalise the masculine virtues in the modern public school by placing them fatally beyond the reach of civilised feminine influence.

The young men of Cambridge, friends and students of G. E. Moore, who were the original nucleus of what was to become the Bloomsbury Group, could never in fact have succeeded in forming so liberated a circle had it not been for the two young women, sisters of Thoby Stephen, whom he introduced to his friends. Certainly, without these young women the group would not so successfully have achieved its almost total rejection of conventional sexual taboos. Quentin Bell has said that 'there had never before been a moral adventure of this kind in which women were on a completely equal footing with men'. What is important is not that they had 'equal rights', whatever that phrase can possibly be taken to mean, but that they were considered equally valuable as human beings.

There had been every expectation that Vanessa and Virginia Stephen would live the ordinary lives of two beautiful, well-born young ladies. That they did not do so is only partly attributable to the fact that they were extraordinarily talented, one a genius. It was rather that with their contemporaries, particularly their brothers, they found the possibility of a different life, and that their father, old when they were born, died when they were young enough to achieve a beginning. Many are shocked to read in Virginia Woolf's diary the statement that, had her father lived, his life would have ended hers. Yet it is a simple statement of truth. The two beautiful young ladies did not, in any case, succeed in society, nor did they care for the proper, eligible young men, though every one of their brothers' friends fell in love with them, even those not by nature seekers of the love of women. Vanessa Stephen, with a reputation for sitting up all night talking to young men (which she did) and for attending balls 'improperly' clad (which she did also) has recorded the moment when she was 'cut' by someone she had known well and felt, with enormous relief, that she need never bother with such people again.

Rupert Brooke is an example of a contemporary of the Bloomsbury Group who, going another way, achieved his apotheosis of manliness. 'This mixing of the sexes is all wrong', he enunciated; 'male is male and female is female … manliness is the one hope of the world'. He was to welcome war, to write its slickest patriotic poems, to sneer at 'half-men' and 'all the little emptiness of love'. Hassall's biography sadly demonstrates that, in a real sense, he had ended his life before it ended. But one remembers that when he had asked Virginia Stephen to swim with him, she had doffed her clothes to do so, and was able to report that his legs were *not* bowed, and that when he had asked her for the brightest thing she knew, she had said immediately: sunlight upon a leaf. The young men of Cambridge who did not go on to glorify war had found in the drawing rooms of Gordon Square that, as Duncan Grant has said, 'they could be shocked by the boldness and scepticism of two young women'.

'What a pity one can't now and then change sexes', Lytton Strachey wrote to Clive Bell. Outspokenly homosexual within his own circle and wishing that one could write frankly about English sexual habits as Malinowski had about the sexual life of the Trobriand islanders (but, Strachey knew, one would have to publish it in New Guinea), he feared no diminution of the masculinity he admired by his celebration of feminine virtues, such as the ability to write good letters. Those who honour the Bloomsbury Group are unable to agree with Anthony Burgess, typical of his generation of writers in America and England, who boasts that he is frightened of submitting himself to a woman author and who must castigate Ivy Compton-Burnett as a 'big sexless nemistic force', and George Eliot as a wholly successful 'male impersonator'. Perhaps those under thirty, now so busy casting off the artificial signs of sexual difference, will be less tempted than their elders have been to reassume the Victorian terror of women and pride in heterosexuality.

With the publication of Holroyd's life of Strachey, the fact of English homosexuality can finally be faced up to. In the past it has been made the basis for much nasty comment – for example by a critic in *Scrutiny* who wrote of Strachey that 'incapable of creation in life or in literature, his writings were a substitute for both' but it was rarely a subject for serious discussion. Goronwy Rees, in *Encounter*, has complained of the failure of anyone, up to now, honestly to confront the matter. Certainly the most culpable here is Sir Roy Harrod, whose biography of Keynes, brilliant in many ways, would not have been so widely mentioned as a practice in hagiography had not Harrod not only ignored Keynes's homosexuality but flatly denied, in his preface, that he had withheld anything whatsoever of importance about 'his hero'. (Written earlier, E. M. Forster's *Goldsworthy Lowes Dickinson* does not commit this fault, but then Dickinson did not have a mother living at the time of the biography's publication.) Whether Englishmen are peculiarly homosexual because of the English public school and university system, which isolates young men from women through the years of adolescence and young adulthood, is uncertain, but Noel Annan has suggested this, and Freud himself recognised the contribution of social factors to the development of homosexuality. In fact, many artistic men *are* homosexual, and perhaps we ought to take a hint from Bloomsbury and cease to regard this phenomenon as mysteriously and fundamentally threatening.

If Virginia and Vanessa Stephen tolerated homosexuality in their friends largely because they knew the rigidly masculine world of their father would never have done so, that fact does not bring into question the extraordinary sympathy which existed between the members of the group, of whatever sexual inclination. Leonard Woolf has criticised Holroyd for taking with appalling seriousness all of Strachey's loud, youthful lamentations about love, which were never as serious as Holroyd seems to think. But when, in the second volume, Strachey has found his name and his identity, the shrill dramatisations of homosexual infatuation give way to the moving expressions of love as genuine as it was unconventional. The love between Strachey and Carrington, for example, however 'abnormal', surely triumphs over all but the most bigoted objections to remind us that love, after all, is love, and scarce enough. 'It is only', Forster writes in *Howards End*,

> that people are far more different than is pretended. All over the world men and women are worrying because they cannot develop as they are supposed to develop. Here and there they have the matter out, and it comforts them.... It is part of the battle against sameness.

Difference – eternal differences, planted by God in a single family, so that there will always be colour.

When Julian Bell, the son of Clive and Vanessa, described the environment of his boyhood: 'Leisure without great wealth; people intent to follow mind, feeling and sense where they might lead', it must have been in the awareness of what envy such a description can arouse. 'Orchard trees run wild', he writes, describing Charleston, his family's home and one of the meeting places of Bloomsbury:

> West wind and rain, winters of holding mud,
> Wood fires in blue-bright frost and tingling blood,
> All brought to the sharp senses of a child.

It required money, of course, and Bloomsbury did not underestimate the value of money. But they had far less of it than is generally supposed, and they never cared for money in itself. Holroyd has demonstrated that for Strachey, the money he made from his biographies represented opportunities to share pleasure with his friends. John Lehmann, who himself came from a wealthy home, has described Charleston in the twenties:

> The half-finished canvases of Duncan Grant, or Julian's mother Vanessa, or his brother Quentin piled carelessly in the studios, and the doors and fireplaces of the old farmhouse transformed by decorations of fruit and flowers and opulent nudes by the same hands, the low square tables made of tiles fired in Roger Fry's Omega workshops, and the harmony created all through the house by the free, brightly coloured post-impressionist style one encountered in everything.... [All] seemed to suggest how easily life could be restored to a paradise of the senses if one simply ignored the conventions that still gripped one in the most absurd ways, clinging from a past that had been superseded in the minds of people of clear intelligence and unspoilt imagination.

Charleston, where Clive Bell wrote *Civilization* and Keynes *The Economic Consequences of the Peace*, still strikes one in the same way. I visited the place one afternoon because I wanted to buy a self-portrait of Duncan Grant, and the sense of life being lived rather than endured still clung about it. Can one describe Charleston by saying that it had been created, not copied, and that no thought had been taken of propriety?

Virginia Stephen had been brought up to observe the proprieties: when she set up housekeeping with her brother in Bloomsbury, and Lady Strachey came to call, the dog Hans made a mess on the hearth rug and neither lady mentioned it. Yet soon Virginia was to take part in the now legendary *Dreadnought* Hoax, in which she, her brother and their friends, disguised as Abyssinians, were piped aboard the admiral's flagship. Questions were later asked in Parliament. But fun was always to be made of any institution, new or old, which attracted pomposity. They all had an enormous sense of fun about everything. When Virginia Stephen accepted Leonard Woolf's proposal of marriage, Strachey wrote to a friend: 'She hoped that everyone would be thunderstruck. Duncan alone came up to her expectations – he fell right over on the floor when she told him: and of course really he had been told all about it by Adrian before'. For a short time Strachey was prepared to think of airplanes as exciting: 'As I was returning from my walk in the afternoon', he wrote to a friend,

> an aeroplane was seen to be gyrating round the house, 3 times it circled about us, getting lower and lower every time. Intense excitement! The farm hands, various females, Olive and her mother, all the cats, and myself, rushed towards it.... Finally the machine came down in a field exactly opposite the lodge gates at the end of the avenue. There I found it – a group of rustics lined up at a respectful distance. I took it upon myself to approach – but in a moment perceived that the adventure would end in a fizzle. No divine Icarus met my view. Only a too red and stolid officer together with a too pale and stolid mechanic. They had lost their way. I told them where they were, asked them to tea which they luckily refused, and off they went. It *might* have been so marvellous.

Everything is here of the Bloomsbury manner likely to make F. R. Leavis wake screaming in the night. But how much else is there beneath the mockery, not least of all the prophetic insight into what dreary and deadly paths the planes would carry us. Some years later a future admiral of the fleet invited Lytton to fly with him. Strachey declared that 'he was the wrong *shape* for flying and that his beard presented a hazard that was likely to foul the controls'. Bloomsbury would never do, or not do anything, except from kindness, unless it chose.

Clive Bell and his son Julian happened to enjoy hunting: they hunted. Although Clive Bell was an important art critic as well as a scholar of Latin and Greek, he was, it is said, 'as good company in brushing room and butts as he was in the National Gallery or the Tate'. None of them bothered with proper clothes; as Virginia Woolf said, an intellectual dresses well, or badly, but never correctly. And one of Forster's characters wrote over his wardrobe the motto: 'Mistrust all enterprises that require new clothes'.

Unquestionably, their greatest gift was for conversation, on all the ponderous and frivolous subjects in the world. They remind us of the inevitable conjoining of gaiety amid kindness. The listener was essential to the speaker: 'Don't you feel', Virginia Woolf said after Strachey had died, 'there are things one would like to say and never will say now?' Whether or not it was the influence of G. E. Moore, with his famous: 'What exactly do you mean by that?' or the remarkable degree to which they were all gifted which gives one such a strong sense of conversation as the apotheosis of human communication, certainly they must have believed that what one says is not more important than how one says it. We are convinced, somewhere in the depths of our beings, that cleverness and insincerity are inextricably combined. It is frequently forgotten of the wittiest of epigrammatists, Oscar Wilde, that he was, until his imprisonment, the kindest of men. Bludgeons are infrequently wielded by the frivolous, and conversational wit is not the handmaiden of cruelty. No member of the Bloomsbury Group was ever nasty in public. True, as Strachey wrote of Walpole: 'It is impossible to quarrel with one's friends unless one likes them; and it is impossible to like some people very much without disliking other people a good deal'. But if Strachey himself sulked when bored, Clive Bell, John Russell has told us, was

> ready to talk about anything: and however feebly the ball might be put up, he would always give of his best. 'Yes', he would say after some notorious *mauvaise langue* had been to see him, 'he spoke a good deal of ill of all of us, but I must say I found him very agreeable'.

Virginia Woolf regretted that all criticism of living authors could not be spoken to them 'over wine-glasses and coffee cups late at night, flashed out on the spur of the moment by people passing who have no time to finish their sentences....'

'I do not know', Auden wrote some years ago, 'how Virginia Woolf is thought of by the younger literary generation; I do know that by my own, even in the palmiest days of social consciousness, she was admired and loved much more than she realised'. Auden must now, one supposes, know how Virginia Woolf is considered by a younger generation: has any important writer, a quarter century after his death, ever been the object of so much cruel yet meaningless vituperation? It is almost as though the present world needs, somehow, to protect itself against her charms. It would be neither fruitful nor enlightening to enumerate the many diatribes against her; one can only hope that the recent blundering account of her essays on the front page of the *New York Times Book Review* may be the nadir. I wonder, not why she is so widely disliked – for reputations, like investments, fluctuate – but why there exists so crying a need to flay her in public. Partly, perhaps, because her husband, in deciding to publish those sections of her diary which deal with her writing, inevitably published the passages in which she was most strained; partly because she was, as T. S. Eliot wrote, the centre, not merely of a group

> but of the literary life of London. Her position was due to a concurrence of qualities and circumstances which never happened before, and which I do not think will ever happen again ... with the death of Virginia Woolf, a whole pattern of culture is broken.

Partly it is that uniting, within her works, the feminine and masculine vision, and in portraying, moreover, what Stephen Spender has called her knowledge of 'how it felt to be alone, unique, isolated', she presented a vision of itself which the world is not, at present, prepared to contemplate. Most writers, if they are honest, Auden suggests, will recognise themselves in her remarks: 'When Desmond praises "East Coker" and I am jealous, I walk over the marsh saying I am I'. But how many wish to experience with her what Auden calls 'the Dark Night', when

> reality seemed malignant – the old treadmill of feeling, of going on and on and on, for no reason ... contempt for my lack of intellectual power, reading Wells without understanding...; buying clothes; Rodmell spoilt; all England spoilt; terror at night of things generally wrong in the universe.

This is the side of her which has been thrust at us, and for many it is unbearable, particularly since she does not lay the blame for her despair on governments, or interviewers, or the distortions of public judgements. She accepts the despair as her personal burden, and yet functions, completing her ninth novel before she takes her life.

Yet for those who remember her – and it is the saddest of ironies – the memory is of gaiety. 'What made her', Rose Macaulay asked, 'the most enchanting company in the world?' Those who have loved a suicide are fated to remember what in her was most alive. 'She was herself', Vita Sackville-West said, 'never anybody else at second hand ... the enormous sense of fun she had, the rollicking enjoyment she got out of easy things'. 'I don't feel Bloomsbury', Virginia Woolf once said to a friend, 'do you feel Marylebone?' William Plomer reminds us how unrecluse-like her life had been: Virginia as a young girl, going in a cab to a ball at a great house; Virginia learning Greek with Clara Pater, the sister of Walter; Virginia printing books and tying parcels for the Hogarth Press; Virginia laughing with her nephews; Virginia asking the Nicolson boys about their day ('What happened this morning? Well, after breakfast ... No, no, no. Start at the beginning. What woke you up? The Sun. What sort of sun?' and she would hand back glittering, Nigel Nicolson wrote, what they had imparted so dully); Virginia 'sitting up all night in a Balkan hotel reading the *Christian Science Monitor* to cheat the bugs'; Virginia witnessing a murder under her window in Euboea; 'Virginia continuing to play bowls at Rodmell during the Battle of Britain, with Spitfires and Messerschmitts fighting, swooping and crashing round her'; Virginia writing her extraordinary letters to friends and to other people because they were sick or lonely or disappointed.

'Virginia was a wonderful raconteur', David Garnett writes:

> she saw everyone, herself included, with detachment.... But alas, while I was living at Charleston, I almost deliberately avoided having a friendship with Virginia, for it would have been impossible without confidences and in the home circle she had the reputation as a mischief-maker.... Thus it was only later on that I became on terms of close friendship with Virginia and then our friendship grew steadily until ... my hair was streaked with grey.... By then she had for me long ceased to be a possible mischief-maker and became the very opposite – a woman on whose sympathy and understanding I could rely when I most needed support.

A reputation for mischief-making, however, is more adhesive than a reputation for friendship. Clive Bell, to suggest her vivacity, remembered

> spending some dark, uneasy, winter days during the first war in the depth of the country with Lytton Strachey. After lunch, as we watched the rain pour down and premature darkness roll up, he said, in his searching personal way, 'Loves apart, whom would you most like to see coming up the drive?' I hesitated a moment, and he supplied the answer: 'Virginia, of course'.

Certainly there hang over her memory vague questions about her sexuality. It is impossible to pin them down. There have been widely scattered intimations similar to Holroyd's, who, giving no source, speaks of her as 'shying hysterically away from sexual intercourse'. Lytton Strachey remarked of *To the Lighthouse* that 'she rules out copulation', an interesting statement about a novel of which the heroine has eight children. Whatever the truth – and the world takes as swift revenge on childless married women as on spinsters – it was perhaps inevitable that her reaction against the aggressive masculinity of the Victorian world should be interpreted as a fear of manhood. Mrs Leavis sneered at her for having no cradle to rock. But one may choose to remember that when Freud, who had greatly admired the works of Lytton Strachey, met Virginia Woolf he presented her with a flower. I have always thought it an act of gallantry and wisdom.

As a woman, I know that Virginia Woolf has uniquely presented some part of the female sensibility: its pain, its impotent awareness, its struggle to be free of the littleness of life, its deep distrust of political parties and the state. She understood creation: Auden mentions a passage in *The Waves* as the best description of the creative process he knows. Stuart Hampshire has explained why her work has been smothered by 'nervous polemics. Her elegant play with language seems to have aroused a sense of social grievance among critics, because her tone and style were taken to be a return to the genteel tradition of *belles lettres.*' Still, Hampshire reminds us, she contributed on one occasion to the *Daily Worker.*

'But', my English student said to me, 'she was mad'. True. I pointed to Trilling's brilliant essay on the madness of the artist in which he declares that, while we may all be ill, the artist alone finds health in the work he completes. Her style, like that of all Bloomsbury, was never to be in a hurry. She took seven years to finish her first novel, which none of her friends thought an extraordinary length of time, and she never wrote more than three hours a day. Yet she completed seventeen books, and essays and stories enough for six posthumous ones, and, it must not be forgotten, cooked dinners ('And now with some pleasure I find that it's seven; and must cook dinner. Haddock and sausage meat.'), set type, talked to friends, travelled, walked with a dog over the downs and by the river.

What astonishes one most about the whole group, perhaps, is how much they accomplished. They had become friends before any of them had done more than learn brilliantly to talk to one another. Yet Keynes became the outstanding economist of his age and ours. Roger Fry and Bell, in their artistic theories, particularly that of significant form, had a profound effect, and also introduced the postimpressionists to an outraged England. The Hogarth Press, under Woolf's direction, became one of the most impressive of publishing houses; Lytton Strachey changed forever the possibilities of biographical art. Forster, if not, as Spender has called him, the greatest novelist of his generation, is certainly one of the most important. Leonard Woolf was a writer, editor and active socialist. Vanessa Bell and Duncan Grant were impressive portraitists, as a visit to the Tate will testify, and they were able still, in the thirties, to shock the bourgeoisie, specifically, as Stansky and Abrahams explain, 'the directors of the Cunard Line, who commissioned Grant to decorate a room on the *Queen Mary* and then having seen the work, decided nervously that it would not do'. Finally, of course, there is Virginia Woolf, a novelist of genius each of whose works was a new experiment in the technique of fiction. Strachey might have been thinking of the Bloomsbury Group when he praised the salon of Julie de Lespinasse:

> If one were privileged to go there often, one found there what one found nowhere else – a sense of freedom and intimacy which was the outcome of real equality, a real understanding, a real friendship such as have existed, before or since, in few societies indeed.

But surely neither the members of that salon, nor of any other, produced so much work, or so greatly transformed the culture of their country, or represented, along the spectrum of intellectual interests, so wide a range.

A word must be said about G. E. Moore, the Cambridge philosopher, whose *Principia Ethica* has mistakenly been credited with providing the entire ethos of Bloomsbury. J. K. Johnstone's book, the only one so far devoted to the group, was written, necessarily, with too little information available; suspecting ritual, Johnstone sought the dogma to explain it. Quentin Bell's new book indicates that, in fact, the group, while admiring Moore's work, used it as justification for its own already held convictions; Keynes's memoir, carefully read, can be seen to admit that the *Principia* provided an expost philosophical justification for immoralism, in Gide's meaning of the word.

What is of more immediate interest about Moore is the sort of man he was: brilliant, gentle, generous of heart and virtuous. His influence on English philosophic thought was, as C. D. Broad has said, out of all proportion to his comparatively small literary output. It was by his discussions, his conversations, mainly with students, that his influence was felt. He never lectured but that he held a discussion class, and a point raised there, Braithwaite tells us, would make him revise in his next lecture what he had previously said. He never took a sabbatical leave, and anyone interested in knowing what Moore was thinking could always find him at Cambridge. His lectures were never the same from year to year, which left him little time for publication, and his most brilliant thoughts were kept for conversation with his pupils. Is there, today, a comment to be made? Except to say, with Péguy, that 'a great philosophy isn't one against which there is nothing to say, but one which has said something'.

The men and women of Bloomsbury were extraordinarily accomplished both in their individual lives and works and in the life of love and friendship they shared. As Brenan said of Strachey, they were 'almost indecently lacking in ordinariness', but they did not wish to persuade the world to share their eccentricities, nor to respond other than good-humouredly to its sneers. They were civilised even if, as Virginia Woolf remarked of Clive Bell's book on that subject, civilisation turns out to be a lunch party at 50 Gordon Square. Civilisation is capable of worse things, and usually achieves them.

Note

1. Here, as at other points in this essay, I have made use of Michael Holroyd's recent monumental biography of Lytton Strachey.

Bloomsbury Bashing: Homophobia and the Politics of Criticism in the Eighties

Christopher Reed

'Bloomsbury Bashing' Revisited

When 'Bloomsbury Bashing' appeared in 1991, I joked that it was all the mean footnotes from my dissertation strung together. It certainly registers the anger of an ACT-UP-generation graduate student confronting homophobic elders authorised by academic titles and scholarly publications. Now that I enjoy such authorisation myself, perhaps I should repudiate my youthful excesses. Instead, I find myself nostalgic for a moment when calling out the prejudices of academic authorities could be imagined to engender social change.

I use the term *engender* purposefully here, because feminism was central to that era's nexus of activism and academia, as reflected in the title of the journal (*Genders*) that published 'Bloomsbury Bashing'. I came to Bloomsbury through feminism generally and more specifically through Carolyn Heilbrun's feminist revaluation of androgyny. My boyfriend at that time (husband at this time) was Heilbrun's student, and the first person, male or female, to petition to substitute Virginia Woolf for Chaucer, Milton or Shakespeare in the 'major author' portion of Columbia University's doctoral comprehensive exams in English. Eager to participate in this gate-crashing enterprise, I set out to read Woolf's novels, and started with *Orlando*. My delight in its gender-bending wit – my first exposure to the Bloomsbury aesthetic I later dubbed the 'Amusing Style' (*Bloomsbury Rooms* 236–77) – collided with the contempt for Woolf and her Bloomsbury colleagues I discovered in scholarship that supposedly celebrated transgression, aesthetic and/or political. I found it particularly 'unnerving' – the essay's term – that

---

'Bloomsbury Bashing: Homophobia and the Politics of Criticism in the Eighties' by Christopher Reed was first published in *Genders* 11 (Fall 1991): 58–80. Reprinted here in its entirety with the kind permission of the University of Texas Press, Journals Division. Copyright © 1991 by the University of Texas Press. All rights reserved.

well-received feminist criticism indulged in gay-bashing rhetoric, including clichés of 'homosexual conspiracy' and the Nazis' 'homosexual brotherhood'. 'Bloomsbury Bashing' sought to reclaim Woolf and Bloomsbury for the register of radicalism in which I initially encountered them.[1]

We now call that register *queer*.

Had I written 'Bloomsbury Bashing' just a little later, I might have combined the term reanimated by Queer Nation (founded in 1990) with the locution of Mike Myers' 'Coffee Talk' drag persona Linda Richman (premiered on *Saturday Night Live* in 1991) in order to challenge common allusions to the 'open homosexuality' of the Bloomsbury Group with this thought experiment: *The 'open homosexuality' of Bloomsbury was neither open nor homosexuality. Discuss.* That discussion would include arguments since made by others, including contributors to this volume, that Bloomsbury's fluid and performative ideas of sex and sexuality exemplified the queer ideals being advanced to contest the 'gay' and 'lesbian' identities that, despite their political activation, retained the essentialist assumptions of 'homosexuality'. It would also challenge still-current assumptions about the nature and value of 'openness', asking what we think we know when we assign sexual-identity rubrics and how identity might derive from discretion.

'The society of buggers has many advantages – if you are a woman' (Woolf, *Moments* 194). Woolf's memoir emphasises that it was reticence about sex that first attracted her to the group. In welcome contrast to the unrelenting articulation of heterosexuality in conventional chatter about fashions, dances, romances and marriages, the young men she met in Bloomsbury discussed philosophical abstractions. At the time, Woolf says, 'It never struck me that the abstractness, the simplicity which had been so great a relief after Hyde Park Gate were largely due to the fact that the majority of the young men who came there were not attracted by young women' (194). When the reserve that meant 'it never occurred to me that there were buggers even now in the Stephens' sitting room at Gordon Square' (194) ended, the resulting openness was not about homosexuality. In the famous anecdote in which 'all barriers of reticence and reserve went down', Lytton Strachey 'pointed his finger at a stain on Vanessa's white dress' and asked the one-word question, '"Semen?" Can one really say it? I thought. And we burst out laughing' (195). If, following this episode, 'the word bugger was never far from our lips' (196), it was not because 'homosexuality' was open, but because, as Michael Warner says, 'in those circles where queerness has been most cultivated, the ground rule is that one does not pretend to be *above* the indignity of sex' (35). Buggery took its place among other deviations from married, monogamous, heteronormativity in Bloomsbury.

To acknowledge the equalising queerness of sex, moreover, can authorise discretion. The hilarity provoked by Strachey's question forestalled any imperative to answer. The disruptive power of laughter de-authorised the dynamics of confessing subject and masterful interrogator that still characterise discussions of sexuality.

Woolf's memoir of Bloomsbury's origins in queer discretion relates to the context of its articulation at a meeting of the 'Memoir Club', a venue in which the group's members shared reminiscences. Here Woolf's memoir openly invoked homosexuality for a closed audience, reinforcing a group identity rooted in its members' shared discretion at a time when publicly identifying living men as 'buggers' would have invited criminal prosecution. Her pledge of allegiance to Bloomsbury takes its place with E. M. Forster's battle-cry for discretion: 'If I had to choose between betraying my country and betraying my friend, I hope I should have the guts to betray my country' (68).

In this context, invocations to openness were invitations to bashers, whether on the streets or in scholarly journals. This was plenty painful at the time, and I remain dismayed, if no longer unnerved, by Jane Marcus's published response to my criticism of Bloomsbury bashing: 'We plead guilty to the charge. But please, sir, we only did it to defend Virginia Woolf from the trivialization her fiction and her ideas suffered under that name [Bloomsbury].... And anyway it was fun' ('A Tale' 12). Leaving aside the entertainment value of exploiting homophobia to buttress what Marcus here characterised as 'a convenient lie' imagined to benefit Woolf's reputation (12), it may be that these performances of pride and prejudice had some upsides, for they revealed what was most radical about Bloomsbury: its determination to live out – with all the connotations of openness 'out' implies – an ideal, not of homosexuality, but of friendship.

As early as 1964, Leonard Woolf countered the tendencies to use 'Bloomsbury' as a term of abuse with the explanation, 'We were and always remained primarily and fundamentally a group of friends' (qtd. in Williams, 'Bloomsbury Fraction' 149). In a brilliant essay exposing how Woolf's phrasing obscured the class privileges that fostered these friendships, Raymond Williams – always fair-minded – acknowledged that one of Bloomsbury's significant contributions to the middle-class culture it sprang from was a pioneering openness to the intellectual and creative ambitions of its female members. Circling back from his acknowledgement to Leonard Woolf's words, we might recognise a challenge to sex/gender norms in the term 'friendship'. He does not say 'friends and relations'. He does not cite the bonds of marriage, though for most readers these would bolster his authority to speak from and for Bloomsbury. He reaches for the gender-neutral, egalitarian, volitional bond, unsanctioned by the church or state, signified with the term *friends*.

Interviewed by a gay magazine in 1981, Michel Foucault challenged assumptions that gay sex or gay identity were in themselves counter-hegemonic:

> two young men meeting in the street, seducing each other with a look, grabbing each other's asses and getting each other off in a quarter of an hour. There you have a kind of neat image of homosexuality without any possibility of generating unease, and for two reasons: it responds to a reassuring canon of beauty, and it cancels everything that is troubling in affection, tenderness, friendship, fidelity, camaraderie, and companionship, things that our rather sanitized society can't allow a place for without fearing the formation of new alliances and the tying together of unforeseen lines of force. (136)

Rather than centring on sex, Foucault, in this interview titled 'Friendship as a Way of Life', focused on a catalogue of productively 'troubling' forms of affinity homosexuality might create beyond 'the form of the couple', if, instead of 'trying to discover in oneself the truth of one's sex', we 'use one's sexuality henceforth to arrive at a multiplicity of relationships' (135–6). Compared to Bloomsbury, however, Foucault's ideal of being '"naked" among men, outside of institutional relations, family, profession, and obligatory camaraderie' (136), seems limited in both its exclusive homosociality and its investment in escaping, rather than re-imagining structures of family and profession. Bloomsbury's men and women together challenged – we might say *queered* – those structures, creating unconventional living units and professional relationships at a time when the risks, including prison and losing one's livelihood or one's children, were substantial.

In a longer essay on 'Bloomsbury as Queer Subculture', I note that though Bloomsbury's experiments in coupling and collaboration were not always in all ways successful, no one who felt slighted ever 'sought adjudication in the courts or vindication by public opinion' (77). This enraged the bashers. I still laugh at Gertrude Himmelfarb's fury at Bloomsbury's 'deliberate suppression' of 'sexual proclivities' so that 'even so perceptive and psychoanalytic-minded a critic as Lionel Trilling was able to write a full-length study of Forster in 1943 without realizing that he was a homosexual' (42). You have to wonder if Trilling was less perceptive or more discreet than she imagined. Himmelfarb's outraged point, however, is that discretion prevailed against temptations to normativity among those in Bloomsbury and its periphery.

Bloomsbury's discretion endured until the invocations to openness of the 1960s. The bashing that followed registered the radicalism of Bloomsbury's challenge to norms of masculinity, and to structures of authority that coerce confession and render judgement on non-normative modes of identity and affiliation. That some politicians today pride themselves on what they call their 'evolution' on gay marriage does not render these structures less prevalent or pernicious. In an era of assimilation to social norms, when 'friend' is reduced to a Facebook status, the most useful legacy of Bloomsbury's queerness may be the group's use of friendship to create a community that enabled, protected and took pleasure in forms of affiliation, erotic and otherwise, they imagined for themselves.

Δ   Δ   Δ

When Duncan Grant died in 1978 at the age of ninety-three, he could not have known that his reputation, along with those of the other artists and critics of the Bloomsbury Group, was on the brink of a remarkable revival. Paintings that were then valued in the hundreds of pounds are now selling for tens of thousands. Charleston Farmhouse, where Grant lived with Vanessa Bell, has been restored and opened as a museum. And the books and exhibition catalogues on Bloomsbury art that appeared in the 1980s would fill a long shelf – not to mention the prodigious proportions of the coffee table that would be needed to hold the glossy art magazines that tell and retell the familiar stories of the exhibitions, decorative arts workshops, country homes and domestic dramas of the Bloomsbury artists. This upsurge of interest in Bloomsbury has proceeded, however, amid a volley of attacks on the group, attacks that are surprisingly vehement and personal, given that their targets live solely in the pages of history. The anger Bloomsbury arouses today suggests that the group continues to stand for something that threatens established beliefs. Yet an overview of the attacks on the group provides no consensus about what that something is. As early as 1968, Quentin Bell noticed that the group 'has been criticized from a bewilderingly large number of points of view' (*Bloomsbury* 10).[2] The past decade saw little change in this situation, as Bloomsbury's name was deployed to signify everything from the English landed gentry to the hippy counterculture, and from free-wheeling sexual liberation to the most oppressive phallocentric conspiracy. This essay sees Bloomsbury's apparently schizophrenic position in modern culture as, in fact, a consistent enforcement of patriarchal prohibitions that – with varying degrees of self-consciousness – determine a wide spectrum of critical practices.

The mutually exclusive nature of the attacks on Bloomsbury suggests a general failure to come to grips with the group in any kind of historical specificity, so that its name can be invoked as a sign for almost any social category the critic finds disagreeable. The vagueness in current perception of Bloomsbury arises, no doubt, in part from the breadth of the group's activities, which ranged from aesthetics to economics, and from the most public of political campaigns to the most private of sexual revolutions. Robert Skidelsky has observed that Bloomsbury was the last intellectual movement to sustain itself in England outside of the university system (248), and its disregard for the boundaries of academic disciplines contributes to the imprecision with which modern commentators, trained within those limits, use the group's name.

Even within the realm of the visual arts, however, Bloomsbury's relationship to contemporary culture is complicated enough to stymie facile analysis. On the one hand, the critical entrepreneurship of Clive Bell and Roger Fry was undeniably central to the promotion and comprehension of modern art throughout the English-speaking world. On the other hand, the group's own aesthetic endeavours have been dismissed from the canons of high modernism, a judgement still heard from journalists untouched by current scholarship. William Feaver's recent repetition of this standard view simply ignores recent scholarship in order to conclude that Bloomsbury's painting was trivial, Virginia Woolf merely a 'dilute James Joyce' and the whole group 'ultimately, a prolonged disappointment' (182).

An overview of the past decade's writing on Bloomsbury, however, finds more behind the attacks on the group than ignorance or the parroting of received ideas. The widely varying assessments of Bloomsbury's cultural position offer a salutary reminder of the power of ideology to inflect history. At the same time, the consistency with which writers at both the radical and reactionary ends of the critical spectrum cast Bloomsbury as the antihero in their tales of modernism suggests that the differences between the academic right and left are contained within a broader ideology. Consistently behind – or metaphorised within – the varieties of intellectual charges made against Bloomsbury is the group's transgression of patriarchy's ultimate prohibition: the feminised man. So primary is this taboo (consider the number of men who wear skirts as opposed to women who wear pants), it can be used to signify virtually any deviance from any critical norm, whether Marxist, neo-Victorian or even feminist. Bloomsbury's subversion of gender prescriptions allows (or provokes?) critics of all ideological stripes to make the group stand for the dangerous 'other' against which their ideological norms are defined. 'Gay-bashing' or 'fag-bashing' is the term law enforcement officials use to describe how gangs of youths, enforcing the rough machismo of the streets, attack men they perceive as effeminate. Bloomsbury suffers an analogous kind of bashing at the hands of academics in the name of any number of critical orthodoxies.

Before analysing the common strategies uniting Bloomsbury's otherwise divergent antagonists, however, it will be useful to outline the phenomenon of the group's renascence, as the differences shaping Bloomsbury's revival in England and America have had an important influence in determining the different critical response on both sides of the Atlantic. Bloomsbury, having few structural connections to the United States beyond Fry's brief tenure as a curator at the Metropolitan, was never the powerful cultural presence there that it was in England. Although important trends in American culture, from Roosevelt's economic policies to Clement Greenberg's aesthetics, descend from Bloomsbury's writers, their influence was felt at some remove and divorced from the identity of the group. Bloomsbury as a group did not emerge as a cultural force in America until the 1960s, when the nascent feminist movement recognised in Virginia Woolf's writings some of its most pressing concerns. Women across the academic spectrum remember Woolf's posthumously published *A Writer's Diary* as a personal and intellectual inspiration. Carolyn Heilbrun's *Toward a Recognition of Androgyny*, first published in 1973, tied Woolf to a broad feminist vision and drew attention to the intellectual community from which she emerged. Today in America, Woolf is without doubt the best-known and most widely studied of Bloomsbury's members, and it is largely in relation to her that the painters and critics of the group have re-emerged into critical currency. By 1980, when an appeal was launched to save Charleston, the farmhouse the Bloomsbury artists lived in and decorated, American donors contributed most of the necessary funds – 97 and 95 per cent of donations in two recent years for which figures are available – from a financially contributing membership made up of more than twice as many women as men.[3]

In England the rise in Bloomsbury's fortunes was less dramatic, less dependent on Woolf, and hence less restricted to literary studies. As a native daughter, Woolf never sank to the level of neglect she experienced abroad; neither does her work seem now to be as widely studied in English universities as it is in America. Meanwhile, other figures in and around Bloomsbury remained active cultural agents into the 1950s. Leonard Woolf continued to publish new political writings, there was a retrospective of Duncan Grant's paintings at the Tate in 1959, and the names of Roger Fry and Clive Bell remained in England much more a part of established art-historical discourse than was the case in America, where the formalism they invented was subsumed into the criticism of the New York school. In England, therefore, the burst of interest in Bloomsbury in this decade, especially as it has been often connected to the appeal to refurbish Charleston Farmhouse and provide financially for its incorporation into the National Trust, seemed to many to smack of old-guard values and the stately-homes-of-Britain set. Waldemar Januszczak, art critic of England's national leftist newspaper the *Guardian*, consistently condemned exhibitions of Bloomsbury art as deviating from the properly industrial aesthetic of modernism epitomised by the Bauhaus. The elitist overtones of Clive Bell's social tracts, which are virtually unknown in America, led Simon Watney to split off Bloomsbury's art, which he treats sympathetically in his *English Post-Impressionism*, from Bell's 'aesthetic eugenics', which, he says, have been instrumental to the 'contemporary recuperation of "Bloomsbury" as a cultural idyll for a middle class which can no longer admit more frankly aristocratic social fantasies' (*English* 3; 'Connoisseur' 69).[4]

The drive to link Bloomsbury with a reactionary social vision is nowhere more apparent than in Charles Harrison's *English Art and Modernism*, which for American readers presents the most sustained leftist critique of the group. Harrison applies a Marxist model of class conflict to present the history of modernism as a competition between 'two significant and contrasting interests' (13). One camp, represented by Ruskin and Morris, Harrison describes as concerned 'for the social function of art', while the other, epitomised by Whistler, represents 'the contrasting point of view that art should be valued in terms of a set of culturally autonomous interests' (13–14). The unwarranted triumph of Whistler over Ruskin – not so much in their legal battle as in the verdict of history, which despite 'the real value of Ruskin's case … has tended to represent [Whistler] as a martyr in the cause of modernism' – Harrison sees as presaging the subsequent triumph of Bloomsbury's formalism over social realism, which becomes a sign of the bourgeoisie's domination of the working class (14).

Harrison's self-proclaimed allegiance to the working class is ultimately vitiated by an exclusive focus on the 'high art' painting and sculpture subsidised by the bourgeoisie. Failing to include the popular culture that might be read as a genuine working-class aesthetic, he is forced to exaggerate Bloomsbury's distance from both the previous generation of Arts and Crafts activists and the group's social-realist contemporaries. Bloomsbury, Harrison says, 'had the southern English gentleman's habit of shrinking from the consequences of industrialization', a remark carefully crafted to avoid outright falsehood while nevertheless conveying the erroneous impression that the group comprised southern English gentlemen (90). Harrison's presentation of Bloomsbury severs its members' roots in the rising professional urban class of Victorian administrators and intellectuals from which Ruskin, Morris, and the Arts and Crafts movement emerged. Yet Vanessa Bell and Virginia Woolf were quite literally the heirs of William Makepeace Thackeray, who published some of Ruskin's most radical tracts. And Roger Fry, who was one generation older than his colleagues in the Bloomsbury Group, as a young man participated in a number of Arts and Crafts guilds, including the Guild of Handicraft, founded by his close friend C. R. Ashbee, and the Century Guild, through which he met his wife. Bloomsbury's establishment of the Omega Workshops, where from 1913 to 1919 young artists were provided a living wage for the cooperative and anonymous production of domestic furnishings, is one measure of its links to the guilds of the Victorian radicals.[5]

In fact, echoes of Ruskin's prose run strongly through Fry's writing, not least of all in their shared revulsion for the consequences of industrialisation. Harrison deals with these connections by belittling them. In what must set a record for the faintest of faint praise, he dismisses Fry's Ruskinian critique of the division between artist and artisan in the 'commercial State' by allowing Fry only 'the suggestion here of an intuition' that 'the high and isolated status which he among others claimed for the fine artist in the modern age might be defensible only in the context of what he would in the end have to recognize as indefensible socio-political circumstances' (90). Among Fry's explicit denunciations of the social construction of art, the following contribution to the straitlaced *Burlington Magazine* is typical: 'There is a certain social class feeling, a vague idea that a man can still remain a gentleman if he paints bad pictures, but must forfeit the conventional right to his Esquire if he makes good pots or serviceable furniture' ('A Modern Jeweller' 170).[6]

The flip side of Harrison's reluctance to acknowledge Fry as anything but a politically reactionary aesthete is his eagerness to portray Walter Sickert as a true son of Ruskin and Morris, a thwarted modernist champion of the worker. To sharpen the comparison rhetorically, Harrison introduces Fry as an 'amateur', linked to 'the intellectual aristocracy of Bloomsbury', and in the short biographical sketch condemns him by his association with New York's Metropolitan, which, Harrison finds time to inform the reader, was 'then under the presidency of the millionaire Pierpont Morgan' (32, 51–2). He does not mention that Fry's employment was terminated when he alone resisted Morgan's practice of taking the museum's best purchases for his personal collection.[7] Harrison presents Sickert, in contrast, as the author of 'workmanlike modern paintings' (26) and carefully advances his few qualified credentials of political correctness: 'It is perhaps significant that he often visited William Morris during the 1880's, in company with his first wife, the daughter of Richard Cobden, Liberal politician and free-trader' (24–5). That nothing came of these meetings, that Sickert moved in very upper-crust circles, that he always justified his work in purely visual terms, vehemently resisting any suggestion of sympathy for the working-class models he painted, that nothing in his imagery challenged his buying public's conception of working-class life as violent and sordid – all of this Harrison ignores or evades. Upholding Sickert's choice of subjects 'representative of "*la moyenne de la vie*"' as 'a powerful criticism' of 'established views', Harrison resists the obvious fact that such brothel and music hall themes were staples of the Impressionist tradition from which Sickert emerged, although his lapse into French might have betrayed its roots (35). It was Sickert who trained in the aestheticising Impressionism of Whistler and Degas, while Fry was exploring Arts and Crafts movement guilds and lecturing workers at Toynbee Hall.

Other such elisions and distortions contribute to Harrison's presentation of Sickert and Bloomsbury as antagonists, a schema that anyone who has read Virginia Woolf's adulatory *Walter Sickert* will recognise as exaggerated. Arguing by buzzword rather than by historical analysis, Harrison reveals less about the artists and critics he purports to describe than about his own highly patriarchal values. Harrison is blind to the implications of women's central place in Bloomsbury, especially in contrast to the formal ban on women in Sickert's Camden Town group. Simple sexism underlies his dismissal of Woolf's ability to contradict Clive Bell's criticism of Sickert (32), while preconceptions about female creativity skew his brief description of Bloomsbury's collaborative Omega Workshops: 'Vanessa Bell's textiles, Grant's painted screens and Fry's pottery were among the more representative products of the workshop' (72). In fact, all three artists worked in all three media, and Bell's *Bathers* screen, now at the Victoria and Albert, is perfectly representative of the best of the Omega's production.[8]

Harrison does not simply ignore the collaborative effort of Bloomsbury's men and women to confront and resist both the aesthetic and social imperatives of patriarchy. He invokes the patriarchal norms Bloomsbury struggled against to belittle the men of whom he disapproves. The 'workmanlike' Sickert is elevated in contrast to an image of Roger Fry as not merely 'amateur' but also satisfactorily effeminate. If Harrison does not actually call Fry prissy, the idea is there in his compulsive repetition of a more polite synonym. Fry, Harrison says, 'nurtured a fastidious distaste' for Sargent's painting (52); his 'sensibility' was 'too fastidious not to be highly selective in the face of experience' (56); he was even 'fastidiously indifferent to German culture' (95). Little wonder that, in Harrison's account, the highroad of masculine accomplishment rapidly passes over Bloomsbury, with its domestic emphasis on 'the renewal of decoration', to go on to the art of 'ideas' represented by the 'new and energetic faction' of Wyndham Lewis and the Vorticists (74).

As in Harrison's treatment of Sickert and Bloomsbury, his class-oriented distinction between Bloomsbury and the Vorticists is exaggerated and infused with the coyness of sexual innuendo. While 'the intimates of the Bloomsbury circle … flirted with radicalism', the Vorticists are described as 'mostly the children of working men, shopkeepers, foreigners or the nouveau riche' (88–9). Harrison leaves vague the relationship among these categories of disenfranchisement, and one can only speculate about how the working-class Vorticists interacted with figures like Lewis, a cosmopolitan Canadian, who was born on his father's yacht and educated at Rugby.

The sexual subtext of Harrison's rhetoric breaks through in his thumbnail comparison of Bloomsbury with Vorticism. Despite the fact that of Bloomsbury's four art critics and painters only Duncan Grant can be described as homosexual, Harrison opens with the generalisation: 'Where Bloomsbury took pride in its considerable homosexual membership, the Futurists and [Vorticists] struck attitudes of aggressive heterosexuality'. This remark is followed by a comparison of the two groups' responses to the war: 'Bloomsbury was on the whole pacifist, and when conscription was introduced many of its denizens took to the country; among the rebels, on the other hand, there were some eager and early volunteers and several uncomplaining conscripts' (90). One might expect that Harrison's leftist politics might lead him to admire – or at least consider the rationale behind – Bloomsbury's staunch opposition to a war that Clive Bell, in a manifesto seized and burned by the government, condemned as a betrayal of the public interest in favour of 'what a small ruling caste considered gentlemanly' (5). Instead, Harrison concludes from Bloomsbury pacifism that

> of the three principal constituent factions within the pre-war avant-garde [Sickert's Camden Town group, Bloomsbury, and the Vorticists] the adherents of Post-Impressionism were thus best placed after the war.... the friendships and connections within the Bloomsbury set had predictably remained largely intact. (145)

With the 'predictably' hinting that domination of the English avant-garde lay behind Bloomsbury's withdrawal from the mayhem of the front lines, Harrison spares himself from considering the connections between Bloomsbury's antinationalist pacifism and its rejection of 'aggressive heterosexuality'.

The links Harrison ignores, however, have been eagerly seized upon by Bloomsbury's critics on the political right. Gertrude Himmelfarb, in her book of essays published as *Marriage and Morals among the Victorians*, attacks Bloomsbury for the 'disaffection from the society and the country at large' that led to its opposition to World War I (49). Himmelfarb is eager to damn all of Bloomsbury's cultural products by their association with the group's deviance from sexual convention. Bloomsbury's painting and writing, she implies, were enervated by 'the extraordinary amount of psychic energy that went into their complicated personal lives' (42). Establishing Lytton Strachey as the 'essence' of Bloomsbury for no other reason than his homosexuality, she links even Keynes's economics, which she characterises as 'based entirely on the short run and preclud[ing] any long term judgements', to 'his homosexuality – what Schumpeter delicately referred to as his "childless vision"' (37). Yet about the Bloomsbury men's refusal to fight in World War I, Himmelfarb can only conclude that it was motivated by a 'contempt for the masses, as well as for the bourgeoisie' (39). This she finds 'dramatically illustrated' by her retelling of the familiar anecdote of how Lytton Strachey, when facing a tribunal empowered to imprison or exempt from service draft resisters, responded to the jingoistic question of what he would do if he saw a German soldier about to rape his sister: 'He solemnly looked at each of his sisters in turn and replied, in his high-pitched voice, "I should try and interpose my own body"' (39).[9]

How the 'masses' were represented by the military establishment Strachey here confronted is here left unexplained, though this was exactly the question Clive Bell's pacifist manifesto was burned for asking. No follower of Marx, Himmelfarb's rhetorical appeal to the 'masses' at this point derives from a letter she transcribes from Skidelsky's biography of Keynes in which Duncan Grant tried to justify his antinationalist pacifism to his father, a major in the army:

> I began to see that one's enemies were not vague masses of foreign people, but the mass of people in one's own country and the mass of people in the enemy country, and that one's friends were people of true ideas that one might and did meet in every country one visited. (Himmelfarb 39; Skidelsky 326)

Anyone genuinely interested in the sexual determination of Bloomsbury's position outside mainstream culture would read Grant's remark – which is quite clearly not about the 'masses' understood as the working class – in the context not only of such obvious historical events as Oscar Wilde's recent imprisonment but also of Grant's other published comments on the subject, readily available in Skidelsky's text. Writing to Keynes from a visit to his family in 1908, Grant said:

> You are the only person I feel I can speak to.... It's not only that one's a sodomite that one has to hide but one's whole philosophy of life.... Here I am surrounded by ... good, honest sort[s] of people but it's so damnable to think that they can only think me a harmless sort of lunatic or a dangerous criminal whom they wouldn't associate with at any price. (Skidelsky 196)

Far from thinking seriously about the impact of homosexuality on Bloomsbury, however, Himmelfarb raises the topic in order to castigate the group for its deviance from the norms of 'Marriage and Morals among the Victorians' she celebrates. Upbraiding Bloomsbury for concealing its sexual behaviour, she simultaneously seethes with the neo-Victorian fury the group's members knew they had to avoid. Himmelfarb complains that Bloomsbury's reticence prevented 'even so perceptive and psychoanalytic-minded a critic as Lionel Trilling' from realising Forster 'was a homosexual' (42), although it is unclear how Trilling would have used this information, given his doubts over the advisability of publishing the original Kinsey Report on the grounds it would promote the behaviours it described. Armed as she is privileged to be with the recently disclosed facts, Himmelfarb herself splutters with sibilants and outraged alliteration as she announces: 'We are only now beginning to recognize how "queer" that world was – not only homosexual but androgynous, near-incestuous, and polymorphously promiscuous' (45).[10]

As Bloomsbury knew, there is no way rationally to engage a Victorian morality that insists these categories are self-evidently damning. Rather than make a case for their immorality, Himmelfarb misrepresents Keynes's 1938 memoir on Bloomsbury 'immoralism'. Grafting onto his words her own catalogue of Bloomsbury's sins – the 'sense of autonomy and liberty, the cultivation of consciousness and feeling, the elevation of the self and the denigration of society, the emphasis on immediate gratification ... narcissism and egoism ... perversity and promiscuity' – Himmelfarb asserts that these 'Keynes himself recognized to be a form of immorality' (45). But when Keynes in a talk delivered as a challenge to Bloomsbury's second generation called the group's original members 'in the strict sense of the term, immoralists', he went to some effort to explain that by this term he does not imply Bloomsbury lacked a code of ethics – a condition of amoralism. Instead, he said, Bloomsbury rejected 'customary morals, conventions and traditional wisdom' and 'claimed the right to judge every individual case on its merits' according to principles

Keynes in retrospect found, if anything, overexact and unnecessarily gloomy. Far from condemning early Bloomsbury for unbridled hedonism, Keynes identified the failure in the group's philosophy as its attribution of rationality to all human action. He noted, however, that it was Bloomsbury's refusal of constituted authority in favour of 'the application of logic and rational analysis' that 'for the outer world ... was our most obvious and dangerous characteristic'.[11] This assessment of the barely post-Victorian establishment of his day is confirmed by the tenor of Himmelfarb's Victorian revivalism.

The refusal to submit to authority lay always at the heart of Bloomsbury's social attitudes, a stance Himmelfarb's clear identification with constituted authority leads her to see as deeply threatening or simply inexplicable. Thus she interprets as mere callousness Vanessa Bell's and Duncan Grant's refusal to claim the authority of age and parenthood by prohibiting what they accurately foresaw would be their daughter's unhappy marriage (45). Belittling Forster's outrage at the censorship of gay books by the British government, Himmelfarb waxes furious over his professed readiness to subordinate loyalty to that government to fidelity to a trusted friend (40–1). Himmelfarb's misapprehension of her subject is not ultimately surprising, however, for her aim is not to understand Bloomsbury but to create an account that will act as a parable for our times, proving the need for a return to Victorian values. Her study is introduced with the observation that 'from the perspective of our own time' an unidentified 'we' have come to 'better appreciate Victorian morality'. In an assertion all the more foreboding for the enigma of its complete lack of reference, she says, 'Today more than ever, we have reason to be wary of the kind of "civilization" celebrated by Bloomsbury' (xiii–xiv).[12]

Whatever the shortcomings of Himmelfarb's text as history, however, her thrashing of Bloomsbury in the interest of reviving Victorian social mores is useful in making explicit what is only implied in Hilton Kramer's more circumspect disapproval, with its measured allusions to the 'great many unpleasant facts' in Bloomsbury's sexual history, and his vague distress that they should 'reject the respectable and the conventional in favour of the perverse and the esoteric'. It was, in fact, one of Kramer's editorial attacks on Bloomsbury in the *New Criterion* that inspired Himmelfarb's piece and provided its strategic model. In 'Bloomsbury Idols', which opened the first issue of 1984, Kramer, rather than condescending to a sustained consideration of Bloomsbury himself, urges someone else to the task. 'Despite the immense number of books, articles, and reviews already devoted to it', he says, Bloomsbury 'has not yet found its writer', and he calls for someone to focus on the group's 'moral rebellion', with the instruction that she or he 'begin ... with that remarkable confession of categorical error which Keynes delivered ... under the title "My Early Beliefs"'. In her book, Himmelfarb cites Kramer's piece approvingly, confirming the collegial connection that would seem to make her denunciation of Bloomsbury as a 'circle of "fellow-travellers" or "sympathizers"' with its own institutionalised mouthpieces in the press (29) seem somewhat hypocritical in the light of her participation in what must be the closest contemporary American equivalent, the circle of conservative intellectuals connected by blood, marriage and ideology who contribute to such journals as Kramer's *New Criterion*. The fact that Himmelfarb, as a popularising historian with a keener eye for a telling phrase than for an accurate quotation, enacts in her modern anti-Bloomsbury group the role of her nemesis, Lytton Strachey, has not been lost on commentators with an eye for irony.[13]

Himmelfarb cites Kramer to buttress her observation that Bloomsbury's creative output was so negligible that all current critical interest must centre on its members' biographies. This assertion of the essentially uninteresting nature of Bloomsbury's art is here supported only by several columns of question-begging rhetoric about aesthetic 'achievement' and 'accomplishments of the mind', leading to a final characterisation of Bloomsbury as a group of 'failed writers and artists' (3). For the specifics of Kramer's objection to Bloomsbury's art, however, one may look to his review of a London Cubism exhibition, first published in the *New Criterion* in June 1983 and then anthologised in *The Revenge of the Philistines*.[14] Condemning the inclusion of such 'peripheral off-shoots' of Cubism as 'Gleizes, Metzinger, Marcoussis, or Villon', Kramer marvels at how long it has taken the English to accept the MoMA-sponsored reverence for Braque, Picasso and a vision of Cubism in which 'there were no theories or manifestos, no politics or ideology, no scientific reasoning or philosophical doctrines' (*Revenge* 81). And Kramer blames England's misapprehension of Cubism on the influence of Roger Fry. As soon as he begins to enumerate the specifics of Fry's deviation from the critical standard, however, Kramer reveals the hollowness of his claim to an aesthetic uninflected by ideology. 'Fry's enthusiasm, shared by many of his Bloomsbury friends, was largely reserved for the more decorative aspects of Cubism', Kramer complains, continuing:

> Far from advancing any real understanding of the Cubist aesthetic, this cozy, decorative use of its more superficial devices only served to blur its artistic importance. The Omega style – so typically Bloomsbury in the way it diluted and distorted modernism in the interests of aesthetic sociability – made Cubism look homey and insipid. (*Revenge* 77)

It is not difficult to isolate the ideology in this passage. To be decorative, cosy, sociable and homey, to actually turn modern art into objects for the home – all of this is incompatible with aesthetic importance. Kramer's is a vision of modernism centred on the mythic figure of the isolated artist-hero, too tough for the feminising pleasures of community and domesticity. Despite his professed abhorrence for manifestos, politics and ideology, Kramer's brand of modernism forcefully replicates the patriarchal bias of the dominant culture.

To challenge Kramer's claim to art without ideology would qualify as a critique of his position were it not that, in less guarded moments, he is happy to affirm the political function of his aesthetics. In a 1986 *New Criterion* essay titled 'Modernism and Its Enemies', Kramer describes modernism as 'preeminently the culture of democratic capitalist society', the artistic expression of 'the bourgeoisie, in other words you and me, and the life of the mind in middle-class capitalist society' (7). Having allied mainstream modernism explicitly with the dominant culture, Kramer sees attacks on its standards as part of 'what the Sixties bequeathed to American culture' (4). He describes how 'we' (presumably the 'you and me' of the bourgeoisie) are still 'digging our way out of the debris' of the sixties, which 'swamped us' with 'the counterculture and the antiwar movement and the sexual revolution' (6). The same chronology opens *The Revenge of the Philistines*, which bemoans the 'betrayal of the high purposes and moral grandeur of modernism in its heyday' (11): 'Twenty years ago it was rank heresy to suggest that modernism might have already entered upon its decline.... Today, however, it is suddenly chic to speak of "postmodernist" art' (1). The same timetable introduces his attack on Bloomsbury: 'It is startling now to be reminded that as recently as 1968 – a year that saw a great many changes in our cultural life – Bloomsbury could still be described, without fear of contradiction, as "unfashionable"' ('Bloomsbury' 1). So determined to attach Bloomsbury's renascence to the events of 1968 is Kramer that he incorrectly assigns to that year the publication of a biography of Lytton Strachey that contained the first candid – though hardly explicit or politically affirmative – acknowledgement of its subject's homosexuality and concludes, 'It was no doubt Mr. Holroyd's biography which set this great reversal in motion' (1).[15]

Simple sexism may account for Kramer's blindness to Virginia Woolf's overriding importance to Bloomsbury's return to cultural prominence – though he does grant her enough attention to belittle her anger at her father's autocratic domestic behaviour, reprimanding her for her lack of gratitude, since 'no orthodox Victorian paterfamilias would have given his daughter the complete freedom of his large and unexpurgated library' ('Bloomsbury' 5).[16] In a textbook enactment of patriarchal attitudes, however, Kramer's inability to recognise a woman's accomplishment and his annoyance at a daughter's insubordination to her father are eclipsed by his fixation on men, his outrage at male homosexuality in particular. For Kramer, the Strachey biography looms over all other examples of Bloomsbury's current cultural manifestations, becoming a talisman of both 'society in a permanent state of orgy and ecstasy' and the 'precipitous decline in criticism that began to make itself felt in the Sixties' ('Bloomsbury 2'). Indeed, any defection from the standards of high modernism, in Kramer's view, can be traced to the subversive influence of male homosexuality. The introduction to *The Revenge of the Philistines* explains that in the triumph of postmodernism, 'no instrument has proved to be more powerful or more pervasive than the attitude of irony we call Camp' (5). And in case anyone should miss the imputation of homosexuality intended when 'we' call something 'Camp', Kramer spells out his allusion in a footnote: 'The origin of Camp is to be found in the subculture of homosexuality. Camp humour derives in its essence, from the homosexual's recognition that his condition represents a kind of joke on nature, a denial of its imperatives' (6). Just as Lytton Strachey is made to personify Bloomsbury, so other gay men are deployed in Kramer's account as the representatives of postmodernism: here Andy Warhol is 'the outstanding example [of Camp] in the visual arts' (7); elsewhere Henry Geldzahler is 'our number one camp curator in the New York Museum world' (in de Antonio and Tuchman 132).

For Kramer, as for Charles Harrison, the spectre of masculine defection from the patriarchal order underlies the threat Bloomsbury represents to the myth of the modernist hero, be he bourgeois or working class. So powerful is this threat that both Kramer and Harrison – though they share little else in common – refuse the support Bloomsbury could give to the ideals they espouse. Kramer ignores Bloomsbury's dedication to the formalist aesthetic he celebrates; Harrison denies the group's commitment to leftist political ideals and its place in the legacy of Ruskin and Morris. In the battle over the cultural meaning of modernism, no one, it appears, wants Bloomsbury on his or her side.

This kind of struggle to claim the heroes of modernism for one ideology or another has been waged, however, in the face of increasingly vocal criticism from feminist commentators alert to the intellectual poverty and ideological violence inherent in the practice of art history as hero worship. One might expect that this generation of feminist scholars, sensitive to gender issues, should have recognised the misogyny inherent in prescriptions against masculine effeminacy and freed itself from the assumptions and strategies of Kramer and Harrison. And initially this was so. Germaine Greer, in her ground-breaking survey of women artists, called the relationship between Duncan Grant and Vanessa Bell 'one of the greatest love stories of our time'. Illustrating one of Bell's many portraits of Grant, she praised their partnership as 'adjusted to allow both the fullest expression of their creativity' and notes the painters' collaborative work on domestic designs and their 'shared … female irreverence for monuments' (57).

The brief account of Bloomsbury art that Greer published in 1979 includes a call for the more detailed studies of the artists that the eighties, with the rapid growth in women's studies, began to provide. The successful institutionalisation of women's studies criticism into the academic establishment seems to have come at some price to earlier feminist principles, however. It is unnerving to watch the openness to Bloomsbury's domestic and sexual choices disappear in the writings of the most prominent academics who, in the eighties, looked at Woolf and Bloomsbury from what they claimed was a feminist standpoint. In contrast to the more sophisticated feminist perspectives that, in academic journals and university press books, have developed around the sexual dynamics in Woolf's texts, the women who address Woolf's biography seem anxious to undermine Bloomsbury's fundamental critique of sexual oppression. In the name of feminism, these influential books reassert the standard patriarchal prescriptions of heterosexual monogamy and the primacy of the nuclear family (albeit slightly inflected by the acceptability of the two-career couple). Unchallenged by other feminists (though basic texts in both American and European feminism offer ample grounding for such a critique), it has been these biographically oriented approaches to Woolf that, released by more mainstream publishers and readily available in paperback re-editions, in the eighties became central to women's studies curricula, while their authors were rewarded by appointments to influential positions at prestigious American colleges and universities. The successful mainstreaming of this brand of feminism cannot be separated from its proponents' enthusiastic adoption of the old gay-bashing strategies of the fathers.[17]

The tendency, in accounts of Bloomsbury, to enforce patriarchal imperatives under the guise of feminist revisionism can be traced back to Phyllis Rose's biography of Virginia Woolf, *Woman of Letters*. Rose describes her account as 'written in sympathy' with its subject, in an attempt at 'an imaginative understanding of a figure who, as the years pass, seems less remote and less aloof' (xix). Though attractive sounding, this methodology boils down to Rose's attribution of her own highly conventional values to Woolf. Reading strongly against the grain of Woolf's own letters, memoirs and fiction, Rose anxiously distances her subject from the homosexuality of her male associates. In her last novel, *Between the Acts*, Woolf offered the following view of women's response to gay men:

> They knew at once they had nothing to fear, nothing to hope. At first they resented.... Then they liked it. For then they could say – as she did – whatever came into their heads. And hand him, as she handed him, a flower. (135–6)

Similar sentiments characterise the autobiographical writings of both Virginia Woolf and Vanessa Bell. The 'freedom' Bell found in Bloomsbury, she said, 'was I believe largely owing to Lytton Strachey':

> Only those just getting to know him well in the days when complete freedom of mind and expression were almost unknown, at least among men and women together, can understand what an exciting world of explorations of thought and feeling he seemed to reveal. ('Notes' 79)

The most negative remark Woolf in her memoirs makes about her gay colleagues is the gently self-mocking passage describing her growing feelings of boredom with the young men she knew because 'there was no physical attraction between us'. There are 'many advantages' for women in 'the society of buggers', Woolf says. 'It is simple, it is honest, it makes one feel … at one's ease'. Nevertheless, with gay men 'one cannot, as nurses say, show off', which 'is one of the great delights, one of the chief necessities of life' (194). This passage Rose glosses as Woolf's 'traumatic encounter with the young men of Bloomsbury' (47). And where Woolf, like her sister, credits the sexual freedom of the gay men in her circle, pre-eminently Lytton Strachey, with revolutionising 'the old sentimental views of marriage in which we were brought up' (196), Rose describes Woolf's 'hurt' at 'her treatment by the Bloomsbury homosexuals', Strachey in particular (65).

To support her position, Rose, like Himmelfarb, invokes the stereotyped conflation of homosexuality and immaturity, describing Strachey as a perpetual 'adolescent' with 'atrophied emotions' (92). Wrapping a feminist rhetoric around another old myth, Rose insists that 'Strachey's homosexuality, which was so much a part of his self-definition, was decidedly misogynist' (77). As evidence for this claim, she describes how E. M. Forster's *Maurice* 'conveys the platonic, Greek spirit of attachments between university men at the turn of the century and their anti-female bias' without acknowledging that the book is a critique of these attitudes (77).[18] And Rose goes on to conclude from the fact that Keynes and Grant are known to have occasionally slept with women that for Bloomsbury's men as a totality 'there was no biological obligation in their youthful preference for men' (77). Thus Strachey's failure to sleep with Woolf can only be explained as a desire to hurt her. In Rose's scenario, Woolf rescues herself from the 'homosexual conspiracy' (46, 78) of Bloomsbury by her 'willed commitment to normality' in the decision to seek out straight male associates and ultimately to marry (67).[19] Rose characterises Woolf's marriage as 'a plunge into reality' that allowed her 'acceptance of herself as a woman' and 'the excitement of … discovering that the ordinary adventures of life [were] open to her' (67–8). In short, Rose seeks to tame Woolf, turning her life into a story of a woman struggling to conform to exactly those 'old sentimental views of marriage' in which a woman is defined through her bond with a man, that Virginia Woolf in her own autobiography claimed, with her gay friends, to have escaped.

This kind of 'feminist' rewriting of Woolf to defuse her challenge to heterosexual privilege continued in the eighties in the writings of Jane Marcus, who perpetuates the correlation between homosexuality and misogyny with a rigid essentialism. Woolf's *Three Guineas*, we are informed, 'was met and is still met by male abuse', although the only attack on the book Marcus quotes is the undeniably female Queenie Leavis's description of it as 'Nazi dialectic without Nazi conviction' (Marcus, 'Liberty' 64, 66). Marcus's determination to ignore the complicating issue of non-feminist women (though she details numerous instances of Woolf's female relatives' promotion of patriarchal values) is matched by her insistence on a single, deterministic idea of men. For Marcus, all men are univocally the patriarchy, a repressive social order of which homosexuality is the ultimate signifier. Claiming that she does not want to 'attack homosexuality itself' (as if sexuality could exist apart from its social inscription), Marcus nevertheless lumps together Woolf's 'forefathers and her friends' as a single entity she calls the 'homosexual hegemony over British culture' (61, 96). By comparing this totality with the Nazis' 'homosexual brotherhood', Marcus is able to assert, 'The Cambridge Apostles' notions of fraternity surely appeared to Woolf analogous to certain fascist notions of fraternity' (67). Marcus's 'surely' notwithstanding, there is no evidence in Woolf's writing for this thesis, which, in its totalising conception of fraternity as homosexuality and homosexuality as fascism, ignores the complexity of relationships between men, belittles the antifascist work of Bloomsbury homosexuals like John Maynard Keynes and insults our memories of the victims of the Nazis' persecution of gay men.[20]

From a purely historical standpoint, the fallacy of Marcus's analysis lies in her blindness to the very real differences between the gay men who were Woolf's contemporaries and the old-guard Apostles, whose sexually sublimated, morally aggrandised homoerotic bonding Forster attacked in *Maurice* and Lytton Strachey mocked as the 'higher Sodomy'. The tendency for modern commentators to use this phrase as Bloomsbury's self-congratulatory characterisation of its own sexual ethic should be checked by the example of its use in one of Strachey's high-spirited letters to Grant, here about Geoffrey Scott: 'He's what I call a "higher sodomite" of the most virulent type … mild, in love, Keynes says, with an impossibly flimsy ideal, with impossibly flimsy balls (added by me)' (L. Strachey to D. Grant, 7 Apr. 1906).[21] These letters reveal that Bloomsbury's 'homosexual hegemony' contributed actively to Philippa Strachey's suffrage work, despite Marcus's completely unfounded assertion that they 'were not like homosexuals of more vulnerable classes, the natural allies of women' ('Liberty' 61). Grant refers to stints collecting signatures on petitions at the polls and licking stamps until midnight, as well as to his work designing posters for the cause.[22] About his sister, who rose to be secretary of the suffragist Fawcett Society, Strachey remarked to Grant: 'I suppose you, no less than me, when life and all its glooms press round you, say, "Thank the Lord there's Pippa!" But then, the Lord is responsible for so many other things as well' (L. Strachey to D. Grant, 12 Apr. 1907).

Marcus's anxiety to distance Virginia Woolf from the men in the close-knit intellectual community now known as the Bloomsbury Group continued through her editorship of two volumes of feminist essays on Woolf criticism, *New Feminist Essays on Virginia Woolf* and *Virginia Woolf: A Feminist Slant*. Dismissing Woolf's self-identification with Bloomsbury, voluminous correspondence with its members and eulogistic biography of Roger Fry, Marcus proclaims her party line in the introduction to the first volume: 'We do not consider "Bloomsbury" as an important influence on Virginia Woolf.... Her work and life ought to be wrenched out of their provincial English Bloomsbury setting' (Introduction xvii–xviii). Marcus claims here to want to place Woolf in a 'European' context of 'Jews, homosexuals, and radicals' (xviii), all identities pertinent to the members of Woolf's chosen circle. And lest one suspect the 'homosexuals' Marcus invokes are drawn from the 'vulnerable classes' she finds 'the natural allies of women', it should be noted that her example is Proust, who, along with Kafka, Brecht and Benjamin, are specified as Woolf's 'real contemporaries' (xviii). This determination to 'wrench' Woolf from her own community and into Marcus's version of feminism (which looks suspiciously like a masculine canon) both exploits and condescends to the woman whose legacy as 'a guerrilla fighter' against patriarchy she claims to retrieve ('Thinking' 1).

Marcus's confidence as Woolf's self-appointed saviour seems all the more misplaced in view of her terrified reaction to Woolf's stated opinions. Foreclosing any broad-based analysis of gender, Marcus rejects as 'premature and optimistic, one thinks' ('No More' 154), Woolf's obviously rhetorical suggestion in *Three Guineas* that the term 'feminism' be consigned to a ceremonial burning: 'The word "feminist" is destroyed; the air is cleared; and in that clearer air what do we see? Men and women working together for the same cause' (185). Here Woolf allies herself with Josephine Butler's claim to be working 'for the rights of all – all men and women', and tells her male correspondent,

> You are feeling in your own persons what your mothers felt when they were shut out, when they were shut up, because they were women. Now you are being shut out, you are being shut up, because you are Jews, because you are democrats, because of race, because of religion. (186–7)

The distance between Woolf and the modern academics who would cut her down to their size is starkly apparent in their rejection of this impassioned call to reject the scapegoating of other afflicted classes and to recognise the potential for coalition and cooperation in confronting the complexities of oppression and empowerment.

The decade's final harvest of the ideological seeds planted by Rose and cultivated by Marcus is Louise DeSalvo's 1989 study of Woolf, subtitled *The Impact of Childhood Sexual Abuse on Her Life and Work*. Starting from Woolf's autobiographical account of her molestation by her half-brothers, DeSalvo enquires into its effects on Woolf's adult life and writing while, somewhat incidentally, she considers how the same (or similar) experiences affected Vanessa Bell's life and career, although Bell herself – despite her frank anger at any other of aspects of her upbringing – never referred to any such suffering. Here and in both Marcus's volumes of collected essays, DeSalvo's work makes the problem of the academic-feminist rewriting of Bloomsbury most acute, because – despite its misstatements, exaggerations and suppressions – her analysis is so clearly inspired by the work of women, working in clinics and battered women's shelters, on the front lines of the struggle against sexual violence. DeSalvo's passionate dedication to the topic of childhood sexual abuse is demonstrated in her numerous citations to the literature currently being generated by the women (and men, too, although DeSalvo makes no mention of it) coming to terms with their sexual abuse, in part by telling their stories in newspapers, books and scholarly reports. It is, quite properly, the aim of writings by and about survivors of abuse to stress the diversity of their stories so that others may, by recognising elements of their own experience, escape a guilty isolation and validate their strategies of recovery. But the sheer variety of manifestations and responses to abuse allows DeSalvo to make it the determining factor in virtually all the Stephen sisters' professional and personal manoeuvres, ultimately confining them to the role of victim and denying them the agency they exercised in reformulating life on their own terms.[23]

This tendency is exacerbated by the overview quality of the chapter DeSalvo devotes to Vanessa Bell, which substitutes for Bell's own accounts of her life as a triumphant break with her patriarchal upbringing (quoted above) a version of her story as a series of passive victimisations. DeSalvo tells a story of a woman who reels from the 'collapse of her marriage to Clive Bell and after her love affair with Roger Fry had ended' into a third tragedy as she 'suffered within the relationship with Duncan Grant, who was a committed homosexual' (74). DeSalvo's imputation of Grant's agency in the description of his sexuality echoes Rose's righteous – if illogical – argument that being gay is just one more thing men do to hurt women. The agency Grant gains here, however, is more than made up for by that denied Bell. For while DeSalvo has combed the records of Bell's life for the tokens of disappointment, frustration and sadness that would seem to describe her as a victim, she has ignored coincident expressions of strength, decisiveness and joy. '[Clive] does know that we must both be free to have what friendships we like and he will in time live up to his principles', Bell wrote in 1911 (V. Bell to R. Fry, 13 Sept. 1911). Later, explaining to Fry why – over his passionate objections – she broke off their affair, Bell wrote:

> I believe our feelings for each other were equal, at any rate enough so to make things easy. Then as you know I changed, but I think really not in feeling but wanting to lead my own life.... The only difference was perhaps that I had made up my mind to look after myself more independently. (V. Bell to R. Fry, 1915?)

Clearly Vanessa Bell did not act as Louise DeSalvo would in her place; DeSalvo in the dedication and acknowledgements of her book foregrounds the fulfilment and empowerment she draws from her own nuclear family, which, like Bell's first *ménage*, consists of a husband, whose surname she shares, and two sons. Without presuming to question the suitability of this lifestyle to DeSalvo, one may, nevertheless, ask whether her pleasure in it – reinforced by readings in therapeutic practices that seek to accommodate individuals to prevailing social norms – precludes her from considering why Bell, a woman who demonstrated the gumption to break with both husband and lover (and keep both as friends), might have maintained a domestic partnership with a gay man for fifty years. For DeSalvo, Bell's behaviour can only be explained as 'inviting trouble and pain for herself' by 'unconsciously reproducing' the sexually exploitative conditions of her childhood home (75). DeSalvo catalogues Grant's 'extraordinary amount of outrageous behavior' in some detail, again selecting carefully from the record to create an unambiguous narrative (75). Excised are Bell's assertions that 'Duncan is simply amazingly good to me' and her attestations to 'the extraordinary delight it is to be with someone so alive and creative' (V. Bell to R. Fry, 2 May 1915, 29 Nov. 1918). Even when forced to acknowledge Grant's affection for Bell and his encouragement of her painting, DeSalvo reacts by attributing what might have been his attractive traits to the basest motives: 'Duncan was assured of the constant services of a woman who ran their household with apparent ease and efficiency at very little cost to himself, other than protestations of continuing affection and unceasing love and unaltered devotion and utter dependence' (76).

DeSalvo's determination to render Bell's history in the grimmest possible terms carries through to her brief analysis of Bell's art. Describing a nursery Bell decorated with jungle animals, DeSalvo insists on a pathological reading of the subject matter. Ignoring the ubiquitous presence of wild animals in children's books and pictures, DeSalvo insists Bell 'avoided traditional images of good cheer. Rather, the nursery was full of beasts of prey' (79). A similarly grim interpretation of Bell's late painting *The Nursery* disregards more positive analyses – even by recent women critics – to make much of the fact that the child looks away from his mother, though even a cursory view at the work reveals a complex interchange of reciprocal glances and gestures as the mother looks at the boy, who (along with the other woman) looks at the baby, who looks at the toy the boy tugs while shuttling the badminton birdie back and forth with his mother (79).[24]

One could go on correcting and amending DeSalvo's account, but the focus should be on the broader issues raised by the type of feminist approach she shares with Rose and Marcus. Running through the work of these writers is a common drive to normalise Bloomsbury, even if this means denying the strength of Bloomsbury's women to imagine a radically different world. Pathologising the unacceptable elements of the broad-based critique of patriarchy Bloomsbury offered, these modern commentators seek to fit the group – or, more specifically, the women in the group – into a feminism that accepts the power conferred by heterosexual privilege in exchange for the reinscription of its norms: heterosexual romance culminating in a permanent and sexually possessive union. Surrendering to the common temptation among the disenfranchised to appeal to the establishment by allying with its oppression of other marginalised groups, these academic feminists will cede to no (straight) man in their condemnation of sex outside marriage or between men. Homosexuality, in particular, is denied all complexity as lived experience and is simply deployed to signify the oppression of women. In this, these academic feminists follow the academic Marxists like Harrison who make homosexuality the badge of evil – in this case the decadent and effeminate bourgeoisie. And, of course, for scholars on the right like Himmelfarb and Kramer, homosexuality functions equally usefully to signify any threat to the authority of bourgeois social norms. Caught amid these conflicting ideologies is Bloomsbury, which, despite its crucial place in the development of mainstream-modernist, leftist and feminist thought, is violently disowned by ideologues of all stripes, who would rather have none of the group's legacy than accept the full implications of its version. The critical literature generated about Bloomsbury during the course of the past decade demonstrates just how radical its vision continues to be.

Notes

For helpful criticism on this piece as it was in progress, I want to thank Robert Herbert, Robert K. Martin, the readers of *Genders*, and those who respectfully challenged certain wording and assumptions following an oral presentation of some of this material at the Fourth Annual Lesbian, Bisexual and Gay Studies Conference (Cambridge, 28 Oct. 1990). My critique of feminist approaches to Woolf was developed in partnership with Christopher Castiglia, who first presented some of these ideas as 'Who's Afraid of Lytton Strachey' (New England MLA Convention, Providence, 25 Mar. 1988). This piece is dedicated, with love, to him.

1. On the feminist repudiation of androgyny in the 1970s, see MacLeod 15–17. For the record, I want to note that 'Bloomsbury Bashing' was welcomed by the editor of *Genders*, Ann Kibbey, who made the most of quite ambivalent readers' reports, and Brenda Silver and Robert K. Martin sent generous and supportive responses to this unknown graduate student. For more on Heilbrun's importance to the American reception of Bloomsbury, see my 'Only Collect'.
2. Bell here echoes his parents' similar remarks, quoted in Rosenbaum 74–5, 86, 90.
3. For two examples of Woolf's influence on the formation of American feminists from opposite poles of the academic spectrum, see Rose xviii and Greenspan. The statistics on donations come from the minutes of the Sixth Annual General Meeting of the Charleston Trust, 27 June 1987.
4. On the British press's reaction to the Bloomsbury artists' renascence, see Watney 'Critics'. Watney's thoughtful treatment of Bloomsbury's art in *English Post-Impressionism* has been recently extended in his *The Art of Duncan Grant*.
5. Bell and Woolf, along with their siblings, inherited various of Thackeray's manuscripts through their father, whose first wife was Thackeray's daughter. For an intelligent discussion of Bloomsbury's sociological background, see Williams 'Significance'. For details on Fry's guildwork, see Spalding, *Roger Fry* 55–9. My dissertation (Reed 'Re-imagining') takes up the group's roots in the Arts and Crafts and the Aesthetic movements in more detail. An overview of the activities of the Omega is provided by the catalogue to the exhibition (see MacCarthy and Collins).
6. Compare Fry, 'The Artist as Decorator'.
7. Harrison misstates the dates of Fry's curatorship at the Metropolitan, giving them as 1905–10, when in fact Fry resigned in 1907, retaining until his fight with Morgan only a loose connection to the museum as an acquisitions advisor. See Tompkins 109–10.
8. Compare Woolf, *Walter Sickert*. Sickert's abrupt letter rejecting Nan Hudson and Ethel Sands from the group is quoted in Baron 34. For an examination of Bell's relationship to Sickert, see my 'Apples'.
9. Notwithstanding the quotation marks, Himmelfarb here paraphrases Schumpeter's obituary notice of Keynes, reprinted in his *Ten Great Economists* 275. Similarly,

the remark she attributes to Strachey was corrected in all editions after 1971 of Michael Holroyd's *Lytton Strachey*.
10. Trilling's review of the Kinsey Report was first published in the *Partisan Review* (Apr. 1948), reprinted in Trilling 223–42. Trilling objected particularly to the report's 'idea that homosexuality is to be accepted as a form of sexuality like another, that it is as "natural" as heterosexuality'.
11. Keynes's essay 'My Early Beliefs' appears with an informative preface in Rosenbaum 48–64.
12. For a brief, insightful analysis of Forster's attitudes, see Herz 121–3.
13. See Thomas.
14. Kramer's assertion of Bloomsbury's lack of aesthetic interest is contradicted by Watney's books, as well as by Collins's meticulous historical study, *The Omega Workshops*, and the related exhibition catalogue (MacCarthy and Collins).
15. The first volume of Holroyd's biography, which treats the most active years of Strachey's sex life, was released in 1967. Kramer's claim that Holroyd's biography celebrates Strachey's homosexuality is belied by the persistently pejorative tone in Holroyd's comparison of Strachey and Wilde (p. 232 of the 1971 edition).
16. This criticism of Woolf is phrased as an attack on Spalding's *Vanessa Bell*, but Spalding merely reports the accounts found in the posthumous collection of Woolf's autobiographical essays, *Moments of Being*.
17. Feminist literary critics often bring a subtle and sympathetic analysis to Woolf's texts, including the lesbianism implicit in *Orlando* (see Knopp; Moore). Even in the more literary studies of Woolf, however, one detects a strong desire to separate Woolf from the rest of Bloomsbury. Critics explicating the feminist implications of Woolf's style often ignore the connections between her 'modernism' and the formalist aesthetics developed by Woolf's Bloomsbury colleagues. See my 'Through Formalism'. Basic feminist texts that could offer the basis for a broader feminist analysis of the relationship between gay men and women in Bloomsbury include Irigaray's '*Des marchandises entre elles*'; and the introduction to Sedgwick's *Between Men*. Although this kind of broader analysis did not inflect studies of Woolf and Bloomsbury in the eighties, there may be hope for the nineties. As this piece was in production, there appeared Mary Ann Caws' *Women of Bloomsbury*. Although Caws does not take on previous feminist critics by name, she challenges in general terms their assumptions, arguing strongly for a more respectful attitude toward the choices made by Bloomsbury's women.
18. To correct Rose's blatant misreading of Forster's *Maurice*, see Martin.
19. The phrase 'homosexual conspiracy' is footnoted to Noel Annan, which does not make it right.
20. Compare Heger; and Plant.
21. For misrepresentations of the term 'higher sodomy', see Himmelfarb 45 and Deacon 65.
22. See Grant, Letters. Grant's sketch and the resulting suffrage poster are fig. 4 and colour plate 1 in Tickner.
23. Various of DeSalvo's errors are exposed in Quentin Bell's 'Who's Afraid for

Virginia Woolf?' Examples of the literature on sexual abuse of boys and men include Grubman-Black; Hunter; Lew; and Sonkin.
24. Gillespie quotes more positive feminist views of Bell's *The Nursery* and adds her own in *The Sisters' Arts* 159.

Works Cited

Baron, Wendy. *The Camden Town Group*. London: Scalar, 1979.
Bell, Clive. *Peace at Once*. London: National Labour, 1915.
Bell, Quentin. *Bloomsbury*. 1968. London: Weidenfeld and Nicolson, 1986.
—. 'Who's Afraid for Virginia Woolf?' *New York Review of Books* 15 Mar. 1990: 3–6.
Bell, Vanessa. 'Notes on Bloomsbury.' In Rosenbaum, *The Bloomsbury Group*, 79.
—. Letters to Roger Fry. 13 Sept. 1911, 1915?, 2 May 1915, 29 Nov. 1918. MS. Tate Gallery Archives. London.
Caws, Mary Ann. *Women of Bloomsbury: Virginia, Vanessa, and Carrington*. New York: Routledge, 1990.
Collins, Judith. *The Omega Workshops*. Chicago: University of Chicago Press, 1984.
Deacon, Richard. *The Cambridge Apostles*. New York: Farrar, 1985.
De Antonio, Emile and Mich Tuchman. *Painters Painting: A Candid History of the Modern Art Scene*. New York: Abbeville, 1984.
DeSalvo, Louise. *Virginia Woolf: The Impact of Childhood Sexual Abuse on Her Life and Work*. Boston: Beacon, 1989.
Feaver, William. 'Bloomsbury Painters'. *Architectural Digest* July 1988: 132–7, 182.
Forster, E. M. 'What I Believe'. 1938. Rpt. in *Two Cheers for Democracy*. New York: Harcourt, 1951.
Foucault, Michel. 'Friendship as a Way of Life'. *Ethics: Subjectivity and Truth*. Vol. 1 of *The Essential Works of Foucault 1954–1984*. 3 vols. Ed. Paul Rabinow. Trans. Robert Hurley. New York: New Press, 1997. 135–40.
Fry, Roger. 'The Artist as Decorator'. *Colour* Apr. 1917: 92–3.
—. 'A Modern Jeweller'. *Burlington Magazine* Apr. 1910: 170.
Gillespie, Diane Filby. *The Sisters' Arts*. Syracuse: Syracuse University Press, 1988.
Grant, Duncan. Letters to John Maynard Keynes. 5 Apr. 1909, 26 Apr. 1909, 12 Jan. 1910. MS. British Library. London.
Greenspan, Elaine. 'A Bloomsbury Bathroom in New Mexico'. *Charleston Newsletter* Dec. 1988: 16–17.
Greer, Germaine. *The Obstacle Race*. New York: Farrar, 1979.
Grubman-Black, Stephen D. *Broken Boys/Mending Men: Recovery from Childhood Sexual Abuse*. New York: Tab, 1990.
Harrison, Charles. *English Art and Modernism, 1900–1939*. Bloomington: Indiana University Press, 1981.
Heger, Heinz. *The Men with the Pink Triangle*. Trans. David Fernbach. Boston: Alyson, 1980.
Herz, Judith Scherer. *The Shorter Narratives of E. M. Forster*. New York: Macmillan, 1987.

Himmelfarb, Gertrude. *Marriage and Morals among the Victorians*. New York: Knopf, 1986.

Holroyd, Michael. *Lytton Strachey: A Critical Biography*. 2 vols. New York: Holt, 1967–68.

Hunter, Mic. *Abused Boys: The Neglected Victims of Sexual Abuse*. Lexington: Lexington, 1989.

Irigaray, Luce. 'Des marchandises entre elles'. In *New French Feminism*. Ed. Elaine Marks and Isabelle de Courtivron. New York: Schocken, 1980. 107–10.

Knopp, Sherron E. '"If I Saw You Would You Kiss Me?": Sapphism and the Subversiveness of Virginia Woolf's *Orlando*'. *PMLA* 103.1 (1988): 24–34.

Kramer, Hilton. 'Bloomsbury Idols'. *New Criterion* Jan. 1984: 1–9.

—. 'Modernism and Its Enemies'. *New Criterion* Mar. 1986: 1–7.

—. *The Revenge of the Philistines: Art and Culture 1972–1984*. New York: Macmillan, 1985.

Lew, Mike. *Victims No Longer*. New York: Perennial, 1989.

MacCarthy, Fiona and Judith Collins. *The Omega Workshops, 1913–19: Decorative Arts of Bloomsbury: Crafts Council Gallery, 18 January-18 March, 1984: A Crafts Council Exhibition*. London: Crafts Council, 1983.

MacLeod, Catriona. *Embodying Ambiguity: Androgyny and Aesthetics from Winckelmann to Keller*. Detroit: Wayne State University Press, 1998.

Marcus, Jane. 'Liberty, Sorority, Misogyny'. *Representation of Women in Fiction: Selected Papers from the English Institute, 1981*. Ed. Carolyn Heilbrun and Margaret R. Higonnet. Baltimore: Johns Hopkins University Press, 1983. 60–97.

—. Introduction. *New Feminist Essays on Virginia Woolf*. Ed. Jane Marcus. 1981. London: Macmillan, 1985. xiii–xx.

—. '"No More Horses": Virginia Woolf on Art and Propaganda'. *Women's Studies* 4 (1977): 265–89. Rpt. in *Critical Essays on Virginia Woolf*. Ed. Morris Beja. Boston: Hall, 1985. 152–71.

—. 'A Tale of Two Cultures'. *Women's Review of Books* 9.4 (1994): 11–13.

—. 'Thinking Back through Our Mothers'. *New Feminist Essays on Virginia Woolf*. Ed. Jane Marcus. 1981. London: Macmillan, 1985. 1–30.

Martin, Robert K. 'Edward Carpenter and the Double Structure of *Maurice*'. *Essays on Gay Literature*. Ed. Stuart Kellogg. New York: Harrington Park, 1985. 35–46.

Moore, Madeline. *The Short Season between Two Silences: The Mystical and the Political in the Novels of Virginia Woolf*. Boston: Allen, 1984.

Plant, Richard. *The Pink Triangle: The Nazi War against Homosexuals*. New York: Holt, 1986.

Reed, Christopher. 'Apples: 46 Gordon Square'. *Charleston Newsletter* June 1989: 20–4.

—. 'Bloomsbury as Queer Subculture'. *The Cambridge Companion to the Bloomsbury Group*. Ed. Victoria Rosner. Cambridge: Cambridge University Press, 2014. 71–89.

—. *Bloomsbury Rooms: Modernism, Subculture, and Domesticity*. London: Yale University Press, 2004.

—. 'Only Collect: Bloomsbury Art in North America'. *A Room of Their Own: The Bloomsbury Artists in American Collections*. Ed. Nancy E. Green and Christopher Reed. Ithaca: Herbert F. Johnson Museum of Art, Cornell University, 2008. 58–87.

—. 'Reimagining Domesticity: The Bloomsbury Artists and the Victorian Avant-Garde'. Diss. Yale Universtiy, 1991.

—. 'Through Formalism: Feminism and Virginia Woolf's Relation to Bloomsbury Aesthetics'. *Twentieth Century Literature* 38.1 (1992): 20–43.

Rose, Phyllis. *Woman of Letters: A Life of Virginia Woolf*. New York: Oxford University Press, 1978.

Rosenbaum, S. P., ed. *The Bloomsbury Group*. Toronto: University of Toronto Press, 1975.

Sedgwick, Eve Kosofsky. *Between Men*. New York: Columbia University Press, 1986.

Shumpeter, Joseph A. *Ten Great Economists*. New York: Oxford University Press, 1951.

Skidelsky, Robert. *John Maynard Keynes*. Vol. 1. *Hopes Betrayed, 1883–1920*. New York: Viking, 1983.

Sonkin, Daniel J. *Wounded Men: Healing from Childhood Abuse*. New York: Harper, 1988.

Spalding, Frances. *Roger Fry*. London: Granada, 1980.

—. *Vanessa Bell*. New York: Harcourt, 1983.

Strachey, Lytton. Letters to Duncan Grant. 7 Apr. 1906, 12 Apr. 1907. British Library. London.

Thomas, Keith. 'A Neo-Victorian Romance'. *New York Review of Books* 28 May 1987: 26–8.

Tickner, Lisa. *The Spectacle of Women: Imagery of the Suffrage Campaign 1907–14*. Chicago: University of Chicago Press, 1988.

Tompkins, Calvin. *Merchants and Masterpieces: The Story of the Metropolitan Museum of Art*. New York: Dutton, 1970.

Trilling, Lionel. *The Liberal Imagination*. New York: Viking, 1950.

Warner, Michael. *The Trouble with Normal: Sex, Politics, and the Ethics of Queer Life*. New York: Free, 1999.

Watney, Simon. *The Art of Duncan Grant*. London: Murray, 1990.

—. 'The Connoisseur as Gourmet: The Aesthetics of Roger Fry and Clive Bell'. *Formations of Pleasure*. London: RKP, 1983. 66–83.

—. 'Critics and Cults', *Charleston Newsletter* Dec. 1986: 25–9.

—. *English Post-Impressionism*. London: Studio Vista/Eastview, 1980.

Williams, Raymond. 'The Bloomsbury Fraction'. 1978. Rpt. in *Culture and Materialism: Selected Essays*. London: Verso, 1980. 148–69.

—. 'The Significance of "Bloomsbury" as a Social and Cultural Group'. *Keynes and the Bloomsbury Group*. Ed. Derek Crabtree and A. P. Thirlwall. London: Macmillan, 1978. 55–8.

Woolf, Virginia. *Between the Acts*. London: Hogarth, 1941.

—. *Moments of Being*. Ed. Jeanne Schulkind. New York: Harcourt, 1976, 1985.

—. *Three Guineas*. London: Hogarth, 1938.

—. *Walter Sickert: A Conversation*. London: Hogarth, 1934.

Camp Sites: Forster and the Biographies of Queer Bloomsbury

George Piggford

'Camp Sites' Revisited

In the years since the publication of *Queer Forster* (Martin and Piggford, 1997) and my chapter in that volume on the influence of Lytton Strachey on the biographical writing of Forster and the Bloomsbury Group, queer theory has gone mainstream in academia. In that volume, my co-editor Robert K. Martin and I asked, perhaps naively, 'Queer? Forster?' on the way toward our central claim and celebration: 'Queer Forster!' If our goal in the various essays in the volume was 'to explore the theoretical implications of juxtaposing "queer" with "Forster"', then it is fair to say that we succeeded in initiating a conversation between queer theory and interpretations of Forster's texts (Introduction 1). My own contribution, 'Camp Sites', examines the queerness of E. M. Forster's biographical writing, specifically its campy tendencies, present in early experiments but all but extinguished by the time he published *Marianne Thornton* (1956). The arch tone in Forster's biographies anticipates and echoes the more famous life writing of Lytton Strachey, and the Stracheyesque can be found not only in Forster's writing, but also in biographical sketches by Clive Bell, John Maynard Keynes and Virginia Woolf. This mode provides an ambiguously gendered subversion of the official patriarchal and Mandarin voice of Victorian biography, a voice closely associated with Virginia Woolf's father Leslie Stephen. Bloomsbury biography in its Stracheyesque mode is a

---

'Camp Sites: Forster and the Biographies of Queer Bloomsbury' by George Piggford was first published in *Queer Forster*, ed. Robert K. Martin and George Piggford, Chicago: University of Chicago Press, 1997. Reprinted here slightly revised by George Piggford with the kind permission of the University of Chicago Press. Copyright © 1997 by the University of Chicago. All rights reserved.

self-conscious send-up of the textual voice of the father: at once ventriloquism and defacement. Especially in their life writing, Forster, Strachey and Woolf were heirs to their Victorian progenitors; at the same time, they made distinct and fundamental contributions to the cultural revolution of literary modernism and laid the groundwork for queer biography.

Δ   Δ   Δ

My reading of Queer Bloomsbury – and E. M. Forster's place in it – does not argue for a privileged and central position for the writers of Bloomsbury in a refigured, revisionist construction of modernism. Rather, I seek to accomplish two goals. First, this essay asserts the importance of the connections among the major Bloomsbury writers – Forster, Virginia Woolf and Lytton Strachey. This project, related closely to a recent re-examination of Bloomsbury inaugurated by the work of Judith Scherer Herz, Perry Meisel, S. P. Rosenbaum and Christopher Reed, argues for the significance of the influence of these writers upon one another and examines their common traits and topoi. Second, I wish to establish the importance of an under-appreciated modernist subgenre explored by the writers of Bloomsbury, a category which I term 'camp biography', particularly Forster's employment of this mode. Generally, my examination of this subgenre serves to show that the writings of the Bloomsbury Group emphasise the modernist forces of parody and irony that have been recently taken up as central terms in the theorisation of postmodernism by numerous critics, most notably Linda Hutcheon. The close proximity of Strachey, Woolf and Forster to the English literary establishment and particularly to the Victorian biographic tradition allowed these writers to examine its faults and fissures and to attack its pretension and sententiousness.[1] Although Forster's writing has not typically been read as campy, his biographical writings share the Bloomsbury camp sensibility that has been labelled 'Stracheyism'.

Bloomsbury and Constructions of Masculinist Modernism

Before any attempt to determine the salient features of Forster's relationship with Bloomsbury and with the biographies composed by writers such as Strachey and Woolf, one must first endeavour to answer a basic question: 'What is the Bloomsbury Group?' I use the present rather than the past tense in phrasing this query because Bloomsbury remains among us as a significant category in the fields of literary criticism, art criticism, history, and even economics and political science.

Although many of its members – including Clive Bell, Leonard Woolf and E. M. Forster – attempted to provide textual portraits of the group,[2] Quentin Bell's characterisation of the group in his *Bloomsbury* maintains an enduring influence. Bell asserts that his topic is 'almost impalpable, almost indefinable' (103); for him, Bloomsbury has 'the dimensions of a whirlpool' and 'the character of a beast that is half chameleon and half hydra' (21). According to Bell, any conception of Bloomsbury must centre on friendship and reasonable talk: Bloomsbury 'talked on the whole reasonably, it talked as friends may talk together, with all the licence and all the affection of friendship. It believed … in pacific and rational discussion' (103–4). For Bell, Bloomsbury is best understood as a group of friends united by a world-view that one might roughly characterise as 'humanist'.[3] Its emphasis on rationality encouraged its members to produce texts and art that combat what the group perceived as the irrational aspects of the modern world – war, racism, censorship and intolerance generally.

Bell further argues that Forster cannot be placed anywhere near the centre of this cluster of friends[4] for two reasons: his reverence and his optimism, neither of which is part of the Bloomsbury ethos (106). Bell points out, however, that 'ethically' Forster 'seems to me altogether on the same side as Bloomsbury: conscious, deeply conscious of the dark irrational side of life but absolutely convinced of the necessity of holding fast to reason, charity, and good sense' (106). Bell's illuminating portrait of the group correctly positions Forster at the margins of Bloomsbury as Bell characterises it. But by choosing to 'leave Bloomsbury linen … unaired' (9), Bell largely ignores a central aspect of Bloomsbury with which Forster closely identified: its queerness.

By downplaying the importance for Bloomsbury of sexuality in all its polymorphously perverse forms – a major topic of rational talk among these friends – Bell misses arguably the most important defining characteristic of the group. It is most likely for this reason that Bell appears to be mystified by writers such as Sir John Rothenstein who view Bloomsbury as a 'criminal association' (Bell 11). In defending Bloomsbury against what he perceives as Rothenstein's unfair and unwarranted attack, Bell apparently forgets that many of the men associated with Bloomsbury engaged in criminalised sexual acts, and almost without exception its other members were guilty of crimes against Christian morality such as adultery and – most notably in the case of Virginia Woolf – sapphism.[5] Woolf herself associated the spirit of Bloomsbury with sexuality, particularly candid sexual talk, in her memoir 'Old Bloomsbury'. When in 1904 Lytton Strachey articulated the word 'semen' in conversation with Vanessa and Virginia, 'A flood of the sacred fluid seemed to overwhelm us. Sex permeated our conversation. The word bugger was never far from our lips' (Woolf, 'Old Bloomsbury' 54). This moment might be read as the birth of Bloomsbury as an enclave in which sexual possibilities might be discussed and explored.

The connection between Bloomsbury and queer sexual practices has been noted by a number of critics, some of whom, most famously Carolyn Heilbrun, celebrate the group's sexual practices and discourses as liberatory and subversive. Usually, however, critics point out Bloomsbury's sexual experimentation in an attempt to condemn its members as effeminate, enervated, decadent buggers. Ezra Pound was one of the first critics to compare unfavourably the feminine, but not necessarily female, textual output of Bloomsbury to the masculine writing of the group often termed 'the men of 1914': James Joyce, T. S. Eliot, Wyndham Lewis and Pound himself. My reading of Poundian 'masculinist' modernism is indebted to Sandra Gilbert and Susan Gubar's *No Man's Land*, particularly 'Tradition and the Female Talent'. Here I expand and modulate Gilbert and Gubar's terms somewhat so that the feminine can represent not only women, but also homosexual men. According to sexologists such as Havelock Ellis and John Addington Symonds, homosexual men, or 'inverts', might be understood to be 'women trapped in men's bodies', feminine men (see Ellis and Symonds). This construction influenced and informed both the formation of homosexual identity in the modernist period and the virulent attacks launched against homosexuals at this time by Pound and others.

In a series of essays, Pound lavishes high praise on the work of his fellow (real) men: Joyce's *Ulysses* provides 'an impassioned meditation on life' (416), Eliot's 'depiction of contemporary life' in *Prufrock and Other Observations* is 'complete' (419) and Wyndham Lewis's *Tarr* 'is the most vigorous and volcanic novel of our time' (424). Pound embeds a harsh critique of Bloomsbury in his reading of the American-born Lewis's energetic, magma-spewing novel. He commends Lewis for attacking the 'Cambridge set' (Bloomsbury, that is), characterised by Lewis as 'the *dregs* of Anglo-Saxon civilization', and its individual members, epitomised by the character Hobson, as crosses between 'a Quaker, a Pederast, and a Chelsea artist' (qtd. in Pound 427). Pound sees Lewis's *Tarr* as a justified attack on a 'frowsy background of "Bourgeois Bohemia", more or less Bloomsbury' (428). This assault on those whom Pound elsewhere termed the 'Bloomsbuggers' (qtd. in Scott 94) represents for Pound Lewis's 'cleaning up a great lot of rubbish' (429).

What we might term Pound's masculinist, phallocentric view of Bloomsbury as the feminine ('frowsy') and inverted (pederastic) dregs of English civilisation became a typical criticism of the group in the 1960s and 1970s, notably expressed in Hugh Kenner's *The Pound Era* (1971). Kenner suggests that the 'shades' moving about the ruins of London – the 'Unreal City' of Eliot's 'Waste Land' – are the ineffectual shades of members of the Bloomsbury Group, in this case Virginia Woolf and Clive Bell (382), whose 'treacly minds' (553) contrast with the massive intellects of Lewis, Pound, Joyce and Eliot, architects of an energetic vortex of change in English art in the *Blast* period (245).[6]

Terry Eagleton presents a similar argument in his 1970 *Exiles and Émigrés*. In it, Eagleton asserts that the English literary establishment needed to import its modernists from the colonies and the provinces, including James, Eliot and Pound from the United States, Conrad from the continent via the Belgian Congo, Yeats and Joyce from Ireland, and the working-class Lawrence from the collieries of Nottinghamshire. This importation was necessary because the close proximity of bourgeois English writers to their literary tradition blunted the revolutionary potential of the modernist urge among them. Eagleton contends that 'the unchallenged sway of non-English poets and novelists in contemporary English literature points to certain central flaws and impoverishments in conventional English culture itself. That culture was unable, of its own impetus to produce great literary art' (10). Although Eagleton's reading of modernism represents an insightful examination of the importance of colonial writing for a transnational understanding of the modernist movement, the gender politics of his analysis warrant careful scrutiny.

In Eagleton's reading, as in other masculinist constructions of modernism, the perceived 'literary elite' of England (read: 'Bloomsbury') is viewed not only as feminine and feminised, but also as second rate. By reading the modernism of Joyce, Eliot and Pound as the necessary influx of aggressive, virile, revolutionary colonial energy that was needed to revitalise the literature of the passive, decadent mother country, Eagleton, in effect, reinscribes a binaristic notion of modernism articulated first by Ezra Pound. Reading within an andro- and heterocentric critical tradition, Eagleton implicitly connects the feminine with the suppressed other of a binary which always already privileges the male, heterosexual subject as the potential revolutionary 'self'.[7]

Post-Lacanian feminist theorists such as Jane Gallop and post-structuralist queer critics such as Judith Butler and Lee Edelman have demonstrated various ways that such simplistic binaries are founded upon pernicious tautological structures of argumentation – structures that erase the complex interaction between phallus and absence of phallus, power and lack of power, signifier and signified, self and other. Gallop's reading of Lacan's seminar of 1972–73 argues that Lacan demonstrates that

> the phallic order and phallic enjoyment are ... a kind of failure: a failure to reach the Other, a short circuiting of desire by which it turns back upon itself. The phallic order fails because, although unable to account for the feminine, it would, none the less, operate as a closure, attempting to create a closed universe that is thoroughly phallocentric. (Gallop 34)

Lacan's phallocentric analysis of gender, in other words, attempts to erase the feminine at the moment that 'the feminine' is articulated as the Other of the phallic order.

Butler and Edelman apply to the category of sexuality a critique similar to Gallop's analysis of gender. For Butler, a sustained querying of the conventional binary demarcating the biological sexes leads to a questioning of the logic of heteronormative sexuality:

> If we call into question the fixity of the structuralist law that divides and bounds the 'sexes' by virtue of the dyadic differentiation within the heterosexual matrix, it will be from the exterior regions of that boundary … and it will constitute the disruptive return of the excluded from within the very logic of the heterosexual symbolic. (Butler 12)

Edelman's reading of the binary of sexuality, like Butler's, calls into question the stability and authority of the 'structuralist logic' that underpins analyses such as Eagleton's.[8] In contrast to readings that rely on the phallocentric logic of structuralism and to feminist readings that ground the notion of difference itself in the notion of gender difference, Edelman calls for a kind of critical writing that inscribes 'homosexual difference'. For Edelman,

> the homosexual difference produces the imperative to recognize and expose it precisely to the extent that it threatens to remain unmarked and undetected, and thereby to disturb the stability of the paradigms through which sexual difference can be interpreted and gender difference can be enforced. (195)

A mode of textual analysis that lays bare this difference at least potentially undermines the binarising logic identified by Butler and exemplified in Terry Eagleton's reading of modernism, which divides modernist writing into a revolutionary masculine self and a feminised and culturally impoverished other.

By privileging one modernism over another, by centring modernism in the textual projects of, in effect, 'the men of 1914', Pound, Kenner and Eagleton reinscribe the privilege of the masculine male and his literary output within a heteronormative construct of literary production.[9] For Eagleton in *Exiles and Émigrés*, the masculine modernists 'dominated' the literature of England in the early twentieth century because they were able to 'grasp … society as a totality' and thereby 'transcend' it (9, 10). The total cultural authority or phallic power of these authors allowed them to achieve 'a point of balance at which inwardness could combine with an essential externality to produce major art' (10). Eagleton contrasts the major art produced by the modernists who had immigrated to England against the minor art produced by native writers such as Woolf and Forster, who, in their 'enclosed and elitist' circle of friends were 'marooned from the world of working relationships and wider social institutions' (13). In Eagleton's reading, the female and feminised upper-middle-class writers exemplified by the members of Bloomsbury were not able to perceive the 'totality' of modern society and are therefore marginal modernists. Indeed, any 'us versus them' approach necessarily effects a (re)materialisation of the phallus and of the phallic logic which numerous queer and post-Lacanian feminist theorists have attempted so strenuously to escape.

As Christopher Reed has so persuasively argued, the sexual, erotic and social connections among the members of the Bloomsbury Group, particularly Woolf's complicated connections to the queer male writers associated with Bloomsbury, have been de-emphasised or even disregarded from the perspective of certain masculinist and feminist critical methodologies. Reed has rightly, I believe, associated a particular reading of Woolf with an attempt to 'undermine Bloomsbury's fundamental critique of sexual oppression' ('Bloomsbury Bashing' 52). That is, a specific tradition of revisionist readings of Woolf, epitomised by Jane Marcus's *Virginia Woolf and the Languages of Patriarchy*, rejects the feminine label given to the male writers of Bloomsbury – by, most famously, a resentful Wyndham Lewis – and instead aligns them with patriarchal authority.[10] This move effectively divorces Woolf from her immediate context, the coterie of close friends who attended informal gatherings for years at which 'buggery' was a main topic of conversation. By accepting uncritically the male/female and masculine/feminine binaries on which constructions of Bloomsbury such as Marcus's are based, this kind of feminist revisionism reinscribes the very patriarchal authority that underpins binaristic logic.[11]

In contrast, Reed's reading of the Bloomsbury Group allows its irregularities, inconsistencies and contradictions to emerge. His understanding of the group as a subculture that 'constructed sexual identity in much the same way it created aesthetic identity: in the realm of the social and relation to the past' ('Making' 190) allows for both an analysis of the anxiety of influence of the Victorian period on the artistic and literary work of Bloomsbury and an examination of the very complex interaction between the group's writings and various theories of sexuality predominant in the early twentieth century. Reed's assessment, which focuses on the influence of the aesthetic tradition (Walter Pater, Oscar Wilde) and of sexological theories (J. A. Symonds, Edward Carpenter) on the group, moves toward a construction of what I would like to term 'Queer Bloomsbury'.

Stracheyism and Bloomsbury Biography

Strachey, Woolf and Forster all utilise irony and camp parody in an attempt to inscribe queer sexualities into their biographical texts. Strachey has been a privileged figure in readings of the Bloomsbury camp mode, which was first identified as 'Stracheyism' by D. H. Lawrence. He writes in a letter to E. M. Forster that he prefers the 'sadness' of Forster's *Pharos and Pharillon* to its 'Stracheyism' (qtd. in Furbank 2:163). Edwin Muir's review of *A Passage to India* asserts that Forster 'is inclined toward the ironical school of which Mr. Lytton Strachey is the instructor' (379). Wilfred Stone labels a number of Forster's short biographical sketches 'Strachey-like' (284). Further, Woolf biographer James King has associated her playful *Orlando* with Stracheyism: 'By introducing fanciful elements into her mock-biography, Virginia, like Lytton Strachey, was attempting to revolutionise the art of biography' (411). For Lawrence, then, Stracheyism represents the comedic belittling of historical figures; for Muir it indicates irony generally; for Stone Stracheyism seems to represent both a style and the brevity of Forster's sketches; for King it suggests 'mocking', parodic elements and a 'fanciful tone'. How might one construct a workable definition of Stracheyism from these disparate sources?

Judith Scherer Herz, in *The Short Narratives of E. M. Forster*, explores the significations of Stracheyism in a helpful way. She associates Stracheyism primarily with irony. Forster's irony is tempered by pathos, a quality that she finds nowhere in Strachey. For Herz the basic tenet of Stracheyism, at least as practised by Strachey himself, is 'irony covers all' (80). Although Herz is correct in pointing to the significance of irony in Strachey's biographies, its most distinguishing feature is parody. Irony is always contextualised by parody in the Stracheyesque mode. Linda Hutcheon has argued that irony often works in parody, is framed by parody. Irony is 'a miniature (semiotic) version of parody's (textual) doubling' (4). Herz accurately points to the fact that Strachey's pathos-free irony differs from Forster's, but it is parody that unites the biographical works of Strachey, Woolf and Forster. In those texts, one might find a shared set of stylistic elements first associated by D. H. Lawrence with Stracheyism. The goal of these elements, discussed below, is to produce an over-the-top imitation of the Victorian biographical voice. It is the overblown nature of the parodic imitations found in Bloomsbury biographies that produce a camp effect in the texts. This campiness, moreover, suggests possibilities of queer desire.

Typical Bloomsbury Group camp is deliberate, contrasted by Susan Sontag in her ground-breaking 'Notes on Camp' to 'naive' camp (281). Strachey, Woolf and Forster knowingly parody established conventions of Victorian biography to belittle and critique them. Their use of camp positions them as members of an elite camp 'cognoscenti', as Andrew Ross defines that group. Camp belongs to those in the know 'who have accredited confidence to be able to devote their idiosyncratic attention to the practice of cultural slumming' (63). Only a writer who is a 'marginal' member of the literary elite is able to utilise the particularly queer parodic mode that is camp, whether that marginality results from one's sex, gender or sexuality. In literary texts, camp writers place their intimacy with the dominant culture and its privileged class in the service of subversive and excessive gestures. The Bloomsbury writers in their biographical writings thereby become what Moe Meyer has termed practitioners of the 'strategy and tactics of queer parody' (9).

According to theorists of camp such as Ross and Meyer, the camp mode produces an effect that critically comments on the sex/gender system of a particular cultural context in unpredictable but readable ways, thereby threatening mainstream social understandings of sex, gender and sexuality and interrelations among these categories. Ross contends that camp plays 'a crucial role in the redefinition of masculinity and femininity' (148). David Bergman likewise thinks that 'camp constantly plays with notions of inside and outside, masculine and feminine, it does not locate truth in these polarities' ('Strategic' 95). The Bloomsbury writers' use of camp does not seek to eliminate the categories of masculinity and femininity, nor of male and female. Rather, it dissociates the gender roles that women and men are generally coerced into playing from the category of biological sex and complicates these with playful intimations of sexual proclivity and identity. In this way, camp inscribes queerness as a sensibility, and the campy moments, or camp sites, in the works of Strachey, Woolf and Forster provide evidence for at least a broad cohesiveness in a subgenre that might be termed 'Bloomsbury camp biography'.

Lytton Strachey, certainly the best-known biographer associated with the group, utilises camp to undermine and to parody his own Mandarin – or official Victorian biographic – style. Barry Spurr has argued that

> introducing the vocabulary and cadence of Mandarin, Strachey proceeds subtly and wittily to pervert and violate its conventions, manipulating the solemnity of the Ciceronian, Gibbonian dialect to produce a voice placed, as it were, midway between the male and female ranges and sounding, at once, like both and neither. (32)

Although I generally agree with Spurr's argument, I would rather describe the interplay of male and female voice in Strachey as an instance of queer parody, a strategy of sexual subversiveness. Strachey's prose parodies the overblown style of Victorian biography. In their impersonation of Victorian panegyric, Strachey's biographies exaggerate its conventions, mannerisms and flourishes. The brevity of Strachey's historical sketches, particularly those included in *Eminent Victorians* and in various periodicals, is perhaps the first clue to their campiness. Rather than the ponderous multivolume works of Victorian biography, Strachey provides short and vivid sketches whose very form undermines the importance of the personages featured in them.

Strachey's campy subversion of pompous Victorian biographic conventions is further revealed in his adaptation of three of its stylistic devices: the aphorism, the utilisation of a series for amplification (employed by Strachey for the 'bathos of deflation') and the use of allusion.[12] Strachey's most famous camp aphorism, which reads much like a Wildean epigram,[13] is found in the preface to *Eminent Victorians*: 'The history of the Victorian Age will never be written: we know too much about it. For ignorance is the first requisite of the historian' (9). Strachey's statement, its comedic effect multiplied by its very baldness and directness, makes clear to any reader of this text that he plans both to insult Victorian biographers and to rewrite the history of the Victorian period. Such aphorisms represent parodic versions of the pithy moralising common in the British biographical tradition. Elsewhere Strachey writes aphoristically that 'It has often been observed that our virtues and our vices, no less than our clothes, our furniture, and our fine arts, are subject to the laws of fashion' (*Biographical* 34). This suggests that the moral laws of any period are illusory and subject to critique, ridicule and revision by writers in successive periods.

Further, rather than using series for amplification or to pile up heroic epithets for his subjects, Strachey employs them to effect the 'bathos of deflation' (Spurr 37). The medieval period, for example, is for Strachey a time of 'prayer, asceticism, and dirt' (*Biographical* 34). He characterises Joseph Addison as 'that charming, polished, empty personality' (*Literary* 246). And Voltaire is 'an artist, an egotist, a delirious enthusiast, dancing, screaming, and gesticulating to the last moment of extreme old age' (*Biographical* 51–2). This triadic structure is pervasive in Strachey's biographical writing and the Voltaire example is especially camp in its measured excessiveness capped by the excessive insistence on finality and age: 'last … extreme old'. Strachey builds up his widely admired subjects only to tear them down and make them appear ridiculous.

A final device utilised by Strachey for camp effect is allusion. He frequently nods to revered texts, including the Bible and Shakespeare's plays, but uses them for comic and deflating effect. Strachey asserts in an inversion of 2 Peter 3:8 that in the 'sight (or perhaps one should say … blindness)' of human beings 'a thousand years are too liable to be not as a day but as just nothing. The past is almost entirely a blank' (*Biographical* 17). Here history becomes a blank page of ignorance. And referring to Cardinal Manning, Strachey presents a camp Hamlet: 'The time was out of joint, and he was only too delighted to have been born to set it right' (*Eminent* 22). Strachey's 'delighted' implies a near-rhyme with Shakespeare's original 'cursèd spite', and Manning's relish at embracing the principles of the Oxford Movement inverts Hamlet's attitude toward his own supernaturally inspired task. Such inverting allusions along with aphorisms and deflating series are to be found throughout Strachey's biographical writings.

In Strachey's pastiche of literary styles, references to queer sexuality are often inserted as subversive gestures, subtle attacks on presumptive heterosexuality. Situated within the multivocal and parodic style utilised by Strachey, isolated sentences appear that at the very least suggest queer possibilities. What are we to make of the statement that Dr Arnold 'was particularly fond of boys' (*Eminent* 197–8)? Or that Albert, the Prince Consort, who 'had a marked distaste for the opposite sex' (*Queen* 136), 'never flirted – no not with the prettiest ladies in the court' (*Queen* 179)? These and other examples clarify Strachey's textual project: to write not only in a campy style, but also in ways that allow the irregularities of desire a forum for expression.

Although Strachey's texts are certainly the most striking examples of the subgenre of Bloomsbury camp biography, Virginia Woolf, too, is the author of a number of works that could easily fit into this category, particularly *Orlando* and *Flush*. With her father's stentorian voice literally ringing in her ears, Woolf, like Strachey, attempted to revolutionise biography. Especially in *Orlando*, Woolf's camp utilises the figure of the androgyne to queer notions of writing biography and of inscribing sexual identity. She, like Strachey, impersonates a Victorian biographical voice only to parody it:

> Happy the mother who bears, happier still the biographer who records the life of such a one! Never need she vex herself, nor he invoke the help of novelist or poet. From deed to deed, from glory to glory, from office to office he must go, his scribe following after. (*Orlando* 14–15).

Orlando utilises this overblown style to camp up the voice of the sententious and florid Victorian biographer.[14]

It is the report by the biographer's voice in *Orlando* of Orlando's abrupt transformation from male to female that clarifies Woolf's parodic reading of discourses of sexual identity. In an attempt to prepare the reader for the radical change, the biographer articulates hesitations and uncertainties about narrativising such an unprecedented metamorphosis:

> The biographer is now faced with a difficulty which it is better perhaps to confess than to gloss over. Up to this point in telling the story of Orlando's life, documents, both private and historical, have made it possible to fulfil the first duty of a biographer, which is to

> plod, without looking to right or left, in the indelible footprints of truth; unenticed by flowers; regardless of shade; on and on methodically till we fall plump into the grave and write *finis* on the tombstone above our heads. (*Orlando* 65)

What Woolf means of course is such is the duty of the official biographer, the Victorian biographer: Leslie Stephen, Woolf's father, editor of the *Dictionary of National Biography*. This passage employs an aphorism that, similar to Strachey's pronouncement about the 'first requisite of the historian' in his Preface to *Eminent Victorians*, proclaims the duty of the biographer with mock gravity: 'to plod … in the … footprints of truth'. The afterthoughts added to this aphoristic statement – 'unenticed by flowers', etc. – emphasise its parodic nature. The final reference to 'the tombstone above our heads' might indeed be as close as any writer in English has ever approached to the camp sublime.

Woolf's biographer, however, strays from this well plodded path:

> But now we come to an episode which lies right across our path, so that there is no ignoring it. Yet it is dark, mysterious, and undocumented; so that there is no explaining it. Volumes might be written in interpretation of it; whole religious systems founded upon the signification of it. Our simple duty is to state the facts as far as they are known, and so let the reader make of them what he may. (*Orlando* 65)

This Stracheyesque passage utilises a series for an ultimately deflating effect. The fact that there is 'no explaining' the coming metamorphosis provides bathetic comedy through its redundancy. Need the biographer note that there is 'no explaining it' immediately after she has indicated that it is 'dark, mysterious, and undocumented'?

The parodic aspects of the passages above are clear. Taken together, they comprise the first announcement of Orlando's coming transfiguration, the text's defining moment of queer sexuality: 'He stretched himself. He rose. He stood upright in complete nakedness before us, and while the trumpets pealed Truth! Truth! Truth! we have no choice but to confess – he was a woman' (137). This seemingly simple alteration from one biological sex to another masks a sustained if playful critique of contemporary discourses of sexuality. As I have argued elsewhere, Woolf's presentation of Orlando's sex change undermines notions of sexual identity, particularly Freud's formulation of narcissistic cathexis.[15] Both Woolf's and Strachey's biographical writings, called by Michael Holroyd 'deviant fantasy' (606), might also be rightly called 'camp biography' because both utilise an over-the-top and parodic style and both inscribe queer characters whose irregular desires implicitly critique simplistic, binaristic notions of sexual identity.

Strachey and Woolf imbue their biographical writings with queer desire through the stylistics of queer parody and by thematising non-normative sexualities. They also likely write their own dissident sexualities into such texts. Strachey's *Elizabeth and Essex*, for example, might represent a veiled inscription of his own relationship with Roger Senhouse. Certainly *Orlando* is commonly read as a disguised celebration of Woolf's love for Vita Sackville-West. Forster does something similar in his fiction. *A Passage to India*, for example, has been read as a rewriting of his relationship with Syed Ross Masood, the friend for whom Forster expressed erotic desire and to whom *Passage* is dedicated. Although Woolf's and Strachey's biographical texts trouble the distinction between reality and fiction – Woolf by writing a fiction as if it were a biography and Strachey, in *Elizabeth and Essex*, by writing a biography as if it were a fiction – their camp biographies claim to maintain some relation to historical fact. *Orlando* is subtitled 'A Biography'; *Elizabeth and Essex* 'A Tragic History'. Forster makes no such claims for his fictional works and, in any case, he does not typically exhibit a camp sensibility in his fictional writings.

It might also be possible to argue that moments in Strachey's and Woolf's lives provide superb examples of camp performance. Strachey's well-known appearance before the Hampstead Tribunal to plead his case as a conscientious objector against World War I provides an iconic camp moment in any history of Bloomsbury. One might term Strachey a camp pacifist, judging from the comments which he expressed at the hearing, prefaced by his histrionic inflation of a seat cushion to protect his tender posterior from the hard wood of his chair. When asked what he would do if he saw a German soldier attempting to rape his sister, he answered simply, 'I should try and come between them' (qtd. in Holroyd 349). This queer, parodic expression of non-violent resistance underscores the strategy of subversive camp with which Strachey hoped to outwit the tribunal.

Woolf, too, engaged in camp performance, most notably through her willing participation in her brother Adrian's '*Dreadnought* Hoax' (see King 161). The hoax involved Adrian and Virginia and a small number of their friends, disguised as the Emperor of Abyssinia and his retinue, insisting on and being granted a close examination of the Royal Navy's *Dreadnought*, 'then the most secret battleship afloat' (King 160). For this hoax Virginia 'wore a turban, an embroidered caftan and a gold chain' in addition to her face being 'blackened with greasepaint' and adorned with a moustache (King 161). These details suggest camp pacifism, camp orientalism and camp androgyny.

No such performance may be found in the biographies of Forster's life; both his pacifism and his anticolonialism were serious and in earnest. In his letters, however, he does at times demonstrate a camp sensibility. Writing about his impressions of Ravello to his friend Edward Dent, Forster notes that 'the noise of people expectorating in the street is wafted up and my mother wails. She cannot get used to the sunny South' (qtd. in Beauman 109). The campiness of this passage is both ironic and parodic. That is, the ironic tone of a cliché such as 'the sunny South' is framed by an overall attempt to imitate a Victorian epistolary style. One need only replace the highly formal 'expectorating' with a term such as 'celebrating', and a typical nineteenth- or early twentieth-century tourist letter emerges. The passage suggests the meeting between North and South which is often expressed with irony and is a constant source of comedy in Forster's novels. Such scenes described in Forster's fiction and non-fiction point to a camp sensibility not foreign to those that underlie the queer parodic performances of Strachey's tribunal appearance or Woolf's participation in the *Dreadnought* Hoax.

Forster's Camp S/Cites

In order to argue for Forster's place in the campy coterie which I have termed Queer Bloomsbury and more specifically as an author whose texts belong to the subgenre of Bloomsbury camp biography, I must begin with an examination of Forster's lesser-known, early non-fictional writing, particularly the short sketches that he published as an undergraduate at Cambridge. In Forster's writing, the Stracheyesque mode is roughly equal to the Apostolic mode.[16] Forster first employed a camp-parodic mode of writing as a Cambridge undergraduate to amuse his fellow students and Apostolic brothers. In early biographical sketches that appeared in Cambridge undergraduate periodicals such as the *Cambridge Review* and *Basileona*, Forster utilises parody and demonstrates a marked camp sensibility. This mode persists in Forster's post-Cambridge biographical writings, although, as his career develops, the parodic Forster comes into conflict with an ever more earnest Forster. A softening of the parody found in Forster's early writings may indeed have contributed to the ironic Forster discerned by Judith Scherer Herz and familiar to other readers of his novels.

Parody is pervasive in Forster's earlier published writing, for example 'On Grinds', 'On Bicycling' and the series 'The Cambridge Theophrastus'.[17] According to S. P. Rosenbaum, Forster in these prose sketches 'begins to connect through parody the present with the classics and history he had been studying' (*Victorian* 274). The butt of the joke of these pieces is R. C. Jebb's bowdlerised 1870 translation of *The Characters of Theophrastus*.[18] In this series, Jebb translates Theophrastus' humorous presentation of thirty types of men: 'The Flatterer', 'The Unpleasant Man', 'The Offensive Man', The Stupid

Man' and so on. In Jebb, the sketch for each type usually begins with a definition of the man's representative quality and then uses various examples to illustrate the relationship between the quality and the man. For example, Jebb's translation of 'The Flatterer' begins:

> Flattery may be considered as a mode of companionship degrading but profitable to him who flatters. The Flatterer is a person who will say as he walks with another, 'Do you observe how people are looking at you? This happens to no man in Athens but you…'. With these and like words, he will remove a morsel of wool from his patron's coat. (Jebb 81)

This pattern is consistent throughout *The Characters*, as is Jebb's stilted and literal style, both of which provide Forster with a blueprint for his earliest satirical writing.

'On Grinds' and 'On Bicycling' broadly mimic Jebb's use of definition and example. 'On Bicycling' begins with a definition of that activity before turning its attention to the dominant characteristics of the typical cyclist. The two sketches titled 'The Cambridge Theophrastus', in contrast, parody Jebb's translation closely. The opening lines of Forster's 'The Cambridge Theophrastus: The Stall-Holder':

> A stall may be defined as a place in which dumb animals are penned, and a stall-holder is one who pens them. She is one who, being at other times generous, straightforward and magnanimous is able, at the call of Charity, to put all these things away from her and devote herself solely to the acquisition of wealth. She addresses herself chiefly to those who are young and in possession of money that is not their own but entrusted to them by their absent parents. (*Albergo* 57)

Forster begins his sketch not with the definition of an abstract quality, as in Jebb's translation of Theophrastus, but with a humorously unnecessary description of a familiar sight in Cambridge. Like Jebb he moves from this definition to the description of a type and includes phrases spoken by a typical stall-holder, for example: 'If you will take both these egg cosies I will reduce them to four and sixpence' (*Albergo* 57). Forster parodies Jebb's style and transfers the personages described in *The Characters* from the ancient world to contemporary Cambridge.

In many ways this is typical undergraduate playfulness, in this case of a series of texts that are already meant to be humorous. It is the humourlessness of Jebb's style that Forster is sending up. Jebb seems oblivious to the comedy inherent in Theophrastus' original text. The humour that is original to Forster's 'Cambridge Theophrastus' lies in his parody of Jebb's pretentiously literal Victorian style. Importantly for Forster, Jebb's translation is bowdlerised, as Jebb explains in his introduction to *The Characters*: 'There are ... in the Characters about a dozen passages or phrases which I was unwilling to translate, and which I have omitted in the English and the Greek' (ix–x). Jebb lists – in Greek – the chapters from which he has excised passages. Looking these chapters up in a recent translation, one discovers quickly that most of Jebb's omissions refer either to bodily fluids or to sexual acts.[19] By parodying Jebb's translation, Forster camps up a text that is exemplary of Victorian prudishness.

The parodic Forster is also evident in a number of his undergraduate writings that are not biographical. In 'A Tragic Interior', for example, Forster presents an exaggerated version of Aeschylus' *Oresteia* that features a cuckolded Agamemnon and an overbearing Clytemnestra. The action in Forster's version of the play takes place entirely offstage (in something of an anticipation of Tom Stoppard's *Rosencrantz and Guildenstern Are Dead*). By focusing on unlikely offstage goings-on, Forster implies the absurdity of Victorian critics who took these tragedies much too seriously from Forster's point of view. He emphasises his critique of Victorian attitudes through a reference in the play to yet another self-serious prude, A. W. Verrall, an 'indefatigable editor of school texts of the Latin and Greek classics' (Thomson 41). When Forster's Agamemnon comments, 'Really now, this play might have been written by Euripides', Clytemnestra replies, 'Or by Dr. V★rr★ll' (*Albergo* 67). Another classical parody is evident in an early short story by Forster, 'The Road from Colonus', a rewriting of Sophocles' *Oedipus at Colonus*. Sophocles' scene of tragedy becomes in Forster's story a site of homoerotic encounter and the panic it induces.

The undergraduate Forster further parodies the Victorian solemnity of R. C. Jebb, A. W. Verrall and their ilk in 'Strivings after Historical Style', which presents humorous versions of four styles typical of 'a certain series of Oxford textbooks' (*Albergo* 77): dramatic, personal, critical and cosmic.[20] The passages that he provides as examples of these styles are rife with bombastic and pompous sentences, clichés and mixed metaphors (see Rosenbaum, *Victorian* 276). Judging from his earliest biographical and non-biographical writing, one might safely assert that Forster the undergraduate employed a parodic mode almost exclusively. His use of this style diminishes as Forster develops the characteristic comic-ironic tone in his novels, with their own strategies of deflating the pomposity and self-importance of characters including Harriet Herriton, Charlotte Bartlett and Cecil Vyse, and the Turtons and Burtons of *A Passage to India*.

Sketches written by Forster for the *Independent Review* shortly after his graduation from Cambridge also conspicuously employ a camp parodic mode.

Short pieces such as 'Cnidus', 'Cardan' and 'Macolnia Shops', all written within a few years after the turn of the century, have been identified as Stracheyesque by critics such as Wilfred Stone and Judith Scherer Herz. Possibly the best example of Forster's utilisation of this mode is 'Macolnia Shops'. This sketch examines the character of Dindia Macolnia, 'a wealthy lady' and resident of ancient Rome, who purchased a toilet case for her daughter which eventually made its way to the Kirchner Museum. There Forster examined it in 1903. Forster utilises a catalogue of heroic and prominent ancients in this short piece in ways similar to Strachey's and Woolf's use of such indicators of importance, to undercut and to parody them through the bathos of deflation:

> Marius was in Rome at the time, or, if not Marius, Sulla, or, if Sulla was dead, Cicero was speaking, or, if Cicero was silent Macolnia might have looked with well-bred curiosity on the face of Augustus Imperator. But Dindia Macolnia was there to shop. (*Albergo* 171)

Shopping, here the accumulation of decorative objects, functions in this sketch to undercut the more heroic associations with imperial Rome.

Also, as in other examples of Bloomsbury camp biography, Forster inscribes queer sexuality into his sketch. Macolnia's gift to her daughter is even for her an antique, a 'Greek work [that] tells the story of the punishment of Amycus by Pollux ... Pollux, the boxer, has vanquished him and bound him naked to a tree, and round them are a group of admiring onlookers' (*Albergo* 171). Forster explains that the decorations on the toilet case represent a paean to friendship, which for him includes the homosocial, the erotic and the sexual.[21] As in Strachey and Woolf, Forster's use of camp allows this queer gesture to signify multivalently, within an overall context of parody. Like an unknowing, un-initiated reader, Macolnia does not understand the import of Forster's erotic interpretation of the toilet case: '"Praise of Friendship!" cries the angry shade of Dindia Macolnia, rising on its elbow out of the quaint Etruscan Hell. "I bought it because it was pretty, and stood nicely on the chest of drawers"' (*Albergo* 173). The scene on the toilet case, with its same-sex sado-masochistic overtones, provides a subversive contrast to the portrait of a 'middle class' consumer who wishes to own and to domesticate it.

Another sketch written for the *Independent Review* utilises a rhetorical mode similar to those in Strachey's and Woolf's biographies. 'Luigi Cornaro' focuses on an Italian Renaissance writer of numerous guides to good living, which suggest that a proper diet is the secret to a happy, long life. Forster's text includes at least one camp aphorism: 'An old man, however advanced, may be a poor companion, and a hygienic old man can be a dreadful bore' ('Luigi' 181). Also included in the text is a deflating series, which occurs in a passage by Cornaro translated by Forster: '"Three bad habits", [Cornaro] says, "have come into this Italy of ours during my lifetime. The first is Formality, the second Lutheranism, and the third overeating"' (179). In a device that will become typical in his later biographies, Forster separates himself from this bathetic passage through the use of quotation marks. He is not the author of such campy passages, but the inclusion of them nonetheless grants them his authority.

Forster generally admires Cornaro for his vitality and assuredness, and possibly also because Cornaro is for Forster in some sense queer. This possibility is raised in a comment that Cornaro makes to the Bishop of Aquileia in a letter. Assuring the bishop that he has a beautiful voice, Cornaro wishes that the bishop would hear him sing, accompanying himself 'meanwhile on the lyre like David'. If the bishop could experience this performance, he 'would be perfectly charmed' (181). As in 'Macolnia Shops' and Strachey's and Woolf's biographies, camp suggests the possibility of irregular desire, characterised in this sketch as 'charm[ing]' a bishop. Forster ultimately grows annoyed with this Renaissance man, 'and longs to feed him forcibly' (182). He 'longs' as well 'To hear the other side – what his wife thought of his singing for example' (182). This humorous passage causes the reader to wonder what Cornaro's wife thought about her husband's desire to charm a bishop through song. Did she realise that she could never be a Jonathan to her husband's David, that Cornaro's fitness regime was meant to catch the eye of a Catholic prelate? This delightful sketch provides a superb example of the playful, Stracheyesque Forster.

Unlike Strachey's and Woolf's biographies, Forster's early biographical writings do not typically examine Victorian figures in great detail or the Victorian era directly. Generally, the early post-undergraduate sketches – most of which are collected in *Abinger Harvest* and *Pharos and Pharillon* – provide Stracheyesque portrayals of historical figures from ancient history. In addition to 'Macolnia Shops' and Luigi Cornaro, these include 'Cardan', 'Gemisthus Pletho', 'Philo's Little Trip' and 'St. Athanasius'. Although he parodies Victorian biographical styles in these pieces, he does not provide an explicit critique of Victorian attitudes. A review from 1910 does, however, suggest that an anti-Victorian stance informs Forster's writing. 'Mr. Walsh's History of the Victorian Movement' is the title that Forster gave to his review of *A Manual of Domestic Economy*, by J. H. Walsh. Forster reads Walsh's manual, which went through several printings in the nineteenth century, as 'not a manual of Domestic Economy but a manual of Victorianism' (*Albergo* 110). In this review, Forster associates Victorianism with 'meanness and naiveté' (112), a world-view that 'condemns every friendship that one has had or is likely to have' (113). Further, he sees the characteristics of Victorianism, which contrast starkly with his own liberal humanism and faith in human intimacy, as a threat to his own post-Victorian culture. Forster fears that 'Victorianism may not be an era at all. It may be a spirit, biding its time' (*Albergo* 116).

Forster uses his later book-length biographies to parody and to undermine this dangerous spirit of Victorianism. In contrast to his earlier short sketches, these works do attempt to rewrite established versions of certain moments and settings in nineteenth-century British history, particularly the world of late-Victorian Cambridge in *Goldsworthy Lowes Dickinson* and the development and decline of the Clapham Sect in *Marianne Thornton*. In these works, Forster does not consistently use an overblown and campy style that undermines established conventions of biography. Indeed, the voice found in Forster's later biographical writings allows, typically, primary sources to speak for themselves through direct quotation. The 'camp sites' in these texts are often simultaneously camp citations, or 'camp cites'.

But texts such as *Goldsworthy Lowes Dickinson* and *Marianne Thornton* do employ many of the strategies of parody exemplified by Strachey's biographies, although the examples are neither as numerous nor as pronounced as they are in Strachey's writing. In his 1934 biography of his mentor and friend Goldsworthy Lowes Dickinson, Forster attempts to parody an overly serious diarist style in recounting an episode that occurred when Forster and Dickinson were travelling together in India. During the trip, Forster notes,

> We kept diaries. 'The extent of the heat may be judged from the fact that, on descending to my cabin, a tube of Kolynos was found in a semi-liquid condition' is a sentence which Dickinson gave me to put into mine. He said it was the ideal diarist style. (*Goldsworthy* 113)

In this passage, the pomposity of the phrase 'semi-liquid condition' is deflated by the reference to a mundane tube of Kolynos, a popular toothpaste brand. This camped version of a traditionally serious diarist style represents Forster's attempt, in his own words, to 'transcribe … nonsense' (*Goldsworthy* 113). Although the passage does not feature overblown and ornate rhetoric, as in Woolf's *Orlando*, it does suggest a similar emphasis on metabiographical parody, and it attempts to undermine the sonorousness of Victorian biography. Its focus on Dickinson's liquefying toothpaste underlines its playfulness. Generally the tone of Forster's Dickinson biography, like Woolf's tone in her biography of Roger Fry, is tender and sympathetic. Only quick flashes such as the one described above clue in the reader to the homoerotic playfulness of Forster's friendship with Dickinson.

The parodic Forster also emerges in his 1956 *Marianne Thornton: A Domestic Biography*, which takes as its subject the Clapham Sect and the aunt whose financial legacy enabled Forster's literary career. Glen Cavaliero has noted that at points in *Marianne Thornton* Forster's 'tone seems about to turn into the patronizing mockery of Lytton Strachey's *Eminent Victorians*' (30), but for Cavaliero it never quite does so. Forster, 'anxious to mediate between one age and another', usually avoids Stracheyism in this work (30). But Forster's biography is more Stracheyesque than it first appears, particularly the final section of the book, which centres on Forster's own birth. Utilising a series for an ultimately deflating effect, Forster describes a letter written by his aunt to his mother: 'It was not exactly a patronizing letter, it was not snobbish … but it left the victim no outlet and was written without the slightest consciousness that it was appalling' (*Marianne* 284). This technique is similar to the Stracheyesque bathetic series. In another passage that utilises Strachey's typically tripartite structure, Forster discusses the relationship between his mother and his hostile Aunt Emily:

> Once [Aunt Emily] gave me a Bible, whereupon my mother sobbed with rage. I learnt afterwards that when Emily disliked people she gave them a Hymn Book, and when she detested them a Prayer Book. So a Bible was the limit of limits. (299)

Finally, Forster, like Strachey and Woolf, inscribes at least the possibility of queer desire into *Marianne Thornton*. The biography includes a reference, in a letter written by his Aunt Marianne, to a close friend of Forster's father, Edward Streatfeild, who accompanied Forster's parents on their Paris honeymoon. Marianne feels that it is unfortunate that Forster's mother must travel with 'no lady companion, except Streatfeild, who is very nearly one I own, but not quite' (285). She later describes Forster's father, despite his wife, as 'old-maidish' (286). Forster's father and his friend are thus the 'old maid' and the 'lady' — certainly a queer pair. As in earlier biographies, Forster separates himself from this camp style through the use of quotation marks. Other camp s/cites might be found in Forster's later biographical writings, but generally these employ fewer strategies of queer parody than do his early work. At the same time, Forster developed for his novels a style that employs mimicry of both the narrative voice of serious Victorian novels and the suburban English voices that surrounded him at home and in his travels. His novelistic style was prepared for and anticipated by the early parodic writings.

Strachey, Forster and Woolf all express allegiance to a humanist philosophy that allows them both to admire and to parody the biographical writings of their literary forebears and to camp the prudish traditions of Victorian literature. The sense of play in texts such as *Eminent Victorians*, *Orlando* and *Marianne Thornton* suggests parodic metafiction, which is frequently asserted as a characteristic of postmodern writing. To argue, from a masculinist perspective, that the texts of Bloomsbury lack vitality and energy misses a crucial point. Although the writers of the Bloomsbury Group enjoyed privileges concomitant with their class positions, they were engaged in a systematic, if playful and parodic, dismantling of the moral and aesthetic underpinnings of the class system that provided such privilege. Strachey's off-hand 'Semen?' arguably marks the conception of this project. My hope is that readings such as this one that find in Bloomsbury a sustained if implicit critique of sexual oppression that crossed and undermined the boundaries between sex and gender, will begin the work of making readable the modernism of Queer Bloomsbury, indeed, the queerness of modernism itself.

Notes

1. Forster, Strachey and Woolf were not the only Bloomsbury authors to evince a camp sensibility in their biographical writings. See, for example, the portrayals of the Council of Four at the Versailles Conference in chapter 3 of J. M. Keynes's *The Economic Consequences of the Peace* and the biographical sketches collected in Clive Bell's *Old Friends*.
2. See the section entitled 'Bloomsbury on Bloomsbury' in Rosenbaum's *The Bloomsbury Group* for an ample sampling of these memoirs.
3. Although 'humanism' has become a disparaging term for many recent theorists, it signified in the late nineteenth and early twentieth centuries above all a critique of a Christian, theocratic world-view. Bloomsbury's humanism was greatly influenced by the philosopher G. E. Moore, particularly his *Principia Ethica*.
4. Judging from a diagram of the Bloomsbury Group provided by Quentin Bell (15), its central members were Duncan Grant, Clive Bell, Virginia Woolf, Saxon Sydney-Turner, Vanessa Bell, Roger Fry and Leonard Woolf. Orbiting at various distances from this central cluster are numerous others, including Lytton Strachey and Maynard Keynes. Two figures, Francis Birrell and E. M. Forster, are positioned at the outermost limits of the diagram. Although Forster was frequently absent from many Bloomsbury gatherings in the first two decades of the century (as Keynes, among others, has pointed out), he was by the mid-1920s a frequent visitor to the homes of prominent members of the group, such as Woolf and Strachey. Roger Poole has demonstrated that Forster's connection with Woolf was particularly strong: Forster was Woolf's most valued critic. Their relationship was also extremely complicated, as Joseph Bristow has shown.
5. On Woolf's sapphism, see James King and especially Suzanne Raitt.
6. Bonnie Kime Scott correctly points out that the major drawback of Kenner's view is related to its masculinist bias against Bloomsbury: a 'Pound narrative of modernism' such as Kenner's does not 'touch in a very productive way upon Bloomsbury' because 'Pound's virile ethos clashed with Bloomsbury' (94).

7. Eagleton presented a quite similar reading of modernism at the 1994 MLA Convention in an essay entitled 'Modernism in Ireland'.
8. Edelman claims, for example, that queer critics should not 'reengage in our critical practice this heterosexually inflected inside/outside, either/or model of sexual discriminations'; rather, queer critical analysis 'might do well to consider Barbara Johnson's description of a criticism informed by deconstructionist insights in order "to elaborate a discourse that says *neither* 'either/or', *nor* 'both/and', nor even 'neither/nor', while at the same time not totally abandoning these logics either"' (203).
9. Admittedly, it is somewhat difficult to assert that T. S. Eliot and Henry James are representatives of the masculine modernist tradition in any uncomplicated way. In *Exiles and Émigrés*, Eagleton includes them in the list of 'the seven most significant writers of twentieth-century English literature', all of whom are, significantly, male: 'Lawrence … Conrad, James, Eliot, Pound, Yeats, Joyce' (9). These writers are characterised by their power to totalise, to grasp 'the elements of a culture in their living and changing interrelations' (10). In his later *The Function of Criticism*, however, Eagleton lists Eliot, James and Forster as 'crippled, marginalized, self-ironizing humanists' (100), suggesting that these authors might not in fact be the exemplars of phallic authority of Eagleton's earlier characterisation.
10. Marcus argues, for example, that 'for women like Virginia Woolf, the homosexual men of Cambridge and Bloomsbury appeared to be, not the suffering victims of heterosexual social prejudice, but the "intellectual aristocracy" itself, an elite with virtual hegemony over British culture' (177). See Reed for a useful critique of Marcus's reading of the role of male homosexuals in Bloomsbury ('Bloomsbury Bashing' 54–6).
11. Bette London incisively points out Marcus's complicity in phallic logic: 'Marcus constructs her revolutionary paradigm as a simple reversal within the terms of the dominant discourse, leaving intact its underlying structures of thought, politics, and meaning' (15).
12. I have borrowed these categories from Spurr's excellent analysis of Strachey's style.
13. Oscar Wilde's camp sensibility and characteristically aphoristic style played a major role in the development of Stracheyism. For an exploration of the important connections between Wildean aestheticism and Bloomsbury, see Reed, 'Making' 203–17.
14. In *Flush*, her biography of Elizabeth Barrett Browning's cocker spaniel, Woolf parodies a Victorian biographical style as she simultaneously attacks Victorian prudery and sexual double standards. After noting that 'Before he was well out of his puppyhood, Flush was a father', the voice of Flush's biographer continues: 'Such conduct in a man even, in the year 1842, would have called for some excuse from a biographer; in a woman no excuse could have availed; her name must have been blotted in ignominy from the page. But the moral code of dogs, whether better or worse, is certainly different from ours, and there was nothing in Flush's conduct in this respect that requires a veil now, or unfitted him for the society of the purest and the chastest in the land then' (13). Woolf seems to be suggesting in

86   GEORGE PIGGFORD

this passage that the moral code of the Victorians, like the moral code of dogs, 'is certainly different' from her own and that of the Bloomsbury circle.
15. See Piggford for a detailed analysis of the relationship between camp and the figure of the androgyne in Woolf's text.
16. The 'Apostolic mode' might be characterised as the mode employed in meetings of the Cambridge Apostles, or Conversazione Society, a secret organisation whose members, including Strachey and Forster, presented blunt, candid and frequently campy papers to each other at monthly meetings. In a talk entitled 'A Roman Society' (presented to a meeting of the Apostles on 9 December 1910), Forster utilises a camp parodic style to describe the Renaissance academy of Pomponius Laetus. This talk might be read as exemplary of the Apostolic style. See Bristow for an analysis of Forster's lifelong attachment to the Apostles.
17. These sketches were all originally published in 1900 and are reprinted along with Forster's other undergraduate writing in *Albergo Empedocle and Other Writings*. In the original publications, the author of these pieces is typically listed as 'Peer Gynt'. The fact that these pieces are 'spoken' through the voice of a persona – the rakish hero of Ibsen's play – suggests an attempt on Forster's part to distance himself from these campy texts.
18. Theophrastus (c. 370 to c. 285 BCE), a student of Aristotle, wrote *The Characters* c. 319 BCE.
19. An echo of this attitude might be found in *Maurice*'s Dean Cornwallis, who instructs the undergraduates in his translation class to 'Omit: a reference to the unspeakable vice of the Greeks' (51) in Plato's *Symposium*.
20. S. P. Rosenbaum accurately describes Forster's use of the 'cosmic' style as 'apocalyptically trite', especially in its wrenching turn from imagery of the biblical Flood to that of fire (Rosenbaum, *Victorian* 276).
21. In *The Longest Journey*, for example, the novel's protagonist, Rickie Elliot, wishes that a 'friendship office' existed where he could officially record his erotically charged friendship with Stewart Ansell, a relationship which he compares to that of David and Jonathan. And in *Maurice*, Maurice's dream of a 'Friend' suggests in the first half of the text John Addington Symond's erotic and idealising, but necessarily sexual, notion of 'Greek love' and in the second half a Whitmanian-Carpenterian vision of 'comradeship', which Robert K. Martin reads as a code for full physical homosexuality. See Martin, 'Edward', particularly 35–8.

Works Cited

Beauman, Nicola. *Morgan: A Biography of E. M. Forster*. London: Hodder, 1993.
Bell, Clive. *Old Friends*. London: Chatto, 1956.
Bell, Quentin. *Bloomsbury*. New ed. London: Weidenfeld, 1986.
Bergman, David E. *Camp Grounds: Style and Homosexuality*. Amherst: University of Massachusetts Press, 1993.
—. 'Strategic Camp: The Art of Gay Rhetoric'. Rpt. in Bergman 92–109.

Bristow, Joseph. '*Fratrum Societati*: Forster's Apostolic Dedications'. Martin and Piggford 113–36.
Butler, Judith. *Bodies That Matter: On the Discursive Limits of 'Sex'*. New York: Routledge, 1993.
Cavaliero, Glen. *A Reading of E. M. Forster*. London: Macmillan, 1979.
Eagleton, Terry. *Exiles and Émigrés: Studies in Modern Literature*. London: Chatto, 1970.
—. *The Function of Criticism: From the Spectator to Post-Structuralism*. London: Verso, 1984.
—. 'Modernism in Ireland'. MLA Annual Convention. Marriott, San Diego. 29 Dec. 1994. Address.
Edelman, Lee. 'Homographesis'. *Yale Journal of Criticism* 3 (1989): 189–207.
Ellis, Havelock, and John Addington Symonds. *Sexual Inversion*. London: Wilson, 1897.
Forster, E. M. *Abinger Harvest*. 1936. New York: Harcourt, 1966.
—. *Albergo Empedocle and Other Writings*. Ed. George H. Thomson. New York: Liveright, 1971.
—. *A Passage to India*. 1924. Abinger Ed. 6. Ed. Oliver Stallybrass. London: Arnold, 1978.
—. *Goldsworthy Lowes Dickinson*. 1934. Abinger Ed. 13. Ed. Oliver Stallybrass. London: Arnold, 1973.
—. 'Luigi Cornaro'. *The Creator as Critic and Other Writings by E. M. Forster*. Ed. Jeffrey M. Heath. Toronto: Dundurn, 2008. 178–83.
—. *Marianne Thornton: A Domestic Biography*. New York: Harcourt, 1956.
—. *Maurice*. New York: Norton, 1971.
—. *Pharos and Pharillon*. Richmond: Hogarth, 1923.
—. *The Longest Journey*. 1907. Abinger Ed. 2. Ed. Elizabeth Heine. London: Arnold, 1984.
Furbank, P. N. *E.M. Forster: A Life*. 2 vols. New York: Harcourt, 1977, 1978.
Gallop, Jane. *The Daughter's Seduction*. Ithaca: Cornell University Press, 1982.
Gilbert, Sandra M., and Susan Gubar. *No Man's Land: The Place of the Woman Writer in the Twentieth Century*. Vol. 1: *The War of the Words*. New Haven: Yale University Press, 1988.
Heilbrun, Carolyn. *Toward a Recognition of Androgyny*. New York: Knopf, 1973.
Herz, Judith Scherer. *The Short Narratives of E. M. Forster*. New York: St Martin's, 1988.
Holroyd, Michael. *Lytton Strachey: The New Biography*. New York: Knopf, 1994.
Hutcheon, Linda. *Irony's Edge: The Theory and Politics of Irony*. London: Routledge, 1994.
Jebb, R. C., ed. and trans. *The Characters of Theophrastus: An English Translation from a Revised Text*. London: Macmillan, 1870.
Kenner, Hugh. *The Pound Era*. Berkeley: University of California Press, 1971.
King, James. *Virginia Woolf*. London: Penguin, 1995.
London, Bette. 'Guerrilla in Petticoats or Sans-Culotte? Virginia Woolf and the Future of Feminist Criticism'. *Diacritics* 21-3 (1991): 11–29.
Marcus, Jane. *Virginia Woolf and the Languages of Patriarchy*. Bloomington: Indiana University Press, 1987.

Martin, Robert K. 'Edward Carpenter and the Double Structure of *Maurice*'. *Journal of Homosexuality* 8.3/4 (1983): 35–46.
Martin, Robert K., and George Piggford, eds. *Queer Forster*. Chicago: University of Chicago Press, 1997.
—. 'Introduction: Queer, Forster?' Martin and Piggford 1–28.
Meyer, Moe. 'Reclaiming the Discourse of Camp'. *The Politics and Poetics of Camp*. Ed. Moe Meyer. London: Routledge, 1994. 1–22.
Moore, G. E. *Principia Ethica*. 1903. Cambridge: Cambridge University Press, 1993.
Muir, Edwin. 'Mr. Forster Looks at India.' Rev. of *A Passage to India*, by E. M. Forster. *Nation* 8 Oct. 1924: 379.
Piggford, George. 'Who's That Girl? Annie Lennox, Woolf's *Orlando*, and Female Camp Androgyny'. *Mosaic* 30.3 (1997): 39–58.
Poole, Roger. 'Passage to the Lighthouse'. *Charleston Newsletter* 16 (1986): 16–32.
Pound, Ezra. *Essays of Ezra Pound*. New York: New Directions, 1968.
Raitt, Suzanne. *Vita and Virginia: The Work and Friendship of V. Sackville-West and Virginia Woolf*. Oxford: Clarendon, 1993.
Reed, Christopher. 'Bloomsbury Bashing: Homophobia and the Politics of Criticism in the Eighties'. *Genders* 11 (1991): 58–80. Rpt. in *Queer Bloomsbury*. Ed. Brenda Helt and Madelyn Detloff. Edinburgh: Edinburgh University Press, 2016. 36–63.
—. 'Making History: The Bloomsbury Group's Construction of Aesthetic and Sexual Identity'. *Journal of Homosexuality* 27.1–2 (1994): 189–224.
Rosenbaum, S. P., ed. *The Bloomsbury Group: A Collection of Memoirs and Commentary*. Rev. ed. Toronto: University of Toronto Press, 1995.
—. *Victorian Bloomsbury: The Early Literary History of the Bloomsbury Group*. New York: St Martin's, 1987.
Ross, Andrew. 'Uses of Camp'. Bergman 54–77.
Scott, Bonnie Kime. *Refiguring Modernism*. Vol. 1: *The Women of 1928*. Bloomington: Indiana University Press, 1995.
Sontag, Susan. 'Notes on Camp'. *Partisan Review* (1964). Rpt. in *Against Interpretation*. New York: Anchor-Doubleday, 1990. 275–92.
Spurr, Barry. 'Camp Mandarin: The Prose Style of Lytton Strachey'. *ELT* 33 (1990): 31–45.
Stone, Wilfred. *The Cave and the Mountain: A Study of E. M. Forster*. Stanford: Stanford University Press, 1966.
Strachey, Lytton. *Biographical Essays*. San Diego: Harcourt, 1969.
—. *Elizabeth and Essex: A Tragic History*. New York: Harcourt, 1928.
—. *Eminent Victorians*. 1918. London: Penguin, 1971.
—. *Literary Essays*. San Diego: Harcourt, n.d.
—. *Queen Victoria*. 1921. San Diego: Harcourt, 1978.
Thomson, George. 'Cambridge Humor'. Forster, *Albergo* 37–43.
Woolf, Virginia. *Flush*. 1933. San Diego: Harcourt, 1983.
—. 'Old Bloomsbury'. Rpt. in Rosenbaum, *Bloomsbury* 40–59.
—. *Orlando*. 1928. San Diego: Harcourt, 1956.

Redecorating the International Economy: Keynes, Grant and the Queering of Bretton Woods

Bill Maurer

'Redecorating the International Economy' Revisited

Since the 2007–08 global financial crisis, there has been a reappreciation of John Maynard Keynes and alternative monetary theory. Keynes's emphasis on public investment, his caution against taking seriously overly dire predictions of long-run effects of government spending, his defence of a strong fiscal state to channel market forces if necessary and his proposals for an international currency all have gained new traction. Unfortunately, however, that traction has not been enough to head off austerity, deflation and its associated rise in nativist populism, the Greek crisis and bailout, or the next credit crisis. When I first started working on this essay, back in the late 1990s, cultural critics generally lumped Keynes together with Bretton Woods, and thereby associated him with IMF-mandated 'structural adjustment' in many countries of the so-called Third World, or just equated him with 'capitalism' *tout court*. This seemed silly to me. I remember arguing with a friend who said, 'He's in the grave where he should be!' To which I responded, 'I want to dig up his corpse and start poking at it!' I wanted to recuperate Keynes's own, unrealised plans for Bretton Woods, to look more closely at the world he sought to create and to think about whether other economies were possible, especially after the implosion of the socialist experiment

---

'Redecorating the International Economy: Keynes, Grant, and the Queering of Bretton Woods' by Bill Maurer was first published in *Queer Globalizations: Citizenship and the Afterlife of Colonialism*, ed. Arnaldo Cruz-Malave and Martin F. Manalanson, New York City: New York University Press, 2002. Reprinted here abridged with the kind permission of New York University Press. Copyright © 2002 by New York University. All rights reserved.

and the unsustainability of neoliberalism – which was borne out by the financial crisis. Keynes was prescient, despite his avowed antipathy toward long-range forecasting. And I didn't just want to speculate on the possibilities of other economies: I wanted a how-to guide. Keynes provided that. The fact that it was an aesthetic as much as a political economic project made it all the more appealing.

Re-reading my essay now, many years after I wrote it, I am struck by how many passages of Keynes's own words seem to be speaking to us directly about all we have learned – and failed to learn – from the Great Recession. I am also struck by how much this essay represented my own effort to break from much of the critical tradition in political economy and anthropology, my continuing foray into the wilds of economic plurality with J. K. Gibson-Graham. There was no turning back after this essay. Were I to rewrite it today, I would probably want to trace out the impact of Alfred North Whitehead on Keynes's theory of probability – Whitehead was one of the readers of his thesis on probability – and explore the resonance between Whitehead and Gibson-Graham. If the problem when I first wrote this essay was an overly reductive approach to economy among critics of capitalism – and overly simplistic modes of queer activism – the problem now might be the enthusiastic enunciations of ontology, and here, Whitehead, via Isabelle Stengers, might help us out. I would also take more time with the alternative mathematics offered by Keynes, to add further weight to the programme of economic plurality and the actualisation of other possibilities in the present. Barring world enough and time for further explorations, however, I instead offer it here in a version shorter and hopefully therefore sweeter than its first rendition.

Δ   Δ   Δ

This essay seeks to develop a perspective on globalisation, and on alternative possibilities, by claiming the queerness of John Maynard Keynes's economics through a recuperation of his aesthetics. I am wary of critical approaches to globalisation that imagine a future world of capital controls and local autonomy and that rely on troubling notions of community. At the same time, I am sceptical of celebrations of globalisation that emphasise the creative possibilities of new technologies like the Internet and new publics like transnational civil societies. Both sets of perspectives often take for granted categories of knowledge, being, space and time that they share with the object of their critique, and rely on problematic notions of causality and the delineation of domains of 'sexuality' and 'the economy' (as well as 'art', 'politics', 'gender' and so forth). Ultimately, queer politics and effective challenges to dominant global visions require new categories that are not bound up in bureaucratic rationality, neoliberal market logic, or nostalgic visions of community or autonomy. Focusing on the interplay of Keynes's economics with the interior design of Duncan Grant, this essay reflects on the notion of creative endeavour that underwrote both Bretton Woods and Bloomsbury in an effort to recover an alternate modernity in response to neoliberal globalisation.

Keynes's theories of aesthetics were developed alongside Grant's art and in the wake of G. E. Moore's *Principia Ethica*, a text that had a profound impact on the shape of Bloomsbury art and philosophising. Both Keynes's aesthetics and Grant's post-impressionist interior design rest on a particular notion of agentive perception and moral action. Keynes's theory of probability, moreover, was a direct outgrowth of his aesthetics and permeates his *General Theory*, which specifically addresses the issues of long-term investment and capital mobility, issues that would preoccupy the Bretton Woods planners. Bretton Woods established the regulatory and theoretical apparatus of the post-World War II international monetary system in institutions like the International Monetary Fund and the World Bank. Keynes's alternative plan for an International Clearing Union resonated with his theories of probability and aesthetics, and can be viewed as a post-impressionist project in the manner of Grant's interior design. Keynes's alternate modernity was not unproblematic, drawing on colonial themes as did Grant's economies of eroticism. Nevertheless, Keynes's and Grant's alternative modernity, which has as its centrepiece a doctrine of non-reductive, non-natural 'organic unity' actively constructed by individuals drawing together disparate objects (localities, points on a canvas, designs in a room) into new, ever-changing wholes, and a rejection of the delineation of separate domains of cultural life, offers avenues for addressing the problem of globalisation and the breakdown of the Bretton Woods system.

Bloomsbury's Economic Theorist

Keynes is often credited with the creation of the theory of the 'national economy', since the components of his *General Theory of Employment, Interest, and Money* are all economic aggregates measured over a given geopolitical space (Radice 112). Hence Keynes's association with Fordism and Fordist nation-based systems of mass production and mass consumption. Also central to Keynes's *General Theory* was the explicit threat, as he saw it, of external forces of instability. Keynes argued for limits on capital mobility, fixed exchange rates and a model of international order based on economically sovereign nation-states interlinked by trade and guaranteed by a spatialised regulatory order (Leyshon and Thrift 73–5). His emphasis on national macroeconomic planning and international regulation through Bretton Woods bureaucracies like the International Monetary Fund and the World Bank has led critics to equate Keynesianism with the disciplinary aspects of Fordist production systems (Harvey).

Yet there is another Keynes in between the lines of the *General Theory*. This is the Keynes of play and magic, the Keynes who wrote that capitalist markets resemble nothing so much as a great 'casino', who quipped that the monetary system is 'a contrived system of pretty, polite techniques, made for a well-paneled board room and a nicely regulated market' (Leyshon and Thrift 33), and who compared investing to selecting the winners of a beauty contest. This is the Keynes of Bloomsbury, whose theories of probability and aesthetics, developed alongside the playful interior designs of his lover, Grant, envisioned an alternative modernity set apart from the bureaucratic apparatus of the welfare state and the naturalised logic of the 'free' market. To the well-panelled board room and the nicely regulated market Keynes would contrast the playful dressing-screen and the enjoyment of art in an economy of pleasure.

Debates on the economics of globalisation intersect with queer politics in troubling ways. Gay and lesbian identities and communities emerged in tandem with the economic restructuring and social dislocation of Fordism (D'Emilio) and were also subject to and, arguably, produced by the disciplinary practices of the normalising welfare state. Transformations in Fordism co-occurred with the rise of new social movements like gay liberation. This does not imply that the end of Fordism heralded the end of the regulation of gay identities, or that post-Fordism promises a free play of bodies and pleasures in any necessarily liberatory sense. Such arguments would rely on assertions about causal relationships between economics and sexualities as putatively separate spheres or cultural domains. Part of *my* project is to demonstrate the utter impossibility of making such claims of autonomy, and of making the kinds of causal arguments that rely on the relative autonomy of separate cultural domains like 'economics' and 'sexuality' (Yanagisako and Delaney).

Post-Fordism does promise just such a free play of bodies and pleasures, but only within the strictures of a neoliberal market logic that renders all bodies into vehicles of consumer choice and all pleasures into gut-level preferences (Strathern). In critiquing a heteronormativity that only became normative through the governmentalities of the Bretton Woods moment, however, does critical queer scholarship share a vision of person and preference with the very neoliberal logic that currently inspires globalisation? To what extent are critical queer perspectives products and promulgators of neoliberal visions of freedom, desire, value and profit?[1] To what extent does undermining neoliberal logic in an effort to challenge globalisation also undermine queer criticism? Or, alternatively, can the emergence of queer politics and criticism in the post-Bretton Woods moment have the potential to recuperate an alternative

Keynesianism that might have been constitutive of another modernity but was a road not taken by the Bretton Woods planners? In other words, can we engage the post-Bretton Woods world without falling into its categorical distinctions between supposed domains like economics and sexuality, and can doing so point toward a new vision for future worlds?

Julie Graham and Katherine Gibson argue persuasively that critiques of contemporary capitalism must not fall into the trap of using for analytical or political purposes the dominant metaphors of capitalism's supposed triumph. As they put it,

> the script of globalization need not draw solely upon an image of the body of capitalism as hard, thrusting and powerful. Other images are available, and … it is important to draw upon such representations in creating an anticapitalist imaginary and fashioning a politics of economic transformation. (Gibson-Graham 138–9)

Revisiting Keynes affords an opportunity to consider alternative representations of capitalism and to think through alternative visions of globalisation. This project is important for queer politics because it counters heteronormative language of globalisation and suggests possibilities for queer rethinkings of capitalism. It is important for anticapitalist politics because it allows a reconsideration of lost economic alternatives that were available when the global visions of Bretton Woods came into focus (Ritter 19).

Keynes's Aesthetics: Organic Unities in Theory and Design

As many Keynes scholars have argued, Keynes's economic theories were the outgrowth of his earlier work in aesthetics.[2] Like others in the Bloomsbury circle, Keynes based much of his thinking on G. E. Moore's *Principia Ethica*, published in 1903 when Keynes was a student at Cambridge. Keynes's reading of Moore resulted in several papers on aesthetics, written between 1904 and 1909. As Robert Skidelsky writes, summarising the thrust of the 'new Keynes scholarship', Keynes's beliefs about political and economic planning are seen as 'expressions of his beliefs about ethics and probability developed before the First World War' (Skidelsky, 'Keynes's Philosophy' 104).

Moore's papers proceeded from his discussion of the relationship between aesthetics and morally correct actions, embodied in his statement that

> By far the most valuable things, which we can know or can imagine, are certain states of consciousness, which may be roughly described as the pleasures of human intercourse and the enjoyment of beautiful

objects. No one, probably, who has asked himself the question, has ever doubted that personal affection and the appreciation of what is beautiful in Art or Nature, are good in themselves; nor, if we consider strictly what things are worth having purely for their own sakes, does it appear probable that any one will think that anything else has nearly so great a value as the things which are included under these two heads…. [But the] mere existence of what is beautiful has value, so small as to be negligible, in comparison with that which attaches to the consciousness of beauty. This simple truth may, indeed, be said to be universally recognized. What has not been recognized is that it is the ultimate and fundamental truth of Moral Philosophy. (Moore 237–8, section 113)

Moore continued, in what became a Bloomsbury slogan, 'personal affections and aesthetic enjoyments include *all* the greatest, and *by far* the greatest, goods we can imagine' (Moore 228, section 113, original emphases). These 'goods', these things of beauty that cannot be disaggregated into their constituents, form 'highly complex *organic unities*', according to Moore (228, section 113, original emphasis). As Keynes wrote in 1938, reflecting on the influence of Moore on himself and his peers,

> Nothing mattered except states of mind, our own and other people's of course, but chiefly our own. These states of mind were not associated with action or achievement or with consequences. They consisted in timeless, passionate states of contemplation and communion, largely unattached to 'before' or 'after'. Their value depended, in accordance with the principle of organic unity, on the state of affairs as a whole which could not be usefully analysed into parts…. The appropriate subjects of passionate contemplation and communion were a beloved person, beauty and truth, and one's prime objects in life were love, the creation and enjoyment of aesthetic experience and the pursuit of knowledge. ('My Early Beliefs' 83)

Keynes's papers on aesthetics considered the nature of these 'organic unities' postulated by Moore, and concerned what he called their 'fitness', or ability to generate 'good' states of mind. However, the doctrine of organic unities presented a paradox. The existence of a 'bad' object like suffering might be necessary to produce a 'good' state of mind like pity, which would inspire good action to relieve suffering (Skidelsky, 'Keynes's Philosophy' 107–8). This paradox might lead to the conclusion that social reformers ought to create deprivation in order to inspire pity and moral actions designed to resolve it. But, Keynes maintained, there are ways to create the good feeling of pity without actively creating situations of suffering or deprivation, for instance by writing melodramas ('Shall We Write Melodramas?'). Melodramas, Keynes wrote, allow people to 'enjoy at second hand, or admire, the noble feelings *without* the evil happening which generally accompany them in real life' (Letter to F. Lucas, 1928, qtd. in Skidelsky, 'Keynes's Philosophy' 108).

If the task is to increase 'fitness' in objects and ontological categories in order to increase 'goodness' in the world, yet fitness inheres in parts of complex organic unities, then how does one conduct social reform? Keynes's answer involved a rejection of empiricism. He did not seek to distinguish objects in the world from ontological categories, since all objects in the world are called forth only in our perception of them. 'Aesthetic feelings', Keynes wrote in 'Miscellanea Ethica', 'are not directly evoked by the objects themselves but by the content of our perceptions' (qtd. in O'Donnell 102). Keynes explicitly left aside the question of whether external objects matter at all — in both a consequential and a substantive sense. 'I am not endeavouring to answer the question of our relation to the external world', he wrote (O'Donnell 102). Our perceptions are relative. 'The beauty of some pictures depends a good deal upon the particular method in which we fix them' (103). Furthermore, 'it is not beauty but only the feelings which beauty can create that are good' (107). What, then, are the entities that the social reformer must work on in order to increase goodness?

Keynes deferred the answer onto the agentive aspects of perception. These are ultimately dependent on context and situatedness in a social and aesthetic space. As Rod O'Donnell summarises, '[b]y adjusting our sense organs and position, we have a certain voluntary control over the perception produced in us. We can see different "aspects" of a painting depending on how we fix it, and from where we view it' (107). For Keynes, aesthetic judgements are not based on 'mental facts supplied by the senses', but only on 'a "certain selection" of these, made either consciously or instinctively' (O'Donnell 107), to produce a 'kind of harmony between our surroundings, as they are presented to us by our senses, our thoughts, and our emotions' (109).

How is one to determine the best 'arrangement' of objects, the best position from which to view objects, or the selection of sense data from which to create harmony? Although Keynes held that '[p]ersons with the finest taste and greatest artistic power see "the most beautiful grouping" of these facts' (O'Donnell 107), he wavered on the standards of 'fine taste' because of his anti-empiricist position on the question of beauty:

> we must refrain from narrowing down too far the fit objects of our senses, and, while it is the delight and duty of all lovers of beauty to dispute ... concerning tastes, we must not impose on the almost infinite variety of fit and beautiful objects ... tests and criteria which

we may think we have established in that corner of the field which is dearest to ourselves; nor must we fail to see beauty in strange places because it has little in common with the kind of beauty we would strive to create. ('Miscellanea Ethica', qtd. in O'Donnell 112)

This emphasis on perception as an active, agentive process found direct expression in the post-impressionist art of Grant. Post-impressionists rejected techniques like palate mixing in favour of techniques like pointillism, in which the spectator's eye resolves a collection of small dots into colour and form depending on the spectator's distance from and position in relation to an object (Reichardt 240). The effect of such painting is to call into question the process of seeing itself, to highlight its contingent nature, and to exploit 'the discrepancy between physical fact and psychic effect' (Alpers, qtd. in Reichardt 239).

Grant, together with Vanessa Bell, brought post-impressionism into interior design, working not with a two-dimensional canvas but the three-dimensional space of living areas. Two- and three-dimensional patterns come together in the spectator's field of vision into surprising and playful patterns, the perception of which is dependent on the spectator's position and movement through a room. One of Grant's most important works, his 1949 *Abstract Kinetic Collage Painting with Sound*, or *The Scroll*, combines the play of perception with the motion of the object and the spectator's position relative to it. It is designed to be viewed through a rectangular aperture as the work is unwound vertically off a yarn-winding machine used in craft weaving, while accompanied by music (Watney 39).

The emphasis of Grant's aesthetics is decidedly non-utilitarian. As Christopher Reed notes, Grant's art served 'as an alternative to the precious materials and machined sleekness of the "heroic" modernism exemplified in the designs of Le Corbusier' (qtd. in Watney 11). Grant's masterwork is not a particular decorative object or painting, but his home, Charleston, where his 'pictures, fabrics, pottery and design work in the type of environment for which they were envisaged, as elements of an overall aesthetic involving the artist in every aspect of an interior' (Watney 9). As Angelica Garnett, the daughter of Duncan Grant and Vanessa Bell, wrote, Grant and Bell's artistic project 'enabled them to make the imaginative leap from seeing walls, doors and fireplaces as a potentially tasteful background to treating them – like canvases – as an opportunity to make a statement of a very personal nature' (71).

Although some of his contemporaries maintain that, as a project opposed to modernism, Grant's interiors presented an 'escape' from a 'life ... increasingly dominated by machines' into a home-space of 'fantasy, imagination, [and] wit' (Todd and Mortimer 28), the work itself undercut the very opposition of home and world central to both modernism and romanticism. Here, Grant was derivative of Vanessa Bell. He relied on elaborate *trompe l'oeils* that confounded the distinction between interior and exterior space. Many of his paintings play on this distinction. His interiors represent an 'increased blurring of the distinction between "inside" and "outside"' the picture-space and the home-space (Watney 53). Doors become canvases; canvases become windows; frames enclose other frames, which in turn open out into other picture-spaces, and so on. As Watney summarises,

> Charleston [itself] was lived in very much as an ongoing process of representation.... At times it seems almost as if Grant were living inside a picture that he was painting, of himself painting the picture in which he was living. (53)

Probability and Possibility in Social Action

Keynes advanced his ideas about aesthetics in his *Treatise on Probability* (1921), which was written during the time of his relationship with Grant (1908–14). In 1908 Keynes and Grant vacationed in the Orkney Islands 'and enjoyed many profitable hours on painting and probability' (Hession 55). Grant believed that Keynes's appreciation of painting derived from their pursuits during this trip; 'in fact he accepted', Grant wrote, 'without me having to point it out, that the painter had a serious job on hand' (qtd. in Skidelsky, *John* 198). Keynes's work on probability was to have a profound impact on *The General Theory* and derives directly from his aesthetics and the concretised embodiment of his theory of aesthetics in the interiors of Grant.

Keynes contended that increasing the goodness in the world entails improving upon what he called 'fit' objects, which were objects or ontologies about which it was possible to have good feelings. But his notions of fitness and beauty were profoundly anti-empiricist. One could not really grasp hold of a fit object without transforming it, as it was always part of a larger organic unity, and its fitness was a consequence of and a condition for one's perception of it in the first place. Furthermore, one's perception ultimately depended on the object's and one's own position in a broader field, much as perception of Grant's *Scroll* depends on a particular viewing point and process of seeing. According to Keynes, therefore, a *fit* object is one to which it is possible, *but not necessary*, to have good feelings or a good mental state; it is 'defined in terms of a possibility, not [an] actuality' (O'Donnell 100).

The claim that *fit*-ness is a possibility led Keynes to a redefinition of probability in his *Treatise on Probability*. For Keynes, probability was not about frequencies of phenomena, or statistical description and projection, but rather 'the formulation of probability judgments in the broadest sense, with arguments and the process of reasoning' (Moggridge, *Maynard* 144; Skidelsky, 'Keynes's Philosophy'). Probability referred to 'the degree of belief it is rational to entertain in given conditions' (Keynes, *Treatise on Probability* 4), not the relative frequency of empirically observable phenomena. Probability is by definition a logical, not empirical, problem, according to Keynes, and uncertainty, having no place in logic, has no place in probability. Our belief that our knowledge of the present gives us some purchase on the future is the product of sloppy thinking about the nature of the universe and a consequence of the empiricist fallacy. We have 'only the vaguest idea of any but the most direct consequences of our acts' (Keynes, 'General Theory of Employment' 213, qtd. in Dow and Dow 49). As Keynes wrote,

> The scientist wishes … to assume that the occurrence of a phenomenon which has appeared as part of a more complex phenomenon, may be some reason for expecting it to be associated on another occasion with part of the same complex. Yet if different wholes were subject to different laws qua wholes and not simply on account of and in proportion to the differences of their parts, knowledge of a part could not lead, it would seem, even to presumptive or probable knowledge as to its association with other parts. (*Treatise on Probability* 277)

Keynes's vision of probability thus recalls the Moorean doctrine of organic unities (Carabelli). Also, like Moore's notion of goodness, Keynes's probability is 'unanalysable, indefinable, non-natural, [yet] directly perceived or intuitive and objective' (Moggridge, *Maynard* 149). It is also, again, profoundly antiempiricist. As Keynes wrote in the *Treatise*,

> If our experience and our knowledge were complete, we should be beyond the need of the calculus of probability. And where our experience is incomplete, we cannot hope to derive it from judgments of probability without the aid either of intuition or of some further a priori principle. Experience, as opposed to intuition, cannot possibly afford us a criterion by which to judge whether on given evidence the probabilities of two propositions are not equal. (94)

Elaborating on the doctrine of organic unities, Keynes explicitly contrasted the 'atomic', methodologically individualist perspective espoused by Bertrand Russell with an 'organic' perspective embodied in his probability, although his probability clearly derived from the mathematical, logical formulations of Russell. According to the 'atomic' perspective, found in the mathematical sciences and in the mathematical social sciences like econometrics,

> [t]he system of the material universe must consist ... of bodies which we may term ... legal atoms, such that each of them exercises its own separate, independent, and invariable effect, a change of the total state being compounded of a number of separate changes each of which is solely due to a separate portion of the preceding state.... Each atom can, according to this theory, be treated as a separate cause and does not enter into different organic combinations in each of which it is regulated by different laws. (276–7)

Much of Keynes's argument in the *Treatise* is aimed at the methodological individualism of mathematical approaches to the social sciences, and is a defence of 'intuition' as opposed to rational calculation (see Davis 'Keynes's' and *Keynes's*). As Keynes put it in the *Treatise*, '[t]he hope, which sustained many investigators in the course of the nineteenth century, of gradually bringing the moral sciences under the sway of mathematical reasoning, steadily recedes' (349). In a later speech, he discredited social science aimed at quantifying human behaviour and sentiment, since human beings and human societies are always more than the sum of their parts.

Keynes's organic perspective, according to Roy Rotheim, provided insight 'not through prior knowledge of "atoms" but through our interacting with reality, with coming to grips with complex things at their own level of being' (87). Rotheim's statement could also be applied to the post-impressionist artists, whose works aimed to upset a methodologically individualist conception of art. In the individualist conception, an artist creates a work for a viewer. The viewer engages with the work only at the level of a distanced observer casting a critical or appreciative eye. The work, in this view, is inert – an object created to be viewed. For Keynes and the post-impressionists, however, the work was just as much a part of an active, lived reality as the viewer and the artist. It is only through interacting with that reality that the viewer and artist come to grips with the complexity conveyed through the work of art.

Keynes's notion of 'evidence' is similar to his view of art – dynamic and complex. What, then, counts as 'evidence'? How can we assess different kinds of 'evidence' and measure them against each other? Keynes answers that the problems of measuring evidence are similar to those of measuring probabilities, which may imply that evidence, like probability, is a logical, not empirical, category (*Treatise on Probability* 77–8; see also Rotheim). If evidence is a logical category, it therefore changes along with changing premises and conclusions. For Keynes, an understanding of temporality was central to assessing the weight of arguments. Conclusions based on an equilibrium model, for instance, ignore the temporality of social life and thus have less 'weight' than conclusions based on more organically conceived probabilistic claims. Take the idea of an economic process 'tending toward' equilibrium. Joan Robinson, in a lecture on Keynes, notes that this idea confuses metaphors, since it involves 'using a metaphor based on space to explain a process which takes place in time' (255). As Rotheim points out,

> words such as tendency, if used in an equilibrium framework, only have meaning if the concept of equilibrium exists, *a priori*. One cannot move in time when the language emanates from an equilibrium system, because in the latter we start with an equilibrium, define the appropriate premise structure, and then rest assured that we will return to the equilibrium unscathed. (98)

He continues,

> When we move into a framework of time, we start with the premises and move forward as we interact along the way causing us to change our premises and change our path. The two thought processes reflect different, incompatible language structures; between those based on atomistic systems where probabilistic statements are valid, and those which are organic, where uncertainty prevails, and where knowledge of the real, social world evolves in an interactionist configuration. (98)

Keynes's probability thus also introduced a particular notion of space-time, reminiscent of the vertigo of Grant's play with enframing devices in interior design, confusing inside and outside as a person moves through living spaces. Logical relationships are reversible. Therefore, for Keynes, so are probabilistic and evidential ones. As Keynes reflected in his 1938 memoir, in reference to his early philosophising,

> Suppose we were to live our lives backwards, having our experiences in the reverse order, would this affect the value of our successive states of mind? If the states of mind enjoyed by each of us were pooled and then redistributed, would this affect their value? How did one compare the value of a good state of mind which had bad consequences with a bad state of mind which had good consequences? In valuing the consequences did one assess them at their actual value as it turned out eventually to be, or their probable value at the time? ('My Early Beliefs' 87)

Keynes evokes a space-time field like that of one of Duncan Grant's interiors, where inside, outside, frame and world dissolve into each other and resolve into new patterns depending on the position of the spectator and movement through space-time. His epistemology, like Grant's design, is based on

> using a variety of logical chains ... with differing starting-points, and taking different parts of the system as exogenous. As a result, the

duality of endogeneity and exogeneity loses its universal application
and becomes specific to the particular chain of reasoning at hand.
(Dow and Dow 59)

This may not seem a very satisfying place to be when determining what course of action one should pursue in the process of trying to bring about social change. Keynes's response to this dilemma has to do with a notion of 'risk' inherent in any action in the world. 'There seems', he writes, 'a good deal to be said for the conclusion that, other things being equal, that course of action is preferable, which involves least risk and about the results of which we have the most complete knowledge' (*Treatise on Probability* 347); or 'a high weight and an absence of risk increase *pro tanto* the desirability of the action to which they refer' (*Treatise* 348). Skidelsky summarises, '[t]he important conclusion for practice is that it is more rational to aim for an immediate good than a remote one, since the first will have behind it both a greater weight of argument and a higher probability of attainment' ('Keynes's Philosophy' 112). As Keynes wrote elsewhere,

> it can seldom be right ... to sacrifice a present benefit for a doubtful
> advantage in the future.... It is not wise to look too far ahead; our
> powers of prediction are slight, our command over results infinitesimal.
> It is therefore the happiness of our own contemporaries that is our
> main concern; we should be very chary of sacrificing large numbers
> of people for the sake of a contingent end, however advantageous that
> may appear.... We can never know enough to make the chance worth
> taking. (qtd. in Skidelsky, 'Keynes's Philosophy' 114)

Keynes thus articulated a vision of political action and history that is profoundly anti-teleological. This has consequences for both Christian and liberal humanist metaphysics and morality (Skidelsky, *John* 153), and, like recent movements in queer criticism, troubles liberal visions of activism and political efficacy.

Queering *The General Theory*

Keynes's notions of space, time and probability came together in some of the most important parts of his economics. Chapter 12 of *The General Theory*, titled 'The State of Long-Term Expectation', provides an account of the state-of-play of the modern stock market and the raising of capital for enterprise. Investments based on long-term expectations of return, Keynes argued, are not based on forecasts or frequency-based probability judgements, the kind of judgements Keynes was arguing against in the *Treatise*. True to his position in the *Treatise*, he writes that '[t]here is ... not much to be said about the state of confidence *a priori*' (*General* 149).

> If we speak frankly, we have to admit that our basis of knowledge for estimating the yield ten years hence of a railway, a copper mine, a textile factory, the goodwill of a patent medicine, an Atlantic liner, a building in the City of London amounts to little and sometimes to nothing. (*General* 149–50).

How, then, are expectations made and investments revalued in the course of market trading?

Keynes's answer came straight out of his thinking on aesthetics and probability. 'In practice', he wrote, 'we have tacitly agreed, as a rule, to fall back on what is, in truth, a *convention*' (*General* 152, original emphasis). The 'convention' that maintains capitalist enterprise is a sort of collective illusion that the current state of affairs, A, will continue into the future state of affairs, A1, and not into an entirely unexpected future state, B. We know full well that this is an illusion. But it serves to bolster our confidence that the present state of affairs, A, is a reasonable one – that existing market values of stocks are appropriate, given assets and current yields. It also serves to guarantee a particular vision of stability and order. In effect, Keynes was saying, the capitalist market is an illusion of our own making, yet it is an illusion with which we can live quite happily, as long as we stick to the conventions warranting its stability. Participation in the illusion is like an invitation to Grant's Charleston: come, participate in this world, setting aside any claims to a 'reality' behind the illusion; so long as everyone plays the game according to convention, only goodness will result.

Convention is upset, however, by certain aspects of the market that encourage speculation. Keynes made a distinction between investment in the hopes of securing a steady income through regular return, and investment in the hopes of making a fast buck through an increase in conventional basis of valuation. The former he termed 'enterprise', the latter he termed 'speculation'. Keynes saw speculating on stock values, putting one's money into the stock market in the hopes that a stock itself will increase in value over the short term, as a form of gambling, rendering the capitalist economy a great 'casino' (*General* 159).

People speculate, Keynes believed, because capitalist markets have made what he termed a 'fetish' of 'liquidity', or the belief that one's money should be able to move and be convertible into any manner of investment quickly and easily. Liquidity, of course, is the cornerstone of contemporary globalising processes. Liquidity only makes sense, Keynes argued, when people are able to approach the market as a gambling operation, and not as a social process designed to increase goodness in the world by helping enterprise accumulate the necessary capital for its endeavours, while distributing profit and risk. Because of the way the market is currently organised, Keynes wrote, 'it is not sensible to pay 25 for an investment of which you believe the prospective yield to justify a value of 30, if you also believe that the market will value it at 20 three months hence' (*General* 155). Speculation need not be harmful when it merely consists of 'bubbles on a steady stream of enterprise' (159). But things get out of hand 'when enterprise becomes the bubble on a whirlpool of speculation. When the capital development of a country becomes a by-product of a casino, the job is likely to be ill-done' (159). 'These tendencies' toward speculation 'are a scarcely avoidable outcome of having successfully organised "liquid" investment markets' (159).

Liquidity encourages investors to make unwise choices. It masks the morally correct relationships of investment, which, for Keynes, are relationships that constitute community over time, not relationships that garner particular individuals wealth in the short term. The issuing of shares in corporate enterprise, Keynes wrote, leading to the separation of ownership from control, has created a whole class of people whose involvement in the stock market is not based on commitment to enterprise but on daily (or hourly) revaluations of stock (*General* 150–1).

> It is as though a farmer, having tapped his barometer after breakfast, could decide to remove his capital from the farming business between 10 and 11 in the morning and reconsider whether he should return to it later in the week. (151)

'Thus', Keynes wrote, 'certain classes of investment are governed by the average expectation of those who deal on the Stock Exchange as revealed in the prices of shares, rather than by the genuine expectations of the professional entrepreneur' (151). Furthermore, the process of investment on the stock market leads individuals, not actually to assess the productive potential of any given enterprise, for instance, but rather to anticipate other investors' choices and gain advantage over them.

Keynes chose the example of beauty competitions to illustrate this logic:

> [P]rofessional investment may be likened to those newspaper competitions in which the competitors have to pick out the six prettiest faces from a hundred photographs, the prize being awarded to the competitor whose choice most nearly corresponds to the average preferences of the competitors as a whole; so that each competitor has to pick, not those faces which he himself finds prettiest, but those

which he thinks likeliest to catch the fancy of the other competitors, all of whom are looking at the problem from the same point of view. It is not a case of choosing those which, to the best of one's judgment, are really the prettiest, nor even those which average opinion genuinely thinks the prettiest. We have reached the third degree where we devote our intelligences to anticipating what average opinion expects average opinion to be. (*General* 156)

Like sexuality and gender, then, investment decisions are performances that are always made in relation to others. Investment/desire is triangulated through third and fourth and *n*th parties.

Keynes provided no specific formula for encouraging people to see that their investments ought to be bound up in an ethic of community. He did, however, write that

> [t]he spectacle of modern investment markets has sometimes moved me towards the conclusion that to make the purchase of an investment permanent and indissoluble, like marriage, except by reason of death or other grave cause, might be a useful remedy for our contemporary evils. (*General* 160)

But such a prospect, he continued, would foreclose the good, productive possibilities of liquidity – just as marriage forecloses the good possibilities of 'personal affections and aesthetic enjoyments'. If the individual investor is assured that his investments are 'liquid', and he can convert them to cash at any time, then he will be 'much more willing to run a risk' (*General* 160) and encourage more investment. Human beings, Keynes believed, contained what he called 'animal spirits' that urge them to movement, change and risk:

> Most ... of our decisions to do something positive, the full consequences of which will be drawn out over many days to come, can only be taken as a result of animal spirits – of a spontaneous urge to action rather than inaction, and not as the outcome of a weighted average of quantitative benefits multiplied by quantitative probabilities. (*General* 161)

Furthermore, these animal spirits could be harnessed toward the creation of goodness in the world, especially when they are combined with hopes for the future and when they help mitigate fears of failure.

> It is safe to say that enterprise which depends on hopes stretching into the future benefits the community as a whole. But individual initiative will only be adequate when reasonable calculation is supplemented and supported by animal spirits, so that the thought of ultimate loss

which often overtakes pioneers, as experience undoubtedly tells us and them, is put aside as a healthy man puts aside the expectation of death. (*General* 162)

Here is Keynes as a high modernist and humanist, fully believing that in putting aside fears and accepting the illusion of the continuation of the present state of affairs into the future, human beings will maintain the conventions necessary to maintain order, while increasing goodness through entrepreneurial and moral progress. At the same time, here is Keynes as a member of Bloomsbury, accepting a non-quantifiable, probabilistic reasoning based on a vaguely hinted at notion of intuition that reveals the illusion of a future to be just that – an illusion, an artifice based on convention, a collective leap into the unknown. We cannot worry too much about the actual future that may come to pass, since that future *is* always unknowable.

> We should not conclude from this that everything depends on waves of irrational psychology.... We are merely reminding ourselves that human decisions affecting the future, whether personal or political or economic, cannot depend on strict mathematical expectation, since the basis for making such calculations does not exist; and that it is our innate urge to activity which makes the wheels go round, our rational selves choosing where we can, but often falling back for our motive on whim or sentiment or chance. (*General* 163)

Contingency occupied a powerful place, then, in Keynes's philosophy of moral action. And that contingency was the logical corollary to his vision of organic unities. In arguing against reformers who would suggest action for the good of the many in the uncertain future, Keynes quipped, 'this *long-run* is a misleading guide to current affairs. *In the long run* we are all dead' (*Tract on Monetary Reform* 65).

The International Clearing Union: Designing Modernity

Put in the context of his aesthetic theory and his probability theory, Keynes's writings on the currency controls and the domestic economy would support neither feudal imaginations nor the bureaucratic calculus of the modern welfare state. Rather, they demonstrate, first, the species of contingency that animated his thinking on social action in the world and, second, a failure of analytical language to describe the future world he was envisioning. Parts of 'National Self-Sufficiency' read like passages out of the *Treatise on Probability*. For instance:

> the new economic modes, toward which we are blundering, are, in
> the essence of their nature, experiments. We have no clear idea laid up
> in our minds beforehand of exactly what we want. We shall discover it
> as we move along. ('National Self-Sufficiency' 768)

Much as Grant's interior design was a process of discovery through movement and no small measure of experiment and blundering, Keynes's discourse on economic transformation relied on a recognition of contingency and a faith in the human combination of intuition and animal spirits to reframe problems in the process of trying to solve them.

At the same time, Keynes came up against the limits of modernist discourses. His writings on exactly how to manage investment, currency control, interest rate reduction and full employment frequently contain references to hybrid entities – Keynes's attempt to move among the discursive possibilities of the modem world that bounded state, market, public, private, domestic, international and other domains. In trying to move through these categories, Keynes leaned heavily on the notions of goodness derived from his aesthetics, and appeals to justice and beauty:

> [P]rogress lies in the growth and recognition of semi-autonomous
> bodies within the State – bodies whose criterion of action within their
> own field is solely the public good as they understand it ... bodies
> which in the ordinary course of affairs are mainly autonomous within
> their prescribed limitations, but are subject in the last resort to the
> sovereignty of the democracy expressed through Parliament. ('End of
> Laissez-Faire' 313–14)

These semi-autonomous, semi-public bodies are nowhere clearly defined. Yet in his concrete proposals for the international monetary order, proposed as Britain was going heavily into debt to the United States to finance the war against Germany, Keynes put forward a model for just such a body in the form of an International Clearing Union. The plans for the Clearing Union formed the basis for discussion in the years immediately preceding the Bretton Woods conference in 1944. Indeed, Bretton Woods itself can be read as a rewriting of Keynes's proposal to benefit the United States and redesign the modernity Keynes had just begun to envision.

Keynes's plans were grand indeed and, to many of his contemporaries, too vague to be practical. Yet what others observed as ill-defined can be readily seen to derive from Keynes's aesthetics and theories of probability, as well as the epistemology of post-impressionism. Keynes wrote,

> The management of an international standard is an art and not a
> science, and no one would suggest that it is possible to draw up a

formal code of action, admitting of no exceptions or qualifications, adherence to which is obligatory on peril of wrecking the whole structure. Much must necessarily be left to time and circumstance. (Qtd. in Moggridge, 'Keynes' 70)

The project hinged on perspective, position and experimentation (Mini 154). 'Bancor', the universal unit of monetary exchange Keynes proposed, for instance, was based on the belief that international currency exchanges exist to serve enterprise, which will generate exports and increase income, spurring imports. Bancor would facilitate long-term investment over short-term speculation. As a central unit of account held in a central, international organisation, it would reflect and embody the organic unity of the whole international capitalist system. And it would emerge in practice, over time, without a set plan governing it but rather borne of experimentation and of active participation in the lived reality of international trade. Here, as in other writing, Keynes laid his faith in a class of 'international civil servants' to manage the Clearing Union (Moggridge, 'Keynes' 79). The vision was of cosmopolitans who continually reposition themselves so that they can capture the whole and, for instance, revalue bancor from the resolution of international payments and currencies exchanges, much as a viewer resolves the dots of a pointillist painting into forms and images. These international civil servants would be like Grant's artist-viewers, thrown into a reality that they continually construct and reconstruct. 'Decision-makers [would] organise their perceptions and their expectations around [several] world views, or paradigms' (Dow and Dow 60), not one. Since 'what is exogenous within one approach, or line of reasoning, is endogenous within another', social reformers could 'tackle each question from a variety of angles, with a variety of methods' (62).

While the Clearing Union plan was an important starting point for the Bretton Woods negotiations, its key features were utterly transformed as the plan became the blueprint for the International Monetary Fund and Bank for Reconstruction and Development, or World Bank. The United States was in a position to dictate the terms of these institutions, for reasons I cannot go into here (but see Crotty; Helleiner *States*; Leyshon and Thrift). Most important here, however, was the United States' success in securing for the US dollar the key position in the new international economy as the unit of account, instead of Keynes's proposed international currency unit. In practical terms, this meant that the United States 'was liberated from the disciplining power of money because balance-of-payments difficulties could be countered simply through an expansion of domestic credit' (Leyshon and Thrift 72). Replacing Keynes's proposed bancor with the US dollar meant grounding international monetary arrangements in one version of the 'real', as if it were a painting with one unchangeable vanishing point from which all perspective is derived, rather than an interior designed to confound any efforts at perspective. Unlike Keynes's proposal, which required that creditor countries' surpluses in the Clearing Union be reinvested in productive enterprise elsewhere, under Bretton Woods creditor countries were under no obligation to contribute to overseas investment. They could very much go their own way, like the 'legal atoms' Keynes derided in his probability theory, without having to account for their place as parts of an organic whole.

Thus, Bretton Woods took Keynes's Clearing Union plan and subverted some of its most radical elements. It did so by turning Keynes's proposed post-impressionist ever-changing masterwork into a realist bureaucratic enterprise. There would be no international civil servants revaluing the unit of account in an ever-changing process of experimentation and engagement with complex lived realities. Nor would that unit of account be the result of the sort of perspective-shifting endeavour of moving through one of Grant's interiors. Rather, it would be the product of one perspective, that of the United States. The Fund would not be a passive force, either, merely balancing accounts against one another to ensure enterprise on a world scale in accord with individual member countries' specific interests. Rather, the Fund would actively interfere in member countries' internal affairs, enforcing frugality and thrift and at the same time encouraging speculation and capital flight. There would not be the multifaceted perspective of diversely positioned international civil servants; rather, the perspective of one member country, the United States, whose money served the dual function of a national currency and an international standard of account, would aspire to become the only available point of view.

We Have Never Had an Alternate Modernity?

There are many reasons to be wary of Keynes's Clearing Union proposal, of course, not the least of which is the poorly delineated notion of cosmopolitanism it relied on. There was a dark underbelly to that cosmopolitan vision, too, which crept into Keynes's thinking on international monetary orders beginning with his first book on the subject, *Indian Currency and Finance* (1913), and culminating in his contributions to the Bretton Woods conference. Where Keynes's aesthetics failed him, he fell back on familiar discourses of bourgeois nationalism and colonial nostalgia in their most antimodern, Romantic form.

His pronouncement at the end of *Indian Currency and Finance*, that 'India, so far from being anomalous, is in the forefront of monetary progress' (182), is reminiscent of Mr Cameron in Virginia Woolf's play *Freshwater*, who sought 'truth' in India and, like other anti-industrialists of the era, celebrated colonial subjects' alternative 'truths' without accounting for their colonial subjection (Woolf 6). Keynes's book studiously ignores the imperial politics of early twentieth-century India. Indeed, there are no 'Indians' in the book – except for the 'Indian tax-payer', who appears in a sarcastic passage about an imaginary Member of Parliament, with little knowledge of India, worrying 'that some cosmopolitan syndicate of Jews was not fattening at the expense of the ryots of India, whose trustee he had often declared himself to be' (Keynes, *Indian* 101–2). At these moments, Keynes sounds, at best, a good deal like the contemporary 'neo-medievalists' described by Eric Helleiner ('International' 60). At worst, he sounds like an anti-Semite. This points up some of the failures of the discursive possibilities opened up by Bloomsbury.

Keynes's probability theory, together with his aesthetics of 'fitness', aimed to circumvent modernity's rational calculus and to discredit the possibility of bureaucratic planning. His theoretical apparatus attempted to replace the methodological individualism of neoclassical economics with an organic, much more Continental and perhaps more mystical conception of social reality and the place of social action in the world. Keynes's theoretical orientation also led him away from the orthodox high-modern variants of Marxism circulating at mid-century. As he recounts in his memoir, speaking of his Bloomsbury circle of friends,

> [We] escaped from the Benthamite tradition. But I do now regard that as the worm which has been gnawing at the insides of modern civilisation and is responsible for its present moral decay. We used to regard the Christians as the enemy, because they appeared as the representatives of tradition, convention and hocus-pocus. In truth it was the Benthamite calculus, based on an over-valuation of the economic criterion, which was destroying the quality of the popular Ideal. Moreover, it was this escape from Bentham, joined with the unsurpassable individualism of our philosophy, which has served to protect the whole lot of us from the final *reductio ad absurdum* of Benthamism known as Marxism. We have completely failed, indeed, to provide a substitute for these economic bogus-faiths capable of protecting or satisfying our successors. ('My Early Beliefs' 96–7)

Keynes's project also left him open to utopianism, which ultimately subverted the radical potential of his theorising. In criticising convention while attempting to use conventions to guide society, Keynes and his compatriots fell back on a dominant modern version of the opposition between reason and convention, modernity and tradition, civilised and primitive, conscious and unconscious. This is clear in his discussion of the 'animal spirits' leading humans to favour action over inaction. But in his later memoirs Keynes reflects on what he considered with hindsight to be his youthful naiveté regarding reason and unreason:

> We were among the last of the Utopians ... who believe in a continuing moral progress by virtue of which the human race already consists of reliable, rational, decent people, influenced by truth and objective standards, who can be safely released from the outward restraints of convention and traditional standards and inflexible rules of conduct, and left, from now onwards, to their own sensible devices, pure motives, and reliable intuitions of good.... In short, we repudiated all versions of the doctrine of original sin, of there being insane and irrational springs of wickedness in most men. We were not aware that civilisation was a thin and precarious crust erected by the personality and the will of a very few, and only maintained by rules and conventions skillfully put across and guilefully preserved. ('My Early Beliefs' 99)

Disillusioned, he surmises, 'The attribution of rationality to human nature, instead of enriching it, now seems to me to have impoverished it. It ignored certain powerful and valuable springs of feeling' ('My Early Beliefs' 101).

World War II and its aftermath jarred Keynes and shook his faith in animal spirits simply trundling along getting things done. Now, these spirits could be seen capable of motivating the darkest of passions sitting just beneath the surface of human reason. Keynes's later reflections sound downright Freudian, as when he wrote in his memoir that he and his Bloomsbury colleagues went through life 'as water-spiders, gracefully skimming, as light and reasonable as air, the surface of the stream without any contact at all with the eddies or undercurrents underneath' ('My Early Beliefs' 103). This tendency toward filling the gaps of his modern vision with the hegemonic modernity's others was present in his work from the start, as it was in the work of Duncan Grant. Keynes's thinking on matters of finance and currency grew from his experience in the Indian civil service and his work on Indian currency reform. Grant's interiors were inspired, in part, by his voyages to Italy and Turkey, where he encountered an East that worked its way into Charleston and Grant's own self-perceptions through erotic self-portraiture. Their attempts to construct an alternate modernity did not shield them from the intense pull of the dominant modernity through its self-constructed others, and led Keynes, at least, to consider gazing down the 'alternative' modern paths of National Socialism.

The Probabilities of Queering Globalisation

Keynesianism was fundamentally inspired by the orientalism, classism and aesthetic sensibilities of early twentieth-century England. At the same time, however, Keynes articulated a discourse that might have provided another model for modernity and for the post-war international economic order. Excavating that model may help provide new possibilities for responding to globalisation in ways that do not replicate the terms of the Bretton Woods world, while avoiding the neoliberal celebration of markets and individualism or the frightening invocations of 'community' that critiques of Bretton Woods often incite.

Like Keynes, critics on the left and the right often locate their opposition to globalisation – which is really shorthand for the breakdown of Bretton Woods institutions – in an imagined local community, bound in time and space, made up of individuals connected by commonality of interest and sentiment. For many gays and lesbians, this can be a terrifying place in which to locate oneself. The Bloomsbury vision of cosmopolitanism and a perspective-shifting experimentalism may hold more promise. Keynes's methodology depended on 'several, parallel, intertwined and mutually reinforcing' logical chains, none of which is objective or positivist but rather contingent and partial (Stohs, qtd. in Dow and Dow 59). His Clearing Union would have been an international yet translocal organisation, linking diverse entities into an overarching pattern that changes depending on the position from which it is viewed, much like one of Duncan Grant's interiors. Perhaps, too, it is the sort of model we have already created for ourselves, in our own translocal communities. This model may only need to be set in motion to new purposes – purposes not explicitly about 'sexuality' or the 'economy', but about challenging the taken-for-granted domains of contemporary and past modern discourses.

Keynes and Grant offer 'alternative scripts or inscriptions of sexual/ economic identity' (Gibson-Graham 139). Whether they might have done so for good or ill, I cannot say. Making explicit Keynes's designs, however, exposes the probabilistic nature of those possibilities that *have* been realised, suggesting that ultimately the apparatus of Bretton Woods, and its breakdown, was never a foregone conclusion. After all, even with the benefit of hindsight, political economists are still hard put to come up with consistent explanations of the collapse of the Bretton Woods system. Perhaps their failure reveals that the system was never quite systemic, was always a little nervous, and always contained unrealised potential, though this has been hidden, as behind a dressing-screen. It also suggests that there may be other possibilities as yet unexplored, to redesign, and to redecorate.

Notes

1. See Gibson-Graham on constructions of desire in globalisation narratives.
2. As Rod O'Donnell, a leading Keynes scholar, writes of this period in Keynes's career, 'aesthetics was not of minor interest in the pre-1914 period but was *one of the foremost preoccupations of his early philosophizing*' (O'Donnell 97, original emphasis).

Works Cited

Carabelli, Anna. 'Keynes on Cause, Chance and Possibility'. *Keynes' Economics: Methodological Issues*. Ed. Tony Lawson and Hashem Pesaran. London: Helm, 1985.

Crotty, James R. 'On Keynes and Capital Flight'. *Journal of Economic Literature* 21 (1983): 59–65.

Davis, John B. 'Keynes's Critiques of Moore: Philosophical Foundations of Keynes's Economics'. *Cambridge Journal of Economics* 15 (1991): 61–77.

—. *Keynes's Philosophical Development*. Cambridge: Cambridge University Press, 1994.

D'Emilio, John. 'Capitalism and Gay Identity'. *Powers of Desire: The Politics of Sexuality*. Ed. A. Snitow, C. Stansell and S. Thompson. New York: Monthly, 1984. 100–13.

Dow, Alexander, and Sheila Dow. "Animal Spirits and Rationality'. *Keynes' Economics: Methodological Issues*. Ed. Tony Lawson and Hashem Pesaran. London: Croom, 1985. 46–65.

Garnett, Angelica. *Deceived with Kindness: A Bloomsbury Childhood*. London: Chatto, 1984.

Gibson-Graham, J. K. *The End of Capitalism (As We Knew It): A Feminist Critique of Political Economy*. Oxford: Blackwell, 1996.

Harvey, David. *The Condition of Postmodernity: An Enquiry into the Origins of Cultural Change*. Oxford: Blackwell, 1990.

Helleiner, Eric. *States and the Reemergence of Global Finance: From Bretton Woods to the 1990s*. Ithaca: Cornell University Press, 1994.

—. 'International Political Economy and the Greens'. *New Political Economy* 1.1 (1996): 59–77.

Hession, Charles. 'Keynes, Strachey, and the Gay Courage to Be'. *Challenge* 36.4 (1983): 53–9.

Keynes, John Maynard. *Collected Writings of John Maynard Keynes*. Ed. Elizabeth Johnson, Austin Robinson and Donald Moggridge. 30 vols. London: Macmillan, 1971–89.

—. 'The End of Laissez-Faire'. *Essays in Persuasion*. New York: Harcourt, 1926. 312–22.

—. 'The General Theory of Employment'. *Quarterly Journal of Economics* 51 (1937): 209–13.

—. *The General Theory of Employment, Interest, and Money*. 1935. New York: Harcourt, 1964.

—. *Indian Currency and Finance.* 1913. Vol. 1 of *Collected Writings.*
—. 'Miscellanea Ethica'. 1905. In O'Donnell, 'Keynes on Aesthetics'.
—. 'My Early Beliefs'. 1938. *Two Memoirs.* Intro. David Garnett. New York: Kelley, 1949. 78–103.
—. 'National Self-Sufficiency'. *Yale Review* 22.4 (1933): 755–69.
—. 'Shall We Write Melodramas?' 1906. In O'Donnell, 'Keynes on Aesthetics'.
—. *Tract on Monetary Reform.* 1923. Vol. 4 of *Collected Writings.*
—. *Treatise on Probability.* 1921. Vol. 8 of *Collected Writings.*
Leyshon, Andrew, and Nigel Thrift. *Money/Space: Geographies of Monetary Transformation.* London: Routledge, 1997.
Mini, Piero V. *Keynes, Bloomsbury, and The General Theory.* London: Macmillan, 1990.
Moggridge, D. E. 'Keynes and the International Monetary System, 1909–46'. *International Monetary Problems and Supply-Side Economics.* Ed. Jon S. Cohen and G. C. Harcourt. London: Macmillan, 1986. 56–83.
—. *Maynard Keynes: An Economist's Biography.* London: Routledge, 1992.
Moore, G. E. *Principia Ethica.* 1903. Cambridge: Cambridge University Press, 1993.
O'Donnell, Rod. 'Keynes on Aesthetics'. *New Perspectives on Keynes.* Ed. Allin F. Cottrell and Michael S. Lawlor. Annual supplement to *History of Political Economy* 27 (1995): 93–121.
Radice, H. 1984. 'The National Economy: A Keynesian Myth?' *Capital and Class* 22: 111–40.
Reichardt, Jasia. 'Op Art'. *Concepts of Modern Art.* Ed. Nikos Stangos. London: Thames and Hudson, 1988. 239–43.
Ritter, Gretchen. *Goldbugs and Greenbacks: The Antimonopoly Tradition and the Politics of Finance in America, 1865–1896.* Cambridge: Cambridge University Press, 1997.
Robinson, Joan. 'Lecture Delivered at Oxford by a Cambridge Economist'. *Collected Economic Papers.* Vol. 4. 1953. Oxford: Blackwell, 1973. 254–63.
Rotheim, Roy J. 'Keynes and the Language of Probability and Uncertainty'. *Journal of Post-Keynesian Economics* 11.1 (1988): 82–99.
Skidelsky, Robert. *John Maynard Keynes.* Vol. 1. *Hopes Betrayed, 1883–1920.* New York: Viking, 1983.
—. 'Keynes's Philosophy of Practice and Economic Policy'. *Keynes as Philosopher-Economist.* Ed. R. M. O'Donnell. London: Macmillan, 1991. 104–23.
Stohs, M. '"Uncertainty" in Keynes' *General Theory.* A Rejoinder'. *History of Political Economy* 15 (1983): 87–91.
Strathern, Marilyn. *After Nature: English Kinship in the Late Twentieth Century.* Cambridge: Cambridge University Press, 1992.
Todd, Dorothy, and Raymond Mortimer. *The New Interior Decoration: An Introduction to Its Principles and International Survey of Its Methods.* London: Batsford, 1929.
Watney, Simon. *The Art of Duncan Grant.* London: Murray, 1990.
Woolf, Virginia. *Freshwater: A Comedy.* 1935. New York: Harcourt, 1975.
Yanagisako, Sylvia, and Carol Delaney, eds. *Naturalizing Power: Essays in Feminist Cultural Analysis.* New York: Routledge, 1995.

Passionate Debates on 'Odious Subjects': Bisexuality and Woolf's Opposition to Theories of Androgyny and Sexual Identity

Brenda Helt

Since 'bisexual' was rarely used to describe a sexual identity type until the 1960s, it might seem anachronistic to use the word to describe the coexistence of sexual desire and affections for both men and women in the same individual in literary work of the early twentieth century. Yet the fact that 'bisexual' was *not* an identity category indicating a type of person in this period is precisely what makes an investigation of Woolf's use of bisexuality and bisexual desire important. Bisexuality has several functions in Woolf's work. Those functions, though, are obscured if desire is conflated with sexual identity, or if Woolf's depictions of desire are understood solely in terms of autobiographical self-expression rather than authorial strategy.

In her work of the 1920s, Woolf challenged trends to construe same-sex desire as a distinguishing characteristic of a sexual type as well as the essentialist ideas about male and female character traits that underlie theories of androgyny. She instead gave voice to a much older understanding of women's same-sex desires as common to *most* women and promoted those desires as epistemologically, aesthetically and politically more useful to women than the bifurcated sexual identities and beliefs about dual-gendered minds promoted by sexologists and some members of the avant-garde.

'Passionate Debates on "Odious Subjects": Bisexuality and Woolf's Opposition to Theories of Androgyny and Sexual Identity' by Brenda Helt was first published in *Twentieth-Century Literature* 56.2 (2010): 131–67, prefaced by a five-page encomium by Linda Hutcheon. Reprinted here abridged with the kind permission of *Twentieth-Century Literature*.

Woolf opposed both the reduction of desire to sexuality and the concept of dyadic (i.e. homo/hetero) sexual identity itself – a concept just gaining currency in the 1920s and '30s. Her work instead frames same-sex desire and sexuality as common, ordinary, harmonious with women's desire for and sexual relations with men, and even useful in achieving marital bliss. Thus she disentangles bisexual desire from androgyny and sexual identity. As she does so, she dispenses with the male-promoting concepts of androgyny and androgynous genius, and recoups the imaginative and creative possibilities associated with bisexual desire for women. With this in mind, I examine the function of bisexual desire in *Orlando* and *A Room of One's Own*, understanding it as a challenge to the new hetero/homo dichotomy that Woolf believed to be producing another social invention: a culturally widespread homophobia that isolated women from other women, emotionally, politically and professionally.

Sex Talk Becomes High Modernist Philosophy

In 'Old Bloomsbury', Woolf narrates the advent of modernism among those quintessential modernists, the Bloomsbury Group. As Virginia and Vanessa sat talking one day in 1906, the drawing room door opened and Lytton Strachey emerged from the shadows, pointing a finger at a stain on Vanessa's dress.

> 'Semen?' he said. Can one really say it? I thought and we burst out laughing. With that one word all barriers of reticence and reserve went down…. Sex permeated our conversation. The word bugger was never far from our lips. We discussed copulation with the same excitement and openness that we had discussed the nature of good. (195)

Bloomsbury's fascination with sexuality was consistent with that of other avant-garde groups now considered modernist. In the inter-war period, women and men who aspired to be avant-garde began to distinguish themselves by openly debating the latest sexual theories in mixed company, and by producing literary and artistic works that openly engaged in these debates. By 1922, Woolf could term this new openness 'a great advance in civilization', one for which, she implied, Bloomsbury was directly responsible ('Old Bloomsbury' 196).

Bloomsbury's ideas about sexuality were heavily influenced by sexual scientists from Otto Weininger to Freud, and both bisexuality and androgyny were key points of debate in these discussions. Though its important role in the epistemological history of sexuality is no longer obvious, bisexuality was central to sexology's congenitalist theories of sexuality and sexual identity.

The mid-nineteenth-century medical study of the physical hermaphrodite – sometimes termed a 'bi-sexual' – initiated hypotheses in Germany that there might be a corresponding type who was psychologically both male and female: a 'psychic hermaphrodite'. Psychic hermaphroditism was understood by some sexologists to account for 'inversion' in general, but for others it explained a type that might have sexual relationships with both men and women: a 'psychosexual hermaphrodite'.

Because late nineteenth-century medical science had presumed that 'hermaphrodites' – the term then used to describe intersexed persons – were either male or female, sexologists such as Havelock Ellis reasoned that psychologically, too, people were either male or female, though in rare cases their psychological sex might not accord with their biological one.[1] In arguing that some rare 'types' of people are born 'sexual inverts' – that is, the sex of their mind is the 'opposite' of that of their body – Ellis eschewed 'third sex' theories popular with German scientists like Hirschfeld and French authors like Gautier to describe people who did not fit into a binary sex/gender paradigm. In so doing, he also dismissed the association of sexual bisexuality with gendered 'bi-sexuality' or 'androgyny' in favour of the hetero/homo dyad.

Freud, too, found the conflation of bisexuality with gender dimorphism as well as sexual bisexuality problematic, since it caused a slippage between gender identification and sexual desire. One of Freud's most significant departures from other sexual scientists was his belief that homosexuality was a neurosis rooted in early childhood developmental problems. Such a theory necessitated the hypothesis that all human beings are congenitally 'bisexual' – born psychologically dual-gendered – and that they acquire an identification with one sex or the other through a complex psychological mechanism by which they come to desire the parent of the opposite sex, and *only* that parent. The fact that both Ellis and Freud found gendered duality (androgyny) and sexual bisexuality incompatible with their theories of homosexuality is characteristic of the general consternation these two concepts with their single signifier were causing among scientists. In London during the inter-war period, then, 'bisexuality' was a floating signifier. Primarily a scientific term, the word rarely referred to a mature adult's sexual attraction to people of both sexes, a state most early twentieth-century scientists, Freud included, believed to exist only in very young children, in people of 'primitive' cultures, or in those passing through a transitional phase between the two true sexual dispositions, heterosexuality and homosexuality.

By the early 1920s the appropriation of sexological theories to valorise homosexuality and bisexuality in men was well established among the well-educated in London, Cambridge and Oxford. So common was this stance at Cambridge that young men like Leslie Runciman felt the need to apologise for their attraction to women (Tindall 47). In later life, Rosamond Lehmann explained Runciman's apologetic attitude about his sexual attraction to women as a response to a trend among young men at Cambridge to prefer sexual relationships with other men, since they were understood to be sexually, because intellectually, more stimulating: 'He thought it was an intellectual disgrace to marry' (qtd. in Hastings 68).

That this particular manifestation of homosexuality among young men at Cambridge in the late 1910s and the 1920s was considered a 'trend' or 'fashion' by first-generation Bloomsberries is clear in a 1925 letter from Woolf to Jacques Raverat:

> Mrs Joad ... now has a room of her own, and walks out with various Cambridge young men, who are not entirely devoted to the fashionable foible of loving their own sex.... Have you any views on loving one's own sex? All the young men are so inclined, and I can't help finding it mildly foolish; though I have no particular reason. For one thing, all the young men tend to the pretty and ladylike, for some reason, at the moment. They paint and powder, which wasn't the style in our day at Cambridge. I think it does imply some clingingness. (*Letters* 3: 155)

Here Woolf's critique of a younger generation's performance of homosexuality as style is similar to that of friends such as Lytton Strachey and E. M. Forster, who scoffed at some men's avowed preference for what Strachey facetiously termed 'the higher sodomy', a pretentious intellectualisation of same-sex but non-sexual relationships that masked a preciosity and misogyny of which they disapproved. (Forster's character Clive in *Maurice* is a higher sodomite, for example.) The persona of the effeminate 'sodomite' performed by some of the Bright Young Things – Cecil Beaton, Stephen Tennant, Edward Sackville-West – also seemed to appropriate sexological theories of inversion that much of first-generation Bloomsbury had rejected in favour of the socialist, feminist and egalitarian theories and practices of Edward Carpenter. Though fascinated and amused by the youthful gender-play of the Bright Young Things, Woolf did not endorse the logic implied by the fashions of inversion that retrospectively were interpreted as evolving sexual identities.

For some inter-war women, this fashion of sexual inversion took the form of the mannish lesbian. Although that persona did not resonate as sexually 'deviant' with the larger public until after the 1928 obscenity trial of Radclyffe Hall's *The Well of Loneliness*, the mannish lesbian was recognisable to groups of the *cognoscenti* prior to the trial, as attested to by her presence in works such as Lawrence's *The Rainbow* (1915) and *The Fox* (1922), Lehmann's *Dusty Answer*

(1927) and Mackenzie's *Extraordinary Women* (1928). The theory of sexual inversion could not account for same-sex attractions in feminine and bisexual women, especially those whose partners were not masculine. Some inter-war women therefore appropriated a competing sexological theory popularised in the scientific community by sexologist Otto Weininger, who hypothesised that those attracted to others of their sex were born neither male nor female, but both: they were 'sexually intermediate types' (5–10, 51). For Weininger, 'the woman who attracts and is attracted by other women is herself half male' and 'homo-sexuality in a woman is the outcome of her masculinity and presupposes a higher degree of development' (66).

Unlike her lover Vita Sackville-West and some of her younger male friends, Woolf disagreed with understandings of sexual desire that were based on gender stereotypes, performed as gender dysphoria, and construed as essential sexual identities. It was specifically these understandings of identity as a problem of gender (or 'sexual') inversion that she termed 'perversion' in a 1930 letter to Ethel Smyth (*Letters* 4: 200). Though Woolf could find cross-dressing and gender-play creative and fun, as *Orlando* illustrates, she did not accept conflations of gender and desire as grounds upon which to construct identity, nor did she endorse the evolving theories that rendered sexuality part of an aesthetics of identity. Ridiculing the self-presentations of Eddy Sackville-West and other 'effeminate sodomites' as 'silly', 'pretty' and 'trivial' in her letter to Smyth, Woolf portrayed such costuming as a cover for shallow thinking (4: 200).

Women's Ordinary Bisexuality

As historians such as Carroll Smith-Rosenberg, Lillian Faderman, Martha Vicinus and Sharon Marcus have shown, there is a long tradition in Great Britain and the United States of positive understandings of women's intimate affective and often sexual relationships with other women. Together, the research of these four scholars demonstrates that the stigmatisation of women's intimate relationships with other women (as indicative of deviant sexual identities) is a fairly recent development. In *Fashioning Sapphism*, Laura Doan argues that the trial of Hall's *Well* crystallised an image of 'the lesbian' as mannish for the general population in England, thereby paralleling for women the stigma the Oscar Wilde trials had generated for men (1–30). Yet even before the Hall trial, Woolf foresaw the danger for women and for feminism of replacing older understandings of women's 'romantic friendships' and undefinable same-sex loves with an easily identifiable masculine-gendered sexual type or with a Freudian understanding of homosexuality as neurotic sexual subjectivity.

In her work of the 1920s, Woolf depicts the eroticism of those long-standing positive portrayals of women's intimate friendships (intimacies that are neither gendered masculine nor exclusive of similar relationships with men) and promotes them as more desirable than exclusively homo- or heterosexual relationships. For example, a major theme of *A Room of One's Own* is the complexity of women's lives and minds, their experiences of desire, their relationships with each other and, importantly, men's inability to understand and depict these. She criticises male scientific presumptions about the desires and minds of women. 'Where shall I find that elaborate study of the psychology of women by a woman?' Woolf asks her audience of educated young women, exhorting them to write such studies (*Room* 81).

Woolf's fictional novelist, Mary Carmichael, begins the work of portraying women's relationships with other women in their full complexity. Woolf considers Carmichael's depiction of two professional women who not only share a laboratory but even *like* each other as entirely new in literature. Chloe and Olivia like each other. But that fact does not preclude their liking men as well, a point Woolf makes explicit. Olivia has two children and a husband, and leaves Chloe at the lab to go home to be with them (87–8). The mention of Olivia's children and husband specifically contradicts the increasingly popular association of lesbianism with feminists and professional women, an association given wide publicity by the Radclyffe Hall trial. Far from hinting that Chloe and Olivia are lesbians, Woolf thus refutes the association of feminism with lesbianism. Woolf does *not* mean to deny that women who work together might also experience erotic feelings for each other, however. Rather she reinforces an understanding that she implies has long been held among women, though rarely documented in print: women's love for other women is a highly desirable and empowering emotive force common to *most* women, and not an identifying characteristic of a rare sexual type.

That so-called 'perversion' and friendship merge into each other, rather than marking women as distinct types, is an important point in most of Woolf's work and is intimated in her letter to Smyth:

> Where people mistake, as I think, is in perpetually narrowing and naming these immensely composite and wide flung passions – driving stakes through them, herding them between screens. But how do you define 'Perversity'? What is the line between friendship and perversion? (*Letters* 4: 200).

For her, 'perversion' is consistent with friendship – these are intimate relationships, which Woolf values, not sexual types. Woolf's criticism in the letter is aimed at the appropriation of scientific concepts of perversion, not at sexual and affective relationships.

Nobody's Androgyny

Both the androgyne and the genius have a heritage privileging men and maleness more generally. Thus Woolf's challenges to sexological theories of gender inversion and dyadic sexual identities necessarily included theories of androgyny popular with modernists and other elite circles. In the companion pieces *Orlando* and *A Room*, Woolf shows that the androgynous mind is presently an impossibility precisely because of the social realities accompanying embodiment. In both works, Woolf takes up but ultimately rejects the prevalent notion that the gifted artist must have an androgynous mind. Woolf shows that what it means to be man or woman depends upon social conditions, and these conditions differ based on the biological sex of the body. One cannot know what it is to be 'womanly' unless one has walked down Whitehall in a woman's body, for example, or tried to engage in intellectual conversation with Milton or Pope while wearing voluminous skirts and decorously pouring out tea. And learned men and men of genius do not, in fact, somehow manage to escape their sex and 'remov[e] themselves above the strife of tongue and the confusion of body' to 'issu[e] the result of their reasoning and research in books which are to be found in the British Museum' (*Room* 25). Woolf's emphasis in *A Room* on the subconscious misogyny of every man writing on 'sex – woman, that is to say', from the honourable Professor von X to 'men who have no apparent qualification save that they are not women', is one she has previously broached in *Orlando* (*Room* 27). Alexander Pope, the genius figure in that novel, becomes enraged when Orlando inadvertently offends him and therefore 'avenge[s]' himself by 'present[ing] her instantly with the rough draught of a certain famous line in the "Characters of Women"' (214).

Although *Orlando* is certainly in part a 'love letter' to Vita Sackville-West, it also furthers a theoretical argument between the two women concerning gender and desire, especially in relation to first-wave feminism.[2] Sexological thinking authorises Sackville-West's essentialism. She herself claimed that she exemplified 'the perfectly accepted theory that cases of dual personality do exist, in which the feminine and the masculine elements alternately preponderate' (qtd. in Nicolson 106). Sackville-West's conflation of sex, gender and sexual desire caused her to believe she was actually a 'different person' – a male person – when she was amorous or sexual with women, and she would often dress according to the sex she felt she was embodying at the moment (qtd. in Nicolson 105). Her purported ability to shift between the two sexes allowed her to claim to be that most rare of types among 'civilised' societies: a 'bi-sexual' or 'psychosexual hermaphrodite' in 1920s sexological parlance, or a *female* androgyne or even androgynous genius.

Orlando disputes this notion that gender has a biological essence. A main contention of the novel is that nobody can know what it is to be either a man or a woman without having lived in the body of one. Putting on trousers and making love to women does not make one a man. *Orlando* should be read, then, as part one of Woolf's two-part contradiction of theories of the writer or artist as androgynous genius, or as member of the intermediate sex or of the third sex, all of which share the same basic premise: men are essentially active and intellectual, women are essentially passive and sensual, and so the ideal gifted type is a biological male born with a touch of womanly sensibilities.

Woolf's theories of gender, sexuality and desire take into account the social reality of living as a woman in society and the ways that reality is formative of one's mind or psyche and, therefore, of one's opportunities and talents. *Orlando* shows that only by living corporeally as both a man and a woman and being understood by both one's society and one's intimates as one and then the other can a person hope to obtain an androgynous mind. Even then, the necessity of always being treated as one or the other would cause a person to think predominantly as one or the other. Because a body will always be interpellated as either male or female, even the sex-changing Orlando can partake only fleetingly of an androgynous mind. For a few days after her sex change, Orlando 'seemed to vacillate' between the two sexes, 'she was man; she was woman; she knew the secrets, shared the weaknesses of each' (158). But for Woolf this momentarily androgynous state is not to be recommended. It is 'a most bewildering and whirligig state of mind to be in', and, immediately after her first experience of being courted by a man, Orlando begins to adopt a woman's perspective and to perform her gender as a woman – a woman the sight of whose legs might even cause a sailor a nasty fall from the mast (158–9).

Woolf shows that the experience of being treated as a woman – and she implies that Orlando's first experience includes the sexual – is responsible for Orlando's move from the temporary and confusing state of androgyny towards a woman's perspective: 'it is plain that something had happened during the night to give her a push towards the female sex, for she was speaking more as a woman speaks than as a man, yet with a sort of content after all' (159). And when Orlando returns as a woman to her family estate in England, her servants and suitors quickly begin to treat her as one. She, in response, develops an interest in decorating the many rooms of the mansion and a care for her dress and person. The social realities accompanying the possession of a woman's body quickly begin to occlude the insights she had garnered living in the body of the 'opposite' sex.

Woolf differed strongly with Sackville-West's ideas regarding what we today might call her 'bisexuality'. Though Orlando changes sex during the novel, just as Sackville-West claimed she felt she did based upon the sex of the person she was in love with at the moment, Orlando's sex is often not the 'opposite' of that of her beloved. Orlando actually changes sex only once; her subsequent changes are changes of clothing only, and seem primarily nods to convention, though her cross-dressing provides opportunities for sexual play. Orlando's desires, though, are consistently free-flowing and completely irrespective of sex and gender. When Orlando is a young man, he is powerfully attracted to Sasha before he is able to discern her sex. Prior to discovering her to be a woman, he notes the 'extraordinary seductiveness which issued from the whole person', a person who looks remarkably like a boy (*Orlando* 37–8). When he believes her to be a boy, he wants to 'tear his hair with vexation' at the thought that he cannot embrace the object of his desire (38). Later, after Orlando becomes a woman, she continues to love Sasha, for

> if the consciousness of being of the same sex had any effect at all, it was to quicken and deepen those feelings which she had had as a man. For now a thousand hints and mysteries became plain to her that were then dark ... and if there is anything in what the poet says about truth and beauty, this affection gained in beauty what it lost in falsity. (161)

Knowing the truth about women through the experience of being a woman makes women more desirable, suggesting that women are ordinarily better judges of women than are men, an idea consistent with Woolf's normalising of same-sex desire in *Mrs Dalloway*, *To the Lighthouse* and *A Room*.

After being courted by men and learning of the limitations that British society places on its women, Orlando takes to changing her sex, figuratively, with her clothing, by which 'device' she 'reap[s] a twofold harvest ... and enjoy[s] the love of both sexes equally' (221). And if her mention of the names of Nell and Kit along with Sasha when musing on love late in the novel is any indication, we can assume Orlando's enjoyment of 'the love of both sexes' included same-sex sexual relations (311). After her marriage to Shelmerdine, a man with whom she is 'passionately in love' (251), and whom she even likes (264), Orlando begins writing exotic, sensual poetry in which girls appear, a fact that can be overlooked by the 'spirit of the age' only because she has 'a husband at the Cape' (265).

The difference I am noting here between Sackville-West's and Woolf's theories of bisexuality is similar to and evocative of two significant differences between sexological theories and Freudian ones, though Woolf goes further than Freud, whose work she did not actually read until 1939.[3] Whereas most of the sexologists conceived of anatomical sex and sexual desire as inextricable, homosexual desire being explained as occasioned by a disparity between the anatomical and the 'true' or psychical sex (or the sex of the 'soul'), Freud's separation of sexual instinct from sexual object and both from sexual aim in his *Three Essays on the Theory of Sexuality* effectively disentangled sex from sexuality. In Woolf's work, unlike Freud's, bisexual desire seems to be the most common experience of *adults*. Furthermore, Woolf's theories of sexuality foreground the ways social realities such as class systems, financial means, physical bodies, epistemologies of sexuality and gender, and hegemonic power structures determine the possibilities for a given individual of bringing desires to consciousness and pursuing them.

Unlike both the sexologists and some of her friends, Woolf was not striving to develop a modernist category or definition of a sexual type. Woolf's approaches to issues of sexuality were instead integrated in a literary focus on what she called 'an ordinary mind on an ordinary day' ('Modern Fiction' 149). Most of Woolf's characters are ordinary; they are not rare types with unusual thoughts and desires. In *Mrs Dalloway*, the importance that the mature Clarissa Dalloway gives to being once kissed by Sally Seton as a young woman epitomises Woolf's focus on the ordinary. Even Orlando, who sometimes seems to imagine himself/herself to be extraordinary, is actually quite ordinary. Orlando is unusual only in her/his fantasy elements: physical sex change, multi-centuried longevity, extreme wealth and privilege as a member of the aristocracy. In *Orlando*, Woolf simultaneously plays with and challenges Sackville-West's contention that she is a rare type because she is able psychically to change sexes, an ability Woolf calls 'something that happens to most people without being thus plainly expressed':

> Different though the sexes are, they intermix. In *every human being* a vacillation from one sex to the other takes place, and often it is only the clothes that keep the male or female likeness, while underneath the sex is the very opposite of what it is above. Of the complications and confusions which thus result *every one* has had experience; but here we leave the general question and note only the odd effect it had in the particular case of Orlando herself. (*Orlando* 189, emphasis added)

Finding oneself intermittently thinking 'like a man' and 'like a woman' is not, for Woolf, an identifying feature of a rare type of person. Everyone does it. Effectively stating that all adults are androgynous, Woolf disrupts both the notion that gender has an essence and the belief that only rare types have the experience of thinking or feeling like both a man and a woman. If everyone is androgynous, then androgyny is nobody's distinguishing characteristic, nobody's rare trait.

If Woolf believes that everyone 'vacillates' between the two sexes, then, does she also believe that everyone also experiences Orlando's 'love of both sexes equally'? The answer, I think, is not to be found in *Orlando*, but in Woolf's earlier novels, in which bisexual desire is experienced by extremely ordinary characters that, in other hands, would be mere stereotypes: Rachel Vinrace of *The Voyage Out*; Jacob Flanders and Dick Graves of *Jacob's Room*; Clarissa Dalloway of *Mrs Dalloway*; Mr Bankes, Mr Ramsay and Charles Tansley of *To the Lighthouse*. What people do with their bodies in respect to fulfilling (or not) their desires depends on socially constituted realities differing by geographical locale, historical moment, economic resources, social standing and biological constraints, including the psychic constraints that the individual develops as a result of being interpellated as a gendered subject. Woolf carefully removes all but the latter of these constraints for Orlando, so that Orlando's story demonstrates that gender is socially constructed, even performative, and that desire is naturally and commonly polymorphous or bisexual when released from social strictures.

A Room of One's Own, too, demonstrates that the daily experience of living in a given sexed body is exactly what makes a mind 'womanly' or 'manly'; nobody can escape the effect of this experience on the psyche. As is typical of her essays, Woolf begins her disquisition by positing a question or placing in question a popular maxim. In the case of the androgyny thesis in *A Room*, the maxim is Coleridge's statement that 'a great mind must be androgynous'. Woolf begins the interrogation of this maxim by maintaining that Coleridge's hypothesis was invoked for her by the sight of a man and woman getting into a taxi, a common enough occurrence, but one which, she pretends, made her speculate as to whether there might be 'two sexes in the mind corresponding to the two sexes in the body', which might

> also require to be united in order to get complete satisfaction and happiness.... It is when this fusion takes place that the mind is fully fertilised and uses all its faculties. Perhaps a mind that is purely masculine cannot create, any more than a mind that is purely feminine. (102)

To most scholars, this passage has seemed to offer clear evidence that Woolf agreed with those who believed in the superiority of the androgynous mind. But Woolf's variations on this theme only begin with the taxi. Less often quoted is a passage just previous:

> For certainly when I saw the couple get into the taxi-cab the mind felt as if, after being divided, it had come together again in a natural fusion. The obvious reason would be that it is natural for the sexes to co-operate. One has a profound, if irrational, instinct in favour of the theory that the union of man and woman makes for the greatest satisfaction, the most complete happiness. (101–2)

In a statement theorising the aesthetic superiority of an androgynous mind, Woolf interposes the figure of the male–female couple and refers to marriage. One explanation for this might be that Woolf enjoyed being married, an idea she facetiously implies to be radically retrogressive not only in her reference to the 'irrational instinct', but also in a 1925 letter to Sackville-West: 'But then, in all London, you and I alone like being married' (*Letters* 3: 221). Her inclusion of male–female love in her consideration of the theory of androgynous superiority therefore could be read as a corrective to this homosocial/ homoerotic paradigm that had elicited so much misogynistic speculation among some young men at Cambridge.

While Woolf may agree with those arguing that it is impossible to find an androgynous mind 'like Shakespeare's' in a woman, her reasons are different from those bandied about among young men at Cambridge.[4] These reasons form the basic arguments of *A Room*, and are the same as those she gives for the dearth of great women writers: the lack of women's financial and material independence, the want of reasonably reputable educational institutions for women, the fact that women are not admitted into the libraries of the great universities, the burden of raising children and caring for men – in short, a history of patriarchal subjection. Woolf writes,

> Coleridge certainly did not mean, when he said that a great mind is androgynous, that it is a mind that has any special sympathy with women; a mind that takes up their cause or devotes itself to their interpretation. Perhaps the androgynous mind is less apt to make these distinctions than the single-sexed mind. (102)

A Room as a whole is engaged in encouraging women to write history, psychology, even science from a *woman's* perspective, not an androgynous one. The mind's ability to 'make these distinctions' is extremely important to Woolf. They make a woman with her 'single-sexed mind' psychologically a woman.

Many of the problems women writers have faced historically are caused by marriage, however, and others are exacerbated by it, as Woolf implies throughout *A Room*. So what are we to make of this apparent privileging of the heterosexual couple in Woolf's riff on androgynous creativity? The answer is inherent in the metaphor itself, which Woolf does not originate, but only exposes as inherently debilitating for women. She elaborates upon it further a few pages later: 'Some collaboration has to take place in the mind between the woman and the man before the act of creation can be accomplished. Some marriage of opposites has to be consummated' (108). The natural result of such a coupling for a man, who here is 'the writer', is that 'once his experience is over', he 'must lie back and let his mind celebrate its nuptials in darkness. He must not look or question what is being done' (108). But the natural result of that coupling for a *woman* is radically different: the carrying, birthing and raising of the child that is the 'artistic creation' in the extended metaphor. Woolf, who hated lectures and didacticism, simply gives her readers the conceptual tools to deconstruct the metaphor of the androgynous mind for themselves.[5] The logic, however, is simple: the metaphorical consummation of the androgynous mind's 'marriage of opposites' invokes a social and biological reality that is different for men and women. The highly limiting material conditions of a woman's life in a patriarchal society – the exposure of which is a main purpose of *A Room* – makes the free and equal union of the male and female a material impossibility.

In *A Room*, then, we can understand Woolf to question the possibility of androgyny for anyone, male or female, since here, as in *Orlando*, material conditions are shown to suffuse the experience of being 'womanly' or 'manly'. 'Intellectual freedom', Woolf writes, 'depends upon material things' (112). And material things are socio-culturally prescribed and proscribed: the way one is required to dress, for instance, which is exposed as a seriously restrictive physical factor in *Orlando*; or the fact that one is denied entrance to libraries or parliamentary buildings, a limitation with which *A Room* is much concerned; or the social mandate to marry and to bear and raise children, an underlying issue in much of Woolf's fiction. Such limitations cause Woolf to set forth what we might term, after W. E. B. Du Bois, a theory of women's 'double consciousness':

> Again if one is a woman one is often surprised by a sudden splitting off of consciousness, say in walking down Whitehall, when from being the natural inheritor of that civilisation, she becomes, on the contrary, outside of it, alien and critical. (*Room* 101)

Since the androgynous mind is the 'undivided' mind (102), and the thinking woman notices the inequities that surround her far too much for her mind to remain undivided, the state of androgyny is currently impossible for women.

Polymorphous Desire and the Flight of the Imagination

In Woolf's work, the female artist is not constructed according to the cultural mythos of genius. Rather, the notion of genius tends to be exposed as a cultural device for maintaining a reverence or mythical fiction about writing, painting and the arts in general that keeps women from attempting to achieve recognition in those arts. But what then are the ramifications of dismissing both 'androgyny' and 'genius' for Woolf's particular theorisations of the woman artist? More to the point, what does bisexuality or bisexual desire have to do with it? To answer this, I want to turn from *A Room* back again to *Orlando*. One might think that the most interesting passage in *Orlando* for a person interested in Woolf's use of bisexuality would be her explicit reference to Orlando's ability to 'enjoy[ ] the love of both sexes equally' (221). But I want to call attention to what is to me a more illuminating passage of the novel, one that underscores Woolf's *aesthetic* use of that polymorphous desire we now term 'bisexuality': her belief in what it does for the artist.

For Woolf, it is not the ability to think both 'like a woman' and 'like a man' that enables artistic creativity and production. In Woolf's work, conscious indulgence of the ability of one's mind to range freely and contemplate openly *all* desires, even those that are socially proscribed, is necessary for full intellectual and artistic freedom. Thinking through desire, not sex or sexuality, is central to Woolf's concept of the artist. Some of the most important lines in Woolf's work for understanding her use of desire – including the desire that causes Orlando to indulge her 'love of both sexes equally' – are those toward the end of the novel, in which the narrator contemplates the way unhampered polymorphous desire enables artistic inspiration:

> So here then we are at Kew, and I will show you to-day ... under the plum tree, a grape hyacinth, and a crocus, and a bud, too, on the almond tree; so that to walk there is to be thinking of bulbs, hairy and red, thrust into the earth in October; flowering now; and to be dreaming of more than can rightly be said and to be taking from its case a cigarette or cigar even, and to be flinging a cloak under (as the rhyme requires) an oak, and there to sit, waiting the kingfisher, which, it is said, was seen once to cross in the evening from bank to bank.
> Wait! Wait! The kingfisher comes; the kingfisher comes not. (293)

Creativity, imagination and inspiration are here symbolised by the kingfisher, a bird whose ability to dive into flowing water and emerge with a fish has made it a symbol of sudden artistic inspiration mysteriously pulled from the depths of the unconscious. Somewhat more complex is the imagery of budding floral life in the passage. The phallic image of the 'bulbs, hairy and red, thrust into the earth' and productive of flowers together with the nipple-like buds of the almond is fairly obviously evocative of the heterosexual reproductive sex act. And yet the image is queered by the fact that the hyacinth has a long tradition of associations with male homosexuality, as well as by the crocus, traditional symbol of a virginally pure and specifically female bliss, a symbol

Woolf has already used in *Mrs Dalloway* to represent Sally and Clarissa's youthful same-sex love.[6] The lush confusion and proliferation of floral sexual imagery here connects both reproductive and non-reproductive sexuality with the creative process of reflection. All these symbols of sex and desire figure into the 'more than can rightly be said' of what the once-male-now-female poet Orlando is contemplating as she performs the modern woman's gender-bending activity of smoking, possibly even a cigar, in a public park while sitting on the ground absorbed in thought, awaiting inspiration. Implicitly, this unfettered contemplation of a polymorphous diversity of desires and dreamed-of pleasures invokes the intellectual depths from which that fish, that inspiration, will come.

Where women's sexual desire is concerned, it is not limited to the heterosexual keeping of 'an assignation for Sunday dusk' with the gamekeeper and 'slipping off one's petticoat', which Woolf has earlier figured as 'love – as the male novelists define it' (*Orlando* 269). 'Love' includes that, surely, and Orlando has a baby boy on the very next page as if to prove it, but it also includes 'the love of both sexes equally' in which Orlando has been engaging throughout the novel. What is more, it includes the seemingly non-sexual 'splendid fulfilment of natural desires for a hat, for a boat, for a rat in a ditch' (294). To return to the language Woolf uses in her letter to Smyth, the 'narrowing and naming' of 'these immensely composite and wide flung passions' does not serve the modern female artist, who depends on her ability to render in her artwork the beauty of desire in its multiple and uncharacterisable forms.

Woolf's juxtaposition of the beauty of uncategorisable desires against the 'dullness' of sexual identities constructed according to what she calls 'physical feeling' is perhaps made clearer in another passage in the letter to Smyth, in which she remarks on the 'illusion' that presses her to create her fiction. After revealing her previous tendency to 'wheel round and gallop the other way' in response to her own merely physical attraction to two or three 'obtuse, gallant, foxhunting and dull' men earlier in her life, she tells Ethel:

> Perhaps this shows why Clive ... always called me a fish. Vita also calls me fish. And I reply (I think often while holding their hands, and getting exquisite pleasure from contact with either male or female body) 'But what I want of you is illusion – to make the world dance'. More than that, I cannot get my sense of unity and coherency and all that makes me wish to write the Lighthouse etc. unless I am perpetually stimulated. Its [sic] no good sitting in a garden with a book; or collecting facts. There must be this fanning and drumming – of course I get it tremendously from Leonard – but differently – Lord Lord how many things I want – how many different flowers I visit.... (*Letters* 4: 200)

For Woolf, what is 'silly', 'dull' and 'trivial' about certain early twentieth-century evolving sexual identities, then, is the overemphasis on the merely physical aspects of desire, an emphasis she understands to be shared by the sexual scientists, the 'effeminate sodomites' and the 'mannish lesbians' alike. On the whole, Woolf's work is far more interested in desire than it is in sex, sexuality and sexual identity. What her biography-writing narrator facetiously states in *Orlando* might be understood as Woolf's personal authorial mantra nonetheless: 'But let other pens treat of sex and sexuality; we quit such odious subjects as soon as we can' (139). Desire is so multiple, so varied, that the search to satisfy it must not be bounded by constructed limitations such as gender and sexuality. And it is that search itself, and not the physical satisfaction of every desire, that engenders the inspiration that makes possible, makes necessary, Woolf's art.

Notes

1. On the medical profession's shift to an either/or understanding of biological sex with regard to 'hermaphrodites', see Dreger 15–45. See also Foucault vii–xvii.
2. Nigel Nicolson calls *Orlando* 'the longest and most charming love letter in literature' in his depiction of his mother's various loves in *Portrait of a Marriage* (202).
3. For Woolf's unwillingness to read Freud until 1939, see Lee 68.
4. The taunt 'Where's the woman Shakespeare?' was a prime *non sequitur* being used in the late 1920s by male undergraduates in the heated debate over granting women full access and equal degrees at Cambridge. For an in-depth discussion of the controversy over women's attempts to be granted full titular degrees at Cambridge in the 1920s, see McWilliams-Tullberg 142–208. For a discussion of the ways in which *A Room* specifically engages in this debate, as well as the ramifications of that engagement for contemporary feminist theory, see Cucullu.
5. Woolf's dislike of lecturing and didacticism is perhaps most ardently set forth in her essay 'Why?', in which she blames these customs for 'incit[ing] the most debased of human passions – vanity, ostentation, self-assertion, and the desire to convert' (231).
6. Woolf's use of the crocus is esoteric, sometimes symbolising female same-sex desire, as in *Orlando*, sometimes symbolising the essence of meaning, such as that a writer attempts to convey in her or his work, as in her essay 'The Patron and the Crocus', sometimes symbolising both together, as in *Mrs Dalloway*: 'a match burning in a crocus; an inner meaning almost expressed' (47). For a discussion of the symbolism in the latter, see Sparks.

Works Cited

Cucullu, Lois. 'Exceptional Women, Expert Culture, and the Academy'. *Signs* 29.1 (2003): 27–54.

Doan, Laura. *Fashioning Sapphism: The Origins of a Modern English Lesbian Culture.* New York: Columbia University Press, 2001.

Dreger, Alice Domurat. 'Doubtful Sex'. *Hermaphrodites and the Medical Invention of Sex.* Cambridge: Harvard University Press, 1998. 15–45.

Ellis, Havelock. *Sexual Inversion.* Vol. 2. of *Studies in the Psychology of Sex.* 3rd ed. Rev. and enlrgd. Philadelphia: Davis, 1915.

Faderman, Lillian. *Surpassing the Love of Men: Romantic Friendship and Love Between Women from the Renaissance to the Present.* New York: Morrow, 1981.

Foucault, Michel. Introduction. *Herculine Barbin. Being the Recently Discovered Memoirs of a Nineteenth-Century French Hermaphrodite.* Transl. Richard McDougall. New York: Random, 1980. vii–xvii.

Freud, Sigmund. *Three Essays on the Theory of Sexuality.* 1905. *Standard Edition of the Complete Psychological Works*, 24 vols. Vol. 7. Ed. and trans. James Strachey. London: Hogarth, 1953. 133–245.

Hastings, Selina. *Rosamond Lehmann.* 2002. London: Vintage, 2003.

Lee, Hermione. *Virginia Woolf.* New York: Random, 1996.

Marcus, Sharon. *Between Women: Friendship, Desire, and Marriage in Victorian England.* Princeton: Princeton University Press, 2007.

McWilliams-Tullberg, Rita. *Women at Cambridge: A Men's University – Though of a Mixed Type.* London: Gollancz, 1975.

Nicolson, Nigel. *Portrait of a Marriage: Vita Sackville-West and Harold Nicolson.* Chicago: University of Chicago Press, 1973.

Smith-Rosenberg, Carroll. 'The Female World of Love and Ritual: Relations between Women in Nineteenth-Century America'. *Signs* 1.1 (1975): 1–29.

Sparks, Elisa Kay. '"A Match Burning in a Crocus": Modernism, Feminism, and Feminine Experience in Virginia Woolf and Georgia O'Keeffe'. *Virginia Woolf: Emerging Perspectives. Selected Papers from the Third Annual Conference on Virginia Woolf.* New York: Pace University Press, 1994. 296–302.

Tindall, Gillian. *Rosamond Lehmann: An Appreciation.* London: Chatto/Hogarth, 1985.

Vicinus, Martha. *Intimate Friends: Women Who Loved Women, 1778–1928.* Chicago: University of Chicago Press, 2004.

Weininger, Otto. *Sex and Character.* London: Heinemann, 1907.

Woolf, Virginia. *The Letters of Virginia Woolf.* Ed. Nigel Nicolson and Joanne Trautmann. 6 vols. New York: Harcourt, 1975–80.

—. 'Modern Fiction'. *The Common Reader: First Series.* Ed. Andrew McNeillie. San Diego: Harcourt, 1984. 146–54.

—. *Mrs Dalloway.* 1925. New York: Harcourt, 1953.

—. 'Old Bloomsbury'. *Moments of Being.* Ed. Jeanne Schulkind. 2nd ed. San Diego: Harcourt, 1985. 179–201.

—. *Orlando: A Biography.* 1928. San Diego: Harcourt, 1956.
—. *A Room of One's Own.* 1929. San Diego: Harcourt, 1957.
—. 'Why?' *The Death of the Moth and Other Essays.* San Diego: Harcourt, 1942. 227–34.

Part Two: New Essays

The Bloomsbury Love Triangle

Regina Marler

'At its best monogamy may be the wish to find someone to die with.'
Adam Phillips, *Monogamy* 28

'They lived in squares and loved in triangles'. The best quip about the Bloomsbury Group, bar none. Almost no Bloomsbury book review is complete without it, no broadcast, no dramatisation, no web page. Before it, journalists just fell back on how snobbish and effete they were, those pesky Bloomsberries, how un-British, how untalented, how queer-seeming (before Michael Holroyd's biography of Lytton Strachey) and then (afterwards) how certainly, damnably queer. Only when that nameless wag, the unsung Pope of our day, hit on the exact, devastating phrasing in its pithy perfection (imagine the trial runs, the 'loved to live in squares…' and 'lived in love triangles') did the lack of such a chestnut strike the literary world and the media at large, henceforth to embrace it like a scrap of Styrofoam in a sea of deadlines and uncertainty. 'What can we say here', editors ask themselves, 'that has been said many times before?'[1]

The joke wouldn't be funny, of course, if it didn't contain a germ of truth. Although there was plenty of serial monogamy in and around Bloomsbury, some open marriages, and even a couple of fairly traditional ones, the triangle seems to have been a default relationship mode for many members of the group and their close friends, especially when young: 'A eating his heart out vainly for B; B breaking hers in vain for C, and so on in interminable interlocking circles of frustration', as David Garnett, or 'Bunny', himself an A and a C in one of the best-known Bloomsbury triangles (with Duncan Grant and Vanessa Bell), characterised the group's approach to love. Any large group of friends is likely to have some romantic overlap, but the triangle is so frequently associated with Bloomsbury that the Wikipedia entry for 'love triangle' refers to the Bloomsbury Group.[2]

'Among the intellectual elite that was the extended Bloomsbury circle, love's preferred form was the serially lived triangle – both homo- and hetero-erotic', writes Lisa Appignanesi in *All About Love: Anatomy of an Unruly Emotion* (150). She credits Bloomsbury's atypical relationships, in part, with the twentieth-century's challenge to those two pillars of Victorian propriety – Repression and Duty. 'Although Bloomsbury forms of coupling were not widespread', she argues,

> their influence, given the prominence of Bloomsbury ideas in the media, on the loosening of conventions in Britain in the aftermath of that vast shaking-up of hierarchies that the First World War produced, was hardly minimal. The new emphasis on 'feeling', on a desire for self-fulfillment, crucially by women as well as men, abutted against older strictures and gradually dismantled the rigid edifice of dutiful marriage, though its idealized ghost remained, ever to be reinvoked by politicians intent on 'family values'. (152)

But the Bloomsbury ideas prominent 'in the media' during their lifetimes were not about how to balance household finances with your live-in lover and live-out husband, or how to remain dear friends with a former boyfriend after you have married a Russian ballerina. There were no *Guardian* features on their home lives. This aspect of their legacy was little known outside art and literary circles in England before the late 1960s, and no friend of the group would have publicised it.[3] Bertrand Russell, their uneasy ally, lost a university teaching post for his book *Marriage and Morals* (1929), which presented the avant-garde ideas by which Bloomsbury also lived; if he'd been gay, he would have risked arrest.[4] How Bloomsbury's unconventional loves eventually reached the public is one strand of my study, *Bloomsbury Pie*, so I won't revisit it here. But by the time the Beat Generation revitalised the Free Love movement in the United States and inspired Swinging London, Bloomsbury had long been perceived as an old and stuffy establishment clique.[5] In other words: squares. Not a triangle in sight. Hence the shock of Holroyd's *Lytton Strachey* (1967–68) and the failure of scholars before the 1970s – especially before Carolyn Heilbrun's *Toward a Recognition of Androgyny* (1973) – to recognise and explore the rich terrain of love, identity and desire in Bloomsbury.

This essay meanders through one aspect of that terrain, their triangular romances, and speculates on why many of the Bloomsberries preferred to divide their affectional – and sometimes their libidinal – energies between two or more partners, why they valued longevity over simplicity in their relationships, and how they benefited from these risky but oddly resilient unions.

Against expectation, the group's triangles would sometimes prove to bolster, as well as complicate, the original dyads. In ways, they were the queerest thing about Bloomsbury.

∆   ∆   ∆

By its simplest definition, a love triangle is 'a situation in which two people both love a third person'.[6] The western concept of romantic love typically admits the triangle as only a brief, painful occurrence, either an interruption of the dyad's bliss, or an uneasy alliance at the beginning or end of coupledom, in which the new relationship serves as a staging platform or an exit strategy. In geometric terms, picture a triangle of any angle – right, obtuse or acute – with unequal sides. In love, there are no equilateral triangles.

Yet the triangle is a remarkably stable structure: the basic structural unit of the universe. To judge from Bloomsbury, this is no less true in social and romantic arrangements than in physics. In the Freudian view, we keep returning to the triangle throughout life, unconsciously recreating the Oedipal triangle between the infant and its parents. 'Love in the face of any taboo, whether of class, religion, race, or family relationship, is, at least in part, a reworking of the original Oedipal taboo', wrote the psychiatrist and psychoanalyst Ethel Person. 'Indeed, all love bears some relationship to the Oedipal'. There is no escape from the Stephen family drama at Hyde Park Gate, it seems, or the other Bloomsbury childhood homes; just endless re-stagings with replacement cast members: 'Triangles are intimately connected with our early lives, and are imbued with profound desires and fears.... In fact, the play between pairings and triangles, whether enriching or depleting, realized or fantasized, is lifelong' (Person). Sigmund Freud's covert affair with his sister-in-law, Minna Bernays, who lived with him and his wife, may have provided insight into the power of such attractions. But since their relationship was secret, it lacks one of the chief attributes of a Bloomsbury liaison: an audience.

The rapt attention of friends and co-conspirators is part of the ongoing conversation that sustained the group over so many decades. 'What they enjoyed most was talk', Frances Partridge recalled, 'talk of every description, from the most abstract to the most hilariously ribald and profane' (*Memories* 76). But their words also kindled action, like the goading letters in that Bloomsbury favourite, de Laclos's epistolary novel, *Les Liaisons dangereuses*. In the best-known example of this characteristic logo-motion, Leonard Woolf returned to London from Ceylon in 1911 with half a mind to marry Virginia Stephen, due to Lytton's teasing letters from two years earlier. Lytton's campaign lasted for months – and included the alarming day or so in February of 1909 in which he found himself engaged to Virginia. 'Your destiny is clearly marked out for you', he insisted to Leonard, having safely disentangled himself, 'but will you allow it to work? You must marry Virginia' (Strachey 185).

During her disappointing courtship *interruptus* with Lytton, Virginia was also involved in the pseudonymous letter-writing game among her group of friends that enabled her to flirt almost openly with her sister's husband, Clive Bell. 'The idea was to produce a novel in letters', wrote Quentin Bell, but 'it was in fact a kind of epistolary *bal masqué* in which the disguises served only to embolden the participants' (Q. Bell 142). And scholars have remarked on the bravado of Vanessa Bell's letters to Maynard Keynes during the early days of her affair with Duncan Grant, when she was eager to show how relaxed she could be about sexual irregularities: 'Did you have a pleasant afternoon buggering one or more of the young men we left for you?' (V. Bell 163). Bloomsbury would not be Bloomsbury if they had not been egging each other on. That circle of voices replaced parental monitoring and influence. Like the orphaned heroes and heroines in children's fiction, many of them had lost their parents early, had only one parent, or had much older parents, like Colonel and Lady Strachey.

The most famous example of an open marriage of the period is not one of the Bloomsbury unions but that of Harold Nicolson and Vita Sackville-West, an arrangement that permitted Vita's relationship with Virginia, and Harold's with the second-generation Bloomsbury critic Raymond Mortimer, and thus the Nicolsons' inclusion here. They married for love in 1913 (although Vita was already in love with a woman friend), but as their sexual identities evolved, they realised that their sanctioned bond also provided cover. As their son Nigel Nicolson argued in *Portrait of a Marriage*, their union 'not only survived infidelity, sexual incompatibility and long absences, but it became stronger and finer as a result' (ix). Vita's tempestuous nature – for a few years, she careened between Harold and Violet Trefusis – did almost sink the marriage early on. A recently discovered poem to Violet conveys something of Vita's ferocity in love: 'in the heavy fragrance of intoxicating night / I search on your lip for a madder caress / I tear secrets from your yielding flesh' (qtd. in Kennedy). The original was – no surprise – in French.

'You are not a person with whom one can associate law, order, duty, or any of the conventional ties of life', Harold wrote Vita in the midst of this intense triangle; 'I never think of you that way' (Nicolson 168). Although this statement could have been made of almost any member of the Bloomsbury Group, the fact that it was made at all demonstrates how different the aristocratic Nicolsons were from shabby, irreverent Bloomsbury, despite their open marriage. The members of Bloomsbury were artists and freethinkers, more closely aligned to bohemia, and presupposed each other's relative indifference to the 'conventional ties of life'.

∆ ∆ ∆

What, then, is a Bloomsbury love triangle, strictly speaking? It is probably too much to demand that all three vertices of the triangle be closely identified with Bloomsbury and significantly involved with each other as friends or lovers. Virginia Woolf's affair with Vita Sackville-West in the 1920s would not meet this narrow definition. Vita and Leonard were only acquaintances, and Vita is not 'Bloomsbury'. But if we expand our study to include non-Bloomsberries as triangular love interests, we have to cast a large net. What about Clive Bell's late partnership with Barbara Bagenal, who had been Saxon Sydney-Turner's lover before her marriage, and remained Saxon's friend and caretaker all his life? Does that verge on triangular? Then there is the one Bloomsbury-centred triangle big enough for the silver screen: the relationship of Ralph Partridge, Carrington and Lytton Strachey, first described by Michael Holroyd and depicted in Gretchen Holbrook Gerzina's *Carrington: A Life* (1990) and Christopher Hampton's film *Carrington* (1995). Strictly speaking, Carrington and Partridge were not Bloomsbury, but Bloomsbury-by-association. Few would argue that this remarkable relationship was not pure Bloomsbury in concept and execution, though, even – perhaps especially – with the addition of Frances Marshall in 1924, which bent the triangle to a trapezoid.

If we can't precisely define a Bloomsbury triangle – except to say, with Justice Stewart, that we know it when we see it – we can at least examine a few, and touch on the pleasures and hazards of these unconventional bonds. First, we must lay a wreath for Duncan Grant: the erotic hub of Bloomsbury. The Bloomsbury detractor Hugh Kenner noted that 'someone once characterized "Bloomsbury" as a congeries of men and women all of whom were in love with Duncan Grant' (161). And who can blame them? Duncan's sensual good looks and sweet nature felled people right and left. Even his passion for his art contributed to his allure, because it made him a little remote. 'His priority was painting', his daughter Angelica recalled, 'human beings with all their subtleties and complications were peripheral' (A. Garnett, *Eternal* 28). But he was maddeningly distractible in love. As his biographer Frances Spalding notes,

> One of his most pronounced charms – a ready responsiveness – may have had a destabilising effect on his relationships, for it enabled him always to move on, a new interest detaching him as swiftly as he had in the first instance become attached. (112)

Duncan himself came to think he conducted his romantic life on a Regency model, freer and more rational than that of the Victorians. His book choice, when he appeared on Desert Island Discs in 1975, was the collected works of Jane Austen.[7]

While kind, Duncan did not promise fidelity, and was sceptical – even, at times, openly contemptuous – of marriage. His father had been unfaithful and his mother had a longstanding romantic attachment outside her marriage. His grandmother, Lady Grant, had two children by a 'Lord of India' who was not her husband, although her husband accepted these offspring as his own (Spalding 11). Among his many other lovers, Duncan was sexually involved with Adrian Stephen, Maynard Keynes, David Garnett and Vanessa Bell, as well as with his cousins James Strachey (briefly) and Lytton Strachey, despite his fabled initial response to Lytton's advances: 'Relations we may be; have them, we may not' (qtd. in Spalding 36). The early affair between Duncan and Lytton from 1905 to about 1907 was coached from the sidelines by Maynard in a way that almost qualifies as triangular: 'I am in love with your being in love with one another', he confessed to Lytton (qtd. in Spalding 38). Later, when Duncan and Maynard actually became lovers, it was Lytton's turn for confusion: 'I copulated with Duncan again this afternoon, and at the present he's in Cambridge copulating with Keynes', he wrote to Leonard Woolf. 'I don't know whether I'm happy or unhappy' (qtd. in Holroyd 201).

But this was not the first Bloomsbury (or pre-Bloomsbury) triangle. Earlier in 1905, Lytton and Maynard had competed at Cambridge for the affections of Arthur Hobhouse, a fair-haired embryo whom each man longed to bring into the Apostles. Maynard won. This ur-triangle caused exquisite pain – Lytton actively hated Maynard for some weeks – but after Maynard's romance with Hobhouse sputtered, Lytton and Maynard grew closer than ever. They even wondered whether they 'might actually be in love with each other' (Holroyd 110). So Lytton had some reason to expect that, with the later 'loss' of Duncan to Maynard, he might not also lose his closest friend.

There is no pattern to Bloomsbury's triangles, except for this privileging of friendship and emotional intimacy over forms and tradition, along with a disinclination to sever bonds. For instance, soon after Clive and Vanessa Bell married in 1907, Clive resumed meetings with his mistress. This was the first step in the Bells' development of an open marriage – a durable, practical arrangement from which, by about 1911, the sex disappeared. Though one can trace Clive and Vanessa's romantic disconnection and disappointment through their correspondence, no blaming letters have survived. They seem to have quickly realised that they could share a home and some degree of family life while in love with other people. Desmond and Molly MacCarthy drifted apart sexually and both had affairs.[8] James Strachey carried on his longstanding off-and-on relationship with Noel Olivier Richards during his marriage, while his wife Alix had an affair with a woman named Nancy Morris. Frances Partridge attended a queer party the women threw in 1930:

> About a hundred people stood close together in a stuffy basement, shouting, bellowing rather, into each other's open mouths, and sometimes twining their arms vaguely about one or two necks at once. The atmosphere was choking, the food and drink good. Almost all were homosexuals – young man after young man pushed his pretty face round the door, and a crowd of truculent Lesbians stood by the fireplace, occasionally trying their biceps or carrying each other round the room. (Partridge, *Memories* 175)

And Carrington, though only partly Bloomsbury, was entirely triangular. Her husband Ralph Partridge, a Bloomsbury fellow traveller, had affairs during both of his marriages. His old friend Gerald Brenan was a committed non-monogamist; for a time, he shared Carrington with Ralph.

Δ   Δ   Δ

Bloomsbury's permissive, often adventurous, sexual ethos is comprised of so many different strands – differently expressed in each member of the group – that there is almost no stating it clearly. In its infancy, that ethos well pre-dates Cambridge and the Apostles, let alone that supposed Bloomsbury bible, G. E. Moore's *Principia Ethica*. It has strains of Wilde and *The Yellow Book*, of the fear engendered by Wilde's 1895 imprisonment for sodomy and his early death, of Roger Fry and Leonard Woolf's disgust at public school cruelty and sexual brutality, of the suffrage movement, of the rational dress movement, of Havelock Ellis's 1897 *Sexual Inversion*, of early feminism, of Voltaire and other Enlightenment figures, and of Edward Carpenter and other members of the Fellowship of the New Life (especially Bertrand Russell and H. G. Wells), the parent organisation of the Fabian Society. Bloomsbury's early reading of the classics was hugely influential, as many scholars have noted. At sixteen, Lytton Strachey first read Plato's *Symposium*: 'with a rush of mingled pleasure and pain … of surprise, relief, and fear to know that what I feel now was felt 2,000 years ago in glorious Greece' (qtd. in Holroyd 40). Late in life, Virginia Woolf recalled her own experience more flatly: 'I had known since I was 16 or so, all about sodomy, from reading Plato' ('Sketch' 104). For the rest of her life, she still thrilled at the thought of traditional boy–girl love, but Jack Hills had carefully disillusioned her about the 'purity' of men:

> He it was who first spoke to me openly and deliberately about sex – in Fitzroy Square, with the green carpet and the red Chinese curtains.
> He opened my eyes on purpose, as I think, to the part played by sex in the life of the ordinary man. He shocked me a little, wholesomely. He

told me that young men talked incessantly of women; and 'had' them incessantly. ('Sketch' 103–4)

This conversation was Virginia's introduction to the sexual double standard that she and Vanessa would both reject so soundly.

'We both of us want a marriage that is a tremendous, living thing, always alive, always hot, not dead and easy in parts as most marriages are' (Woolf, *Letters* 497). So wrote Virginia to Leonard in May 1912. Her ideal, as her niece Angelica wrote, was 'a passionate commitment to an intellectual companionship, which depended for its success on mutual honesty' (A. Garnett, *Eternal* 16). The Bloomsbury critique of marriage had old radical roots, and the group was not alone in wanting to shed Victorian hypocrisy. Their close contemporary Augustus John, the archetypal bohemian, is rumoured to have had so many children, only nine of them legitimate, that an accurate tally is impossible. 'Max Beerbohm estimated over ninety-nine', Virginia Nicholson notes in her entertaining study of the artistic demi-monde (69). For a time, his wife and mistress raised their children together.

Augustus John's circle included the painter Henry Lamb, who followed him to Paris in 1905 and fell deeply in love with John's wife, Dorelia. This did not hamper the younger man's affairs with Helen Maitland (soon to move in with the Russian mosaicist Boris Anrep) and Lady Ottoline Morrell, nor prevent Lytton Strachey from falling in love with him. Seeing Henry enter a 1910 party with the resplendent Lady Ottoline, Lytton reported that he 'was never so astonished, and didn't know which I was in love with more' (qtd. in Holroyd 224). By that winter, they had formed a triangle, with bawdy, moody, heterosexual Henry at the throbbing apex. By spring, Ottoline had taken two new lovers: Bertrand Russell and (briefly) Roger Fry. The Morrells' open marriage needed a swing door, but they were deeply devoted. 'Even in civilised mankind', as Bertrand Russell put it, 'faint traces of a monogamic instinct can sometimes be perceived' (81).

Not everyone in the group warmed to triangular love. Roger Fry seems to have been serially monogamous. He was only unfaithful to his wife Helen (née Combes) after she was committed to a mental institution; he enjoyed – and then mourned – a passionate two-year affair with Vanessa Bell, and much later settled down with Helen Anrep, who remained (nominally) married to the artist Boris Anrep. Molly MacCarthy would gladly have done away with Betsy Reyneau, Desmond's great passion in his fifties. 'Free Love' had not served Molly well, she felt.[9] Her acute jealousy was 'a source of angry scenes which became an unhappy feature' of her life with Desmond (Cecil and Cecil 161). Morgan Forster's forty-year triangle with the policeman Bob Buckingham and his wife May was important and ultimately supportive, but he would have preferred an exclusive relationship with Bob. For his part, Bob seems never to have admitted his sexual relationship with Morgan to his wife. Saxon Sydney-Turner turned down Barbara Hiles's offer to remain his lover after her marriage to Nick Bagenal. And no one would accuse Leonard Woolf of triangulating; he seems to have been an ardent pair-bonder: with Virginia, of course, then, after her death, with Trekkie Parsons. Because Trekkie was married, however, Leonard did spend his later years in a triangle. She and her husband Ian Parsons eventually shared his London house with him. Often, Trekkie stayed with Leonard during the week at Monk's House – chastely, she always insisted when asked – then returned home for weekends with her husband, whose lover was the publisher Norah Smallwood.

Some argument can be made that Vanessa Bell was also a serial monogamist, in that her relationship with Roger Fry overlapped her sexual relationship with her husband, Clive Bell, only briefly, if at all, and that she broke off her affair with Roger soon after falling in love with Duncan Grant in 1913. That she remained married to Clive all her life, however, enjoying the social status and material comforts of a married woman, often sharing a house with Clive, and attributing Angelica's paternity to him, necessarily triangulates her attention and identity. And Vanessa not only shared Duncan Grant with David Garnett during the Great War, but was the third wheel – the third side of the triangle – in Duncan's many romantic relationships with men after he called off the sexual aspect of his relationship with Vanessa in late 1918. Still in love, Vanessa provided a home for Duncan and remained his close companion all her life. 'One may see in her attitude either passion or possessiveness, complaisance or tolerance or more likely an illogical mixture', their daughter Angelica remarked (A. Garnett, *Eternal* 27). But Vanessa seemed to divine what Duncan needed from her. They travelled together and were regarded as a couple – Virginia called it a 'left handed marriage' (*Diary* 124) – by those in their circle and in the London and Paris art worlds.

As an equal-opportunity flirt, Virginia Woolf represents a special case. Although not the most carnally adventurous of the group (her passionate affair with Vita Sackville-West in the 1920s was her only known extramarital extravagance), her early flirtation with her sister's husband was a classic triangle set in newlywed Eden. Whether Adam and Eve were played by Clive and Vanessa or by the two sisters is uncertain. The identity of the snake is also up for debate. This has to be included among Bloomsbury's failed triangles, for it seriously damaged the sisters' relationship. On the other hand, as Hermione Lee points out, it did not distance them:

> Their feelings towards each other became more explicit, as well as less trusting. Virginia's courtship of Vanessa through Clive freed her to

make more direct demands in her own letters to Vanessa: 'Shall you kiss me tomorrow? Yes, Yes, Yes'. (Lee 250)

This may have been the most emotionally incestuous attachment in Bloomsbury, but it was just one among their many endogamous triangles. They loved what they saw every day. The closet was a factor, as well, for the Bloomsbury men, not all of whom were adept at cruising strangers, or comfortable with the risks. Lytton used to wonder why he had never fallen in love with Leonard, having fallen for nearly every other Y chromosome of his acquaintance. And of course he fell, briefly, for Carrington, with whom he then spent the rest of his life in an asexual but amorous relationship. (The impossibility of living openly as a gay man in England allowed, paradoxically, for more bisexual experimentation than the identity politics of a later era might permit. You did not have to surrender your gay card.) Romantic relationships within the circle stirred jealousy, naturally, but also connected the friends more deeply. They knew each other's history. Often, they *were* each other's history.

Whether within or outside the group, the triangle permitted interesting new constellations – frequently same-sex – and cemented some alliances that might otherwise have been fleeting. The presence of a desirable woman in the triangle sometimes allowed romance to bloom between a homosexual man and a mostly-straight man, a psychosocial opportunity well known to readers of Eve Kosofsky Sedgwick.[10] Less predictably, in the case of both major Bloomsbury love triangles – the arrangement reached by Lytton, Ralph and Carrington at Mill House (and, later, Ham Spray) and Vanessa and Duncan's Charleston *ménage* with Bunny – the presence of a desirable straight-ish man could allow love to deepen between a homosexual man and a woman.

Of course, primary heterosexual relationships, even celibate ones, also nicely concealed whatever same-sex adventures might be taking place behind a closed bedroom door, at a time when sodomy was a felony. The Bells' marriage also permitted Vanessa to live more or less openly with Duncan for almost fifty years without losing servants to 'scandal'. There is nothing new about sheltering behind such constructs, whether to avoid gossip or prosecution; this is the least interesting aspect of the Bloomsbury's unconventional amours. What is arresting, so to speak, and more characteristic of the group, is the honesty within these relationships, and within the circle as a whole. There were no simple bearding arrangements in Bloomsbury – in other words, no relationship formed or enacted solely as a heterosexual front – and it was rare for partners not to disclose their outside attractions to each other, or even submit them to the group for comment and analysis. Within their circle of friends, they jettisoned shame and (largely) secrecy, and thus avoided the homosexual scandals of their parents' generation.[11]

The Bloomsbury emphasis on honesty – on searching conversation and disclosure – can't be overstated. Even its major lapse, the secret of Angelica's parentage, bears on this point, for why would anyone otherwise question Clive and Vanessa's decision, which was entirely conventional?[12] The Bloomsbury devotion to truth-telling effectively redefined intimacy between partners: not fidelity but honesty marked their closeness. Between this insistence on truth and the grounding of their sexual relationships in friendship, the Bloomsberries rarely 'moved on' when passion was spent; they remained involved. Maynard Keynes, for example, settled an annuity on Duncan Grant in 1937, although their sexual affair had ended long before, and relations were frosty between Charleston and the Keynes' home Tilton, only a field away. Similarly, Ralph Partridge brought his new partner Frances Marshall to live part-time at Ham Spray, in lieu of divorcing Carrington and breaking up his household with her and Lytton Strachey. Through these extended involvements, celibate unions came to attain the same importance as sexual ones, and were far more lasting.

Arriving late on the scene, Angelica (Bell) Garnett did notice as she grew up that the conventions of married life – grounded in sexual possession – were not observed at Charleston. 'In her own everyday life sex shone by its absence', she wrote of her alter ego, Bettina, in a lightly fictionalised story:

> The beds, most of them uncomfortable, were also single. No one shared one with anyone else. Neither Howard nor Jamie gave Maman more than a peck on the cheek when they returned from an absence. No one unnecessarily touched anyone else. No one exuded that desirable and mysterious quality that belonged only, it seemed, to Mr Darcy or Mr Rochester. There was safety in this probably, but no thrill and no warmth. She lived in a paradise from which the serpent had long ago departed. (A. Garnett, *Unspoken* 35)

Small wonder, perhaps, that Angelica responded so strongly to David Garnett's pursuit. Here was the possessive masculine love that she had missed from Clive and Duncan. Angelica and Bunny became lovers in 1938 while his wife Ray was dying of cancer; they married, over Duncan and Vanessa's objections, in 1942. The version of their courtship Angelica offers in her 1984 memoir, *Deceived with Kindness*, is not very flattering to Bunny; nor are her later reflections in fictional form in *The Unspoken Truth*, where he features as her much older lover, Bartle: 'She loved him, though not as she would love someone she intended to spend the rest of her life with' (59). Bunny had re-imagined his side of the story in his 1955 novel, *Aspects of Love*, which lives on as a successful Andrew Lloyd Webber musical. Dedicated to Angelica, the book describes a triangle between desirable Rose (the Angelica figure), her dashing young lover Alexis, and her older admirer, George, whom she marries. But Bunny has cast himself as the young lover, rather than as George, and suggests the sexual initiative was all hers.[13]

Angelica and Bunny's marriage began to come apart in the early 1960s. Staying at their home in Hilton, Frances Partridge recorded her sadness at

> the sudden new feeling of their being two quite disconnected people. Bunny told me something of this and it's evidently true … those grey eyes look at him very coolly now; I would be frightened if I were him. (*Other* 57)

After a move to London, away from their shared home, Angelica seems to have offered Bunny a reprieve: some kind of Bloomsbury-like continuance. No more sex, though. Frances tried to persuade Bunny that it 'might be well worth preserving even without the sexual element', but the physical rejection hit him hard (*Other* 203). 'I love her and want to express my love', he told Frances, who reflected, 'Does this mean he simply won't have her except on his own terms?' (207).

Perhaps if Bunny had agreed to a sexless union, they might have entered into a partnership like that of his own parents, Constance and Edward Garnett,[14] or like Clive and Vanessa, and seen each other into old age. Witnessing Clive's enduring attachment to Vanessa, Angelica thought Clive loved her 'for a depth which, when added to her tenderness and humour (even when not addressed to himself), gave her a distinction and mystery he never found elsewhere'. She remained 'the only woman in whose house he could live with some semblance of contentment' (A. Garnett, *Deceived* 141). Vanessa also enjoyed a rich friendship with her ex-lover Roger Fry: 'With Roger', Angelica wrote,

> Vanessa had found too much excitement, sympathy and tenderness to cut him out of her life entirely; neither of them wanted such a thing – the sacrifice would have been disproportionate, and they had too much in common for it to be possible. For the rest of his life there remained between them the flavour of a past love affair, as though neither of them would ever quite admit that it was over. (*Deceived* 32–3)

But Angelica's penetrating, beautifully written memoirs are like sweet and sour candy. She has to conclude this affectionate passage by reminding us that Vanessa clung to her loved ones 'like a limpet'. Angelica can also be counted on to underscore the fear of abandonment and loss that motivated some of Vanessa's life choices – and, I would add, those of her friends. The group had been cemented, after all, in the wake of Thoby Stephen's shocking early death, from typhoid. In holding on to past loves, accommodating new ones, scrupulously negotiating and maintaining a web of intimate and domestic relationships, the friends at the core of Bloomsbury were letting go of nothing.

This meant, of course, living with jealousy – the scourge of companionate unions, no less than of highly passionate ones, like that of Frances and Ralph Partridge.[15] Vanessa's correspondence with Duncan shows the couple absorbing the impact each time Duncan fell in love elsewhere. Angelica believed that Vanessa 'clung to a hope that all problems could be solved by rationalizing them, and that there was somewhere a perfect system that would do away with threatening or painful situations' (*Deceived* 19). Sensitive to her feelings, Duncan would sometimes conceal an affair to buy time or, alternatively, urge her to meet his lovers. 'My one object at the moment is neither to get nor to give pain to others', he wrote (qtd. in Spalding 276). After one anxious letter to Duncan, Vanessa wrote again to apologise: 'I think I know always that as far as anything can be permanent, my relationship with you is, for it seems to me to depend on things that aren't likely to change until we're old and doddering' (V. Bell, *Selected* 297n2).

There was also a kind of corporate jealousy in Bloomsbury, a resistance to outsiders – specifically, to new love interests. 'Rows, jealousies, and sharp differences of opinions add a lively counterpoint to the generally smooth melody of friendship', observes Richard Shone; 'Invariably, such upsets were caused by the introduction of a new element – a new activity or a new friend – which threatened the established pattern of life' (15). Lydia Lopokova is an obvious example. Vanessa found her entertaining but childlike, and advised Keynes to keep her as a mistress. But he married Lydia and was faithful to her.[16] Other 'new friends' included Vita Sackville-West, Mary Hutchinson and Carrington. One only has to read Frances Partridge's bracing diaries to see how she slipped through the barricades and was accepted at once; it probably helped that she was not in love with Lytton.

The intensity of Carrington's passion for Lytton suggests that she might have settled monogamously with him if he were fully available to her. After agreeing to marry Ralph – and hearing a raft of painful Woolfian gossip from him, which he must have repeated in hopes of damaging her ties to Lytton and his intimates – she told Lytton she 'cried to think of a savage cynical fate which had made it impossible for my love ever to be used by you. You never knew, or never will know the very big and devastating love I had for you' (Carrington 177).

No one reading Carrington's surviving letters or diary can doubt how profound a connection she felt with Lytton. If his unavailability was part of the attraction, it seems churlish to dwell on it. Nevertheless, love denied can remain fresh: constantly needing care, stratagems, ingenuity. Triangles can function this way, as well, by introducing novelty and danger. And however innovative the original arrangement – like the Ham Spray household – its failure provokes the same feelings of rage and resentment. Ralph exploded when he learned that Carrington was secretly involved with his old friend Gerald Brenan; decades later, when Carrington's posthumous show at the Barbican was panned by a reviewer from the *Evening Standard*, Frances Partridge revelled in the attack on Carrington's 'obstinate chastity' and her abuse of her husband. 'At last', as her biographer Anne Chisholm characterises her view, 'someone had seen Carrington clearly'. She quotes Frances's diary:

> I for so long had repressed the fact that I too thought she treated Ralph cruelly.... It is two days since I read the Standard and I have only just realized it myself but this little piece of psycho-analysis has produced a curious calm. Why? Because I have faced a piece of the truth. (355)

Δ   Δ   Δ

The Bloomsbury Group's embrace of unconventional amours is as much a part of their modernist project as Vanessa Bell's radical abstract paintings or the stories collected in Virginia Woolf's *Monday or Tuesday* (1921). Here, too, is the 'smashing of glass' that Molly MacCarthy described hearing: 'the strong, rose-coloured glass of the nineteenth-century conservatories cracking up' (31). Despite its risks, I read the Bloomsbury triangle not as a failure of love, but as a creative adaptation: a way to accommodate both attachment and new desire, to remain open to the erotics of artistic collaboration and rivalry, and to honour Bloomsbury as a family of choice, a charmed semi-closed cluster. Pairing off is exclusionary. The triangle connects. It permits the extenuation of love and connection. These were bold experiments. But the Bloomsbury triangle can also be seen as a protective adaptation. It made for loves that would bend but not break.

Notes

1. The quip is so clever, in fact, that it is now widely attributed to the brilliant Dorothy Parker, even on the Charleston website, although it was probably the work of Kingsley Martin. I would like to thank Kevin Fitzpatrick of the Dorothy Parker Society, and Ellen Meister, who helped me confirm that Parker did not say this. (Email and Twitter messages to the author, 2014.)
2. 'Love Triangle'. *Wikipedia: The Free Encyclopedia*. Web. 7 Jul. 2015.

3. For a fuller account of Bloomsbury's influence and afterlife, see my *Bloomsbury Pie*.
4. 'The psychology of adultery has been falsified by conventional morals', Russell insisted, 'which assume, in monogamous countries, that attraction to one person cannot coexist with a serious affection for another. Everybody knows that this is untrue' (141). Russell's own parents, Viscount and Viscountess Amberley, had a somewhat open marriage, but since they both died before his fourth birthday, Russell may not have known this during his formative years.
5. For example: 'To the new writers, [Bloomsbury] means quite simply a society pledged before all else to an ideal of elegant style in conversation, art, life itself; a society in which the liberal and aristocratic are subtly blended' (Fiedler).
6. 'Love Triangle'. *Cambridge Dictionaries Online*. Web. 7 Jul. 2015.
7. Forster also proclaimed himself a 'Jane Austenite', and Carrington recorded that she and Lytton read all of Jane Austen each winter.
8. Clive Bell got a leg over Molly MacCarthy, which Desmond felt freed him to pursue other women. Molly regretted the arrangement. See Cecil and Cecil 165.
9. The sexual disconnection of the MacCarthys soon after the birth of their three children was an ongoing source of sadness and anger for Molly, and Betsy in particular drove her insane with jealousy. See Cecil and Cecil.
10. See especially Sedgwick, *Between Men*.
11. During Virginia and Vanessa's childhood, for example, their mother's first cousin, Lady Henry Somerset, discovered her husband's infatuation with a young man and sued him for custody of their son. After their divorce, he fled England to avoid prosecution, and she was ostracised for having dared to expose him. See Kaplan 205–13.
12. In their horror at her engagement to Bunny, they also may have failed to tell her that he'd been Duncan's lover. Maynard tried to dissuade Angelica, but she would not hear it.
13. Contrast with his much-quoted letter to Lytton on first seeing baby Angelica: 'Its beauty is the most remarkable thing about it. I think of marrying it: when she is twenty I shall be 46 – will it be scandalous?' (qtd. in Spalding 215, and Knights 138). However, Sarah Knights underscores the importance of understanding the context of the letter as gay badinage between two friends, one of whom (Lytton) disliked talk of babies and the trifles of domesticity: 'It was a piece of light-hearted whimsy which Lytton … would have enjoyed. It was a means of conveying a piece of "family" news without recourse to the usual details of baby's weight and duration of labour' (138).
14. The Garnett marriage had been sexually unsuccessful, and Edward Garnett eventually lived openly with his mistress, Nellie Heath, apparently with Constance's permission (Knights 11).
15. Frances's surviving papers show some irritation with Ralph's infidelities. 'Of course she had not liked it', she told her biographer, 'but that she never doubted that it was her Ralph needed and loved. She had never thought that sex was the most important element in marriage' (Chisholm 157).

16. 'Despite early conflicts over Keynes's desire to maintain a male lover, they made each other very happy. Keynes never stopped desiring beautiful men, but he was physically beguiled by Lopokova and settled into a very uxorious husband' (Mackrell).

Works Cited

Appignanesi, Lisa. *All About Love: Anatomy of an Unruly Emotion*. New York: Norton, 2011.
Bell, Vanessa. *Selected Letters of Vanessa Bell*. Sel. and ed. Regina Marler. New York: Pantheon, 1993.
Bell, Quentin. *Virginia Woolf: A Biography*. San Diego: Harvest-Harcourt, 1972.
Carrington, Dora. *Carrington. Letters and Extracts from Her Diaries*. Ed. David Garnett. New York: Holt, 1970.
Cecil, Hugh, and Mirabel Cecil. *Clever Hearts: Desmond and Molly MacCarthy*. London: Gollancz, 1990.
Chisholm, Anne. *Frances Partridge: The Biography*. London: Weidenfeld, 2009.
Fiedler, Leslie. 'Class War in British Literature'. *Esquire Magazine* Apr. 1958.
Garnett, Angelica. *Deceived with Kindness*. London: Chatto, 1984.
—. *The Eternal Moment*. Orono: Puckerbrush, 1998.
—. *The Unspoken Truth: A Quartet of Bloomsbury Stories*. London: Chatto, 2010.
Garnett, David. *Aspects of Love*. New York: Harcourt, 1955.
Holroyd, Michael. *Lytton Strachey: The New Biography*. New York: Farrar, 1994.
Kaplan, Morris B. *Sodom on the Thames: Sex, Love, and Scandal in Wilde Times*. Ithaca: Cornell University Press, 2005.
Kennedy, Maev. 'Vita Sackville-West's Erotic Verse to Her Lover Emerges from "Intoxicating Night"'. *Guardian* 29 Apr. 2013. Web. 22 Apr. 2015. <http://www.theguardian.com/books/2013/apr/29/sackville-west-lost-poem-lover-trefusis>.
Kenner, Hugh. *A Sinking Island: The Modern English Writers*. Baltimore: Johns Hopkins University Press, 1989.
Knights, Sarah. *Bloomsbury's Outsider: A Life of David Garnett*. London: Bloomsbury, 2015.
Lee, Hermione. *Virginia Woolf*. London: Chatto, 1996.
MacCarthy, Mary Warre Cornish. *A Nineteenth-Century Childhood*. 1924. London: Constable, 1985.
Mackrell, Judith. 'Niall Ferguson Should Know That JM Keynes's Marriage Was Happy – With Plenty of Sex'. *Guardian* 6 May 2013. Web. 22 Apr. 2015.
Marler, Regina. *Bloomsbury Pie: The Making of the Bloomsbury Boom*. New York: Holt, 1996.
Nicholson, Virginia. *Among the Bohemians: Experiments in Living, 1900–1939*. New York: Morrow-HarperCollins, 2002.
Nicolson, Nigel. *Portrait of a Marriage. Vita Sackville-West and Harold Nicolson*. 1973. Chicago: University of Chicago Press, 1998.

Partridge, Frances. *Memories*. London: Clark, 1982.
—. *Other People: Diaries 1963–1966*. Vol. 4. London: Flamingo, 1993.
Person, Ethel S. 'Love Triangles'. The Atlantic.com. Atlantic Monthly Group. Feb. 1988. Web. 22 Apr. 2015.
Phillips, Adam. *Monogamy*. New York: Random House, 1997.
Russell, Bertrand. *Marriage and Morals*. 1929. London: Routledge, 2009.
Sedgwick, Eve Kosofsky. *Between Men: English Literature and Male Homosocial Desire*. Ithaca: Cornell University Press, 1985.
Shone, Richard. *Bloomsbury Portraits*. Oxford: Phaidon, 1976.
Spalding, Frances. *Duncan Grant: A Biography*. London: Chatto, 1997.
Strachey, Lytton. *The Letters of Lytton Strachey*. Ed. Paul Levy. New York: Farrar, 2005.
Woolf, Virginia. *The Diary of Virginia Woolf*. Vol. 3. Ed. Anne Olivier Bell. New York: Harcourt, 1980.
—. *The Letters of Virginia Woolf*. Vol. 1. Ed. Nigel Nicolson and Joanne Trautmann. New York: Harcourt, 1975.
—. 'A Sketch of the Past'. *Moments of Being*. Ed. Jeanne Schulkind. New York: Harcourt, 1985.

Duncan Grant and Charleston's Queer Arcadia

Darren Clarke

Tucked behind the front cover of the guidebook to Charleston is not a family tree but a relationship tree – a chart linking the key members of the Bloomsbury Group to each other and to their significant others, with various coloured lines indicating the different kinds of relationship. At the centre of this network are Vanessa Bell and Duncan Grant. Their names are in vibrant green ink to signify that they are original members of the Bloomsbury Group. The names of parents, children and partners who are not members of this informal group of friends are printed in black. Around some of the couples are pale green lines indicating a legally recognised heterosexual marriage. Red lines link children to their parents. Yellow lines indicate heterosexual love affairs, dark blue lines indicate homosexual relationships and lavender lines are for just good friends. Duncan Grant appears at the root of a trident of dark blue lines that connect him with his cousin Lytton Strachey, with Vanessa Bell's brother Adrian Stephen, and with John Maynard Keynes, all original members of the Bloomsbury Group, and another line to David 'Bunny' Garnett. It is a chart that seeks to rationalise emotion, to categorise love, lust and queerness.

What might it mean to say that Charleston, the rural Sussex home of artists Vanessa Bell and Duncan Grant for fifty years, is a *queer* place? Does the fact that homosexual relationships were once as welcome there as straight ones queer a place forever? Or the fact that a gay artist lived and worked there most of his life? George Chauncey has argued that the queerness of a place is transient, that it does not become an integral part of a building and its architecture. It is only queer activity in the present tense that makes a space queer. Charleston challenges that notion, as the queer seems to have permeated this place in a very permanent way. Today, Charleston is like a stage set for queerness, waiting for the drama to be re-enacted, but it is difficult to look back and find specific acts, difficult to pin down the scenes. They were fleeting and secret, leaving little or no trace. Duncan Grant's bedroom, for example, a constant throughout the artists' time in the house and the room he shared with his lover David Garnett during the First War, is seemingly heteronormatised within the current narrative of the space: visitors are told it is the place where Vanessa Bell gave birth to her and Grant's child. Evidence of homosexual acts and queer attitudes at Charleston must be sought in other forms. Acts and emotions are memorialised in letters, diaries and documents, words on paper that leave no impression on the space itself. But Charleston's queerness is physically and visually preserved, as well, for Grant often used his art to re-imagine Charleston as a queer, homo-edenic place, to code queer representations in the permanence of paint. Grant created a visionary rural idyll in Sussex that was an arcadia of sexual dissidence and homosexual society, a utopian, private space, free from external interventions.

Queer Beginnings

Bloomsbury's tenancy at Charleston is rooted in queerness. Vanessa Bell took the lease in 1916, at the height of the First World War, to provide a home for Grant and his then lover David Garnett, or 'Bunny', while they worked on a nearby farm to avoid military conscription. It was then not only the home of a *ménage à trois* that included a same-sex couple, but a home for pacifism and conscientious objection, attitudes that deviated from the general feeling of national pride and belief in authority and traditional masculinity – attitudes being queered by politically motivated and nationally sanctioned jingoism, as Mark Hussey shows in this volume (pp. 240–57). This philosophical deviance from normative social and political beliefs was mirrored in the personal and domestic situation of the inhabitants, as well as in their interior designs for Charleston and in their artwork, particularly that of Grant.

A full-time home for the remaining years of the Great War, Charleston became a part-time country residence in the 1920s and '30s when the artists, freed from state intervention, could resume their metropolitan and European lives. With the advent of the Second World War, Charleston once again became the artists' primary home. After the war there were bolt-holes in London, rooms or small flats taken for their convenience and economy, but Charleston maintained its status as home. Vanessa Bell died at Charleston in 1961; Duncan Grant continued to live there until 1978, when he died while staying with his friend Paul Roche. The two artists are buried next to each other in the churchyard of the neighbouring village of Firle.

Figure 1. Charleston. Courtesy of the Charleston Trust. © Penelope Fewster

The outside of the former farmhouse at Charleston barely hints at its interior (Figure 1). The solid rendered walls and steep, terracotta tiled roof, yellowed with lichen, present an orthodox and vernacular countenance. But the eye perceives small deviations from the norm. On the gateposts that flank the entrance to the garden from the lane are large, double-handled urns designed by Vanessa Bell's son Quentin in 1952. Their distinctive, asymmetrical and uneven shape announces to the discerning visitor that this is an off-kilter place. Glimpses of sculptures – plaster heads along the eastern wall of the walled garden, a life-size cement figure with a bucket of terracotta apples securely balanced on her head at the end of the path, a leaning figure on the far side of the pond and a 'levitating lady' at its north side – provide further evidence that something unusual has been going on.

Once through the pink and grey painted solid front door, all suspicions are confirmed. Painted under the window in the study on the right of the hallway are long, thin-stemmed flowers floating in glass tumblers and rummers; the fireplace is decorated with circles, crosses and lines in vibrant colours; the yellow and green walls are hung with paintings and drawings; an eclectic collection of furniture and textiles fills the room. The dining room on the left of the hallway has black painted walls decorated with diamonds and chevrons, and a round, highly decorated painted table in the centre of the room is surrounded by simple but elegant red dining chairs designed by Roger Fry to be sold at the Omega Workshops in 1913. And so this aesthetic continues, room after room.

The house does not shout; it is not emphatic, it is not macho. It welcomes visitors, seduces them and calms them while simultaneously stimulating the senses, vision taking the lead, with touch and smell not far behind. Truth in the physical world, in the décor of the rooms in which life was played out, was important to Bloomsbury, echoing the moral, philosophical and intellectual experiments made by the group. Christopher Reed describes Charleston as 'a provocative early model of coalition across the lines of gender and sexual orientation' ('A Room' 160). There is no master bedroom at Charleston, for example; constructions of patriarchy are irrelevant. Rather, Bell and Grant made decisions about the designs, décor and furnishings with the aim of encouraging comfort, relaxed intimacy and playful creativity in each room.

Charleston was a space that could accommodate alternative desires alongside alternative formations of domesticity, though never without the risk of unbalancing the scales. There were unwritten conditions regarding who was welcome at Charleston and who was not, for instance. A dance of manners, a choreography of etiquette prevailed. The 'buggers' of Old Bloomsbury – Lytton Strachey, E. M. Forster, John Maynard Keynes – were almost always welcome, as were the ingratiating next generation, including Raymond Mortimer, Angus Davidson and Peter Morris. But there were threats to this innovative domestic 'coalition'. Grant's love for the American artist George Bergen led to a crisis for Bell in 1930. Grant was hoping to restructure his domesticity to include Bergen, mirroring the triangular relationship established during 1916, but both Bell and Bergen were unwilling or unable to adapt. In the post-war period of the 1940s and '50s, Paul Roche, who would remain Grant's friend and companion until the end of the artist's life, was excluded from Charleston, forcing him to resort to camping on the South Downs when visiting Grant in Sussex.

For sixty years the house was a hub of creative activity, but it remained a private place. Other Bloomsbury residences and interiors designed by Bell and Grant appeared in glossy magazines and books as examples of modern living, providing a legitimate alternative aesthetic to an emerging International Modernism. Charleston often appeared as the setting or subject for paintings, but was rarely named.

A Home for Creating Public Art and Private Lives

Charleston first appeared in the media in a 1964 *Sunday Telegraph* article written to coincide with an exhibition at London's Wildenstein Gallery called 'Duncan Grant and His Circle'. A large number of early works were exhibited for the first time – experiments in abstraction and collage, colour and form made half a century before. The show was a great success. Many fine examples of Grant's work now in public collections were first seen at this exhibition, which coincided with a renewed interest in the work of Grant and his contemporaries, a movement that had fallen out of fashion in the post-war period but was being 'discovered' by a new generation of artists and historians interested in the beginnings of British modernism. The illustrated article, titled 'A Past That Lingers', marks something drawing to a close, coming to an end, both a life and a place. It depicts the seventy-nine-year-old artist as Charleston's sole inhabitant who 'lives alone, looked after by housekeeper and gardener' (Wallis 20). But the brief *résumé* of his life and career that accompanies the few illustrations omits a key defining aspect of Grant's life: his homosexuality. This situation was about to change. In 1967, the year the Sexual Offences Act decriminalised homosexual acts between men over the age of twenty-one in England and Wales, Michael Holroyd published the first volume of his biography of Lytton Strachey. This ground-breaking work placed homosexuality at the centre of the narrative, demonstrating how queerness had greatly influenced all the members of the Bloomsbury Group. The private lives and sexual relationships of the 'buggers' of Bloomsbury were exposed, making way for a flood of biographies, volumes of letters, diaries and analysis of the group.[1]

Charleston has both benefited from and played its own part in this retelling. The house, saved for the nation by the Charleston Trust after Grant's death, is now a public space – a heritage site that welcomes visitors to see the formerly private rooms and to hear the former residents' private histories. Charleston has achieved a kind of queer permanence as a museum, held in trust, restored and conserved. Charleston is a lone survivor, a past that lingers and the only complete example of a Bloomsbury home and interior. This permanence was predicted by Quentin Bell in a short play that he wrote and performed in as part of his birthday celebrations at Charleston on 30 August 1936. In *A Hundred Years After or Ladies and Gentlemen*, Quentin Bell, wearing his mother's dress and fur coat, played an American tourist named Miss Helena B. Conker visiting Charleston museum in 2036. 'She' is taken on a tour of the house by a guide played by Christopher Strachey. The members of the audience were employed to play various pieces of furniture; for example, Clive Bell was an eighteenth-century chair, Virginia Woolf a tall writing desk and John Maynard Keynes a safe. Employing Lytton Strachey's queer, knowing take on biography and historical reputation, the twenty-six-year-old Bell predicted the interest there would be in his Bloomsbury elders and the misinformation that would prevail. Thus, Lydia Lopokova was described as a 'soviet parachutist' and Virginia Woolf became Virginia Sackville-West, wife of 'Sir Clive Bell the famous sportsman and wit' (Q. Bell, 'A Hundred'; Spalding, *Vanessa* 267–8).

The longevity of Charleston and of Bell and Grant's tenure there was also anticipated by Virginia Woolf, who wrote to her sister in September 1916, 'I'm sure if you get Charleston, you'll end up buying it forever. If you lived there, you could make it absolutely divine' (*Letters* 2: 119). But while divinity was achieved, eternity was often in question. Its survival as a Bloomsbury house has not always been assured. After Grant's death in 1978, Bloomsbury's presence was in jeopardy. Before the Charleston Trust was formed, plans had been made to strip out the decorative elements, the painted doors and fireplaces, deposit them in a museum and to modernise the house. As early as 1923, the land agent from whom Bell had rented Charleston wanted the house back. Bell began looking for another home for her extended family with the possibility of a Georgian house for sale in Essex. This was sold before she had time to view it but the thought of permanence appealed to Bell. She wrote to Grant: 'I was tempted by the thought of having a permanent house which one could do as one like to & I think we must take steps to look for something' (Letter to D. Grant, Apr. 1928). Thankfully, a long lease was negotiated and Bell and Grant could stay, doing as they liked to the building and the grounds.

In the spring of 1918, Grant began work on a painting that would memorialise relationships at Charleston during wartime. Titled *Interior*, it is set in the dining room, the heart of communal domesticity.[2] Here, the room does not yet have the distinctive black walls of later years, but the greyish paint of Bell's first decorative endeavours. On either side of the picture are Grant's two lovers. Vanessa Bell sits on the window seat to the left of the composition, painting a still life, her canvas propped against the back of a chair. To the right, equally intent on his labours, David Garnett leans over a white sheet of paper, his pen poised over the surface. Grant, unseen but seeing, is present as observer between the other two corners of the relationship triangle. All three are engaged in creative acts, confined by the walls and large expanse of ceiling surrounding them. While Grant's omnipotence depicts productive equilibrium and domestic harmony in the painting, the reality was an ever-shifting and continually unbalanced scale as the trio asserted and accommodated their own and their partner's feelings and emotions. By 1918 this *ménage à trois* with Grant at the centre, shared like wartime rations by Bell and Garnett, had existed for three years.

The public face of the trio that this painting projects, one of professionalism and industry, masks the more intimate, private pictures of the same period. Grant drew and painted Bell naked, he drew her bathing while pregnant; he drew and painted Garnett naked, he drew him shaving. Ablutions in the company of another heralds a new stage in a relationship. The daily process of cleaning becomes ceremonial, charged with resonance, when it is performed, observed and recorded. Bathing is central to several life-changing events in Grant's life. Vanessa Bell wrote to Roger Fry (her current lover) in 1911,

> what do you think happened? I had my bath in his [Grant's] presence! You see he wanted to shave and I wanted to have my bath ... and he didn't see why he should move and I didn't see why I should remain dirty ... I felt no embarrassment and I think perhaps it was a useful precedent. (Bell, *Selected* 112)

Grant too had bathed in a lover's presence in commencement of their sexual relationship – Maynard Keynes, in his case. Grant relayed the story to Paul Roche in 1973. It was, as he remembered, the first time that he and Keynes had properly talked and been together after a chance meeting in a pub near Victoria Station:

> I went back with him to his flat – he was living in Victoria Street. I was very dirty and he asked me if I'd like to have a bath.... He continued his conversation with me, on the edge of the bath. (Roche, *With Duncan* 8)

This demonstration of intimacy is characteristic of Bloomsbury's blending of the sensual with the everyday habits of living.

Despite the calm concentration portrayed in *Interior* and the new intimacies performed in private, reality was sometimes painted a different hue. If the artists' early years at Charleston were a 'model of coalition', it was one forged in a furnace of jealousy and intense physical hardship. Rationed food and demanding physical labour amplified the inherent cracks in the relationships. Charleston was a pressure pot; its physical isolation, the enforced labour of conscientious objection and Grant's jealousy of Garnett's affairs with women all added to the chances of explosion. The end of the war and the birth of Grant and Bell's daughter diffused much of the domestic tension; Garnett's departure in the spring of 1919 dispelled far more.

Painting Domesticity Queer; Queering Domesticity in Paint

Garnett was only one of the long-term serious lovers Grant attempted to incorporate into the *ménage* at Charleston. Simon Watney has written of Grant that 'Throughout his long life he was periodically attracted by and was vulnerable to heterosexual and bisexual Narcissists including David Garnett, George Bergen, and others, and he suffered considerable anguish as a result' ('Duncan' 6–7). George Bergen was born in Minsk in 1903, his family later emigrating to America. By the late 1920s Bergen was in London pursuing his career as an artist. Grant met him at the end of 1929 and the two soon became lovers. The relationship echoed Grant's with Garnett, including the threat to his domestic and professional relationship with Bell. For eighteen months Bergen was at the centre of Grant's life, and once again Charleston became the theatre for negotiations, advancements and retreats. In February 1930 Bell retreated to London from Charleston to allow Grant and Bergen to negotiate the parameters of their relationship. If Grant was hoping to engineer a domestic threesome, he was unsuccessful, but the intensity of the relationship with Bergen eventually waned and equilibrium was restored.

In the years following the Second World War another of Grant's narcissists, Paul Roche, would find himself exiled to the Downs when visiting Grant in Sussex. Grant met Roche while crossing Piccadilly Circus one July afternoon in 1946. Roche almost immediately became the artist's model, muse, friend and lover. Like David Garnett, Roche was predominantly heterosexual and would later marry and start a family, but the bond between the two men dominated the latter part of Grant's life and he would die in Roche's home in 1978.

Roche is a fascinating figure, difficult to pin down, a self-confessed risk taker. He was dressed in a sailor's uniform when Grant met him, but later admitted to being a Catholic priest. He had been ordained in 1943 and was serving as a curate at St Mary's, Cadogan Gardens, London. He was also almost thirty years old, not the teenage youth that Grant took him for. Even his name was difficult to pin down, as he preferred to be called 'Don' rather than 'Paul'. Maybe it was this kind of subterfuge and play-acting, of dressing up and imagining, that Grant found exciting and that instilled mistrust in Bell. Roche recollected that Bell

> never said 'oh, I hope Don will come visit us at Charleston', she never said anything like that … I thought I better keep out of the way, that's the one thing I thought, so that's when I went to live on the hills behind Charleston when Duncan and Vanessa were there together. (Roche, personal interview)

Roche would sleep on the Downs, catching and cooking rabbits, he and Grant communicating clandestinely by leaving notes in hollow trees for each other.

In contrast, Grant and Roche's life in London was one of domestic intimacy. Grant had found Roche a first-floor front room at 1 Taviton Street, Bloomsbury, in the flat of Grant's cousin Margery Strachey, into which he later also moved. The street is adjacent to Gordon Square, near number 46, the house that Bell had moved her siblings to in 1904. In the late 1940s and early '50s Taviton Street became a focus of creativity. Grant repeatedly, obsessively, drew, photographed and painted Roche in his room.

In a sequence of paintings, Grant attempted to resolve and unite the two seemingly opposing worlds of life in Sussex with Bell and his life with Roche in London by altering the architecture of Charleston to include the architecture of Taviton Street. Pictorially, Grant opened up the front of Charleston, knocking through the wall and inserting the tall, glazed doors and wrought iron railings familiar to him and Roche in London. When one of these paintings came up for auction in 2004 it was titled *The French Windows*, the catalogue stating that it was a 'composite view' of Charleston elements, but the painting actually shows a composite view of Charleston and London. The painting was first exhibited in 1954, when it was signed and dated by the artist. This was also the year that Paul Roche left for America with his new wife and their first child. It is therefore a painting representing loss, but Grant has left this door open for Roche, a portal between Charleston and the outside world, the New World. But even here Bell's presence remains on the threshold, the constant figure in Grant's life. She is at home; her hat lies on the table. It would not be until after her death in 1961 that Paul Roche and his family would return to England and Roche would be free to visit Charleston.

This merging of London and Charleston highlights the division of town and country. The pleasures of male sexual intimacy were brought down from London like coffee, which was bought from the Algerian Coffee Stores in Old Compton Street. Unlike the countryside, the metropolis offered different social circles of homosexual and persuadable heterosexual men. Grant's conquests were legendary; the exclamation that 'Duncan's gone criminal again' has been recorded (Turnbaugh, *Duncan* 67). It was the recounting of his complicated affairs over dinner at Charleston (in Grant's absence) that gave Vanessa Bell her first smile after the death of her eldest son Julian in July 1937 (Spalding, *Vanessa* 284). In later life Grant recalled some of his early sexual encounters in London; one was as a teenager in front of Bronzino's *An Allegory with Venus and Cupid* in the National Gallery, where he was approached by a man who 'rubbed his hand against my penis'. Further encounters occurred 'in various places', including 'among the crowd of people listening to the sermons in Hyde Park. Here people stood so close to each other that it was easy to have contact without being seen' (Grant, qtd. in Spalding, *Duncan* 28).

Homo-Edenic Bathing and Charleston's Pond

As well as museums, open air swimming places provided opportunities to look at bodies and to meet men. The Serpentine in Hyde Park was a well-known location for male bathing and the setting for one of Grant's first artistic successes, *Bathing*, which shows seven male figures in various acts of diving into the water, swimming and climbing into a boat (Figure 2).

Originally titled *Bathers in the Serpentine*, the large decorative panel was part of a group commission in 1911 for the dining room of the Borough Polytechnic. The public spectacle of bathing in the Serpentine allowed for different perspectives and interpretations. The 1911 Baedeker tourist guide

Figure 2. Duncan Grant, *Bathing*, 1911, oil on canvas, © Tate, London 2015

for London describes a scene of 'men and boys, most of them in very homely attire', whom the visitor could see 'undressing and plunging into the waters, where their lusty shouts and hearty laughter testify their enjoyment', while John Addington Symonds' memoirs reveal a queer eye questing for more than just spectacle: 'I would rise from a sleepless bed, walk across the park, and feed my eyes on the naked men and boys bathing in the Serpentine. The homeliest of them would have satisfied me' (qtd. in Cook 35–8).

The Times considered that Grant had 'used all his remarkable powers of draughtsmanship to represent the act of swimming rather than any individual swimmer' ('Wall'), an effect Simon Watney states was the artist's intention (*Art* 31). But this interpretation denies the image its expression of the joy of a same-sex society, the 'lusty shouts and hearty laughter'. To telescope the seven figures into one helps heteronormatise the gaze, allowing the viewer to be untroubled by the sight of naked male bodies together in pleasure.

Bathers and bathing would continue to be a theme in Grant's work, and the pond at Charleston would serve as a background for his imaginary all-male societies of bathers, transposed from London to Sussex. The pond played an important role in both Bell's and Grant's visual culture and folklore; it acts as a reservoir of memory and narrative. It is repeatedly recorded in the artists' work, in their paintings and designs, charting the artists' developing pictorial styles and depicting different ideas of family and community. The pond was the location for celebrations, for play, for theatricals, for alchemy and for quiet contemplation. It is written about in letters and diaries. It was a space for exploration and presentation of gender, queerness and displays of familial existence, a place for shifting narratives and self-revelations. Grant was responsible for many interventions and temporary displays of queer dissidence at and in the pond – some accidental, many imagined. For him, it was a space of possibility for artistic distortion, subversion and re-imagining, as in his 1917 plan to keep flamingos on the pond, or the time he set fire to its surface after knocking over a bucket of petrol during the annual fireworks display celebrating Quentin Bell's birthday.

The pond was the setting for Grant's 1923 painting *The Hammock*, now in the Laing Art Gallery, Newcastle-upon-Tyne. *Vogue* magazine described it as 'Miraculously rich in colour and highly original in design, it deserves the most affectionate study' ('Duncan Grant'). The painting has Vanessa Bell at the centre of the composition, lying in the eponymous hammock surrounded by her two sons and daughter. In the foreground is the boys' tutor, Sebastian Sprott. As with the earlier painting *Interior*, Grant is present as observer, viewing apparently another idealised version of Bloomsbury domesticity. It suggests an edenic world with Bell at the heart. But as Christopher Reed has noted, Charleston was 'a secular, somewhat awkward Eden' (*Bloomsbury*

Rooms 192). Sebastian Sprott was the lover of Keynes, considered by Bloomsbury, for a while, to be married to the economist. Keynes was engaged to the Russian ballet dancer Lydia Lopokova and for a while it seemed he had plans for a Bloomsbury *ménage*, but she persuaded him otherwise (Mackrell 202–4).

In 1921, while he was preparing this coded vision of the familial Eden, Grant was also producing two sexually charged paintings of bathers by the pond that exclude the familial, celebrating instead the alternative and the inverted, and presenting a society of freedom: *Two Bathers* and *Bathers by the Pond*. For these, he used a more muted palette than other paintings of the period such as *The Hammock*, a palette suggestive of the haze of a sultry summer's day, a fantastic, dreamlike environment removed from the everyday: a kind of Arcadia.

The two young men of *Two Bathers* have finished their swim and are resting on the edge of the pond.[3] The geography of the pond, the intersection of water and land, gives licence to physical pleasure and experience. The emerging of the body from clothed to naked, the submerging of the body from dry to wet. The figure on the left faces away from the viewer, drying his back with a towel in a pose drawn directly from Renoir. While this figure appears oblivious to the viewer, the prone body on the right catches one's eye. Stretched out horizontally across the canvas, a naked youth lies on his back and stares out of the picture frame. Richard Shone suggests that it is 'a more chaste and cooler vision' than Grant's other bathing painting (202), but I would propose that the reclining figure cannot be viewed as chaste. He looks out from the scene at the viewer, his head upside down. He is inverting physical space, inverting social protocol, opening up a space for behaviour outside of the socially acceptable. He can be read as the son of Adam from Grant's highly criticised 1914 painting *Adam and Eve*. The painting, destroyed in the 1920s, showed Adam on the left standing 'on his hands with his body and legs, knotted and gnarled and twisted like an old oak tree, sticking up in the air' next to Eve, who was described by an unnamed reviewer in the *Observer* as 'suffering from elephantiasis on her right side' ('Art'). Bell explicitly compared Grant's inversions and distortions to queer sex:

> Of course your Adam and Eve is a good deal objected to, simply on account of the distortion and Adam's standing on his head […] I believe distortion is like Sodomy. People are simply blindly prejudiced against it because they think it abnormal. (*Selected* 154)

There is a queerness to the artist's vision, as some critics at the time perceived.

In *Bathers by the Pond*, six men, naked or wearing bathing trunks, relax in and around a pond (Figure 3). The languid attitudes of the bathers have their

Figure 3. Duncan Grant, *Bathers by the Pond*, 1920–21, oil on canvas, Pallant House Gallery, Chichester. © 2015 DACS, London.

antecedents in Cézanne's *Bathers at Rest*, which Grant would have had the opportunity to study at the 1910 exhibition 'Manet and the Post-Impressionists' at the Grafton Gallery. Grant's painting echoes the central recumbent figure lying across the front of the composition, but here the facial characteristics and small moustache are similar to Keynes's, possibly a playful reference to his affair with Grant.

The painting could be an illustration of Vanessa Bell's imagining of life in Sussex when she is away, as in the lengthy description of homosexual activity she includes in a letter to Keynes in 1914:

> Did you have a pleasant afternoon buggering one or more of the young men we left for you? It must have been delicious out on the downs in the afternoon sun ... I imagine you ... with your bare limbs entwined with him and all the ecstatic preliminaries of Sucking Sodomy – it sounds like the name of a station. (*Selected* 163)

The naturalising and normalising of 'sodomy' and homosexuality by Bell, placing it in the sunshine, in the Sussex countryside, as an activity to occupy a 'pleasant afternoon' like going for a walk or having a cup of tea, is reflected in the figures in Grant's painting with their relaxed, uninhibited and almost mundane society.

While freedoms existed within the safety of the Bloomsbury Group, caution was exercised with the outside world. Neither of the bathing paintings was exhibited publicly at the time of its production. As an artist, Grant had licence to record his desires, to make them public as long as they remained framed by an art historical discourse that sublimated any homoerotic interest or attraction. But as Christopher Reed observes, despite being 'authorized as art by Grant's elegant evocation of Seurat's poses and pointillist style', *Bathers by the Pond* was 'still too risky for Grant to exhibit during his lifetime' (*Art and Homosexuality* 135). It remained in Grant's possession until very late in his life, when it was given to Paul Roche, and was not exhibited publicly until 1975. *Two Bathers* went straight into the collection of John Maynard Keynes and was not exhibited until 1983.

However, another group of painted naked young men bathing became public in 1933. *The Bathers* shows nine naked men in and around the pond

Figure 4. Duncan Grant, *Study for The Bathers*, c.1920–21, gouache on paper, courtesy of the Charleston Trust. © 2015 DACS, London

at Charleston.[4] At the centre of the composition are two men wrestling, the athletic sporting act legitimising the other figures and the viewer's gaze, like the sculpture of athletes in the British Museum. The painting was challenging for Grant and took seven years to complete. A second version of the painting remained in Grant's possession and there are numerous support studies (Figure 4).

Robert Medley, who modelled for the painting with his boyfriend, the ballet dancer Rupert Doone, described a two-way process between artist and model in which the roles were fluid and interchangeable: 'we used to draw Rupert and then Duncan would draw Rupert and I, and then I would draw Rupert and we all ended up by drawing each other' (Medley 39). John Rowdon observed Grant's working method when he was preparing the painting, describing how he moved the cut-out elements of the composition, taking 'a leg off by cutting it out, and then one side of a face, and so on. It is with these limbs on cut-out pieces of paper that he builds up the final painting' (28). Using cut-outs and acting as both model and artist, Grant enacted a choreographed collage of figures and space.

Queer Icons in the Garden and Queer Erotica under the Bed

In 1948, these painted male figures became solid (temporarily) when Grant placed a statue of Antinous, the drowned lover of the Roman Emperor Hadrian, on the eastern edge of the pond. It was one of a group of plaster casts that Grant had purchased from Lewes School of Art when it closed in 1931. These he placed all around the garden at Charleston; they included 'the Hermes of Praxiteles, the Venus de Medici, the dying gladiator, all in plaster, pitted by the rain and sometimes so much worn away that one might find a cavity big enough to house a thrush and its brood' (Bell and Nicholson 147). Quentin Bell described how the 'life-size Antinous, wandered from place to place, from the middle of the orchard to the side of the pond' (Q. Bell, 'Charleston Garden' 100). The site became one of gradual loss and decay, however, as the plaster torso weathered away until 'for some time the legs of Antinous stood without any body to support' (100). The drowned Antonius eventually dissolved into the pond, the plaster hero conquered by rain and wind, echoing his corporal body's fate.

Possibly these plaster figures reminded Grant of encounters in the British Museum. Matt Cook explains that the statue galleries were 'a place where it was legitimate to look at sculptures of naked men: they were associated with an Hellenic ethos of self-realisation and control rather than "modern" urban debauchery' (33). Here 'a middle-aged gentleman' once engaged the young

Grant in conversation as the artist was copying the sculpture *Discobulus*. This heralded the beginning of a short-lived sexual affair (Spalding, *Duncan* 31).

Antinous is a queer icon. Bell reflected on this fact when she wrote of Grant's plans for the statue:

> I think it would be lovely but will make us almost too peculiar. However, I suppose that doesn't matter. Our black dining room is surprisingly successful with the natives, who are full of admiration, and so perhaps Antinous reflected in the pond would appeal to them too. (*Selected* 516)

Sarah Waters has charted Antinous' importance to the late nineteenth-century self-identified homosexual culture. Thomas Waugh describes the ubiquitous image of the 'homo statuary postcard genre, from Antinous to David, well represented in every pre-Stonewall collection I have examined' (36). Grant's collection was no exception and Antinous' presence was felt inside Charleston too. Grant owned a small, broken plaster sculpture of the *Capitoline Antinous*, the original found in Hadrian's villa in Tivoli. Its fragile fractured body dances on the thin wire armatures that support its torso. It stands on the desk in Grant's bedroom, next to the window that looks out across the pond. There are also two early twentieth-century photographs of statues of Hadrian's beloved in the collection – classical pin-ups.

Like many homosexuals of the time, Grant sought out images of men that the queer imagination could own and interpret as homoerotic. He accumulated nineteenth-century photographic studies that echoed classical compositions and societies, for instance, and he took the British naturist magazine *Health and Efficiency*. His friend and former lover Maynard Keynes made reference to the German sport magazine *Sportszeitung* as a source of homoerotic imagery, and photographs of boxers in the national newspaper the *Daily Mirror* gave Lytton Strachey *frissons* of excitement. After the Second World War, the artist procured a number of physical culture magazines, many sent by Paul Roche when he was working in America in the 1950s, but also similar British publications. Genital nudity was banned, the models wearing posing pouches or swimwear in full-frontal poses, though often naked in poses where the genitals were obscured. Douglas Blair Turnbaugh describes how Grant 'had some amusement in "restoring" male genitals. He liked to paint penises and testicles on photographs, over the cache-sex of otherwise nude models' (*Private* 16). Grant's painted genitals both covered and removed the model's textile fig leaf, a 'regenitalisation'.

The magazines were also a source of inspiration for a large but concealed body of work. Seams of erotic art representative of the tensions between public persona and private thoughts and feelings lay in out-of-the-way places.

Turnbaugh describes a large collection of erotic drawings in a "'mouse-chewed and ratty'" cardboard box under Grant's bed in his 1970s London flat (Reed, 'Only Collect' 73) and a big envelope of drawings marked 'PRIVATE' (Turnbaugh, *Private* 9). Grant gave an earlier collection to his friend and fellow artist Edward le Bas for safekeeping.

Grant always drew on whatever material came to hand – the backs of letters, on envelopes, in the endpapers of books – but there is something more spontaneous in his erotic drawings, something clandestinely made and secretly circulated which makes visible that which was forbidden. Christopher Reed regards the often 'furtive and hasty production' of Grant's hidden pictures,

Figure 5. Duncan Grant, *Erotic Study*, c.1950, pen and gouache on paper, courtesy of the Charleston Trust. © 2015 DACS, London

frequently executed 'in ballpoint pen on scraps of paper', as 'undercut[ting]' the 'fanciful erotica' that 'At Grant's best' combine 'sexual exuberance with dancing lines and splashes of colour' (Reed, *Art and Homosexuality* 135). The edges of the paper are often ragged and uneven, ripped in haste; couples are entwined, legs and arms folded over each other – a fragmenting, doubling and serialising of body parts. These couples are painted onto pages from magazines, the text appearing through the lighter areas of paint, the paint coming through the reverse of the page, displacing the original textual intention of the support (Figure 5).

These rapidly executed drawings and gouaches are partly informed by photographs, partly taken from life, partly sheer imagination. One of Grant's erotic drawing sessions is recorded in a story 'passed from hand to hand': written down by Francis King in his autobiography, told to him by his partner David, who had posed with a black friend for Grant at Charleston, where 'they were soon invited to strip off and to glue themselves together in increasingly provocative embraces' (King 265–6). On the couple's next visit Grant played the role of seducer and encouraged the models to enact scenes of light sado-masochism while he 'was sketching frenziedly' (266). Once again Grant positioned himself as both agent and voyeur, both inside and outside of these images. A small selection of these erotic images became public in 1989, when Turnbaugh published *Private*. Turnbaugh recalled the amusement and disbelief Grant expressed when he had told the artist fifteen years earlier that one day his secret erotic art would be made public (Reed, 'Only Collect' 74).

∆   ∆   ∆

Duncan Grant lived until 1978, and so had a glimpse of the public freedoms to come. He lived to see the decriminalisation of male homosexuality in 1967 – a partial reversal of the Criminal Law Amendment Act, better known as the Labouchère Amendment that had criminalised all male homosexual sex, which had been introduced in 1885, six months before Grant was born. In the late 1960s he met a new generation of young, openly gay men who would take the private freedoms that Grant and Bloomsbury had advocated into the public arena. Simon Watney, then a student at Sussex University, became a regular visitor to Charleston in the late 1960s and early 1970s, and took Grant to Gay Liberation Front meetings in Brighton. Grant's new friends found at Charleston a model forged in the past that could be cast for the future, not only in the environment that the artists had created, but in the negotiated freedoms within their relationships, this time to be played out on a public stage.

Notes

1. Reactions to these publications are charted by Regina Marler in *Bloomsbury Pie*.
2. Duncan Grant, *Interior*, 1918, oil on canvas, Ulster Museum, Belfast.
3. Duncan Grant, *Two Bathers*, 1921, oil on canvas, King's College, Cambridge.
4. Duncan Grant, *The Bathers*, c.1926–33, oil on paper on plywood, National Gallery of Victoria, Melbourne, Australia.

Works Cited

'Art and Artists: The Grafton Group.' Rev. of the Grafton Group's Second Exhibition at the Alpine Club Gallery. *Observer* 11 Jan. 1914: 7.

Bell, Quentin. 'Charleston Garden: A Memory of a Childhood'. *Charleston: Past and Present*. Ed. Quentin Bell, et al. London: Hogarth, 1987. 84–103.

—. 'A Hundred Years After or Ladies and Gentlemen'. MS. British Library. London.

Bell, Quentin, and Virginia Nicholson. *Charleston: A Bloomsbury House and Garden*. London: Lincoln, 1997.

Bell, Vanessa. Letter to Duncan Grant. Apr. 1928. MS. Tate Gallery Archive. London.

—. *Selected Letters of Vanessa Bell*. Ed. Regina Marler. Berkeley: Moyer Bell, 1998.

Chauncey, George. *Gay New York: The Making of the Gay Male World*. London: Flamingo, 1995.

Cook, Matt. *London and the Culture of Homosexuality*. Cambridge: Cambridge University Press, 2003.

'Duncan Grant at the Independent Gallery'. *Vogue* June 1923: 56.

Hussey, Mark. 'Clive Bell, "a fathead and a voluptuary": Conscientious Objection and British Masculinity'. *Queer Bloomsbury*. Ed. Brenda Helt and Madelyn Detloff. Edinburgh: Edinburgh University Press, 2016. 240–57.

King, Francis. *Yesterday Came Suddenly*. London: Constable, 1993.

Mackrell, Judith. *Bloomsbury Ballerina*. London: Phoenix, 2009.

Marler, Regina. *Bloomsbury Pie: The Making of the Bloomsbury Boom*. London: Virago, 1997.

Medley, Robert. Interview by Andrew Lambirth. *National Life Stories: Artists' Lives*. Tape and transcript. 1994. C466/19/02 F4109 Side A. British Library. London.

Reed, Christopher. *Art and Homosexuality: A History of Ideas*. Oxford: Oxford University Press, 2011.

—. *Bloomsbury Rooms: Modernism, Subculture and Domesticity*. New Haven: Yale University Press, 2004.

—. 'Only Collect: Bloomsbury Art in North America'. *A Room of Their Own: The Bloomsbury Artists in American Collections*. Ed. Nancy E. Green and Christopher Reed. Ithaca: Cornell University, 2008. 58–87.

—. '"A Room of One's Own": The Bloomsbury Group's Creation of a Modernist Domesticity'. *Not at Home: The Suppression of Domesticity in Modern Art and Architecture*. London: Thames and Hudson, 1996. 147–60.

Roche, Paul. Personal interview. 30 Aug. 2007. Disc 4. Firle [Charleston]: Charleston Trust Oral History Archive.
—. *With Duncan Grant in Southern Turkey*. London: Honeyglen, 1982.
Rowdon, John. *Revaluations*. London: Marks, 1934.
Shone, Richard. *The Art of Bloomsbury*. London: Tate, 1999.
Spalding, Frances. *Duncan Grant: A Biography*. London: Pimlico, 1998.
—. *Vanessa Bell*. Stroud: Tempus, 2006.
Turnbaugh, Douglas Blair. *Duncan Grant and the Bloomsbury Group*. London: Bloomsbury, 1987.
—. *Private: The Erotic Art of Duncan Grant 1885–1978*. London: Gay Men's Press, 1989.
'Wall Paintings: Interesting Experiment at the Borough Polytechnic'. *The Times* 19 Sept. 1911: 9.
Wallis, Nevile. 'A Past That Lingers'. *Sunday Telegraph Magazine* 20 Nov. 1964.
Waters, Sarah. '"The Most Famous Fairy in History": Antinous and Homosexual Fantasy'. *Journal of the History of Sexuality* 6.2 (1995): 194–230.
Watney, Simon. *The Art of Duncan Grant*. London: Murray, 1990.
—. 'Duncan Grant and Queer Bloomsbury'. *Canvas: News from Charleston* 14 (2005): 1–7.
Waugh, Thomas. *Hard to Imagine: Gay Male Eroticism in Photography and Film from Their Beginnings to Stonewall*. New York: Columbia University Press, 1996.
Woolf, Virginia. *The Letters of Virginia Woolf*. Ed. Nigel Nicolson and Joanne Trautmann. 6 vols. 1975–80. Vol. 2. New York: Harcourt, 1976.

Nailed: Lytton Strachey's Jesus Camp

Todd Avery

> [S]ome brothers may think it queer that I of all people should want to be religious. Such a thought would be an empty thought and a fallacy in perception; for, don't you see? the great beauty of the new religion is that it admits of so much that is varied, and ridiculous, and strange.
>
> Lytton Strachey (1903, *Unpublished Works* 73)

In the spring of 1913, Pius X lay ill in Rome and an English traveller there sent home a letter suggesting an improbable successor. 'The Pope is dying', he wrote. 'Shall I apply for the post? Then you could come and stay with me at the Vatican' (Holroyd, *Critical* 2: 87). The author of this letter was Lytton Strachey, who possessed few of the necessary qualifications for the priesthood and, if possible, even less interest in the Pionine motto, 'Restore all things in Christ'. In the event, his claim to the Papal Tiara was marginally weaker than that of Giacomo della Chiesa, elected Benedict XV in September the following year. Would he really have wanted the Hat anyway? The standard critical view of Strachey's attitude toward religion is that, as Michael Holroyd writes,

> established religion was a farrago of fantastic superstitions.... At best, religious belief was inspired nonsense; at worst, dangerous, cruel and seductive humbug.... Theological motives and spiritual struggles ... held no reality for him, and he reduced them to a series of comically futile gymnastics in the void. (*Critical* 2: 279)

Strachey certainly harboured no deep sympathy for conventional religiosity. He thought the metaphysical business of religion ridiculous, its moral business pernicious, an 'atrocious fog of superstition that hangs over us and compresses our breathing and poisons our lives' (Strachey, *Letters* 594). He also saw little to celebrate in organised Christianity's production of that noxious cloud of superstition that for nearly 2,000 years had poisoned basic, inevitable, multifarious, pleasurable and enthralling human sexual desires and practices with suspicion, fear and contempt. Given these facts, the case of Religion v. Lytton Strachey seems to close with a resounding finality: guilty as charged.

But is it true that Lytton Strachey did not admit the reality, if not of theological truth, then at least of spiritual struggles? His religious subjects – his eminent Victorians and many others – may have been absurd gymnasts, but notwithstanding his own claim to be 'neither a saint nor an acrobat' (Strachey, *Letters* 647), did Strachey really possess no feeling for religion? Was he truly incapable of understanding others' religious beliefs? Was religion merely, for him, an opportunity for ridicule? Critical consensus, a type of appearance, can deceive. The reality of Strachey's engagement with religion was more complex than it seems. Notwithstanding his reflexive hostility to religion, he hardly ignored it. Strachey understood how religious beliefs had helped to shape the world that he inhabited; he studied those beliefs; and however much he may have wished that fog of superstition to have evaporated in the sun of rationality, he believed that the legitimation of alternative sexualities and the achievement of a new sexual ethic demanded a serious critique of an abiding Christian moralism. In a word, religious discourse was for Strachey very much alive, and the lingering vitality of Christian moralism offered him a multifaceted opportunity. This was an opportunity for sharp social and ethical critique. But Christian discourse and iconography also offered the opportunity for ethical self-work, and for a richly symbolic self-transformation, at a time in his life when he was increasingly adamant that he and his work 'do some good to the world ... make people happier' (Strachey, *Letters* 594). And it was an opportunity of a very queer sort. Strachey's aestheticism was a queer aestheticism, which emerged from repeated engagements with Christian moralism and, near the end of his life, found expression in a conceptually complex and manifestly queer act of *imitatio Christi*.

What was the precise nature of these engagements? And what was so queer about them? From a parodic sermon that is the earliest of his known Cambridge University papers, to the sado-masochistic crucifixion experiments that he engaged in with his last romantic partner in the early 1930s, Strachey demonstrates a steady interest in Christianity and, more importantly, in spiritual questions that he shared with many of his aestheticist and decadent forebears and modernist contemporaries. Like so many aesthetes and decadents before him, Strachey was no mere iconoclast: he was a serious ethical thinker who wished to do good in the world at least as much as to ridicule religiously inspired moral intolerance. The imagining of what he called the 'new world' of sexual liberty demanded a critique of Christian moralism, and across his range of works and activities, Strachey queers Christianity in the service of an ethical ideal of friendship and intimacy unfettered by moral convention.

What I mean by Strachey's queering of Christianity is that his engagement with religious themes and iconography challenges moral norms, and even the idea of moral normalcy, while opening a discursive and practical space for the pursuit of alternative ethical positions and sexual desires. Also, his efforts to open this space and to legitimise conventionally denigrated sexual practices and alternative notions of community rest in part on a critique of Christian moralism. It is not exclusively in his engagements with religion that Strachey develops a queer sexual ethics. But these engagements were crucial to his ethical thinking, whose specific character cannot be understood apart from them. Strachey's attitude toward religion is queer in a critical sense because it challenges the very idea of theological, moral or sexual normalcy. His attitude is queer in a more constructive or creative sense, too; religious language offers him a vehicle for imagining an alternative ethic of intimacy and community based not on conformity to moral rules but, as he puts it in one of his early essays, on a recognition of 'the true values of things' – and specifically of things 'varied, and ridiculous, and strange' (Strachey, *Unpublished* 72–3). For Strachey, moral rules fail to acknowledge such worth, because they cannot abide the complexities of lived experience. By contrast, he celebrated both in his writings and in his life the varied and strange.

Strachey's sexual ethic was grounded in his assumption of the supreme value of friendship – what he called, simply, 'the love of man', as opposed to 'the love of God' (*Unpublished* 72). The seeds of this ethic were planted in Strachey's late adolescence, when he first read Gibbon and Plato. They grew at Edwardian Cambridge when, as a member of the Apostles and other discussion groups, he 'began to interrogate accepted religious ideas, to question the Victorian morality which had been so central in his youth, and to explore new approaches to sexuality and to art'. This was also when he began to 'demand … far more openness of discussion on questions about sexuality.… The papers he read to the Apostles allowed him to question many accepted religious, moral, and sexual ideas and values' (Caine 134). Had he lived centuries earlier, Strachey writes in his Apostles essay 'Godfrey, Cornbury, or Candide?' (1912), his sense of vocation may have led him to

> live for the glory of God! If one could find eternal crowns hereafter, and reconciliations and fulfilments in the bosom of Christ! But that sort of thing is no longer done. Crowns are no longer worn, and heaven is out of fashion. (*Really* 68)

Heaven may indeed have been out of fashion in the early twentieth century, but the language of heaven, and of the spirit more generally, captivated Lytton Strachey's imagination. In an irony befitting one of British modernism's most fluent ironists, he found a vehicle in this language for an ethically generous alternativity.

At the *fin-de-siècle* and in the first years of the twentieth century, Strachey began crafting the 'perverse' ethic that, by fostering a new sense of the spiritual possibilities of intimate relations, 'cuts', as Michael Warner puts it, 'against every form of hierarchy you could bring into the room' and thus represents a fundamental 'premise of the special kind of sociability that holds queer culture together' (35). This ethic was devoted to 'sexual autonomy', which requires

> making room for new freedoms, new experiences, new pleasures, new identities, new bodies…. Variation in this way is a precondition of autonomy – as much as it is also the outcome of autonomy. Pleasures once imaginable only with disgust, if at all, become the material out of which individuals and groups elaborate themselves. (Warner 12)

In later years, Strachey's enduring commitment both to exposing religious prejudice and to publicly affirming an alternative set of spiritual values would find expression in his biographies, essays and short fiction, and, not least, in doing the very thing that was no longer done – namely, adopting the persona of Christ as a way of experiencing physical ecstasy and, through it, a profound self-transformation that he understood in religious terms.

Robert Caserio locates Strachey among those modernists who were 'inspired' by 'the progressive political potential of queer sexuality' – where 'queer' is understood as a way of thinking that 'questions common assumptions about human sexuality, especially if that is thought to be definitively anchored in social, historical, legal, or medical "certainty"' (201). Furthermore, Caserio's description of the ideological force exerted during the early twentieth century by same-sex challenges to dominant assumptions about human sexuality may be read as a gloss on Virginia Woolf's famous recollection of 'the long sinister figure of Mr. Lytton Strachey [standing] on the threshold' at 46 Gordon Square and effecting a 'sacred' 'advance in civilisation' by uttering the single word, 'Semen?' (195–6). For, much like Strachey in a doorway of the hotbed of cultural and sexual unconventionality that was Bloomsbury, 'Homosexuality as we know it arrives at the centre of modernism's revolutionary challenge to cultural repertories' (Caserio 203). Again, as with the lean Mephistophilean figure in the doorway, the sinister instigator of semengate, 'homosexuality shows itself' at this time as 'a queer force, an ally in a wilful derangement of established order' (203). And finally, where

Woolf attributes the impetus behind the revision of 'many customs and beliefs' among the Bloomsberries either directly or indirectly to Strachey's outrageous question, Caserio sees the arrival of homosexuality and of 'queer' sexualities in general on the threshold of modernism as representing a 'challenge … so comprehensive that modernism seeks to break with religion, nationality, and the state' (203).

Almost a decade before appearing so sinisterly in the doorway at Gordon Square, the adolescent Strachey substantially broke with religion and adopted a 'strong anti-Christian bias' (Holroyd, *Critical* 1: 70). At that time, he discovered a new religion in Plato's *Symposium* – or rather, he found a philosophy of male friendship and love and an ethic that legitimised and sustained his increasingly conscious and open homosexuality. A few years later, Strachey would, as Leonard Woolf thought, 'corrupt … Cambridge just as Socrates corrupted Athens … for it seems to have completely broken out into open sodomy' (qtd. in Taddeo 32). The New Style of Love inspired by Plato represented, in Alexandra Peat's terms, an opportunity to think spiritually 'larger than the self' (2). The Edwardian Apostles' eager embrace of physically active same-sexuality and of the more intellectualised version that they called the 'Higher Sodomy' also went hand-in-hand with a fervent rejection of organised religion – even while they continued to operate within a society whose rituals and argot parodied it. Their inspiration for a new and more tolerant civilisation came from Plato, who painted them what Clive Bell calls an 'exquisite picture … of an exquisite way of life' (94). Or, as Strachey saucily told Leonard Woolf, 'I have … an obsession for Paganism – but I prefer it (thank you) Greek' (*Letters* 5).

Writing of Strachey's hostility toward the religiosity and moralism of the late-Victorian society in which he grew up, Julie Anne Taddeo mentions that the 'revolt against bourgeois Christianity is the theme of several of Strachey's essays delivered before the [Apostles or Conversazione] Society' (157n17). It is more accurate to say that the driving purpose of many of the papers that Strachey read during his Cambridge years not only to the Apostles but also to the Midnight Society and the Sunday Essay Society was to articulate what Leonard Woolf calls a 'revolt against a social system and code of conduct and morality which, for convenience sake, may be referred to as bourgeois Victorianism…. [W]e were struggling against a religious and moral code of cant and hypocrisy' (152). Strachey does this in the essays that Taddeo specifies – 'Is Death Desirable?' (1903) and 'Will It Come Right in the End?' (1908) – and in a dozen or so essays, dialogues and stories, some of them only recently published, that address Christianity from a variety of perspectives. The constant topic of these early works is Christian moralism; their dominant theme is how Christian moralism had over the centuries defined proper and improper desires and impeded the fulfilment of the latter, both in the realm of aesthetics and in that of sexuality. Strachey sums up his point of view with an understatement in his 1905 Apostles essay 'Shall We Take the Pledge?': 'the peculiarly Christian standpoint is never mine' (*Really* 131).

Strachey's impassioned defence of lasciviousness in art and life in 'Will It Come Right in the End?' embodies a profound sense of reverence toward innate, convention-perplexing – in a word, 'queer' – desires. He argues that to 'give copulation a fair chance' means to

> conjure up a whole world of strange excitements ... one must imagine the shock and the pressure of bodies, and realize the revelation of an alien mind, one must find oneself familiar with miracles and, assuming an amazing triumph, swim in glory through a palpitating universe of heavenly and unimaginable lust. (*Really* 79–80)

To give copulation a fair chance means not just vulgarly 'to allow the whole world to fuck and bugger and abuse themselves in public and generally misbehave to their hearts' content', but, ultimately, and more spiritually, to 'dwell among new braveries and fascinations, to come smiling into surprising paradises, and to experience serenely God knows how many extraordinary loves' (80–1). To do this is to achieve the 'miracle' of 'heaven'.

In such essays as 'Shall We Take the Pledge?' and 'Will It Come Right in the End?' Strachey's rhapsodic sexual and ethical anarchism and his celebration of other bodies and 'alien minds' recalls the aestheticist tradition. In particular, it gestures to the central statement of art for art's sake in British aestheticism, Walter Pater's conclusion to *The Renaissance* (1873), which figures as ethical reprobation the failure fully to cultivate one's attentiveness to and reverence for other people. 'Not to discriminate every moment', Pater writes, either the 'tragic parting of forces' in 'the face of a friend' or 'some passionate attitude in those about us ... is, on this short day of frost and sun, to sleep before evening' (237). In its ethical emphasis, Pater's conclusion also represents a preface to Strachey's own notorious preface to *Eminent Victorians*, which asserts aesthetically that in the writing of biography the 'value' of individual human beings 'must be felt for its own sake' (4). Strachey's refusal, like Leonard Woolf's, 'to accept or swallow anything or anyone on the mere "authority" of anyone' also echoes Pater's antinomian argument regarding the invalidity of uninvited social or moral convention:

> The theory or idea or system which requires of us the sacrifice of any part of [our] experience, in consideration of some interest into which we cannot enter, or some abstract theory which we have not identified with ourselves, or of what is only conventional, has no real claim upon us. (237–8)

Just as Strachey's insistence on the intrinsic value of individual human beings echoes Pater's on the ethical importance of attending to the faces of others, so too Pater's rejection of convention as an ethical guide finds an echo in Strachey's prefatory defence of the biographer's 'freedom of spirit' (4).

In his Cambridge society papers, Strachey's persistent critique of Christian moralism possesses a deadly serious intent. Its purpose is to open an ethical space within which to cultivate, naturally and freely, a mode or style of life in accord with his sexual inclinations and preferences – and thus to model for others the ethical and social legitimacy of conventionally denigrated sexual practices. Strachey desired 'to do some good to the world – to make people happier' (*Letters* 594). He hoped 'to go into the wilderness, or the world, and preach an infinitude of sermons on one text – Embrace one another! It seems to me the grand solution' (*Letters* 74–5). He encouraged Leonard Woolf, 'Let us forgo … our Crucifixions, we shall be content with a few more hours of quiet laughter and happy affection, of kisses, and remembrances, and human warmth' (*Letters* 99). All such ambitions affirm his desire to deliver a 'New Age' that would have forgotten 'the word "unnatural," which is the root of all evil, muddling and tomfoolery' (*Letters* 44). They also set the dawning freedoms of the New Age against the stifling repressions of religiously informed moral convention.

But if the intention is serious, the strategy is seldom solemn. To be sure, when the occasion demanded, Strachey understood the importance of being earnest. This is shown in his appearance before the Hampstead Tribunal in 1916. Not in his response to the question about what he would do if he saw a German soldier trying to rape his sister – 'I should try to come between them' – which is as arch as arch can be. But in the statement spelling out his reasons for conscientious objection, explicitly on ethical and not religious grounds (*Really* xiii). More often than not, however, and almost always when he is writing of Christianity, even when Strachey's intention is earnest his rhetorical strategy is imbued with the spirit of camp – with what Susan Sontag calls 'the exaggeration of … personality mannerisms'; 'the theatricalization of experience'; a being 'serious about the frivolous, frivolous about the serious' (279, 286, 288). The ultimate purpose of camp, Sontag argues, is to work as 'a solvent of morality', and as such to create new sensibilities that 'relish, rather than judge, the little triumphs and awkward intensities of "character"' (290, 291). To translate Sontag's formulation into Stracheyan terms, the final purpose of camp is to relish the triumphs and intensities of individual human beings, who, for all their littlenesses and awkwardnesses, nevertheless possess intrinsic and inalienable value. Camp, far from being merely a matter of style, possesses a genuine, if often playfully expressed, ethical dimension. 'The whole point of camp', Sontag writes, 'is to dethrone the serious' (288).

But in its manner of expressing 'a kind of love, love for human nature', this dethroning possesses a serious intent (291). Its deeply ethical 'love for human nature' is a love that refuses to be bound by conventional standards of taste or morality.

Strachey carefully honed this style over the course of thirty years. As George Piggford writes in his discussion of Bloomsbury's 'camp sites', this style embodies the 'Bloomsbury camp sensibility that has been labelled "Stracheyism"' (65). For Piggford, who focuses on Strachey's, E. M. Forster's, and other Bloomsberries' biographical writings, the aim of Stracheyism is 'to inscribe queer sexualities into [Bloomsbury's various] biographical texts' (71). In addition, Piggford argues, Strachey employs a camp style to show that 'the moral laws of any period are illusory and subject to critique, ridicule and revision' (73). To expand Piggford's observation – Strachey deployed a camp style to expose the historical constructedness and cultural relativity of all moral standards; to critique those standards which claim transcendent or eternal justification; and, in terms borrowed from Gilles Deleuze, to replace their implicit oppositions of values with new modes of aesthetic and ethical existence (Deleuze 73–4).

Barry Spurr identifies the purpose of Strachey's prose style as the 'indirect presentation' of 'subversive ideas', and 'especially his radical views on religion and sexuality' (34). In the 1930s, Cyril Connolly had listed Strachey among the most notorious practitioners of the elevated, ceremonious, highly aesthetic 'Mandarin' style (46–7). Riffing on Connolly, Spurr dubs it 'Camp Mandarin' – 'it is Mandarin in drag … in which Strachey impersonates its mannerisms and humorously exaggerates its gestures, even as he reveals a residual affection for them' (35). Strachey withholds affection from dominant religious beliefs and sexual standards. At the same time he enjoys the artistic productions that express them and the rhetorical strategies that subvert them – the soaring pillars and gorgeous stained-glass windows of Chartres, the 'elegant cadences' and the 'order and balance' of Gibbonian prose (Spurr 32). He does this in the interest of articulating 'conclusions that are markedly heterodox' on religion and sexuality (34).

Never was there a more unlikely priest than Lytton Strachey. Yet for at least one brief moment at Cambridge, he imagined himself into precisely that vocation. In May 1900, shortly after entering Cambridge, Strachey delivered the mock 'Sermon Preached before the Midnight Society'. His performance reveals both a fascination with religious discourse and his early fluency in the camp style that he would continue to use with such devastating effect. His subject is the 'doubt and hesitation' of the present age, an age 'of struggle, of confusion, of infidelity', in which 'the nations of the earth are disturbed by new doctrines and dangerous knowledge' (*Unpublished* 5).

Addressing himself to 'my brethren', and more particularly to any 'one – one lost sheep (Matthew 10:6) who has strayed, if even for a moment, from the safety of the fold', Strachey brings 'words bearing with them a message of encouragement and hope' at a time when

> more than ever do we feel the stress of ... spiritual battle, now when the whole world has been deluded and snared by foul depths of idolatry and superstition, or cankered and corrupted by the false glamour of what has been called the gospel of science. (*Unpublished* 5)

The world holds many snares, for

> The world is strong – they say – those deluding voices – the world is powerful, the world is great; the world with its empires, and its palaces, and its pomp; the world with its dazzling streams of riches, its fleets laden with precious merchandise, its mighty armies trampling with horse and foot, its towering mountains, its great rivers, and the enormous sea. (6)

The world also ensnares with its 'stores of knowledge and wisdom'; and it ensnares with its beauty, crying, 'Enjoy the world and all the beauty that you find there; the poets, the painters, the forests and the flowers, the breath of the west wind, and the calm blue of the middle sea' (6–7). To these temptations, the young Father Lytton – 'The Strache', as his friends called him, in ecclesiastical drag – opposes 'the divine teaching of the gospel' and 'the unerring guidance of the Holy Ghost'; 'the golden harps, the white robes, and the shining pavement of the City of God'; and 'God, whose transcendent wisdom has conceived the mystery of the Trinity, the crowning proof of the superhuman mind' (7). The final snare, which inspires the preacher to invoke the Synoptic Gospels' command 'Get thee behind me, Satan!' and which inspires his most fervent expression of belief, is that of sensual pleasure and human intimacy: 'Rejoice in wine, in friends and laughter, and the human warmth of love' (7). To avoid this snare, one need only possess 'The love of God, which, as has been so justly said, passeth all understanding. That love for which all else must be given up, more sacred than the ties of friendship or of home – transcendent in its mystery' (7).

The combination of immorality and religiosity is one of the defining characteristics of Bloomsbury. In one of the central self-mythologising texts of Bloomsbury, John Maynard Keynes looked back on his Apostolic days from a distance of more than thirty years and recalled the ethos which had been inspired by G. E. Moore and remained, well into the 1930s, 'nearer the truth than any other that I know' (91). Keynes is speaking here of Moore's 'religion', by which he means a particular 'attitude towards oneself and the ultimate' (86). Even more than his ethics – by which Keynes means 'one's attitude towards the outside world and the intermediate' – it was this aspect of Moore's thinking that, according to Keynes, attracted these young men (86). What Moore's core beliefs in the supreme value of the appreciation of beauty and of the pleasure of human intercourse, in all its many forms, offered them, Keynes writes in an excited sentence, 'was the extreme opposite of what Strachey used to call *funeste* [fatal, funereal]; it was exciting, exhilarating, the beginning of a renaissance, the opening of a new heaven on a new earth, we were the forerunners of a new dispensation' (85).

As an expression of heightened emotion or exquisite pleasure, there is nothing unusual about divine ejaculation – Oh, God! – or plain cussing: Jesus Christ! But is Keynes's use of a religious vocabulary here merely rhetorical convention, or, what amounts to the same thing, just the heightened expression of his longstanding and vital conviction as to the value of Moore's thinking? 'It is still my religion under the surface', Keynes writes in 1938 (91). Lest there be any doubt about his opinion as to the relative merits of Mooreism and Christianity, he adds the *coup de grâce*, 'The New Testament is a handbook for politicians compared with the unworldliness of Moore's chapter on "The Ideal"' (92). The young proto-Bloomsberries, Keynes thinks – religious zealots of a sort – had 'remained … altogether immune from the virus, as safe in the citadel of our ultimate faith as the Pope of Rome in his' (94).

At the time that Keynes is remembering, Strachey had envisioned himself and his Cambridge friends in terms more rhapsodic, hyperbolic and, for good measure, more absurdly narcissistic than Keynes's. But he captures much of the same spirit of ecclesiastical exhilaration and speaks to a shared set of aesthetic and ethical concerns. 'I sometimes feel', he writes to Leonard Woolf in late 1904:

> as if it were not only ourselves who are concerned but that the destinies of the whole world are somehow involved in ours. WE are – oh! in more ways than one – like the Athenians of the Periclean Age. We are the mysterious priests of a new and amazing civilisation…. What is hidden from us? We have mastered all. We have abolished religion, we have founded ethics, we have established philosophy, we have sown our strange illuminations in every province of thought, we have conquered art, we have liberated love. (*Letters* 32)

Also at this time, the mysteriously priestly but plainly horny Strachey appears to have had some trouble deciding whether 'a physical feeling in my abdomen' was evidence of 'merely lust' or 'spiritual affection' (*Letters* 31).

Keynes and Strachey use religious language partly for the purpose of expressive intensification. They also use it as a way of giving shape to their emotional, intellectual and sexual experiences. So much so that notwithstanding their patent atheism, their vigorous commitment to rationality, their general unorthodoxy in social, intellectual, moral and spiritual matters, the question arises as to how seriously their use of religious language might be taken as evidence not only of their efforts to craft a new, alternative spiritual vision but also of a lingering religiosity – evidence of a residual emotional attachment to a tradition that had helped to shape their identities but which they nevertheless genuinely derided as noxious and from which they strove to break. Keynes sees the Mooreism of his generation of Apostles as a religious belief, while also asserting, 'We repudiated entirely customary morals, conventions and traditional wisdom. We were, that is to say, in the strict sense of the term, immoralists.... [W]e recognised no moral obligation on us, no inner sanction, to conform or obey' (94). Strachey shared this view, along with all of Bloomsbury. But while disregarding Christian moralism, at the same time Strachey retained a certain interest in the figure of Christ himself.

Notwithstanding a short-lived plan in the late 1920s to write a biography of Jesus, Strachey found him less continually absorbing a figure than did many of his aestheticist and decadent predecessors (Holroyd, *New* 564). But, then, Strachey's subjects were individual human beings and, as for Jesus, 'Oh, I put him on one side as inhuman' (Strachey, *Letters* 2). Given his aestheticist adherence to the alternative religion of Mooreism which Strachey understood in part as a justification of alternative sexualities, another question emerges: is it possible that Strachey's very immoralism – his queering of conventional morality in the domain of sexuality – possesses a spiritual impetus? More precisely, how does Strachey's performative engagement late in his life with religious iconography both mock the fundamental theological assumption of the divinity of Christ upon which Christian moralism rests, and poach on that assumption toward the articulation of a queer ethics? In a letter from mid-1919, Strachey regales Carrington with some snippets of conversation from a party he had just attended and which he describes as 'the queerest affair you ever saw'. 'Somebody', he had overheard with relish, 'said Mr Strachey looked like Our Lord, but I said he looks like [the] Devil trying to look like Our Lord' (*Letters* 438). Which of these enduringly fascinating figures does Strachey ultimately more closely resemble? Is he really more Mephistophelian than Christ-like? Or can a case be made for the reverse? 'A devil?' as he asked of Voltaire – 'or perhaps an angel? One cannot be quite sure' (Strachey, 'Voltaire' 90). A few months later, he asked Ralph Partridge, 'By-the-bye, why is it that the relics of the holy are never of the more intimate regions of the body? Surely Christ's prick would be highly edifying, and the buttocks of

St John the Divine would attract many worshippers' (*Letters* 451). What is the relation between Strachey's gleefully naughty attitude toward the buttocks of the author of Revelation and the penis of the Son of Man, on the one hand, and his ethical immoralism, on the other?

Benjamin Jowett once remarked of Euripides, 'he is immoral when he is irreligious and when he is religious, he is more immoral still' (qtd. in Annan 72). Might the same be said of Lytton Strachey – with a twist: that when he is irreligious he is immoral, but when he is truly blasphemous he is the very image of ethical spirituality? The answers are to be found in an improbable but real image at a moment late in his life when, still looking like the Devil in Jesus drag, he swapped priestly simulation for divine impersonation. Lytton Strachey is hanging on a cross, wounded and erect. The crucifixion had come to tug thrillingly on his sexual, aesthetic and ethical sensibilities. The questions themselves emerge from a singular letter that Strachey wrote in the summer of 1930 to Roger Senhouse describing a night they'd just shared. 'My own dearest creature', Strachey begins:

> Such a very extraordinary night! The physical symptoms quite outweighed the mental and spiritual ones.... First there was the clearly defined pain of the cut ... and then the much vaguer after-pangs of crucifixion – curious stiffnesses moving about over my arms and torso – very odd – and at the same time so warm and comfortable – the circulation, I must presume, fairly humming – and vitality bulking large ... where it usually does – all through the night, so it seemed. But now these excitements have calmed down – the cut has quite healed up and only hurts when touched, and some faint numbnesses occasionally flit through my hands – voilà tout, just bringing to the memory some supreme high-lights of sensation.... What blessedness! The wretched thing was that the certitude of your affection, which had been quite solid in me for years, began (about three or four months ago) to weaken and waver – with sad results. The anchor had lost hold, and I was drifting.
>
> Now that is entirely right again.... I had failed before to imagine with proper sympathy your states of mind, and my own had become out of tune in consequence. I hope things may improve.... With love on both sides all must be well really. To me, our relations have been among the greatest blessings of my life.
>
> You were a perfect angel last night. (*Letters* 625)

Strachey wrote this letter at a time when he wondered that the Victorians had found it 'necessary to take up the fight against Christianity all over again' (605); when, as his brother James said, he was going 'to write one more biography then "burn his boats" by declaring his homosexuality, and campaigning for sexual egalitarianism' (Holroyd, *New* 632); and above all when, he told Senhouse, he 'long[ed] to do some good to the world – to make people happier – to help to dissipate this atrocious fog of superstition that hangs over us and compresses our breathing and poisons our lives'. During the last two or three years of his life, Strachey embraced a spiritually inflected sense of social mission and identified with Judeo-Christian civilisation's iconic emblem of death and rebirth, rejuvenation and transformation, in a way that renders him a queer sort of Devil – one who was most queer at his most religious, and most ethical at his most blasphemously queer.

What precisely Lytton Strachey saw when he looked at the cross, it is impossible to know. It is pretty certain, though, that Jesus himself did not imagine the cross, forestalling his late-aestheticist imitator, as a vehicle for 'supreme high-lights of sensation'. Unlike Jesus, Strachey did not foresee his death – though, like His, it was soon in coming. Nor, unlike his eminent predecessor in crucifixion, does he appear to have harboured messianic pretensions; he certainly did not imagine himself as the Son of Man or the Son of God, the embodiment of divinity. But even though we do not know exactly what Strachey thought of the cross, he clearly saw it as a technology of eroticism, a sexual machine.

Despite the obvious and basic differences, the crucifixion of Jesus, as it is told and interpreted in the New Testament, and the crucifixion of Lytton Strachey, as read from an ethical perspective through the lens of queer theory, share some key characteristics. In the passion sections of the Gospels, Jesus, much like Socrates in the *Apology*, is described as a threat to religious orthodoxy, a 'perverter of the nation' (Luke 23:2, 9) and a 'blasphemer' (Mark 14:64; John 19:7). Leonard Woolf had compared Strachey to a Socratic perverter; and Strachey clearly held perverse and even blasphemous attitudes toward orthodox opinion. But the more significant connection between the crucified Jesus and Lytton Strachey on the cross is to be found in the Pauline gloss on the crucifixion. St Paul writes, in his Epistle to the Colossians, that through the crucifixion Jesus 'Blot[ted] out the handwriting of ordinances that was against us, which was contrary to us, and took it out of the way, nailing it to *his* cross' (Colossians 2:14, original emphasis). The crucifixion of Jesus is the sacrificial moment in which the Son of Man's death conquers death and makes eternal life available, demonstrating the full extent of His divine love toward humanity. The crucifixion is also the way that Jesus retrieves for fallen humanity, if only in a nebulous hereafter, the God-given capacity for joy and delight that Adam and Eve had possessed in the prelapsarian Garden of Eden. It is the event of martyrdom in which he becomes, as Paul writes in his Epistle to the Hebrews, 'the author and finisher of *our* faith; who for the joy that was set before him endured the cross, despising the shame' (Hebrews 12:2, original emphasis). And it is the event in which, according to Pauline theology (not all of the Gospels or early Christian theologians agree on this), Jesus cancels and supersedes the rules and doctrines of the Mosaic law, confirming the birth of a new law.

Whatever his psychological motivations may have been, Strachey's decision to engage in a sado-masochistic crucifixion to intensify pleasurable sensations bears a more general symbolic significance than just another effort to satisfy his idiosyncratic sexual tastes. When Strachey mounted his cross, revelling in the pleasure at least as much as enduring the pain, he experienced, as he testified, a redemptive blessedness in his relationship with Roger Senhouse. When he mounted his cross, he also discovered a way of translating into physical action his critical project of 'destroying authority by depicting it in [his] own terms', as the painter George Condo describes the purpose of his recent series of crucifixion images (qtd. in Tomkins 64). As a biographer, Strachey's intention and method was to re-imagine a life from a specific, generally ironic, point of view, while preserving his freedom of spirit (*Eminent* 4). So too here, the effect of his actions is freely to rewrite the central event in Christian mythology while rejuvenating – making 'entirely right again' – the 'blessedness' of love. Beyond the strictly personal redemption of this event, what better opportunity could there be for a broadly resonant and relevant symbolic inversion than that offered by the crucifix, what Oscar Wilde termed 'the world's most eternal symbol' (924)?

Paradoxically, however, in performing this act of symbolic inversion and perversion, Strachey is imitating Jesus – the spirit of the crucifixion – as much as he is mocking the central event in the story of Christian redemption from sin and shame. In mounting his cross, Strachey transforms, as Jesus had done, a tool of pain, shame and death into a technology of pleasure, joy and a richly intensified life. Strachey and Senhouse's queer use of this eternal symbol shows its semantic fluidity, its openness to resignification. The crucifixion of Lytton Strachey then appears as an opportunity for self-transcendence and self-refashioning – for a new life and a resurrected love – at a time when, if James Strachey is right, he was on the threshold of turning his attention away from biography and toward gay political activism. Thus, the cross was also for Strachey a site of self-transformation preceding broader social transformation – a camp site for not only mockery but also, and even more importantly, reverence. Camp mocks, but not meanly: it loves the thing it mocks.

Strachey's campy reverence is not for God, the idea of which he thought ridiculous. Nor is it for a man on a cross who, according to the popular view, saw himself as God. It is, rather, for a man on a cross who 'Blot[ted] out the handwriting of ordinances that was against us ... nailing it to *his* cross'. For

Strachey, crucifixion was an invitation to pleasure; it also signified an effort to transcend the moralism and heteronormativity found in 'the handwriting of ordinances that was against us' – in, to be more precise, Section 11 of the Criminal Law Amendment Act of 1885, the Labouchère Amendment – toward the articulation of a new sexual ethic that paradoxically retains a spiritual impetus that it shares with the event and the person in whose name so many adherents of that moralism and heteronormativity ground their opposition to sexual difference. One invariably gains by submitting oneself to the pain of sexy crucifixion some hard-won self-knowledge. The knowledge that Strachey gained, as his 'blessedness!' letter to Senhouse testifies, shows at least as explicitly as any of his writings his commitment to the pursuit and legitimation of modes of existence beyond the reach of shame, and which would supplant any calcified system of moral judgement, leaving it nailed to the cross on a blessed, euphoric, heavenly morning after.

As a spiritually inflected contribution to queer ethics – an act of sexually counternormative ascesis performed as religious rite – the crucifixion of Lytton Strachey represents the physical extension of his early critiques of Christian moralism in the interest of a new sexual ethic. In a portrait of Strachey, Clive Bell recalls that 'His attitude to life, and therefore his art, was based on a critical appreciation of the past, an interest in the present, and a sense of human possibilities – the amalgam bound together and tempered by a fine pervasive skepticism' (34). What Bell says of Strachey's attitude to life may be transposed with only slight modifications to a description of his attitude toward religion. He possessed a critical appreciation of various cultural productions of Christianity (without of course accepting any of its metaphysical assumptions as intellectually legitimate). As a man of twentieth-century tastes, he was also interested in the ways that, as he saw it, orthodox religious moralism poisoned modern lives, at the same time that he was open to the potential use of religious iconography for advancing a new vision of human relations and intimate possibilities – that is to say, a new ethical vision. And he preserved toward religion a skepticism whose thoroughness was equalled only by a fineness of sensibility that, as in his Apostles essay 'Should We Have Elected Conybeare?', discovered in a Christianity purged of its rules and superstitions a viable spiritual framework.

It is an old and critically convenient fiction to regard Lytton Strachey either as a simple scourge of religion or as someone who was fundamentally 'indifferent' to it (Rosenbaum, *Victorian* 256). What Strachey's letters and early papers reveal, though – and what his life embodies – is a much more complex state of affairs. For Strachey, a vigorous critical and performative engagement with religious discourse and iconography was a necessary first step in the marshalling of aesthetic and sexual energies toward the construction of a new, queer polity, 'a really beautiful and vigorous and charming civilization' with a 'new religion … that … admits of so much that is varied, and ridiculous, and strange' (*Unpublished* 73). He thought, felt and lived human relations outside of conventional religiosity and within a new one – in camp sites of queer blessedness.

Works Cited

Annan, Noel. *The Dons: Mentors, Eccentrics, and Geniuses*. Chicago: University of Chicago Press, 1999.
Bell, Clive. *Civilisation and Old Friends*. Chicago: University of Chicago Press, 1973.
Caine, Barbara. *Bombay to Bloomsbury: A Biography of the Strachey Family*. Oxford: Oxford University Press, 2005.
Caserio, Robert. 'Queer Modernism'. *Oxford Handbook of Modernisms*. Ed. Peter Brooker, Andrzej Gasiorek, Deborah Longworth and Andrew Thacker. Oxford: Oxford University Press, 2010. 199–217.
Connolly, Cyril. *Enemies of Promise*. New York: Persea, 1983.
Deleuze, Gilles. 'Ethics Without Morality'. *The Deleuze Reader*. Ed. Constantin V. Boundas. New York: Columbia University Press, 1993. 69–77.
Holroyd, Michael. *Lytton Strachey: A Critical Biography*. 2 vols. New York: Holt, 1967–68.
—. *Lytton Strachey: The New Biography*. London: Vintage, 1995.
Holy Bible. King James Version. N.p.: Zondervan, 2002.
Keynes, John Maynard. 'My Early Beliefs'. *The Bloomsbury Group: A Collection of Memoirs and Commentary*. Ed. S. P. Rosenbaum. Toronto: University of Toronto Press, 1995. 82–96.
Pater, Walter. *Studies in the History of the Renaissance*. 1873. Oxford: Oxford University Press, 2010.
Peat, Alexandra. *Travel and Modernist Literature: Sacred and Ethical Journeys*. New York: Routledge, 2011.
Piggford, George. 'Camp Sites: Forster and the Biographies of Queer Bloomsbury'. *Queer Forster*. Ed. Robert K. Martin and George Piggford. Chicago: University of Chicago Press, 1997. 89–112. Rpt. in *Queer Bloomsbury*. Ed. Brenda Helt and Madelyn Detloff. Edinburgh: Edinburgh University Press, 2016. 64–88.
Rosenbaum, S. P. *Victorian Bloomsbury: The Early Literary History of the Bloomsbury Group*. London: Palgrave, 1994.
Sontag, Susan. 'Notes on Camp'. *Partisan Review* (1964). Rpt. in *Against Interpretation and Other Essays*. New York: Anchor-Doubleday, 1990. 275–92.
Spurr, Barry. 'Camp Mandarin: The Prose Style of Lytton Strachey'. *English Literature in Transition* 33.1 (1990): 31–45.
Strachey, Lytton. *Eminent Victorians: The Definitive Edition*. Ed. Paul Levy. London: Continuum, 2002.
—. *The Letters of Lytton Strachey*. Ed. Paul Levy. New York: Viking Penguin, 2005.

—. *The Really Interesting Question and Other Papers*. Ed. Paul Levy. New York: Capricorn, 1974.

—. *Unpublished Works of Lytton Strachey: Early Papers*. Ed. Todd Avery. London: Pickering, 2011.

—. 'Voltaire and Frederick the Great'. *Biographical Essays*. London: Chatto, 1960. 80–105.

Taddeo, Julie Anne. *Lytton Strachey and the Search for Modern Sexual Identity: The Last Eminent Victorian*. Binghamton: Haworth Park, 2002.

Tomkins, Calvin. 'Portraits of Imaginary People: How George Condo Reclaimed Old Master Painting'. *New Yorker* 17 Jan. 2011: 56–65.

Warner, Michael. *The Trouble with Normal: Sex, Politics, and the Ethics of Queer Life*. Cambridge: Harvard University Press, 2000.

Wilde, Oscar. *De Profundis*. *Complete Works of Oscar Wilde*. Glasgow: HarperCollins, 2001. 873–957.

Woolf, Leonard. *Sowing: An Autobiography of the Years 1880–1904*. Orlando: Harcourt, 1975.

Woolf, Virginia. 'Old Bloomsbury'. *Moments of Being*. Ed. Jeanne Schulkind. 2nd ed. San Diego: Harcourt, 1985. 179–201.

'[T]here were so many things I wanted to do & didn't': The Queer Potential of Carrington's Life and Art

Gretchen Holbrook Gerzina

In the nearly thirty years since I wrote what remains the only full-length biography of the artist Dora Carrington, interest in her life and work has only increased. In 1994, Jane Hill published the somewhat controversial *Art of Dora Carrington*, then the next year curated the 1995 Barbican Art Gallery retrospective 'Carrington: The Exhibition', which brought together Carrington's paintings, crafts and home movies. More recently, Nancy Green and Christopher Reed curated the exhibition 'A Room of Their Own: The Bloomsbury Artists in American Collections', which travelled to six universities from 2008 to 2010 and revealed treasures held in private collections.[1] All of these displayed previously unknown or 'lost' works by Carrington.

Carrington has remained a source of inspiration for study and analysis by academic and other writers. She figures prominently in Anne Chisholm's *Frances Partridge: A Biography* (2009), and Chisholm is collecting and editing a new collection of Carrington's letters, including many previously unpublished and unknown to scholars. David Boyd Hancock's *A Crisis of Brilliance*, about the Slade artists Carrington, Mark Gertler, C. R. W. Nevinson, Paul Nash and Stanley Spencer, was published in 2009. In 2013, Nicholas Delbanco published *The Art of Youth: Crane, Carrington, Gershwin, and the Nature of First Acts*. Although much has been written about her before, in recent years new evidence and materials have come to light about Carrington's relationships with women. Emily Bingham has completed a biography of her great-aunt Henrietta Bingham, Carrington's only known female lover, and Chisholm has unearthed new letters to others – both make possible a more complex and nuanced understanding of Carrington's sexuality.

In light of these new discoveries, it is a propitious time to look again at Carrington's short life, and also to get a new perspective on the way it unfolded, breaking it down into several parts and seeing how each led to the next. Surely few women other than Virginia Woolf and Dora Carrington have had their very private sexual lives aired so publicly, and it seems peculiar to Bloomsbury studies that so many of them have been subjected to this sort of intimate analysis, even by their own family members and friends, let alone by scholars, admirers and filmmakers. However, it is also now possible to see how Carrington, like Woolf, fits into what Christopher Reed calls Bloomsbury as 'queer subculture', which he describes as 'linguistic high jinks [that] came to characterize Bloomsbury's epistolary style' (Reed 75). It involved humour, flirtation, self-deprecation, innuendo and irony as a way of expressing a countercultural ethos that did not always find expression in physical acts.

Early Life and the Slade School of Art

Carrington was born in Hereford on 29 March 1893, but was largely raised and educated in Bedford, although the family later moved to Hurstbourne Tarrant and then to Cheltenham. At first glance, she seems to have been part of a fairly conventional pre-war family, living a suburban life. Her father retired from service in India, and married a much younger, yet far more conventional woman. She raised their five children with an eye to what the neighbours might think of them, and with highly conservative values that did not even allow a married woman to be pronounced 'pregnant'. Her father, however, was a different story; quite deaf and suffering a stroke in 1908, he was adored by his second daughter (the first, Lottie, had left home to become a nurse), and sat for her patiently after her artistic talents became apparent. Carrington hated her mother, and while it is not known what her mother thought of this highly unconventional daughter, it is clear that both parents encouraged her interest in art, furnishing her with supplies and taking her to exhibitions. They also, like many middle-class Victorians, encouraged an active outdoor life of cycling, fishing and games. Whatever she rejected in her later life, she remained committed to the natural world, to cycling and riding, and to the drawing that her parents encouraged in place of the more common musical training, although she gave her mother little credit for these efforts.

Her talent for drawing was discovered by teachers in Bedford, where she won prizes in art, before heading off at seventeen to the Slade School in London. Because of her difficult relationship with her mother, she had already developed a tendency toward secrecy that would continue throughout her short life. Her brother Noel, closest to her in age, noted that 'keeping secrets from one's parents was almost the ultimate sin. Even before she went to London Carrington's friendships and letter-writing became a source of disturbance, especially as she was incurably careless in leaving letters securely hidden' (*Letters*

503). Toward the end of her life she wrote to Augustus John's daughter Poppet, with whom she carried on a very flirtatious illustrated correspondence,

> I say miss what do you think I found in the Bath Room at Mallard Street on a shelf, open to the Public [picture of an eye]. A spider? No. A piece of soap? No. A letter from Carrington to Poppet? <u>Yes</u>. What can you say to <u>that</u>? (Letter to P. John, n.d.)

London and the Slade would completely change her world-view, and her view of herself. In some ways it is easy to see her life as a microcosm of what was changing in the English world, both in terms of social mores and, by extension, in the world of art. In these last years before the Great War, experimentation with gender norms grew, and the New Woman – that freethinking, independent, emancipated feminist who smoked and drank, had a career, and sexual liberation – exactly coincided with her early life. By the time she arrived in London and met other like-minded women, she was ready to lead them in cutting off her hair and putting her art at the forefront of her life. Shortly after her arrival, she encouraged her new friends Barbara Hiles and Dorothy Brett to follow suit. What she perhaps had not anticipated, however, was the way that men would fall in love with her, and apply nearly unrelenting pressure on her to reciprocate.

One of these was fellow Slade student C. R. W. Nevinson, known as Richard or 'Chips', whose parents were political activists who moved from the slums of Whitechapel, where they worked, to literary and artistic Hampstead. His mother Margaret was a suffragette and his father an often-absent journalist. 'Revolutionaries at heart', they could not have been more different from the Carringtons (Hancock 39). Noel Carrington believed that it was in her visits to the Nevinson household that his sister began to develop

> her later dislike for feminine weakness and for the restrictions which custom then imposed upon women.... It was almost certainly at the Nevinsons' house in Hampstead that she began to acquire the feeling that a woman's role in life must not be one of subservience. (Qtd. in Hancock 101)

While Nevinson, no doubt encouraged by her letters to him, dared to dream that she might be as in love with him as he was with her, his was one of a string of broken hearts she left behind, including that of the painter and Slade student Paul Nash.

The most persistent of these was the painter Mark Gertler, whose long and fraught love affair with her has been much written about – and continues to be. Gertler, a Jewish boy born in London but whose family moved back to Galicia for a time before returning, was an outsider at the Slade. Fiercely talented and stunningly good-looking, his persistent and even obsessional pursuit of Carrington succeeded for some time, but also ultimately succeeded in driving her away. His insistence on a sexual relationship was not unusual for a 'liberated' artistic young couple, but while she eventually relented, unhappily, the more he insisted and pressured her, the more secretive she became. They were an incredibly handsome couple, and her friend Nina Hamnett wrote the following to Nevinson in 1912:

> She had fair hair which was cut like an Italian page. She was one of the first women in England to cut off her hair and was very much stared at as she never wore a hat. I invited them both to tea and felt rather as if I had invited a god and goddess. Carrington appeared in one red shoe and one blue. We talked about Art and the future, and I preserved Gertler's tea-cup intact and unwashed on the mantelpiece. It remained there for about a month; I felt that it ought be given to a museum. (Qtd. in Hancock 112–13)

Indeed, throughout life her hair remained a visual synecdoche of what she appeared to promise: sexual freedom, artiness, inventiveness and a counter-cultural sensibility. Everyone who knew her described her bell of thick golden hair that she never changed once she cut it off in 1910.[2] All this seems to have suggested an openness to sex that she simply did not feel, either because of her upbringing, or much more simply because she did not have the sexual urge that Gertler possessed.

> Only I <u>cannot</u> love you as you want me to. You must know one could not do, what you ask, sexual intercourse, unless one does love a man's body. I have never felt any desire for that in my life ... I do love you, but not in the way you want. Once, you made love to me in your studio, you remember, many years ago now. One thing I can never forget, it made me inside feel ashamed, unclean. Can I help it? I wish to God I could. Do not think I rejoice in being sexless, and am happy over this. It gives me pain also. (*Letters* 17)

Apparently 'she had annoyed him by her "inability to really get interested"', according to David Garnett, who edited the published collection of her correspondence: 'Subsequent letters show that sexual relations with Gertler were, for Carrington, always a wretched failure' (Carrington, *Letters* 50). The problem was a lack of interest in the sexual act with a man, but it was also her unwillingness to let Gertler go. Whenever the relationship seemed to be coming to an inevitable end, she reeled him back.

It was Gertler who, through his increasing reputation as a painter, made friends in wider circles and introduced her to Lady Ottoline Morrell and her MP husband Philip at their country house, Garsington Manor. Mark's complaint to the Morrells that Carrington was unwilling to sleep with him ended with Carrington being harangued about her virginity by Philip, then later being 'seized' by Ottoline, who, she wrote to Lytton, 'talked for an hour and a half in the asparagrass [sic] bed, on the subject, far into the dark night' (*Letters* 33).

As is still true today, Carrington's attitudes toward sex turned out to be a subject for public discourse. If we put this into the context of a young woman, no matter how rebellious, who was raised in a Victorian family where 'any mention of sex or the common bodily functions was unthinkable' (*Letters* 504), and who left home as a teenager in 1910, it is easier to understand why she found it difficult to take a step that others found entirely natural. For Carrington, it appeared impossible to make the leap from freedom to desire and, *au fond*, she did not love Gertler. Love, however, changed the story: what Gertler did not know was that it was not to him that she had eventually surrendered her much-discussed virginity, but to someone no one ever imagined.

In 1915, Carrington and her friend Barbara Hiles spent a weekend at Virginia and Leonard Woolf's Sussex retreat, Asheham House, with a large group of guests: Barbara, Vanessa Bell, Duncan Grant, Lytton Strachey and Mary Hutchinson. The Woolfs were away, but even so this was Carrington's first extended introduction to Bloomsbury. An early riser and rather domestic, she went off for long walks over the Downs each morning, only to return to find the others still sleeping. Since the servants were away, she and Vanessa handled the cooking, and everyone took their meals in the kitchen. She wrote all this to Gertler but, true to her secretive nature, she did not tell him the whole truth about the walk she had taken with Lytton Strachey, a central Bloomsbury figure who, despite his ill-considered marriage proposal to Virginia years before, was attracted only to men. Yet something about the much younger Carrington, with her sturdy figure, bohemian clothing that sometimes included trousers, and short hair, attracted him. Quickly disabused of his initial perception of her as a boy, Strachey began to join her for long walks. One day he suddenly stopped and tried to hold and kiss her. She recounted this later in horror to Barbara, and plotted revenge. She slipped into his bedroom that night while he was sleeping, intending to cut off his beard. Instead, he opened his eyes, and she fell deeply, and permanently, in love.

Love, Three Ways

So much has been written about Strachey, and about the unlikeliness of this partnering, that it is worth taking a moment to understand why they did in fact make sense as a pair. There is no denying their obvious differences. He was a tall, lanky, flamboyant Cambridge student and long an insider with those who made up early Bloomsbury. Adrian Stephen, Clive Bell, Leonard Woolf, Maynard Keynes and Strachey had all been at university together, sharing membership in the 'secret' society of the Apostles. Duncan Grant was his cousin (and apparently the first one on whom he practised French kissing). They spent long evenings in the company of Virginia and Vanessa Stephen. They were all extremely well-read, had some independent income, eschewed Victorian and Edwardian conventionality, and revelled in oftentimes cruel gossip. They had razor wits and loved wordplay and languages. Dark-haired Lytton became very proud of the red beard he grew, and of his occasionally flamboyant dress.

While modern critics make comparisons to Oscar Wilde and take the discussion of Bloomsbury and sexuality very seriously, they often miss two things. For one, 'homosexuality' was not a word that anyone in Bloomsbury used. Although their private conversations and coded letters express an often cheerful gay aesthetic, 'the criminalization of "gross indecency" between men in Britain precluded open acknowledgment of homosexuality and exposed even subtle expressions of homoerotic feelings to threats of blackmail – as Bloomsbury's men knew from experience' (Reed 71–2). The subjection of language to this political and social reality did, on the other hand, give them an imaginative field for humour, a point that many in their earnest scholarly evaluations miss. It is no mistake that Virginia Woolf's recounting of the day that Lytton entered a room, pointed to a spot on Vanessa's dress, and asked 'Semen?' presents it as the moment when language was released and everything changed for them.

Seen this way, Carrington encountered a Bloomsbury that was half a generation older and more comfortable in life than she was. Busily throwing off the shackles of suburban life, she could both see through what seemed like their pretensions ('What poseurs they are really!') and was domestically competent (qtd. in Gerzina 70). She envied their independence from families who required lies and deception in order to get away; at twenty-two her life was a tangle of deliberate misrepresentations to lovers and friends. Yet she had more in common with Lytton than it might have seemed. Both came from Anglo-Indian backgrounds, which was something much of Bloomsbury shared. Lytton's father spent decades in colonial Indian administration, as had Carrington's father, who survived the 'Mutiny' or 'Rebellion' and was involved in building the railway. They were part of Bohemian London, but with a foot remaining on the side of middle-class respectability. Her sturdy, boyish body and golden hair, turned-in toes and gasping voice somehow attracted the taller, older, Strachey, with his distinctive Strachey family voice that leapt from bass to falsetto in mid-sentence. As a writer and an artist, they understood the value of the arts and were close to those who created them, even though she was woefully under-educated. As it turned out, he could educate her and she could provide a home for him.

But Lytton and Carrington also shared a sense of humour, which quickly found its pitch in Bloomsbury's 'queer epistolary performances', and 'camp' or 'that much-debated "deliberately exaggerated and theatrical" style associated with sexual subculture since the first decade of the twentieth century' (Reed 75). Carrington's imaginative letters to Lytton, with their wonderful illustrations, matched in private their more public conversations, and he responded in kind. She openly mocked his age and hypochondria, referring to him as 'grand-père' and drawing pictures of him trembling on his deathbed, or wrapped in a blanket and shivering by the fire as he soaked his feet.

They kept their budding relationship a secret and, on a trip to Wales together in 1916, they likely attempted a physical relationship. They planned further trips together, and Carrington gave free rein to the possibilities of her androgyny. In one drawing, 'a vision', she illustrated a walking tour they could take together. She had spent hours in front of a mirror strapping her breasts down and pushing her hair behind her ears, 'trying to persuade myself that two cheeks like turnips on the top of a hoe bore some resemblance to a very well nourished youth of sixteen'. The dangers of a boy travelling with a man were as great as a young woman travelling with a man, and in the last years of the war 'those cursed military authorities make the other rather more difficult, as the life of a village policeman is so dreary, that the sight of a fat cheeked Boy and German Bearded spy would throw him into a spasm of alertness' (*Letters* 81).

Strachey burned with the secret of his surprising new liaison, and even though their relationship is generally portrayed as being one-sided, he later confessed to his friend David Garnett 'that he thought he was in love with Carrington':

> This was told me in a hesitating mixture of eagerness and deprecation. He had burst out because he needed to make a confidence. And then came the fear that he had been indiscreet. I was asked to swear not to repeat what he had told me to either Duncan or Vanessa. Duncan would tell Vanessa, and she would relate it in a letter to Virginia, and the fat would be in the fire. Ottoline would hear of it, which would be fatal. I did not breathe a word of Lytton's secret. (Qtd. in Gerzina 84)

Because Carrington too feared disclosure – as a single young woman, she had her parents to consider – she kept their deepening closeness to herself, and continued to string Gertler along. Somehow their affair limped along, with her limiting her sexual favours to him to three times a month: enough to placate him, and not too much to upset her. Lytton believed that the reason Carrington and Gertler's love affair never worked 'was due to Gertler's violence and Carrington's worry and disgust over contraceptives. The real reason was that she was not in love with him, but with Lytton. Blaming herself did not improve matters', Garnett later wrote (qtd. in Gerzina 84).

When Gertler finally realised what was happening he attacked Lytton on the street after a St Valentine's Day party in London. He was led away by Maynard Keynes and two other friends, but he apologised the next day when he was sober. This unfortunate incident forced Carrington and Lytton to have a frank discussion. She recorded in her diary a long conversation between herself and Lytton, discussing what to do about their obvious sexual and age differences. For once she seemed clear and unequivocal: she loved him, and was willing to forego a conventional relationship in order to build a life of some kind together. Neither would be tied to sexual fidelity (*Letters* 96).

Another aspect of her clarity is important, however. She wrote little about her brother Sam or her sister Lottie, but her older brother Teddy, the subject of one of her finest portraits, had been reported missing in the war just a year earlier. She and Noel as the two youngest were the two closest, but Carrington adored her elderly and infirm father and her older soldier brother, although she opposed the war. He was missing throughout the time that her love for an older, and sexually unavailable, man grew. Soon Carrington was riding her bicycle throughout the countryside, scouting for a rural retreat where she could paint and Lytton could write. On 16 October 1917 she found just the place, and just two days later, as she sat in her parents' house, a letter arrived declaring Teddy officially deceased. 'It's rather worse being here with all his books and things about, and where I saw him last and the remoteness of my parents', she wrote to Lytton in her loneliness and sorrow. 'Forgive me for writing but I wanted you so badly. One is not even left alone to cry. Dearest Lytton I love you so much' (*Letters* 81).

Carrington and Lytton moved into Tidmarsh Mill House, in Pangbourne, only weeks later, and in many ways this set the script for the rest of Carrington's life. She lied to her parents, telling them she was sharing a house with female friends, and stripping their house in Hurstbourne Tarrant of any furnishings, linens and vegetables she could cart away. Her artistic talents were put to work painting murals on walls and making a proper home. Here Lytton had a comfortable place to write and entertain friends in comfort, and it was here that he finished writing *Eminent Victorians* and became famous. One of Carrington's best-known paintings is of the mill house from the rear, with the fantastical addition of black swans on the river. Lytton's friends streamed through, and both he and Carrington were frequently in London seeing their various friends, yet few of Lytton's thought to include Carrington in their invitations to him.

It was a year into this settled new life that a new name, Ralph Partridge, began to appear in Carrington's letters, and the next of several love triangles began. This time it was to appease Lytton rather than herself that Ralph (pronounced Rafe) became a steady and crucial part of their lives. By late May of 1921, Carrington had married him, but Ralph was a central figure in the mill house long before that. It may be that Lytton was the only one happy with this arrangement.

New Arrangements

Ralph Partridge, originally named Rex but renamed by Lytton, first met Carrington through her brother Noel when they attended Christ Church, Oxford, before the war. The three of them, along with a female friend, made a trip to Scotland, and it was during this holiday that Carrington warmed to him and wrote enthusiastically to Lytton. She was initially disparaging of his looks – there was nothing of the frail artist about him at all – but soon wrote admiringly about the athletic physique and military bearing that caused everyone to refer to him as 'the major'. Her letters about him intrigued Lytton, and this was one of the ways she retained Strachey's affections as his newfound fame increasingly brought him into a wider social and literary world. With the death of her father in 1918, her world shrank further. As Lytton had with the death of Teddy, Ralph seemed to appear just when an important male void opened in her life.

Ralph, perhaps predictably, fell in love with her. Anne Chisholm reports a visit Carrington made to Noel in Oxford, where the three of them

> swam in the river by the Trout Inn, and she helped him with a lunch party in his rooms ('cocktails and salmon'). After lunch, 'Noel went back to his studies and I continued my investigations'. At this point she added a small drawing of an erect penis. (Chisholm 61)

Soon he was part of the Tidmarsh household, where Lytton was just as taken with him as was Carrington. He loved having another man in the house, one capable as Carrington, and Ralph too was learning a new way of life that differed from his much more conventional upbringing. Ralph quickly fell into their habit of teasing sexual banter, a 'queer' humour that permeated Bloomsbury conversation and aesthetics. His family never took to Carrington, even after she married him, and she commented that they found her an odd sort of wife. But it was also an odd sort of marriage (Figure 6).

Figure 6. From left to right: Carrington, Ralph Partridge, Lytton Strachey, Oliver Strachey, Frances Marshall (later Partridge). Photograph by Lady Ottoline Morrell, 1923. © National Portrait Gallery, London

Partridge was as jealous as Gertler had been in the past, and once again Carrington felt someone wanted to own her. Lytton wanted him to stay, to add balance to their life and home, and ultimately she caved in to the pressure, describing the marriage in the saddest possible terms. Whatever they imagined marriage might be, it soon involved affairs on both sides, Carrington with Partridge's close friend Gerald Brenan, and Ralph with a series of women. At first Ralph did not seem to mind, but then he made it clear that infidelity was fine for him, but not for his wife.

There has been much speculation over the years about this three-way relationship. Was it a *ménage-à-trois*? Carrington mentions them all talking in bed, but this alone is not evidence of sexual activity. Frances, who married Ralph after Carrington's death, always maintained that Ralph was completely heterosexual. Yet Anne Chisholm, in her biography of Frances Partridge, suggests that it was perhaps possible that a bit of experimentation might have occurred early on:

> although Ralph was to have many warm friendships with homosexual men, and was always keenly interested in their lives and loves, there was never any hint of homosexual behavior from him apart from during the years he was closest to Lytton. (Chisholm 65–6)

By the time Ralph met Frances in London, they knew that his marriage was broken, but also that in order to allow Carrington to continue her life with Lytton, some new kind of arrangement must be made. As all this was being sorted, Carrington fell in love, or in complete infatuation. This time it was with a woman.

Flirtations, Loves and Losses

Carrington was always very clear about her deep dislike of her female body, and tried to be very clear about this with her lovers. Gertler seems to have found her sexual reluctance wilful rather than innate, and it is likely that his roughness and pushiness increased her dislike of the physical expression of love. Brenan found himself equally pushed and pulled by her 'divided self'. Her brother said that Carrington 'never overcame her shame at being a woman, and her letters are full of references to menstruation':

> Although her sexual desire had greatly increased between her affair with Mark Gertler and that with Gerald Brenan, and although she was in love with Brenan as she had never been with Gertler, they follow a curiously similar pattern: almost the same deceptions, excuses and self-accusations are repeated in each relationship. And in each it was the hatred of being a woman which poisoned it. (Noel Carrington, qtd. in Carrington, *Letters* 12)

Even in a time of great social upheaval and in the Jazz Age, a young woman could be bullied and pressured into having relationships that she neither quite desired nor quite shunned.

By the time Carrington was in her thirtieth year, she had been with Ralph for four years, many of them unhappy. She easily tolerated his relationship with Frances Marshall, as she had with his other lovers. Because his jealousy did not allow her the same freedom, he made her share the letters she received from Brenan, though she held back the separate, private, postscripts. She was beginning to feel older, and lived with two men who took lovers, while Brenan, her own lover, was preparing to leave the country for a life in the Andalusian mountains.

Into this turmoil stepped a true Jazz Age woman from America. Henrietta Bingham was the daughter of a self-made Kentuckian, now a politician and newspaper mogul, an Anglophile who loved hunting to hounds and fishing, and who was more than half in love with his own headstrong and beautiful daughter. As a child she had witnessed her mother's tragic death in an automobile accident, and even though her father remarried twice more – always to women with money – the father and daughter's mutual attachment kept them chained to each other throughout their lives. Even as a small child, her violet blue sloe eyes and forthright stare marked her as sensual and even perhaps predatory. She arrived in London at twenty-two, along with a young woman, Mina Kirstein, who had been her professor at Smith College, with steamer trunks of clothes, cookbooks, cocktail shakers and ingredients from Prohibition America, phonograph records of African American music, and an ability to dance the Congo Grind and Black Bottom (Bingham 56). Carrington and the others had never seen anything like her.

The two American women entered Bloomsbury via the bookshop that David Garnett and Francis Birrell ran. Garnett and Kirstein hit it off immediately and began seeing each other, even though Kirstein was also Bingham's lover. When Garnett learned that they were looking for a house to rent, he arranged for the young women to visit Tidmarsh Mill, as the occupants were thinking of going away for a while. They pulled up in a blue Sunbeam – Henrietta was an excellent driver who later persuaded Carrington to learn – and Carrington, working in her studio, was prepared to dislike them, after having seen, and disapproved of, *An American Revue* in Covent Garden. But Carrington thought twenty-six-year-old Mina 'lovely', 'tall with an olive skin, dark shining eyes like jet beads, and a perfect slim figure, short black curling hair'. But Henrietta was 'my style, pink with a round face, dressed in mannish clothes, with a good natural smile'.

> While take-charge Mina did the talking, Henrietta remained cool, catching Carrington's gaze and holding it. Henrietta left Carrington oddly shaken, and she watched the car pull away with regret. Nearing her thirtieth birthday, the painter imagined that these 'lovely creatures' took 'about as much interest in me as if I'd been the housekeeper.' But when they phoned with an offer Strachey refused. He 'couldn't bear to have' them living in his home. (Bingham 84–5)

They were destined to meet again, quite soon, when Garnett held a birthday party for Duncan Grant.

Henrietta arrived bearing a birthday cake decorated with an illustration of Garnett's book *Lady into Fox*, and set up a bar. But the fatal blow, as far as Carrington was concerned, came when the records died down and Henrietta picked up a mandolin and began singing 'Water Boy', an African American chain gang song, 'channeling rebellion and blackness, sorrow and sex, pursuing and being pursued' (Bingham 85–6). Carrington wrote to Brenan, 'I became completely drunk and almost made love to her in public. To my great joy Garnett told me the other day she continually asks after me and wants me to go and see her' (*Letters* 254). Over the summer, views toward Henrietta softened. Lytton met her brothers at a party and had a friendly conversation, and Henrietta later either delighted or shocked them all when she climbed on top of a piano and played the saxophone (Bingham 102).

It was not until the following summer, when the Binghams returned, that Carrington was able to see her again. By this time Henrietta was closely involved with and nearly engaged to the sculptor Stephen Tomlin (called 'Tommy'), and they dropped by for an unexpected visit to Tidmarsh Mill. Carrington's Slade friend Barbara Bagenal was mentioned: '"Charming girl," Henrietta pronounced boldly, "have you ever made love to her, Carrington?" That weekend, the seed of Carrington's attraction, sowed at David's birthday party a year before, suddenly germinated' (Bingham 115).

Carrington, Bingham's senior by eight years, began to make an effort to improve her often of late dowdy appearance. Getting her hair professionally washed, she headed to the house that Henrietta had taken in Knightsbridge and decorated for friends who had not yet arrived, and there Henrietta, with her 'low husky Southern voice' (Brenan 75) and penetrating gaze, seduced her. Their affair went on throughout the summer, and for the first time in her life Carrington felt ecstasy and no shame, and no dislike of her own body. It may have been then that Carrington began a portrait of Henrietta, with a dove (Figure 7).

Her friends' responses to this affair are fascinating, and show how misogyny crept into what otherwise seems a very sexually open group. Brenan, far from being jealous initially, actually offered them his rooms for their trysts. He had always found her sexual interest in him 'unpredictable' (Brenan 85), and did not view her as a lesbian, despite her intense fling with Henrietta. Ralph worried that she would be hurt, for Bingham had a reputation for seducing and abandoning both men and women, but he showed none of the possessiveness he had about other men. Lytton too worried that her heart would be broken, as seemed inevitable, since her emotional investment seemed so great. And Frances Partridge later told me that although she had no problem with

Figure 7. Carrington, *Reclining Nude with Dove in a Mountainous Landscape* (portrait of Henrietta Bingham), c.1924. Private collection

homosexuality among men, she was squeamish about it with women; she did not respond positively when Carrington later flirted with her, a fact which did not improve the relationship between the two women, or, surely, Carrington's sense of self-worth.

    There were other changes that summer. Tidmarsh Mill was being left behind for another house, Ham Spray. Carrington marshalled their friends to come help for several weeks. Lytton marvelled at the way Henrietta 'whitewashed unceasingly and never said a word'. Carrington wrote that she 'never a drop spilt on the floor, and so economical that one pot of paint lasts her a whole day' (qtd. in Bingham 118). During breaks the two women went for long walks, where Carrington intriguingly went 'deep into formative sexual memories she had never shared – bedwetting, a spanking, a peeping

Figure 8: Carrington, Drawing of Henrietta Bingham in heels, c.1924. © Devonshire Collection, Chatsworth. Reproduced by permission of Chatsworth Settlement Trustees

Tom – which Henrietta may have asked her lover to consider in relation to her overwhelming physical shame' (Bingham 119). Henrietta herself was undergoing intense psychoanalysis with Ernest Jones, who was convinced that he could 'cure' her of her lesbianism, as Mina Kirstein claimed he had done for her. Carrington drew her lover that summer in the nude, with elongated legs ending in high heels (Figure 8).

It was the summer of her awakening, but also a summer of heartbreak and sexual merry-go-round. Mina and Henrietta had not completely broken off, but Mina slept with both the married David Garnett and with Clive Bell. Henrietta had Mina, was seriously involved with Tommy, and was also sleeping with Carrington. Gerald realised that he 'half lost' Carrington to Henrietta:

> What I did not then know was that Carrington was basically a Lesbian too and that her affair with Henrietta would affect her physical relations with me by giving her a feeling of guilt which made her react against me afterwards. I was to pay dearly for her having met this American girl. (Brenan 75)

Carrington, deeply in love, later explained that she was not completely lesbian; that, she thought, would have been easier than being so divided.

Brenan was certain late in his life that this was her only lesbian affair, but it was life-changing. Carrington wrote at length to Brenan on 21 July 1925 about what she had been trying to figure out all these years.

> You know I have always hated being a woman ... I am continually depressed by my feminineness. It is true that *au fond* I have a female inside in me, which is proved by my liking to make love, but afterwards a sort of rage fills me because of that. I literally cannot bear to let my mind think of it again. It is partly because Ralph does not any longer treat me like a woman that the strain between us has vanished. All this became clear last summer with Henrietta. I had more ecstasy with her and no feelings of shame afterwards. You pressed me out of myself into a hidden suppressed character, but when I returned I turned against this character and was filled with dread at meeting you again. It is really something unconnected with you, a struggle in myself between two characters.... Probably it would have been easier if I had been completely Lesbian.... In the past everything has gone wrong for this reason – always this struggle between two insides, which makes one disjointed, unreliable and secretive. (*Letters* 323–5)

Henrietta, seen as 'dangerous' by Lytton (Holroyd 541), finally dropped Carrington, who wrote during that 1924 summer of love to Brenan that 'Henrietta returns my affection almost as negatively as you find I do yours' (*Letters* 296). Carrington devised her own ritual to mark the end of the affair: 'she occupied an entire spring afternoon at Ham Spray House constructing an elaborate cardboard coffin for a cocktail shaker Henrietta had left behind. Snowdrops surrounded the cold reflective corpse; the coffin's lid bore an inky cross and "RIP DC"' (Bingham 144). Brenan eventually moved to Spain, and Partridge moved on with Frances. At Lytton's insistence they worked out a schedule whereby the new couple spent many weekends at Ham Spray, but Lytton travelled more often and was frequently in London. Carrington found herself more and more alone.

Loneliness, Flirtation and the Ultimate Loss

In her early thirties, Carrington could not have known she had only a few more years to live, of course. Her wonderful letters continued, with new correspondents. One of the most important of these was Poppet John, one of the lovely daughters of the famous painter Augustus John. The Johns moved in 1927 to a country retreat, Fryern Court, which was within driving distance of Ham Spray, and Carrington was a frequent welcome guest there of Augustus and his second wife, Dorelia. At home, in addition to painting the tiles, glass pictures and signboards that earned her a bit of income, Carrington continued to paint more seriously, keep up the house, and ride her horse Belle. The Johns also kept horses, and had delightful evenings of conversation, drink and games, and her life among them was a godsend.

Carrington was nineteen years older than Poppet and in 1928, when Carrington was thirty-five and Poppet was sixteen, she wrote to Brenan that 'Poppet and Vivien [John] are my only correspondents. And the level I assure you is, although infinitely amorous, infinitely low' (*Letters* 398). She acted the older aunt with them, but although she wrote as though they were still children, the sexual flirtatiousness of the letters to Poppet is often striking. The playfulness she had always incorporated into letters to Lytton might appear to some contemporary readers uncomfortably seductive in letters sent to a teenaged girl, but the Johns' household was as free and open as that at Charleston. In one she wrote from Ham Spray,

> My Darling Poppinmouth, It seems a terribly long time since we lay together in that sweet embrace in the taxi on Monday … I suppose a hundred lips have pressed yours since I last drove in that romantic taxi to Chelsea. But mine I assure you madame have been surrounded by wire netting ever since. (Letter to P. John, n.d.)

The tone suggests innocent kisses, and later letters refer happily to Poppet's engagement. The letters are all play and, as she suggested to Brenan, contain none of the intelligence or *sturm und drang* of her letters to her lovers. Instead, Poppet is drawn as a nude wood nymph hugging a tree (a reference to an inside joke).

For the most part these letters contain gossip, or small news: she has been at the British Museum helping Lytton select pictures for his *Queen Elizabeth*; Pansy and Mary Lamb came to lunch; she (Carrington) has too often been to parties and lunches and drank too much ('I still dream of that dream-like party. I wish I hadn't been quite so boozed for there were so many things I wanted to do & didn't, one was kiss you a hundred times secretly upstairs' [Letter to P. John, n.d.]). Others are even more suggestive (Figure 9):

Figure 9. Carrington, Drawing in undated letter to Poppet John. © Dora Carrington. Reproduced by permission of the Estate of Dora Carrington c/o Rogers, Coleridge & White Ltd, London

Figure 10. Carrington, Drawing in undated letter to Poppet John. © Dora Carrington. Reproduced by permission of the Estate of Dora Carrington c/o Rogers, Coleridge & White Ltd, London

Darling Poppet Sweetie. Thank you very much for your charming letter. You were a dear to write me one so soon as it was a great consolation for the sadness of leaving you. I was miserable at that lovely party coming to an end. I longed to slip up stairs & hide myself in your bed.... I do not know quite why this abandoned creature & Tiber [Carrington's cat] have crept in to this letter. (Letter to P. John, n.d.)

Their kissing makes its way into other letters as well: 'Now I must get the car to start as I've got to drive in to the station. My Fondest Love my sweet, sweet sweetie, and a great many Passionate Hugs. Your devoted C' (Letter to P. John, n.d.) (Figure 10). And there is evidence that these kisses were not all imaginary, as an undated photograph of Poppet and Carrington shows (Figure 11).

Figure 11. Carrington (on right) and Poppet John. Private collection

As a woman approaching middle age, Carrington cheerfully and openly addressed her bisexuality, with none of the angst she had expressed with Brenan much earlier. Poppet made no demands upon her; indeed, she was about to be engaged to a man whom Carrington liked. Because of their sexual insistence and her own uncertainties, Carrington had always triangulated her previous relationships with Gertler, Brenan and Partridge, or had been forced to be part of a three-way liaison. Now with Poppet she could be the amusing and attractive mature woman whose playfulness was appreciated, with no loss of independence. But these letters also mask an increasing loneliness, as Lytton spent more and more time away with his lovers and his work, and Ralph and Frances lived mostly in London and were lost in each other when they came to Ham Spray. Carrington's time spent at Fryern Court with the Johns or elsewhere with Poppet became increasingly precious to her in her increasing solitude.

And Lytton, the mainstay and deepest love of her life, was about to leave her. His various ailments, long a source of amusement to his friends who thought him a hypochondriac, were finally diagnosed as stomach cancer. As Lytton lay dying at Ham Spray, Carrington attempted suicide by climbing into the back of their car and running the engine with the garage door closed, only to be found and revived by Ralph in time to witness Lytton's death. Completely devastated, she shot herself two months later.

Lytton had not only formed the core of her adult life, but gave her a new way to relate to the world. Word play, love, new ideas of 'home' in a changing world were what they shared. If Lytton's writings altered biography, inserting a new tone into a dreary, overwritten art, Carrington's letters and drawings breathed new life into the dailiness of existence. 'Recent scholarship on Bloomsbury shows how easy it becomes for biographers and critics to pass authoritative judgments that enforce highly normative values', writes Christopher Reed (81). 'Much about Bloomsbury – and 1920s culture more generally – surprised and discomfited later generations, as evidenced by reactions to less stylized (more explicit, less campy) explanations of Bloomsbury's attitudes toward sexuality when these appeared decades later' (Reed 77). Carrington, in her life and art, and even in her death, challenged all normativity.

Notes

1. See the exhibition catalogue (Green and Reed). The exhibition website is at http://museum.cornell.edu/bloomsbury/home.htm.
2. I may be one of the only living people who actually saw and held her hair. Noel's

wife, Catharine, had a lock she placed in my hand. It was heavy and almost coarse, and closer perhaps to a very light brown than strictly blonde. It later disappeared and she was never able to discover what happened to it.

Works Cited

Bingham, Emily. *Irrepressible: The Jazz Age Life of Henrietta Bingham*. New York: Farrar, 2015.
Brenan, Gerald. *Gerald Brenan's Personal Record (1920–1972)*. New York: Knopf, 1975.
Carrington, Dora. *Carrington: Letters and Extracts from Her Diaries*. Ed. David Garnett. New York: Holt, 1970.
—. Letters to Poppet John. n.d. [c. 1928–32?] MS. Harry Ransom Center, Austin.
Chisholm, Anne. *Frances Partridge: The Biography*. London: Weidenfeld, 2009.
Delbanco, Nicholas. *The Art of Youth: Crane, Carrington, Gershwin, and the Nature of First Acts*. New York: Houghton, 2013.
Gerzina, Gretchen. *Carrington: A Life*. New York: Norton, 1989.
Green, Nancy, and Christopher Reed, eds. *A Room of Their Own: The Bloomsbury Artists in American Collections*. Ithaca: Herbert F. Johnson Museum of Art, Cornell University, 2008.
Hancock, David Boyd. *A Crisis of Brilliance: Five Young British Artists and the Great War*. London: Old Street, 2009.
Hill, Jane. *The Art of Dora Carrington*. New York: Thames and Hudson, 1994.
Holroyd, Michael. *Lytton Strachey: The New Biography*. New York: Farrar, 1994.
Reed, Christopher. 'Bloomsbury as Queer Subculture'. *The Cambridge Companion to the Bloomsbury Group*. Ed. Victoria Rosner. New York: Cambridge University Press, 2014. 71–89.

Making Sense of Wittgenstein's Bloomsbury and Bloomsbury's Wittgenstein

Gaile Pohlhaus, Jr and Madelyn Detloff

When we originally toyed with the idea of proposing an essay on Wittgenstein for *Queer Bloomsbury*, two objections repeatedly surfaced: Was he queer (enough)? And was he Bloomsbury (enough)? These questions in themselves evoke particular themes in Wittgenstein's later philosophy, especially regarding the concepts of certainty, family resemblance, 'aspectual perception' and 'queerness' as Wittgenstein uses the term (meaning sometimes 'remarkable' and at others 'strange' or 'askew'). We hope to make clear that, although Wittgenstein had his own unique and idiosyncratic way of presenting his ideas, his thinking, especially in his later work, resonates deeply with key concerns raised in Bloomsbury aesthetics (regarding the function of art or the function of words), literature (most significantly in Woolf's philosophical fiction) and value theory (most notably Keynes's macroeconomics). Moreover, it is not lost on us that Wittgenstein's reconceiving of philosophy as an *activity* that ought to work on the philosopher so as to dissolve quests for origins, foundations and/or essences bears resemblance to contemporary queer theory's emphasis on the 'performative' *doing* rather than foundational *being*. Queer Bloomsbury, as a cognitive, geographical and historical space, operates as a generative nexus of ideas on meaning, understanding, valuing and living, and Wittgenstein's philosophical activities can be said to inhabit that space alongside the ideas of his peers, sometimes friends and rivals, who are more recognisably associated with Bloomsbury. In what follows we first address the questions of Wittgenstein's relation to Bloomsbury and his sexuality. We then consider themes within his later work relevant to Bloomsbury, the 'queer' and queer Bloomsbury.

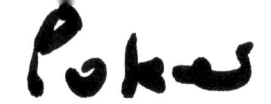

The Bloomsbury Question

Wittgenstein held a peculiar position in Bloomsbury. Throughout his life he was in several homoerotically charged close friendships with men who were key figures in the Bloomsbury Group, including John Maynard Keynes, who anecdotally referred to him as 'God', and Frank Ramsey, a mathematician who was revered by Julian Bell (who, in Bloomsbury fashion, became involved with Ramsey's wife, Lettice).[1] If anything, Wittgenstein was an irritant – a grit of sand in the oyster that was Bloomsbury. During the time that, according to Ann Banfield, the Cambridge philosophers (especially G. E. Moore and Bertrand Russell) were most intensely interacting with Bloomsbury ideals, Wittgenstein was studying with Russell at Cambridge. Ray Monk's biography of Wittgenstein depicts a very intense intellectual engagement between the two men, with Wittgenstein practically stalking Russell after lectures to argue about the more intractable problems of logic, especially 'Russell's paradox' and the search for 'atomic propositions'. Banfield goes so far as to define Bloomsbury's philosophical genealogy in terms of Russell and Wittgenstein:

> Bloomsbury's preoccupation with epistemological questions thus places it squarely within the period of Russell which ends with Wittgenstein's ascendancy. Leonard Woolf, explaining why Virginia had not attended Wittgenstein's lectures says 'nor did I and I don't think many of the older people did' (*Letters LW*, 539). We can thus take the rise of Wittgenstein's influence as a kind of cut-off point for the philosophical background of Bloomsbury. (9)

From this perspective Wittgenstein appears to be something of a Mordred figure who barges into Camelot and causes the philosophical Round Table to splinter. To be sure, he was a mercurial presence at Cambridge. He was elected an 'Apostle', only to resign, only to be re-elected as an 'Angel' member when he returned to Cambridge after the Great War. Second-generation Bloomsbury member Julian Bell derided him in a parodic long poem circulated at Cambridge in the early 1930s. Wittgenstein was himself a cosmopolitan who relocated throughout Europe more than average, yet was awkward in the bohemian atmosphere of London's Bloomsbury neighbourhood. It is safe to say that he was as intensely disliked by some members of the *milieu* as he was intensely admired by others. He left his mark, that is, not only on the men he favoured (Keynes, Ramsey) but also on those women and men whom he irritated (Lady Ottoline, the Woolfs and eventually Moore and Russell). For all of these reasons we think Wittgenstein was an important figure in the network of interpersonal relations we call Bloomsbury – albeit a perplexing and thus often neglected one.

The (Homo)sex Question

If Wittgenstein's relationship to Bloomsbury is perplexing and complicated, the question of his sexuality is even more so. While Wittgenstein avowed no sexual relationships publicly, he did maintain intense attachments to particular men. Moreover, his awkwardness with women was generally known. Indeed, the only recorded encounter between Wittgenstein and Leonard and Virginia Woolf was soured by Wittgenstein's rudeness to Lydia Lopokova, the wife of Maynard Keynes, one of the men to whom Wittgenstein was intensely attached. It would be mere speculation to suggest that jealousy played a part in Wittgenstein's behaviour to Lopokova. Still, such jealousy would not be out of character for Wittgenstein, who acted like a possessive husband on his honeymoon when he and David Pinsent were on their homoromantic excursion through Iceland (Monk 58–61). On the other hand, it is possible that Wittgenstein's behaviour toward Lopokova was simply a manifestation of his general refusal to practise social niceties, a refusal that would have stood out as a breach of gender roles (men of a certain class were expected to be polite toward women of that class). Such behaviour might have struck others as callous ingratitude, since Lopokova and Keynes, themselves newlyweds, were Wittgenstein's hosts. It is difficult to tell whether Wittgenstein's treatment of women such as Lopokova was fuelled by misogyny or by his impatience with the social mores he associated with mixed company. Wittgenstein did hold great respect for some women, including his student Elizabeth (G. E. M.) Anscombe, to whom he entrusted the translation of his posthumously published *Philosophical Investigations*. However, following fellow Austrian Otto Weininger (for whom Wittgenstein harboured a kind of hero worship), Wittgenstein regarded women whom he respected as 'honorary' males (Monk 20, 498).[2]

After the publication of W. W. Bartley's biography of Wittgenstein in the early 1970s, his sexuality became the subject of fierce debate. Bartley suggests that during Wittgenstein's stay in Vienna after release from an Italian prisoner of war camp (1919–20), the philosopher was in the habit of cruising the Prater Park meadows for 'rough young men [who] were ready to cater to him sexually' (40). Bartley also claims that later in life Wittgenstein would occasionally slip away from the 'fashionable and intellectual young men [at Cambridge] who might have been ready to place themselves at his disposal, in favor of the company of tough boys in London pubs' (40).

At the time, these revelations were not well received by many of Wittgenstein's admirers and close friends. In a letter to the *Times Literary Supplement* that bears a remarkable generic similarity to the catalogue of excuses that Eve Sedgwick identified for ignoring evidence of same-sex erotic attachments, Anscombe pointedly asks 'nine questions' of Bartley disputing his evidence of Wittgenstein's homosexual activities (Sedgwick 52–3). Anscombe's letter is interesting insofar as she does not refute any of Bartley's claims, but rather charges him with not having the calibre of evidence required for biographies. Most of Bartley's evidence was derived from fieldwork he did, interviewing Wittgenstein's former elementary school pupils and interviewing patrons of Vienna's gay bars who would have been around during the early 1920s. Same-sex sexual activity was illegal in Austria until 1971, and indeed at the time of Bartley's fieldwork in 1969, sex between men was illegal in most countries of Europe. Hence it is not very surprising that Bartley did not name his sources or provide the kind of contextual detail (where, when, what sort of person was interviewed, and so on) that Anscombe demanded as verification of Bartley's claims.

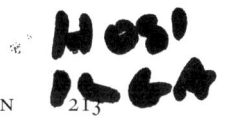

Question 5 of Anscombe's letter begins with a passage from Bartley quoted (more accurately) above:

> 'similarly in later years in England he was from time to time to flee the fashionable and intellectual young men who were ready to place themselves at his disposal in Cambridge in favour of the company of tough boys in London pubs'. A list of Cambridge students who were particularly interested in Wittgenstein is readily available. Which of these could be called 'fashionable'? What evidence is there that these people were 'ready to places themselves at his disposal' in the sense indicated? Exactly how did Professor Bartley obtain evidence that Wittgenstein was ever in a London pub at all; or that he was ever in one for that purpose? Does he claim that a friend of Wittgenstein told him this or that he has seen documents to prove it? Or (as he hints in the preface) has he learnt it from some 'aging homosexual in his own special pub'? If the latter, how did Professor Bartley come to get what story and how establish its truth – how to make the identification, for example?

For the record, we do not really care what Wittgenstein did or did not do in Prater Park or in any number of London pubs. We are not ascribing a sexual identity to Wittgenstein. It is Anscombe and her peers, in fact, who depend upon linking sexual acts to *kinds* of people (in other words, Wittgenstein could not have gone cruising because he was not that *kind* of a person). Instead, we are interested in the sheer incredulity with which Bartley's claims have been met. So Wittgenstein apparently slipped out of Cambridge to hang out in a London pub where men seeking men hung out. Such a statement would be a mere aside if it concerned something other than sexuality. If Bartley had claimed that Wittgenstein occasionally slipped out of Cambridge to see a B-movie at a London cinema, for example, it would be nonsensical for scholars to object: *Show me the ticket stubs! How do you know that he was ever in a London cinema?* As to the shocking assertion that the young men at Cambridge might be more 'fashionable' or more 'intellectual' than the locals at a London pub, picture for a moment the line of investigation that Anscombe proposes in order to verify the accuracy of such an apparently outlandish claim, asking former Cambridge students: *Do you consider yourself fashionable? Are you intellectual, or relatively more intellectual than an average London pub-goer? Would you have put yourself at the disposal (sexually speaking) of your former teacher Wittgenstein? Oh really? What's your name and address in case anyone asks me to back up my story?*

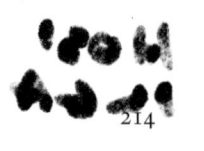

Why would we ever imagine that testimony gathered through Anscombe's proposed method would be more reliable than anonymous testimony whose sources were protected? Given how harshly Anscombe and Wittgenstein's other literary executors attacked Bartley, do we really believe that former students of Wittgenstein would have been inclined to 'tell all' about their mentor? Why is it so unthinkable that Wittgenstein might have preferred men sexually and sought out venues to put himself in contact with 'tough boys'? Are we really surprised that he didn't document such excursions for posterity? Or that someone who might also have frequented such places for the purposes of procuring anonymous sex might prefer to remain anonymous? The real question provoked by Anscombe's 'nine questions' is not whether we can be absolutely sure that Wittgenstein went cruising in Prater Park or London pubs, or even whether he and David Pinsent actually got naked together on their romantic holiday to Iceland in between their steamy conversations about logic, but rather, to quote Wittgenstein, 'whether it can make any sense to doubt it' (*On Certainty* §2).

Wittgenstein and the Queerness of Philosophy

This returns us to Wittgenstein's later work, its resonances with queer theory, with ideas explored by Bloomsbury members, and thus with the idea of 'queer Bloomsbury' itself. Wittgenstein's later philosophical work moves through a variety of 'language-games', including those within which words such as 'knowing' and 'doubting' make sense.[3] Moreover, the driving force behind much of Wittgenstein's later work concerns problems of intelligibility – what it does and does not make sense to say. Wittgenstein's writing proceeds, however, in a way that is unconventional to philosophy: not with an eye for establishing the truth of things, but rather with empathy for the desire for absolutes such as 'the truth of things', and with an understanding that, if human needs are ever to be met, they are not to be met once and for all.

In what follows, we take as a given Virginia Woolf's observation in *A Room of One's Own* that 'masterpieces are not single and solitary births; they are the outcome of many years of thinking in common, of thinking by the body of the people, so that the experience of the mass is behind the single voice' (68–9). Not only is this observation relevant to the 'years of thinking in common' of the Bloomsbury Group, but also to an entire generation of associated thinkers and artists who, arguably, matured to the fullness of their creative and intellectual powers in the decades following the Great War. Woolf's observation resonates deeply with Wittgenstein's own remarks in the preface to his *Philosophical Investigations*, where he characterises his work as 'the precipitate of philosophical investigations which have occupied me for the last sixteen years' and which had been 'conveyed in lectures, typescripts, and discussions' (3–4).[4] He continues, 'For more than one reason, what I publish here will have points of contact with what other people are writing today. – If my remarks do not bear a stamp which marks them as mine, then I do not wish to lay any further claim to them as my property' (4). With these thoughts in mind it is possible to see Wittgenstein's work not as the 'cut-off point' of Bloomsbury's engagement with philosophy, as Banfield contends, but rather as a bridge between Bloomsbury and late twentieth- and early twenty-first-century thought now associated with queer theory.

The unique form of Wittgenstein's *Philosophical Investigations* is more akin to the polyvocal structure of much of Virginia Woolf's fiction (for example *The Waves* and *Between the Acts*) than to standard philosophical prose.[5] Wittgenstein's text presents its reader with multiple voices that 'criss-cross in every direction over a wide field of thought' (3). Some of these voices express a desire to know and define reality in a general manner typical of traditional philosophy, while others direct the philosopher in a variety of ways back to the world of ordinary existence. Hence the latter voice asks the 'philosophical' voice: 'is the word ever actually used in this way in the language in which it is at home? – What *we* do is to bring words back from their metaphysical to their everyday use' (§116, original emphasis). The former voice functions as a phenomenology of the philosopher, an expression of what it is like to want for the kinds of things a philosopher wants. The latter voice persistently articulates those wants and needs as they might be experienced in the everyday world. That is, the latter voice brings the desires of the former back 'to their everyday use'. This re-orienting practice is very similar to Bloomsbury's attention to the quotidian and to the extraordinary within ordinary experience – for example in the everyday epiphanies of Woolf's novels or in the beautiful, yet functional, designs produced by the Omega Workshops.

Curiously, for our purposes, when Wittgenstein's two voices meet in the *Investigations*, he often makes use of the German words *seltsame* and *merwurkdig*, both of which Anscombe in the first English edition of the *Investigations* chose to translate as 'queer'. Indeed, in Anscombe's original translation the word 'queer' or one of its variants (queerer, queerest, queerly) appears fifty times. However, in the revised translation of the fourth edition of *Philosophical Investigations*, Hacker and Schulte translate *seltsame* and *merwurkdig* as 'odd', 'strange', 'curious', 'remarkable' and/or 'extraordinary'. Hacker and Schulte offer reasons for other alterations to Anscombe's original translation, but the choice to erase the word 'queer' from Wittgenstein's text is simply stated in the translator's preface as though it needed no explanation (xiii). And perhaps it doesn't. Wittgenstein's references to 'queer feelings', 'queer experiences' and so on indicate moments that might strike one as odd, peculiar, perhaps even uncanny, but not as recognisably homosexual. Moreover, the text itself pre-dates the theoretical use of the word 'queer' in philosophical treatments of gender and sexuality. In this sense the newer translation (2009) merely corrects the use of a dated word, replacing it with one that does not carry a sexual connotation. Nevertheless, at these moments when Wittgenstein gives voice to experiences and feelings previously translated by Anscombe herself as 'queer', we find distinct resonances to queer theory as we understand it today. For example, these references to *seltsame* and *merwurkdig* in the *Investigations* often concern the force of normativity and human precarity, particularly in the face of questions of intelligibility and even liveability. Moreover, these concerns are often conveyed in tones characteristic of queer theory. That is, they are arch, wry, generative, playful and even perhaps (just a little) erotic.

Like Wittgenstein, Judith Butler, the contemporary philosopher most associated with queer theory, is concerned with questions of intelligibility – what it means to be culturally intelligible and, more pointedly, what it costs (in terms of human dignity) to be unintelligible in a culture. 'If gender is a norm', explains Butler, 'it is not the same as a model that individuals seek to approximate. On the contrary, it is a form of social power that produces the intelligible field of subjects, and an apparatus by which the gender binary is instituted' (*Undoing Gender* 48). Butler calls us to shift our perspective so that we can see concepts such as masculinity, femininity and even the binary understanding of biological sex (male or female) as elements of a meaning-making system, a set of rules for the language-game we call 'gender'. This is not to say that the game of gender is not deadly serious, especially for those who do not fit within the rules of the game and thus are rendered unintelligible or non-human. Butler makes this clear in her 1999 preface to *Gender Trouble*, noting that the stakes of the effort to 'open up possibilities' for different ways to live one's gender would be obvious (that is, 'in plain view') to those who understand 'what it is to live in the social world as what is "impossible", illegible, unrealizable, unreal, and illegitimate' (*Gender Trouble* viii).

Butler came to her paradigm-shifting understanding of gender as performative rather than foundational through a number of engagements with philosophers from Hegel, to Kristeva, Foucault and Derrida, but as our example above makes clear, there are Wittgensteinian resonances in her work as well. We might even say that Wittgenstein's engagement with problems of intelligibility bears a 'family resemblance' to a number of conceptual moves that are characteristic of queer theory.[6] For example, in his later work, Wittgenstein describes how we become captivated by pictures of how things are, or must be – 'A picture held us captive. And we couldn't get outside of it, for it lay in our language, and language seemed only to repeat it to us inexorably' (*Philosophical* §115). When we are held captive by apparent truisms that repeat themselves over and over, we become insensitive to what is right before us. Butler's theory of performative gender dislodges our fixation on the apparent truism that biological sex must necessarily be binary (male or female). That fixation, or 'aspectival captivation' (to use David Owen's shorthand), prevents us from noticing non-binary instances of gender, such as intersexuality (among other gender variations), even though non-binary variations are plainly there.[7]

Among the many captivating pictures Wittgenstein works to dissolve is the idea that analysing (taking things apart to reveal their components – in one of his examples, describing a broom as a broomstick and a brush) will reveal the truth of a thing (the essence of the broom, for example). 'Does the former lie concealed in the latter, and is it now brought out by analysis?' (*Philosophical* §60). For Wittgenstein, it does not make sense to say that the phrase 'broomstick and brush' is more true to the essence of what it means to be a broom than the object's everyday name, 'broom'.

This observation may seem banal, but when we use other names, say 'man' or 'woman', or 'homosexual' or 'bisexual' or 'queer', the urge to take apart and analyse in order to get to the 'truth' of things is almost overwhelming. Michel Foucault called this urge *scientia sexualis* (the science of sex) and describes its invasiveness, its pathologising effects, its propagative force, in Volume 1 of *The History of Sexuality*:

> Not only did it [*scientia sexualis*] speak of sex and compel everyone to do so; it also set out to formulate the uniform truth of sex. As if it suspected sex of harboring a fundamental secret. As if it needed this production of truth. As if it was essential that sex be inscribed not only in an economy of pleasure but in an ordered system of knowledge. Thus sex gradually became an object of great suspicion; the general and disquieting meaning that pervades our conduct and our existence, in spite of ourselves.... (69)

Analysing a person's interests, beliefs, body parts, personal history, hormonal composition, even brain structure had become a cottage industry for churning out expert professions throughout the nineteenth century and early twentieth centuries, but for Foucault, as for Wittgenstein, that analysing activity does not get us any closer to the truth of the thing, in this case the 'truth of sex'.

For Wittgenstein, the work of philosophy is not to uncover some buried or hidden truth, but rather to shift the attention of the philosopher in order to see what is already there in plain view, since as he insists, 'nothing is hidden' (*Philosophical* §435, §559). Foucault employs a similar tactic in his counter-intuitive depiction of the 'repressive hypothesis' in the opening of *The History of Sexuality* (3–13). Rather than exposing the concealed 'truths' of sexuality (and thus participating in the project of *scientia sexualis*), Foucault re-orients our perception of Victorian sexuality through the careful work of 'assembling reminders' (Wittgenstein, *Philosophical* §109). Naming our captivation the 'repressive hypothesis', Foucault challenges the presumption that the Victorian era was an era of sexual silence, reticence and concealment. With the 'repressive hypothesis' dislodged as a totalising view of Victorian sexuality, Foucault is able to call attention to how sexuality was discussed prolifically and new ideas about sex disseminated widely throughout Victorian society. As this example shows, and as Owen has argued further, there is significant affinity between Wittgenstein's thought and Foucault's genealogical method.

Insofar as Wittgenstein continually returns to voices not 'at home' within our practices of intelligibility, his work provides a certain kind of resource to those for whom habituated collective attention makes life unliveable, but not the sort of resource that provides a guiding metanarrative that would order our living once and for all. Rather, Wittgenstein's peculiar form of philosophy gives us something that we were never lacking to begin with. That is to say, nothing special or foundational or definitive or absolutely certain is needed here, but rather a willingness to work, and re-work, our ways of making sense together.

Instead of a metanarrative, Wittgenstein offers a non-coercive set of prompts to his reader. These prompts are open-ended invitations to the reader to proceed with the realisation that 'Now I can go on!' (*Philosophical* §151). As he admits at the end of his preface to the *Investigations*, 'I should not like my writing to spare other people the trouble of thinking. But if possible, to stimulate someone to thoughts of his [sic] own' (4). In a similar vein, Woolf offers the following advice in 'How Should One Read a Book?':

> The only advice, indeed, that one person can give another about reading is to take no advice, to follow your own instincts, to use your own reason, to come to your own conclusions. If this is agreed

between us, then I feel at liberty to put forward a few ideas and suggestions because you will not allow them to fetter that independence which is the most important quality that a reader can possess. (258)

The relation between writer and reader in Wittgenstein's and Woolf's remarks here is non-'tyrannical', which is to say it is ethical in the Levinasian sense (involving something like a face-to-face engagement).[8] The writer is open to the reader's freedom to take his or her words in new directions.

This openness is in stark contrast to the kind of empty materialism that Woolf criticises in 'Modern Fiction'; that is, a descriptive realism that compulsively details (in an attempt to perfectly mimic) life:

> The [materialist] writer seems constrained, not by his [*sic*] own free will but by some powerful and unscrupulous tyrant who has him in thrall, to provide a plot, to provide comedy, tragedy, love interest, and an air of probability embalming the whole so impeccable that if all his figures were to come to life they would find themselves dressed down to the last button of their coats in the fashion of the hour. ('Modern Fiction' 160)

As Woolf notes, this impulse 'more often misses rather than secures the thing we seek' (160). Wittgenstein, too, is critical of the ordering impulse. Even when describing the human capacity to follow a 'rule', he cautions against likening this capacity to being set upon 'rails invisibly laid to infinity' (*Philosophical* §218). For in such a case, '"All the steps are really already taken" means: I no longer have any choice.... But if something of this sort really were the case, how would it help me?' (§219).

At issue here is the difference between inevitability (for example, the inexorable predictability of a computer processing a formula) and sense-making within a constrained but open-ended ecology, such as a language-game or economic system. In this sense, Wittgenstein's attention to the grammar (or 'workings') of our language-games from within shares an affinity with Keynesian economics as discussed by Bill Maurer in this volume. In other words, just as monetary value ought not be ordered by some formula external to local economies, but rather situated dynamically among shifting and changing perspectives within the economy, so too are meanings to be found within the diversity of our everyday uses of words and the practices within which they are interwoven. 'And this diversity is not something fixed, given once and for all; but new types of language, new language-games, as we may say, come into existence, and others become obsolete and get forgotten' (*Philosophical* §23). While the precarity of locating meaning and value within a multitude that does not remain fixed might drive one to seek for such things in the 'purity of logic', the cost is high in both cases. For the language user who seeks to secure meaning outside of language, the cost is sense. For the macroeconomic system that attempts to secure monetary value outside particular economies, the cost is fairness.

In Lieu of a Conclusion

Having articulated Wittgenstein's (and Bloomsbury's) preference for open-endedness, it would be inappropriate to end with a neat summation of Wittgenstein's legacy for queer Bloomsbury. Rather, to quote Woolf, 'One can only give one's audience the chance of drawing their own conclusions as they observe the limitations, the prejudices, the idiosyncrasies of the speaker' (*Room* 4). Woolf's words bespeak a core Bloomsbury value of critical generosity, or (sometimes ruthless) fair play in the 'commons' Bloomsbury created through its intentionally designed living, thinking and creating spaces.[9] Whether these intentionally designed spaces were brick and mortar, such as Charleston or Gordon Square, or conceptual, such as the *Nation and Athenaeum* or the Hogarth Press, they shared an ethos of purposeful living, where purpose cannot be determined by external measures, nor by inherited conventions, but rather by the action, or more precisely the arts, of living. Wittgenstein shared that ethos, although the architecture he designed (for his sister in Vienna) or the living spaces he meticulously arranged, or the discussions he hosted in his rooms at Cambridge, were more spare in line and stark of embellishment than his Bloomsbury counterparts' spaces.[10]

Starting from that ethos of critical generosity and purposeful living, we can, rather than concluding, indicate some potential pathways that open before us when we think queer and Bloomsbury and Wittgenstein together. One route returns us to the ordinary landscapes of the everyday, shifting our attention to extraordinary, remarkable, even 'queer' (in its older sense of unusual or strange) aspects of living. Another assembles reminders for the purpose of jolting us out of ruts in our thinking. We would call this the 'queer theoretical' path if not for our sense that queer theory makes up just one possible segment within a larger network of anti-foundational byways. Like trails, rather than roads, these ways are forged, altered and connected through use – not through external design. We come to know them by walking them. Importantly, for our purposes, we come to know them differently by walking them together. As idiosyncratic a person as Wittgenstein may have been, then, his philosophical practices align with Bloomsbury thinking far more than we may have previously realised. What is queerest about him, in the contemporary philosophical sense of the term, may also be what was most Bloomsbury about him – his concern for making sense of the world in a way that opens us up to possibility, rather than binds us to fixed ideas.

Notes

1. Peter Stansky and William Abrahams date the beginning of Bell's love affair with Lettice Ramsey 'autumn of 1931', which would have been more than a year after the death of Frank Ramsey (140). The Ramseys had an open marriage. When they did become lovers, Lettice and Julian also had an open relationship.
2. In *Sex and Character*, Weininger contends that 'genius declares itself to be a kind of higher masculinity, and thus the female cannot be possessed of genius' (111).
3. A good deal of *Philosophical Investigations* is concerned with 'language-games'. The first instance of the term occurs in section seven (§7) of the text.
4. Unless otherwise indicated, all citations are from the revised fourth edition of *Philosophical Investigations*.
5. For a reading of Woolf's fiction from a postmodern vantage which makes connections to Wittgensteinian thought, see Caughie.
6. Wittgenstein describes 'family resemblance' as 'a complicated network of similarities overlapping and criss-crossing: similarities in the large and in the small' (*Philosophical* §66). For antifoundational feminist readings of Wittgenstein, see O'Connor, Scheman, Scheman and O'Connor, and Heyes.
7. Owen coins the term 'aspectival captivation' in 'Genealogy as Perspicuous Representation' (82). Fausto-Sterling calculates that the frequency of intersexed births is about 1.7%, although other scientists estimate the frequency as lower – around 0.018%, based on different definitions of intersexuality. Regardless of the frequency, it is clear that intersexed people do exist, and that aspectival captivity regarding sex as exclusively binary results in many painful and often unnecessary 'normalisation' procedures being performed on intersexed infants in order to make their bodies conform to the bodily norms of one sex or the other within the binary system, or language-game, of sex difference. See Sax for the dispute about the frequency of intersexed births.
8. Melba Cuddy-Keane discusses Woolf's non-coercive narrative style at length in *Virginia Woolf, the Intellectual, and the Public Sphere*.
9. On Woolf's active cultivation of public thought in the commons, see Detloff, *The Value of Woolf*, 'Epilogue'.
10. On Wittgenstein's brief stint as an architect, see Monk 235–8.

Works Cited

Anscombe, G. E. M. 'Wittgenstein'. Letter. *Times Literary Supplement* 16 Nov. 1973.
Banfield, Ann. *The Phantom Table: Woolf, Fry, Russell and the Epistemology of Modernism*. New York: Cambridge University Press, 2000.

Bartley, William Warren, III. *Wittgenstein*. 2nd ed. LaSalle: Open Court, 1985.
Butler, Judith. *Gender Trouble*. 10th anniversary ed. New York: Routledge, 1999.
—. *Undoing Gender*. New York: Routledge, 2004.
Caughie, Pamela. *Virginia Woolf and Postmodernism: Literature in Quest and Question of Itself*. Urbana: University of Illinois Press, 1991.
Cuddy-Keane, Melba. *Virginia Woolf, the Intellectual, and the Public Sphere*. New York: Cambridge University Press, 2003.
Detloff, Madelyn. *The Value of Woolf*. New York: Cambridge University Press, 2016.
Fausto-Sterling, Ann. 'Table 3.2, Frequencies of Various Causes of Nondimorphic Sexual Development'. *Sexing the Body*. New York: Basic, 2000. 53.
Foucault, Michel. *The History of Sexuality: An Introduction*. Vol. 1. 1976. Trans. Robert Hurley. New York: Vintage, 1990.
Heyes, Cressida J. *Line Drawings: Defining Women Through Feminist Practice*. Ithaca: Cornell University Press, 2000.
Monk, Ray. *Ludwig Wittgenstein: The Duty of Genius*. New York: Penguin, 1991.
O'Connor, Peg. *Oppression and Responsibility: A Wittgensteinian Approach to Social Practices and Moral Theory*. State College: Penn State University Press, 2003.
Owen, David. 'Genealogy as Perspicuous Representation'. *The Grammar of Politics: Wittgenstein and Political Philosophy*. Ed. Cressida J. Heyes. Ithaca: Cornell University Press, 2003: 82–96.
Sax, Leonard. 'How Common Is Intersex? A Response to Anne Fausto-Sterling'. *Journal of Sex Research* 39.3 (2002): 174–8.
Scheman, Naomi. *Shifting Ground: Knowledge and Reality, Transgression and Trustworthiness*. New York: Oxford University Press, 2011.
Scheman, Naomi, and Peg O'Connor, eds. *Feminist Interpretations of Ludwig Wittgenstein*. State College: Penn State University Press, 2002.
Sedgwick, Eve Kosofsky. *Epistemology of the Closet*. Berkeley: University of California Press, 1990.
Stansky, Peter, and William Abrahams. *Julian Bell: From Bloomsbury to the Spanish Civil War*. Stanford: Stanford University Press, 2012.
Weininger, Otto. *Sex and Character*. New York: G. G. Putnam, 1906.
Wittgenstein, Ludwig. *On Certainty*. Ed. G. E. M. Anscombe and G. H. von Wright. Trans. Denis Paul and G. E. M. Anscombe. Oxford: Blackwell, 1969.
—. *Philosophical Investigations*. Rev. 4th ed. Trans. G. E. M. Anscombe, P. M. S. Hacker and Joachim Schulte. Malden: Wiley Blackwell, 2009.
—. *Philosophical Investigations*. 1st ed. Trans. G. E. M. Anscombe. Malden: Blackwell, 1953.
Woolf, Leonard. *Letters of Leonard Woolf*. Ed. Frederic Spotts. San Diego: Harvest-Harcourt, 1989.
Woolf, Virginia. 'How Should One Read a Book?' *The Second Common Reader*. Annotated ed. Ed. Andrew McNeillie. New York: Harcourt, 1986.
—. 'Modern Fiction'. *The Essays of Virginia Woolf*. Vol. 4. Ed. Andrew McNeille. London: Hogarth, 1984.
—. *A Room of One's Own*. New York: Harcourt, 1957.

Deviant Desires and the Queering of Leonard Woolf

Elyse Blankley

In 1904 Leonard Woolf received a letter from his close friend Lytton Strachey: 'Your letter was wonderful, and I was particularly impressed by the curious masculinity of it. Why are you a man? We are females, nous autres, but your mind is singularly male' (Strachey 32). The qualities in Leonard's letter that Strachey professed to admire also characterise what we might now call Bloomsbury's queer universe. Strachey's observation is playful and productively ambiguous: who, exactly, are the 'we others' in this comment? Is Strachey drawing a boundary around his Cambridge subset of talented homosexual men, including novelist E. M. Forster and economist Maynard Keynes, leaving Leonard Woolf, the heterosexual, on the periphery? Or is he rather envisioning an intimate bond between Woolf and himself, voicing his amazement that Woolf and he share a radical gendered kinship *despite* Woolf's heterosexuality? Lytton's letter sexualises their friendship by hinting at shared minds and bodies; Leonard was unlikely to reciprocate with his body, but neither would he judge or dismiss Lytton with a homophobic rebuke. Thus an interesting space opens up in the discourse between these men – not a lack but a pause, a threshold: a place of possibility.

These permeable zones of sexual desire constitute an important dimension of modernism in general and Bloomsbury modernism in particular. Because the inherent straight/gay asymmetry of Leonard's and Lytton's early friendship coexisted within the homosocial symmetry of their shared gender, their lack of mutual erotic desire could function as a queer space for writing modernist masculinity into existence. Eager to disrupt emerging *fin de siècle* prescriptions about sex and identity, Strachey helped give birth to Bloomsbury camp style, as scholars such as George Piggford and Todd Avery have explained.[1] Concurrently, Leonard was questioning heteronormativity, a topic he explores in his 1914 novel *The Wise Virgins*, which offers both conventional and contradictory portraits of masculinity that added to Bloomsbury's revolutionary sexual politics. This is not to imply that the challenges facing these men were equivalent or parallel. Nonetheless, Lytton and Leonard were each drawn to qualities in the other that were forged in response to intriguingly overlapping social conditions of repression and fear. Leonard had everything to gain by embracing his gender privilege as a heterosexual male, but his trajectory toward manhood forced him to question those guarantees. This tension is frequently occluded in critical work on Virginia Woolf's life and writing, which often places Leonard in a very *un*-queer role. Virginia, by virtue of her deep affiliation with and love for women as well as her foundational critiques of gender, embodies a shifting self that is infinitely amenable to our contemporary ideas of 'queer'. In contrast, Leonard's role seems fixed. Whether he is the strict caretaker who rigidly polices his wife's health or the long-suffering husband of a mentally unstable spouse, both are variations on a sexual binary in which the husband is patriarch to his fragile (albeit brilliant) infantilised wife. These versions ignore the fact that Leonard, particularly as a young man, spurned the oppressive role of husband/paterfamilias and searched for alternative ways to be a straight, queer man. His fictions and letters reflect both obedience to and profound dissatisfaction with the socially enforced gender ideologies that put strict and artificial boundaries on personal identity.

Queer is a fuzzy term because it can describe any identity formations that destabilise gender binaries, whether those instabilities are literally manifested in the body or linguistically registered in style (Love 745). One might well ask whether 'queer straightness' is a contradictory indulgence and a gross misappropriation because it intrinsically side-steps the word *queer*'s degrading history. It is imprecise because it is anachronistic; *queer* as a point of political recuperation and linguistic resistance post-dates the Bloomsbury Group by at least fifty years. The word's current usage carries with it utopian beliefs in a self that is always in transition, but it is burdened with a very specific history of secrecy and shame that haunted some of Bloomsbury's members (Strachey, Keynes, Grant, Forster) but not others, including Leonard Woolf. *Queer* nonetheless can help us recognise how Woolf and his friends were rethinking gender *avant la lettre*. Cambridge-Bloomsbury was archly self-aware of its unconventionality and celebrated it within the relatively safe spaces of closed doors and secret societies. It was always more than the bulwark of buggers vilified by D. H. Lawrence, the Webbs or, later, the Leavises. Woolf was not the group's only straight man but may have been the one most acutely aware of gender's role in making identity. Through his four years at Cambridge and seven years abroad as a civil servant in Ceylon, he would perfect, perform and even discard several different versions of British masculinity. In arguing that Leonard Woolf, a straight man between and among Bloomsbury's homosexual and bisexual members, was also a 'queer' man, I mean not to reinstate his heterosexual privilege but to suggest that Leonard's sense of himself as a straight male was never entirely predictable. I am emboldened to describe Woolf's shared sense of gender fluidity as queer because I believe it characterises Leonard's construction of masculinity, even when – especially when – that masculinity ostensibly conforms most closely to late-Victorian heteronormativity. Woolf carried these ideas into his colonial service, where his capacity to 'perform' as the ultimate emblem of British masculinity was continually on display in Ceylon even while he maintained a vigorous correspondence with Strachey that both enacted this model of imperial masculinity and self-consciously undercut it as well.

At Cambridge, most of Leonard's close friends were bisexual or homosexual. To our modern eyes, this is interesting but hardly remarkable; to Woolf, it would have seemed normal after his own experiences in boys' schools, which reinforced homosocial and homoerotic relations (as well as misogyny) among males. Lytton Strachey was his closest friend and confidant. Strachey's biographer, Michael Holroyd, claims Lytton's choice of Leonard as confessor during their late teens and twenties was only partially successful because Leonard was such a puritan, whom Lytton teased by suggesting, for example, that Leonard join a League for the Advancement of Social Purity (Holroyd 60). Given Lytton's puckish tone, one suspects this matter of licentiousness versus restraint was more a convention of badinage between the two men (Lee 297). A good deal of the background banter in letters between Lytton and Leonard from 1904 to 1911 is sexual – not surprising between close male friends but curious by virtue of the mismatch between their objects of desire, even as the nature and notion of desire itself overlapped. Writing was a way to transgress and paradoxically to deconstruct transgression. Leonard's letters frequently reference catamites, sodomites and 'Morocco' (their code for homosexuality), alongside flirtations with young English women fresh from the metropolis, details of erotic expatriate intrigues or laments about his dissolute slide into 'whoring' with local female prostitutes (L. Woolf, *Letters* 67, 76). He is also, at times, irritated with, ironic about, and dismissive of Lytton's attempts to transform Cambridge into Sodom (Glendinning 84). Lytton, for his part, regales his absent friend with tales of lustful conquest and unrequited desire. On 23 October 1905, he writes with delight, for instance, of the synchrony of his and Leonard's mutual sex, in response to Leonard's letter of 1 October from Ceylon describing a night of 'degraded debauch' (102), which occurred nearly simultaneously with Lytton's 'incredible rapture' in the arms of Duncan Grant, a coupling so profoundly ambiguous that Strachey couldn't be sure 'whether one was buggering, or being buggered!' (Strachey 82). Of his night of 'degraded' coupling, Leonard states, 'the pleasure of it is of course grossly exaggerated certainly with a halfcaste whore', then states, 'Are you appalled or enraged' (L. Woolf, *Letters* 102). Read together, the letters reveal layers of crossed boundaries. Lytton quite literally becomes indistinguishable in desire from Duncan but also figuratively so from Leonard, by virtue of the synchronicity. Leonard questions (half comically, half seriously) whether Lytton will be 'enraged', most obviously because he has lain with a half-caste who is also female (and not Lytton!); his tone is amused, boastful and slightly apologetic at the same time. Hermione Lee suggests that the structure of their relationship made some 'eroticism' possible between them, that their tenderness speaks to 'some androgyneity in Leonard' (297, 298). Their correspondence at times certainly confirms this. In their own way, Strachey and Woolf were probing and performing masculinity between and for – and even with – each other.[2]

Existing in tandem with their erotic difference was also the issue of caste and race, most specifically Leonard's status as culturally outside the core Bloomsbury circle. Leonard's fiction and his autobiographical writings show how he understood identity in terms of particular social markers, which in his case included his class, his sexuality, his education and especially his upbringing as a Jew: 'Most people are both proud and ashamed of their families, and nearly all Jews are proud and ashamed of being Jews' (L. Woolf, *Sowing* 196). Leonard inherited not just a particular family but the entire Jewish community, a group increasingly the object of late-Victorian and Edwardian xenophobia as large numbers of Russian Ashkenazi refugees resettled in London's crowded East End, fuelling fears of social unrest and disease. Anti-Semitism was not, of course, new. As historians Eitan Bar-Yosef and Nadia Valman have observed, '"the Jew" was overdetermined: infinitely wealthy and yet abjectly poor; refusing to assimilate and yet assuming a false English identity; cosmopolitan and tribal; "alien" and yet almost overly familiar; ideal colonizer and undesirable immigrant; white but not quite' (3). Leonard's personal circumstances would superficially seem to have offered some distance from these stereotypes as his family was relatively privileged: his father was admitted to the Bar and became a member of the prestigious Queen's Council, giving the Woolfs access to the aspirational western edge of Kensington, where they lived with the accoutrements of upper-middle-class gentility (footmen, maids and so forth). Nonetheless, the family was not fully assimilated within its class, and Leonard suffered anti-Semitism at St Paul's public school (Glendinning 34). All his life he endured what Lara Trubowitz has called the polite English version of 'civil antisemitism' (294), most famously suggested in Virginia's multiple notes to friends announcing that she'd just married a 'penniless Jew'. Leonard bore a racial marker from the first moment he entered Virginia's consciousness via her brother Thoby, who described his wonderful new Cambridge friend to her as a trembling, 'violent' and 'misanthropic' Jew (V. Woolf, 'Old Bloomsbury' 166).

In *The Wise Virgins* (1914) Leonard Woolf satirically deconstructs the stereotypical image of the Semitic interloper through his protagonist Harry Davis, whose outbursts and passionate ramblings underscore his anxious sense of otherness. Harry is romantically drawn to two young women who couldn't be more different: the first, Camilla Lawrence, is the product of a self-confident, sophisticated urban family; the other, Gwen Garland, is literally the suburban girl next door, described as a 'creature' with a 'simple outlook' on life (77). Neither is Jewish, nor is anyone else in the novel outside the Davis family. The Jew and his 'passions' are introduced early when Harry and Trevor Trevithick, a friend of and frequent visitor to the Lawrence household, discuss Camilla and her sister, Katharine, after a visit to their home. Harry probes Trevor for more information about the sisters but is met by Trevor's smiling, composed 'pale face, smooth of all passions and desires ... like the face of some sexless ascetic' (58). What follows is revealing:

> Harry turned on him. 'You're a Christian', [Harry] said contemptuously, brutally.
> 'I hope not', Trevor smiled.
> 'I'm a Jew.'
> 'Yes, I know. Well?'
> 'You can glide out of a room and I can't: I envy you that! But I despise you.... I admire your women, your pale women with their white skins and fair hair, but I despise them'. (59)

Harry's bluntness seems comically inept in the face of Trevor's sangfroid, but it also functions as a form of compensatory masculinity in the scene. In responding so heatedly, Harry exposes his passion as being both racialised and sexualised, but instead of eclipsing Trevor's cool 'sexless' Christian detachment, it only feeds Harry's alienated outrage. 'I'm a Jew': in a curious mixture of passivity and aggression, he confesses/declares he is a public spectacle – he can't just 'glide out of a room'. More than an admission of social awkwardness, this declaration also appears to suggest that his absence only calls attention to his disruptive presence as the Jew, the outsider. Simultaneously, Harry casts those around him as abject (I 'admire' but also 'despise' you and your 'pale women'), a neat substitution that underscores his own abjection. His choice of words implies that he and Trevor are men who 'have' or have control over women (as in, '*your*' women), but instead of strengthening the homosocial connection between himself and Trevor, it widens the gap that separates them, despite the fact that the scene began with Harry feeling 'extraordinarily intimate with Trevor' (58). The differences between them are confirmed when Trevor asks, 'Do most Jews feel like that?', to which Harry responds,

> 'All of them – all of them. There's no life in you, no blood in you, no understanding. Your women are cold and leave one cold – no dark hair, no blood in them. Pale hair, pale souls, you know. You talk and you talk and you talk – no blood in you! You never *do* anything.' (59, original emphasis)

What Harry senses is that Trevor and other non-Jews need not 'do' anything because they are self-contained in what they already 'know'. 'I'm a Jew.' / 'Yes, I know.' What *does* Trevor know? The unspoken issue here is the explosive presence of anti-Semitism, by which everyone 'knows' the Jew. By 'turn[ing] on' Trevor, Harry splits open a weak seam in the logic of oppression that threatens to feminise him. He exits the scene 'at a great pace', while Trevor 'walked away in the opposite direction, humming a little tune' (59).

In her Preface to the 2007 reissue of *The Wise Virgins*, Victoria Glendinning suggests that Harry faces multiple conflicts in this 'raw and angry' book, including his ambivalence about being a Jew, his distaste for his family's vulgar suburban habits and his increasingly urgent 'animal lusts', thwarted by the novel's proper young Victorian virgins (vii–xiii). These conflicts would appear to address separate issues but are in fact inextricable. Consider, for instance, the fact that Harry, a Jewish man self-consciously aware of his desires, is surrounded by Christian half-men who are either sexless, impotent, feminised, or combinations of all three. This was in fact one of Strachey's complaints about the novel, that Katharine and Camilla, two splendid women, had mostly second-rate men at their bidding (Glendinning 166). The older generation of parents is predictably neutered, and the young or youngish men in Harry's company are disembodied. Mr Macausland, the Richstead vicar, is a pompous guardian of Christian morality, easily outraged by the indecent embraces of a couple in a punt. 'Lion' Wilton, another of the Lawrence circle, possesses a woman's face and a Byronic air, but as the narrator dryly informs us, 'Hockey and women's suffrage had, however, spoilt his market, which was still fairly large among married and older women who have not entirely lost their love of submission and of being ill-treated by the male' (L. Woolf, *Wise* 99). The only exception is the barrister/literary critic Arthur Woodhouse, a suitor rejected by Camilla, whose 'fat, round little body' and 'little, round, fat mind' complement his small mental and moral stature (98, 99). Arthur accuses Harry of being passionless: 'You don't mind my saying so, but it's a characteristic of your race – they've intellect and not emotion; they don't feel things' (107). This appeal to stereotype (the 'knowledge' of the Jew that Trevor Trevithick also possesses) is performed by Arthur in front of Camilla because he sees Harry as a rival. Later, when Arthur has satisfied himself that Harry poses no threat, he gathers Harry into masculine confidence, declaring that

> 'I wonder if any woman understands what it means to a man. They don't realize that we've got bodies. That's what makes it so intolerable: unless they are loose and vile they have not passions. What's noble in us is vile in them.' (110)

To be sure, Arthur is speaking for Harry but also divulging intimacies that reveal a great deal about his view of Harry, whom he seeks to control discursively by deciding when to emasculate him and when to re-sexualise him. In this way, Harry is not only a man wrapped in his own self-important search for identity (after all, he, too, is one of the 'virgins' in the title, albeit a foolish one). He can function metonymically as sex itself, a displacement that lets other characters speak sex and knowledge under the sign of the Jew.

By the late nineteenth century, sex and race had begun to resonate within the cultural imagination with more complexity than even these scenes with Harry Davis suggest. Longstanding stereotypes about Jewish masculinity were being 'grafted onto emerging discourses of race and sexuality' (Boyarin et al. 2–3) that brought together homophobia and anti-Semitism, which took shape in two infamous miscarriages of justice: the trials and imprisonment of Alfred Dreyfus and of Oscar Wilde. Writing of this period more than fifty years later in his memoir, Woolf would claim that the Dreyfus affair in France had nearly 'cosmic' importance, as meaningful to him as the trials of Socrates and Christ:

> we already felt that we were living in an era of incipient revolt and that we ourselves were mortally involved in this revolt against a social system and code of conduct and morality which, for convenience sake, may be referred to as bourgeois Victorianism ... struggling against a religious and moral code of cant and hypocrisy which produced and condoned such social crimes and judicial murders as the condemnation of Dreyfus. (L. Woolf, *Sowing* 151–2)

If Dreyfus defined the Jew, then Wilde, as Lytton Strachey knew too well, defined the sodomite. Lytton, writing to Leonard in 1905 after seeing a Wilde play, asked Leonard,

> Do you think that someday people will wonder at [Wilde's imprisonment], as they wonder now at the story of Calas? Are we the Voltaires of the future – freers of the emotions, as he freed the intellect? Dear me! We hardly take ourselves so seriously. And the case is rather different; for what do the affections matter, so far as the world is concerned? They are only good in themselves. (Strachey 46)[3]

That Leonard and Lytton might be marginalised by intersecting patterns of prejudice was not recognised by either. Leonard would not, for example, have known of the 'secret dossier' in the Dreyfus trial that alleged Dreyfus was a homosexual as well as a traitor. Yet both Leonard and Lytton were 'queered' within public discourses of hatred, which defined Jews and homosexuals with similar contradictions. Both could be viewed as figures of sexual excess – predatory, menacing, aggressive – and, paradoxically, as figures of sexual lack – effeminate, passive. In this way, homophobia and anti-Semitism shared a vocabulary (Gervais et al. 143), which could shape populist perceptions and potentially lead to ugly consequences.[4] By increasingly defining Jews as a race and thereby biologising or naturalising their difference, *fin de siècle* anti-Semitic rhetoric used the same 'scientific' logic then being marshalled to identify sexual inversion. Anglo-European fears about unruly metropolitan Jewish or homosexual bodies could in this way be calmed if the danger posed by those bodies – which occupied a space between binary extremes – could categorically be contained by language that pathologised and hence managed these fluctuating identities (Freedman 336).

As Daniel Boyarin and others have argued, the late nineteenth-century emergence of the modern Jew and the modern homosexual is 'more than historical coincidence' ('Strange Bedfellows' 2, 3). Both gays and Jews were viewed through the same phobic lens as having threateningly permeable – that is to say, *queer* – identities.[5] They could assimilate or pass; they could not reliably be identified physically (despite the persistence of stereotypes); they could penetrate the highest places of national significance – government and finance – yet still might claim an overriding allegiance to their subgroup; they enjoyed privileges denied other minorities; they came from no clear identifiable 'place' to which they could be repatriated; they were 'geographically mobile' (Jakobsen 79). Thus Leonard and Lytton shared sexualised bodies whose desires were out of place, even if both men were only partially aware of the specific historical agents creating these ideologies. They might lust – and long for affection as well – but to what extent could either man consider his desires as 'simply' natural? How does one excavate affection from under the weight of binaries that focus instead on crudely biological acts, as the hetero/homo divide does? For Strachey, the legal regulation of homosexual bodies reconfirmed prevailing opinion that those bodies were driven by lust, not love. In 1904, Lytton wrote to Leonard of a conversation he'd had with his mother about whether some of Shakespeare's homoerotic sonnets might, as Sidney Lee had proposed, have been written for a patron or a catamite: 'I think that this is true, and of course absurd. It's quite clear to my mind that one *can* be in love with a man without having sexual feelings about him', Lytton mused. 'It really does seem the apex of idiocy to make everything turn on the wretched physical movements of our unhappy bodies – but this is the only point of the anti-sodomy movement' (Strachey 44). Strachey questions the logic that equates desire with gender identity, but despite his very real belief that the closeted, sexless 'high' sodomy of his classics tutors must be replaced with a 'low' sodomy that admits the pleasures of the body (Reed 71), he also calls those erotic acts 'degradations and horrors' (Strachey 44). The flesh would not and could not be ignored, but its pleasures still bore the legacy of Victorian morality despite proto-Bloomsbury's eagerness to reinvent its moral foundations. This paradox is legible when we remember that while at Cambridge, these young men viewed the world of ideas as 'supreme' and all physical manifestations of life, especially bodies and the trivia of living, as 'phenomena'. Strachey in fact apologises at the end of this letter, admitting that it was mostly 'phenomenal' (Strachey 45). Leonard would much later assert that this early talk was a bit of bluffing by young men who

> had all the inexperience, virginity, seriousness, intellectual puritanism of youth.... In 1914 little or no attention was paid to [G. E.] Moore's fifth chapter on 'Ethics in relation to Conduct', and pleasure, once rejected by us theoretically, had come to be accepted as a very considerable good in itself. But this was not the case in 1903. (*Sowing* 156)

Whereas Lytton's desires were culturally and legally forbidden, Leonard's were sanctioned only insofar as they conformed to expectations of caste and law. The whole of *The Wise Virgins* can be read as a referendum on straight sexual desire and gratification; it is a parodic autobiography that imagines a younger, pre-Ceylon version of Woolf who might easily have lost his nerve, as Harry Davis does, in the face of society's regulation of sexuality. More specifically, it reinforces the expectation that a good Jewish son must follow the fifth commandment and obey his parents (127), which in this case means he must not humiliate his family: 'you've disgraced me – d-d-disgraced us all' stutters Mrs Davis after Harry sleeps with a respectable young (gentile) lady (258).[6] Harry initially congratulates himself that sex with Gwen proves his successful passage into heterosexual gender identity – 'Thank God, I'm a man!' – but his relief quickly turns to disgust when the plot deteriorates into middle-class melodrama: 'I ruined her, or she ruined me – well, we ruined each other, and now we're to marry' (254, 272).

Betrayed by what Strachey would call the 'wretched physical movements of our unhappy bodies', Harry Davis is incapable of pursuing a queerer life with Camilla, although her family and friends disdain philistine morality. It is Mr Lawrence, after all, who advocates alternative domestic and erotic relationships. In retelling the story of a man whose son commits suicide after his wife runs off with someone else, Mr Lawrence opines that the son's grieving father 'thinks that chastity – where he isn't concerned – is the most important quality in a wife. Yes. *I* think we've got beyond that, and the Victorian view of marriage. Conventions, my dear Davis; I'm afraid you're still what they call hidebound by them'. (270)

Harry bristles at this suggestion although it is fundamentally true. He reclaims the moral high ground when he recognises that Mr Lawrence's radical ideas go no further than drawing-room talk (his Christian name is Acton, but he never quite acts on anything). Before 'ruining' Gwen, Harry too is a jangle of talk about passion, desire and women bearing children out of wedlock, progressive social ideas of the day that figured in works by Wells and Shaw, for instance. Now Harry can judge the Lawrences' moral cowardice more harshly than his own because at least he has acted on his passion, if not his convictions. Still, Harry cannot marry Camilla in this novel because *The Wise Virgins* can only identify what it *doesn't* want relationships to be; its protagonist can't implement alternatives. In this regard, part of Camilla's appeal is that she nudges the discourse in a very different direction. Not only does she fear the 'pettinesses and the conventionalities' of marriage, which 'seems to shut women up and out' (267), but she has made no secret of her lack of passion for Harry, as did Virginia to Leonard in response to his offer of marriage.[7] This is a deviant option beyond even Jonathan Ned Katz's important insight that sex identity is completely changed once the reproductive mandate is replaced by desire. If sex as a biblical imperative to procreate becomes instead sex for recreation, then heteronormative sex loses its teleological inevitability (Katz 13–14) and alternative, deviant or 'queer' selves can be imagined. Camilla recoils from desire and by doing so introduces the radical possibility that desire may not figure at all in intense interpersonal relationships – and, what's more, that sex, desire, procreation, reproduction and self-realisation are inconsistent with marriage, the ritual through which culture reifies heterosexuality. Desire outside marriage, intimacy without sensuality: Camilla, the wise virgin, will resonate with unexplored possibilities long after Harry's ardour for Gwen extinguishes itself.

Harry and Gwen are neither deviant nor conforming until their bodies act; and when they act, they quickly settle within a rigid gender classification. Harry may think he has been appropriately 'sexed' by this act of passion, but he has been ironically re-sexed by it because he fails to exercise any personal choice and goes along with the consequences as blindly as does Gwen, who as a late-Victorian woman isn't expected to have any choices. This slippage between desire's ability to confirm gender or to undercut it parallels the permeability of Jewish male identity in the body politic. 'Thank god, I'm a man' suggests Harry's relief at losing the burden of virginity. And yet at this moment he is already being unmanned. In a novel where Harry acts very little yet insists that Jews, unlike Gentiles, are compelled to do things (such as 'make money', as he facetiously tells Camilla), Harry begins to act – that is, to perform a role, to pass. He reframes his virile radicalism to fit the model of suburban marriage that will please his socially aspirational mother. At the same time, he may potentially incur the wrath of the Jewish patriarch who forbids miscegenation, a theme that Roger Poole has argued is never too far from the surface of this novel and which was a real issue in Leonard's marriage to Virginia.[8] For Strachey, who read the book in manuscript, the move toward marriage was inexplicable: 'One isn't prepared to feel [Harry's] decision to marry is inevitable, in his character, from what we know of him'. More important, Strachey wondered why Harry couldn't make his claim to 'having Camilla' (qtd. in Glendinning 166). Harry must either reconfigure marriage or repudiate it altogether to suit his ideals and desires, which lay beyond its scope. This mismatch is arguably the novel's central flaw. By denying Harry the complex life-experience Woolf himself had gathered in the years between 1904 and 1911, Woolf has created an anti-hero limited by lust and sentimentality in spite of his restless desire for alternatives.

Part of this failure can be attributed to the genre itself, the novel of manners and romance. Unlike the books Harry presses on Gwen – *The Master Builder*, *Crime and Punishment*, *The Idiot* and works by Conrad – this plot is recognisably Austenian in its focus on money, marriage and class. Although Harry tutors Gwen in modernity, his own ideas about desire are anchored in the ambiguous language of Victorian fiction, with repeated references to 'the romance and adventure of life' (80). From the opening pages where she is reading a book called *Youth and the Prow*, we learn Gwen is transported by 'silly novels' despite her elder sister Ethel's admonition, 'But, Gwen, dear, it's a book. I don't think I want things to happen to me like that' (8). Harry attracts Gwen because he appears to lift the veil between fiction and life; with him, she might speak 'more like people talked in books' (83) and indulge fully in 'those rare regions, which novels had opened to her in imagination', where 'life beat[s] with a quicker pulse' (207). But Harry, too, is steeped in literary conventions, although his have the sensual quality of the Pre-Raphaelite writers and painters. On the morning after his night with Gwen, we find him ecstatically reciting the opening verses of Lucretius's *De rarum natura* as well as lines from Swinburne's 'Dolores – Notre-Dame des Sept Douleurs', 'A Match' and 'The Garden of Proserpine'. Swinburne was a particular favourite of Woolf and friends at Cambridge; in 1917 Lytton recalled sitting up all night at Trinity College 'chaunting Dolores and the Forsaken Garden, until the sun rose, and we issued forth' (Strachey 340). In *Sowing*, Woolf recollects the same incident but apologises for how 'silly and sentimental' it all must seem. Nonetheless, he defends it as proof of youthful exuberance, the 'passion' of young men who haven't yet had their desires 'castrated' by maturity and disillusionment (168). A large measure of Swinburne's appeal to the proto-Bloomsberries must no doubt have been the heavy swoon of decadent desire in these poems, which are carnal, tortured, hungry and even sado-masochistic, although Woolf in later life remarked only on their wonderful 'distilled lyricism' (*Sowing* 170). 'On thy bosom though many a kiss be, / There are none such as knew it of old. / Was it Alciphron once or Arisbe, / Male ringlets or feminine gold?': the gender fluidity of passion in these lines from 'Dolores' would have resonated deeply albeit elliptically among Woolf's queer young friends, and the lines find a receptive ear in Harry, whose tortured desire for Camilla has been exchanged for a night with Gwen, now refigured as Swinburne's 'queen of pleasure' (the *belle dame sans merci*) to Harry's 'king of pain'.

One of the novel's ironies is that Camilla instructs Harry in the limits of the sex/gender system, but Harry mistranslates the lesson for Gwen, a mistake that leads to the novel's (and Harry's) climax. Gwen is susceptible to Harry's scathing analysis of bourgeois marriage, with its prohibitions that 'rule … their women's lives' (204). 'You can have a child without being one of "those women"', Harry assures her (all the while fingering the fringe of her scarf in an act that suggests sublimated foreplay) (205). The political dimension of these ideas may not have come from Harry's reading of Ibsen but from Camilla's analysis of suburban Richstead. In a righteous feminist outburst, Camilla critiques not just the boredom of the bourgeoisie but the 'injustice' of men against the 'poor pale-eyed girls … waiting, waiting for those abominable young men in straw hats and that disgusting clergyman to come up and ask them to marry them' (156). This same social system makes women like Gwen 'uneducated, purposeless, sterile – and all for them' (157). Harry appropriates part of this rhetoric, not to foster Gwen's independence but to promote his longing for the 'fierceness of love, mental and bodily', which can only be figured obliquely as 'child-bearing' (47, 46).[9] Clearly, Harry has found the limits of discourse available to him in the heterosexual romance.

The dual-sexed polarity itself is under subtle siege in the novel. On the evening he accompanies Camilla to her bus stop and chastely holds her hand, Harry floats in a romantic haze that is both overwrought ('if he died that instant … he would have died after walking by those famous elms with Camilla's hand in his') and self-critical ('Was he a fool, a damned, sentimental fool for feeling like this because he had held Camilla's hand in his for two minutes?') (168). Flushed with success and feeling 'more of a man', he encounters a prostitute in the park, whose carnality disgusts him: 'In the end she abused him in amazingly foul language, and he escaped…' (169). These discordant events leave Harry's lust in limbo. The virgin/whore trope, so influential in nineteenth-century thinking about sex and gender, exerts pressure both on Harry's view of Camilla and on his view of himself. He, too, is virginal (sentimental) and whorish (lusting), yet the terms are decoupled from their binary positive/negative valences. Woolf uses 'sentimentality' inconsistently – it can mean love, affection, emotion and deep feeling – but it is clearly a term of derision,[10] as it was among Woolf's Cambridge confrères, who reviled sentimentality because it suggested middle-brow taste and, more importantly, the culture of women. The sentimental man is degraded because he is implicitly feminised. On the other hand, the lustful man provides no countervailing site of value for Woolf during his youthful quest for masculine identity because lust degrades the spirit. These gendered (and, for Harry, racialised) qualities are further complicated by Arthur's diagnosis that Camilla really wants 'to be a man; and – damn, damn, damn – she never will be' (111). Natania Rosenfeld observes that Arthur considers Camilla so 'redundantly asexual' that she is almost masculinised (67); but one might also argue that her masculinity comes from her refusal to yield, which Harry misattributes to her hyper-femininity as a fine lady or 'Dresden china' (119). In this slippery world of masculine and feminine identities, Harry struggles to find a foothold.

The novel's one clear-eyed character is also its most sexually ambiguous: Gwen's sister Janet, a 'sporting' girl who favours tweeds and golf. Janet rebukes Harry's cowardice by embodying an unsettling counternarrative to the question of identity. Described as 'hanging like Mohammed's coffin between the nineteenth and twentieth centuries, between the soft, subservient femininity of Victorian women and the new woman not yet fully born', Janet has a 'startlingly and provocatively sexless' face and 'hardened' muscles, and her 'rough jacket and rough skirt' might 'at any moment change into trousers', revealing a 'boy of eighteen' underneath (13). With a body that resists classification and a mind indifferent to cant and hypocrisy, Janet can see through Harry's impotent posturing as the man who both tarnishes and saves her sister. 'I don't think you're a cad, but I believe you behaved like one … you're a jolly sight too clever, Harry, that's what's wrong with you' (281). As a woman who eschews motherhood by choice, not by chance, Janet finds integrity and self-fulfilment outside the heterosexual order, from which she can neutralise Harry's lust and critique his romanticism. 'My good fellow, don't let's get sentimental', she responds tartly to Harry's presumption that she despises him (281). Were the novel simply a parade of Gwen-like women, Harry's maladjustment to the bi-sexed social order would seem nothing more than a case of nerves over the prospect of growing up and moving on. But women like Janet and Camilla relieve the pressure in Harry's thinking that's as tightly locked as two continental plates. Here is where even Lytton's conciliatory suggestions to improve the manuscript could not help, because Lytton would want Harry to 'have' Camilla within a system of exchange value, when in point of fact Woolf recognises how heterosexual sentiment and desire demand re-imagined social arrangements and a language more radical than the one Harry currently speaks.

Some biographical facts put this difference between Woolf and Strachey in an interesting light. In 1909, Lytton began to lobby long distance for Leonard, in Ceylon, to marry Virginia. The marriage didn't happen until 1912, but as soon as Leonard told Lytton in 1909 that he would press his suit with Virginia, Lytton responded

> You are perfectly wonderful, and I want to throw my arms around your neck.... Isn't it odd that I've never really been in love with you? And I suppose I never shall.... The day before yesterday I proposed to Virginia. As I did it, I saw that it would be death if she accepted me, and I managed, of course, to get out of it. (Strachey 173)

This odd letter reveals much about Lytton's guilt, anxiety, vanity and ambivalence toward Leonard's heterosexual suitability for marriage, an institution that Lytton describes in clearly misogynistic terms:

> If I were either greater or less I could have done it and could either have dominated and soared and at last made her completely mine, or I could have been contented to go without everything that makes life important. (173)

Women are to be dominated, heterosexual males are to be libidinally disowned: the plot only thickens when we realise that both Lytton and Leonard were arguably in 'love' with Virginia's brother Thoby, who died in 1906, thereby making this triangle an incestuous quadrangle of sorts.

In later years, Woolf said he 'could never think of plots' for stories (*Downhill* 90), and his fiction hews closely to his own experiences. This is true of *The Wise Virgins*, but only up to a point. Although the novel fails to reconcile spiritual selfhood with sexual passion, its value may lie in what it doesn't or won't say about alternatives, at the very moment Leonard stood at the cusp of his own fruitful and eccentric marriage. The context of queer Cambridge–Bloomsbury, especially his intimacy with Lytton Strachey, had given him breathing room to rethink his gender and race, behind his closely guarded façade of Enlightenment rationalism. The answers were not clear, but the questions were the gift of his youthful friendships and his entry into a new world with Virginia.

Notes

1. See Piggford, 'Camp Sites', and Avery, 'Nailed', in the present volume.
2. In his Double Preface to *Lytton Strachey: The New Biography*, Michael Holroyd pointedly wonders why Woolf's own autobiography 'silently passed over the fact that so many of his friends were homosexuals' (xxx). The editor of *Encounter* asked this in a questionnaire sent to Woolf and other critics/chroniclers. Woolf replied that his friends' sexuality was irrelevant to his autobiography, especially because he wasn't gay. Moreover, he had no desire to 'reveal facts which might be painful to living people unless it was absolutely vital to mention them' (Holroyd xxx and 706n10). Woolf's privileging of his allegiance to his friends speaks to core liberal humanist Bloomsbury values. Woolf's omissions also 'straighten' Bloomsbury for a 1960s audience primed by the Leavises to regard it as insular and decadent.
3. Describing emotions as only 'good in themselves' bears the imprint of G. E. Moore's *Principia Ethica*, which powerfully influenced Woolf's generation of Cambridge Apostles. Calas was an eighteenth-century Huguenot convicted by a Catholic court in France and broken on the wheel for allegedly killing his son, whose shameful suicide the family was hoping to protect. Voltaire led the legal campaign to have Calas exonerated posthumously, much as Zola, who published his famous defence of Dreyfus entitled 'J'accuse', argued for Dreyfus's exoneration (Zola's outburst led to his own imprisonment for defamation).
4. For a complex historical analysis of the way anti-Semitism stereotypes Jewish male sexuality as excessive or defective, see Boyarin, *Unheroic Conduct*.
5. In *Modernity and the Holocaust*, Zygmunt Bauman calls this the 'viscosity' of the Jew, who serves as an emblem of modernity because of the Jew's fluctuating meanings that elude stable categories (40; qtd. in Schröder 299).
6. Mrs Davis's brother Oscar also ruined a girl, but she rationalises that something 'had gone wrong with him', and he was shipped off to America. The implication here is that the woman in question was lower class and not a member of the social set with whom the family was trying to ingratiate itself. In contrast, 'Nothing had gone wrong with Harry; he was honest, upright, moral' (264).
7. Virginia confessed to Leonard shortly before their marriage that 'I feel angry sometimes at the strength of your desire. Possibly, your being a Jew comes in also at this point. You seem so foreign' (1 May [1912]; V. Woolf, *Letters* 496).
8. Poole, 74–102. Schröder more specifically identifies Leonard's anxiety about miscegenation as the curse of his own deceased paternal grandfather, whose will stipulated that heirs who married outside Judaism would be disinherited (312).
9. Edward Arnold, Woolf's publisher, demanded that Woolf omit language deemed too coarse for the reading public. Woolf refused to alter the 'question of children discussed by Gwen & Harry'; to do so would render 'Gwen's act at the crisis [to be] one of mere lust' (L. Woolf, *Letters* 199).
10. The exception is, ironically, Harry's assertion to Camilla that 'the only thing that a Jew is sentimental about is Judaism' (127).

Works Cited

Avery, Todd. 'Nailed: Lytton Strachey's Jesus Camp'. *Queer Bloomsbury*. Ed. Brenda S. Helt and Madelyn Detloff. Edinburgh: Edinburgh University Press, 2016. 172–88.

Bar-Yosef, Eitan, and Nadia Valman, eds. *'The Jew' in Late-Victorian and Edwardian Culture: Between the East End and East Africa*. London: Palgrave, 2009.

Boyarin, Daniel. *Unheroic Conduct: The Rise of Heterosexuality and the Invention of the Jewish Man*. Berkeley: University of California Press, 1997.

Boyarin, Daniel, Daniel Itzkovitz and Ann Pellegrini, eds. *Queer Theory and the Jewish Question*. New York: Columbia University Press, 2004.

Boyarin, Daniel, Daniel Itzkovitz and Ann Pellegrini. 'Strange Bedfellows: An Introduction'. Boyarin et al. 1–18.

Freedman, Jonathan. 'Coming Out of the Jewish Closet with Marcel Proust'. Boyarin et al. 334–64.

Gervais, Pierre, Romain Huret and Pauline Peretz. 'Une relecture du "dossier secret": homosexualité et antisémitisme dans l'affaire Dreyfus'. *Revue d'histoire modern et contemporaine* 55.1(2008): 125–60.

Glendinning, Victoria. *Leonard Woolf: A Biography*. New York: Free, 2006.

Holroyd, Michael. *Lytton Strachey: The New Biography*. New York: Farrar, 1994.

Jakobsen, Janet R. 'Queers Are Like Jews, Aren't They? Analogy and Alliance Politics'. Boyarin et al. 64–89.

Katz, Jonathan Ned. *The Invention of Heterosexuality*. 1995. Chicago: University of Chicago Press, 2007.

Lee, Hermione. *Virginia Woolf*. New York: Knopf, 1998.

Love, Heather. 'Introduction to the Cluster on Modernism: "Modernism at Night"'. *PMLA* 124.3 (2009): 744–8.

Piggford, George. 'Camp Sites: Forster and the Biographies of Queer Bloomsbury'. *Queer Forster*. Ed. Robert K. Martin and George Piggford. Chicago: University of Chicago Press, 1997. 89–112. Rpt. in *Queer Bloomsbury*. Ed. Brenda Helt and Madelyn Detloff. Edinburgh: Edinburgh University Press, 2016. 64–88.

Poole, Roger. *The Unknown Virginia Woolf*. Atlantic Highlands: Humanities, 1982.

Reed, Christopher. 'Bloomsbury as Queer Subculture'. *The Cambridge Companion to the Bloomsbury Group*. Ed. Victoria Rosner. Cambridge: Cambridge University Press, 2014. 71–89.

Rosenfeld, Natania. *Outsiders Together: Virginia and Leonard Woolf*. Princeton: Princeton University Press, 2000.

Schröder, Leena Kore. 'Tales of Abjection and Miscegenation: Virginia Woolf's and Leonard Woolf's "Jewish" Stories'. *Twentieth-Century Literature* 49.3 (2003): 298–327.

Strachey, Lytton. *The Letters of Lytton Strachey*. Ed. Paul Levy. London: Penguin, 2006.

Trubowitz, Lara. 'Concealing Leonard's Nose: Virginia Woolf, Modernist Antisemitism, and "The Duchess and the Jeweller"'. *Twentieth-Century Literature* 54.3 (2008): 273–306.

Woolf, Leonard. *Downhill All the Way: An Autobiography of the Years 1919–1939*. San Diego: Harcourt, 1967.
—. *Letters of Leonard Woolf.* Ed. Frederic Spotts. San Diego: Harcourt, 1989.
—. *Sowing: An Autobiography of the Years 1880–1904*. London: Hogarth, 1960.
—. *The Wise Virgins: A Story of Words, Opinions, and a Few Emotions*. 1914. New Haven: Yale University Press, 2007.
Woolf, Virginia. *The Letters of Virginia Woolf*. Ed. Nigel Nicolson and Joanne Trautmann. Vol. 1. New York: Harcourt, 1975. 6 vols. 1975–80.
—. 'Old Bloomsbury'. *Moments of Being: Unpublished Autobiographical Writings*. Ed. Jeanne Schulkind. London: University of Sussex Press, 1976.

Clive Bell, 'a fathead and a voluptuary': Conscientious Objection and British Masculinity

Mark Hussey

> [M]any people still regard the CO's as a bit queer, but it was a queerness they could tolerate.
>
> Harold Frederick Bing, reel 11

> Any English boy born with fine sensibility, a peculiar feeling for art, or an absolutely first-rate intelligence finds himself, from the outset, at loggerheads with the world in which he is to live. For him there can be no question of accepting those conventions which express what is meanest in an unsympathetic society.... The hearty conventions of family life ... arouse in him nothing but a longing for escape ... all his finer feelings will be constantly outraged; and he will live, a truculent, shame-faced misfit, with *John Bull* under his nose and *Punch* round the corner, till, at some public school, a course of compulsory games and the Arnold tradition either breaks his spirit or makes him a rebel for life.
>
> Clive Bell, 'Order and Authority II', 131–2

'We were all C. O.'s in the Great war', wrote Virginia Woolf in an unpublished memoir of her nephew Julian Bell (Q. Bell, *Virginia* 258). While not strictly true (Leonard Woolf, for example, was not a conscientious objector), her remark summarises the prevailing ethos among members of Old Bloomsbury towards the First World War. Julian's father, Clive Bell, played an active and persistent part in the emergence into public consciousness of the figure of the CO during the First World War, but his involvement has to a large extent been eclipsed both by his more familiar identification as an art critic and by the tendency of his friends and contemporaries, including Woolf herself and Lytton Strachey, to disparage him as a *bon vivant* and philanderer.

Clive Bell, however, was a 'rebel for life'. His tireless championing of individual liberty as the paramount value of political and social organisation, and of subjective experience as the only proper basis for aesthetics, pervades his writings on art, society, history and politics. His cast of mind changed very little with circumstances, carrying him from proselytising for the radically new art of the early twentieth century to pacifism before and during the First World War, on to excoriating the puritanical strictures of post-war England and into appeasement and stubborn adherence to untenable ideals in the late 1930s and the Second World War period. In his close identification with the CO issue, Bell is representative of Bloomsbury's challenge to heteronormativity and the patriarchal family: as Lois Bibbings explains, the CO was regarded as 'an unnatural man, a pointless man, an aberration who is not only unmanly and possibly an invert, but is also less than a woman' ('Images' 347).

My title comes from a post-war spat between Bell and Bernard Shaw in the *New Republic* initiated by Bell's derisive criticism of Shaw's *Back to Methuselah*. Shaw began his rebuttal by calling Bell 'a fathead and a voluptuary' ('Shaw's Comment' 361). In 'The Creed of an Aesthete', Bell wrote that

> the people who really care for beauty do not care for it because it comes from God or leads to anything. They care for it in itself; what is more, that is how they care for all the fine things in life. (241)

The doctrine of art for art's sake had long been closely associated with Oscar Wilde, whose aphorisms and, in particular, introduction to *The Picture of Dorian Gray* had come under withering attack by Edward Carson, counsel for the Marquess of Queensberry whom Wilde sued for libel in 1895 (Holland 80 and *passim*). Wilde's notorious claim that 'There is no such thing as a moral or an immoral book' (Holland 80) is reflected in the 'aesthetic emotion' central to Bell's *Art* (published in February 1914) that carries the perceiver out of life and into ecstasy. The public quarrel between Shaw and Bell is entertaining, but Shaw's description of Bell as a 'voluptuary' might have recalled for many readers the late-Victorian English anxiety over proper masculinity and fears of degeneration still prevalent in the first decade of the twentieth century. Some readers of the *New Republic* in 1922 might have also remembered a well-known sketch by the *Punch* cartoonist Leonard Raven-Hill titled 'A Voluptuary' that appeared in the late nineteenth-century compendium *Pick-Me-Up*. The voluptuary depicted clearly suggests the figure of Oscar Wilde (Figure 12). A 4 May 1918 cartoon by Frank Holland in the bellicose *John Bull* depicted the conscientious objector as what Bibbings describes as 'a dandified figure, bearing a passing resemblance both to Wilde and to L. Raven-Hill's sketch' ('Images' 346). Headed 'AN "OBJECT" LESSON', the caption is

A VOLUPTUARY
"To rise, to take a little opium, to sleep till lunch, and after again to take a little opium, and sleep till dinner, *that* is a life of pleasure."
By L. Raven Hill

Figure 12. Leonard Raven-Hill, 'A Voluptuary', *Pick-Me-Up* 12.288 (1894): 233. The caption reads 'To rise, to take a little opium, to sleep till lunch, and after again to take a little opium, and sleep till dinner, *that* is a life of pleasure.'

'This little pig stayed at home' (Bibbings, *Telling* 102). 'The "pig" objector is depicted as a floppy haired, dandified figure, lazing whilst others around him labour for the war' (116). Calling Bell a 'voluptuary', then, summoned both an iconography and a discourse that put in question 'proper' masculinity in the context of war-making.[1]

Christopher Clark observes a 'crisis of masculinity' (358) evident in the writings emanating from those European chancelleries that took the world to war in the summer of 1914. It is 'striking', he continues, 'how often the key protagonists appealed to pointedly masculine modes of comportment and how closely these were interwoven with their understanding of policy' (359). The 'invocations of *fin-de-siècle* manliness are so ubiquitous in the correspondence and memoranda of these years that it is difficult to localize their impact. Yet they surely reflect a very particular moment in the history of European masculinity' (359–60). By the 1890s, fears of degeneracy, crystallised in many respects by the Wilde trial, led to a reaction against the codes of gentlemanly behaviour that had been promulgated by, for example, Newman and Mill. Newman, after all, had described 'gentleness and effeminacy of feeling' (210) as necessary to the civilisation that his *Idea of a University* sought to foster. In *Manful Assertions*, Michael Roper and John Tosh also refer to a 'crisis in masculinity' as 'precisely what many male office clerks experienced in the late Victorian period, as they saw their somewhat ambivalent occupational status undermined still further by the recruitment of female office clerks' (19). Drawing on the work of Richard N. Price, Roper and Tosh assert that 'it was men from just this kind of background who formed the mainstay of the Jingo crowd' (19). A young man educated in a British public school at the end of the nineteenth century, then, was inculcated with notions of 'proper' masculinity that stood ready to be appealed to in a time of war. Peter Parker has explained that by 1914, 'notions of chivalry and patriotic duty combined with the various other elements of the public-school ethos to inspire a generation' (105). At Marlborough, which Clive Bell attended from 1895 to 1899, 'the public-school code of conformity was clearly in operation ... according to the official history of the school's O[fficer] T[raining] C[orps], "by 1913 almost every able-bodied boy had joined"' (Parker 65).

It is, therefore, not surprising that in July 1914 Ottoline Morrell described some of her Bloomsbury friends (among them Eddie Marsh and Lytton Strachey) as 'desperately jingo, longing to rush in to the war at once' (Seymour 195). Clive Bell, in Jonathan Atkin's account,

> described the prospect of war to [James][2] Strachey as like being a compulsory spectator at a university match – a match which was expected to last for three years. The only way of mitigating the boredom was to come down from the terraces and 'take a hand in the game'. (Atkin 32)

Bell had expressed an interest in applying 'for a possible job in the Army Medical or Service Corps' (Atkin 32), but James Strachey told him in September 1914 that the War Office was not looking for any recruits (J. Strachey). A week before Strachey wrote, John Waller ('Jack') Hills, the widower of Vanessa Bell's half-sister Stella, had written to Clive that the best he could do would be to ensure that his application to the War Office was not overlooked, but that he had no influence and that, in any case, there was not even any use for himself at that time (Hills).[3]

When it became apparent, early in the course of the First World War, that the volunteer army upon which Britain prided itself would be inadequate to the government's aims, propaganda was necessary to impel a sense of moral obligation to sign up. And when it quickly became clear that such obligation would not suffice, conscription was introduced, in 1916, following the failure of the Derby scheme. With conscription came the recognition that there was a fundamental contradiction between 'fighting for freedom' and compelling young men to do so: hence, the conscience clause. As Lois Bibbings has pointed out, conscientious objectors comprised only 0.33% of men who were conscripted, but the widespread attention brought about by their publications and by coverage in the press has given them a prominent place in the history of the war (Bibbings, 'Images' 341).

To ensure that only the most tenacious and thick-skinned men would avail themselves of the conscience clause, the CO was feminised and pilloried in the jingo press, and his supporters regarded as seditious elements who must be suppressed to preserve the nation. Cartoons such as those that appeared in *John Bull* and the *Daily Sketch* represented the CO as what Bibbings terms a 'cultural criminal', shirking not only his responsibility as a soldier but,

Figure 13. Archibald English, 'The Conscientious Objector at the Front!', 1916 postcard

implicitly, as a man (Figure 13). Bibbings points out how frequently the local tribunals to which those claiming a conscientious objection to the war had first to apply commented on the applicant's 'presumed moral degeneracy and cowardice or laziness' ('Images' 346).

Talk of conscription long preceded the declaration of war,[4] but by August 1914 it was being debated in Parliament in earnest. In the preface to his 1917 parliamentary history of the conscription debate, Richard Lambert wrote that 'Voluntary service lies at the root of Liberalism, just as Conscription is the true weapon of Tyranny' (iv). Clifford Allen, co-founder of the No Conscription Fellowship, believed that conscription embodied the philosophy that 'exalt[ed] the State as an entity, distinct from its citizens', one of the causes of war (Graham 22). In January 1915, Clive Bell told the readers of the *Nation* that during the previous three months he had spoken with numerous young men of the middle and wage-earning class who did not feel a moral obligation to join the army. 'As the quintessential symbol of Britain's domestic freedom', according to Nicoletta Gullace, 'the volunteer army was a cornerstone of Liberal commitment to consensual governance' (7). The ensuing months of 1915 would see the sinking of the *Lusitania* (on 7 May), the publication of the Bryce Report on German atrocities in Belgium, fuelling the gendered narratives of savagery against women and children that the British press used to shame men into service, and continuation of the zeppelin raids that had begun in England that January. As the Brocks write in their edition of the letters of H. H. Asquith to Venetia Stanley, the conviction that 'Prussianism' must be stamped out and 'the war fought to a finish whatever the cost' led the Conservatives in the British government to doubt whether 'Asquith and his Liberal colleagues [were] capable of ruthless, "all out" war-making. Conscription was the touchstone' (Asquith 597). Bell argues against conscription in terms that echo the pervasive internationalism characteristic of liberal thinking in the early twentieth century: 'The difficulty of patriotism has ever been that it makes morality conterminous [*sic*] with frontiers' (Bell, *Nation* 16 Jan. 1915). He thus aligns with the thinking of, for example, Margaret Llewelyn Davies, secretary of the Women's Co-operative Guild. The 'Woman's Page' of the *Co-operative News* called for a 'true patriotism' that 'is only expressed rightly when it sets out to safeguard the whole world instead of one bit of it' (qtd. in Berman 129). Bibbings recounts the anecdote of CO Arthur Gardiner, who said at his tribunal hearing, when challenged about his patriotism, 'I have no country' (Bibbings, *Telling* 61).

In his letter, Bell points out that some of his writings could be published in Germany but not in England, where censorship and puritanism would prevent it. The greater political freedom that obtains in England may be of less relevance to 'things that have absolute value' than the freedom to say and do what one likes. Furthermore, 'the spectacle of the rich and old, with their instinctive patriotism and great possessions, forcing to the front a reluctant and rational proletariat would be a not very edifying spectacle' (Bell, *Nation* 16 Jan. 1915). Or, as Lytton Strachey would say succinctly to his brother James in March 1916, 'God blast, confound, and fuck the Upper Classes' (L. Strachey 27).

In this and subsequent letters, Bell adumbrates the argument which he lays out in *Peace at Once*, a pamphlet published by the National Labour Press in September 1915. His position, as one would expect from someone who had initially been ready to take part, is not against war in general, but against this war; it is not even against those who wish to go and fight, but it is vehemently against the notion that the government has the right to 'send men to die for the things in which [the government] believes', for if this right were to be granted then the government would have 'over them precisely the same right that the owner has over his slave – the power of life and death' (Bell, *Nation* 16 Jan. 1915). H. W. Massingham, the editor of the *Nation*, drily responded in a note at the foot of Bell's letter that Bell was mistaken to see no difference between the German and British governments as they were currently constituted.

That summer, Bell again wrote to the *Nation*. If conscription is instituted, 'we shall emerge from the war with a full-fledged military system controlled by the governing class' (*Nation* 26 June 1915). By the autumn of 1915, Bell was a 'marked man' (Atkin 33), joining others who had run afoul of the Defence of the Realm Act and whose works had been confiscated and destroyed. By then, London had become 'the worst of jingo places' (Millman 57). Open meetings of pacifists had become impossible, under threat of violent disruption. Printers, publishers and other businesses were wary of any connection to dissident movements, but in Manchester the National Labour Press was willing to disseminate pacifist literature. Bell's was one of several publications confiscated and ordered destroyed following a raid on the National Labour Press offices and a subsequent raid on the London offices of the Independent Labour Party. The initial moves toward censorship had come at the instigation of the Unionist MP Sir Edward Carson (who had cross-examined Oscar Wilde in 1895), the Attorney-General in Asquith's coalition government (Millman 64–5). Bell did not attend the trial in Manchester but was one of 'nineteen owners of publications taken from the ILP's London office who answered a summons to the Mansion House on 13 September' (Beechey 8). On that occasion the Lord Mayor, Sir John Knill, again ordered destruction of *Peace at Once*.

Bell's letter to the *Nation* published on 4 September 1915 (dated 25 August) concerning the destruction of his pamphlet appears below one from 'A. G. W.', who wrote from York that 'an enforced silence is frequently mistaken for agreement with a policy which we loathe'. A. G. W. expressed worry about 'the Prussianizing of free England'. For his part, Bell also pointed out that the suppression of his pamphlet should concern 'those who hold that the particular brand of tyranny under which Germans are said to groan is more evil and oppressive than that which we enjoy in this country'. Does the *Nation* still believe, in light of this suppression of free speech, 'that we are fighting for freedom?' (Bell, *Nation* 4 Sept. 1915). On the same day, the *New Statesman* published a letter from Bell in which he argued that if the *New Statesman* agreed his pamphlet should have been suppressed, then 'it is a good deal less tolerant than the German Government' (Bell, *New Statesman* 4 Sept. 1915). Returning to an earlier theme, Bell restated his belief that the German government was more liberal than the English 'in matters of Art, Thought, Morals and Religion'.

Such a point of view was not unusual among Bloomsbury intellectuals and artists. Duncan Grant, for example, told his father in 1916 that he

> had become I suppose in a sense unpatriotic, as most artists must do. I began to see that one's enemies were not vague masses of foreign people, but the mass of people in one's own country and the mass of people in the enemy country, and that one's friends were people of true ideas that one might meet and did meet in every country one visited. (Skidelsky 326)

When James Strachey at his tribunal hearing said that he would be willing to 'repel savages, negroes' but not to repel Germans, the bewildered chairman turned to John Maynard Keynes, whom Strachey had brought as a character witness, for an explanation of what he meant. Keynes asserted that he did not agree with Strachey's view:

> I do not think it is very reasonable. I do not share Mr Strachey's views, but I see it is an opinion that could be held, among civilised peoples – as to the actual degree of civilisation of the Germans I have a different opinion – but that for people who have the customs of Western Europe, it is a great moral evil to act in this way. (Sherbo 338)

A week after Bell's letter about the destruction of *Peace at Once*, Bernard Shaw wrote to the *Nation* in Bell's defence. In all wars, he said, both sides assume that men will 'submit rather than die', but there must come a point at which one country determines that what was worth dying for is no longer worth dying for.[5] Surely Mr Bell was right to expect 'all freeborn Englishmen to rally round freedom of the press' because such liberty is supposedly one of the crowning values which Britain is fighting to preserve? However, Shaw concludes that he had better keep his own ideas about 'what England ought to do' 'safe in my desk' as evidently some ideas are not allowed to be heard. In the *New Statesman*, E. S. P. Haynes pointed to Bell's apparent 'blissful ignorance' of the fact that a similar pamphlet under German rule would 'instantly result in his being shot or hanged' (Haynes, *New Statesman* 11 Sept. 1915). Haynes had perhaps not read *Peace at Once*, where Bell acknowledges that what he is writing is 'not far short of a hanging matter' (*Peace* 20).[6] Another correspondent that day, writing from Bloomsbury's Mecklenburgh Square, pointed out that the 'secret trial and sentence of death' pronounced on Bell's pamphlet would result only in more interest in whatever he wrote next. The government has 'chosen to destroy a certain writing instead of trying to answer it' (Bracher, *New Statesman* 11 Sept. 1915). G. K. Chesterton returned to the attack in the *Nation* on 18 September, eliciting another defence of Bell from Shaw the following week, where he wrote that 'when you do get down to these plain facts of sin and death, Mr Clive Bell was right' (Shaw, *Nation* 25 Sept. 1915).

In *Peace at Once* Bell attacks generalisation, abstraction, just as Virginia Woolf does in her 1917 sketch 'The Mark on the Wall' (Hussey 19). With wit and verve, Bell skewers the pomposities by which politicians seek to justify their orders that young men should leave their lives behind and go to war:

> A nation has no reality apart from the individuals that compose it. Therefore when you speak of 'the English', 'English honour', 'English interests', either you mean Englishmen, women, and children, their honours, their interests, or you mean nothing. This is just what most politicians and journalists do mean. They are for ever prating of an abstraction called 'the English nation', which, apparently, has little or nothing to do with the people who live in England. For that abstraction they are willing to sacrifice everything, except, perhaps, themselves. It is as though a shepherd should believe that there was such a thing as *a flock of sheep* which had a real existence of its own quite apart from the sheep that composed it. (*Peace* 19)[7]

Generalising is essential to war-making, as are abstractions. But Bell asks his readers to think of a nation as comprising people – people like 'James Smith, a gardener, his wife and three children' (*Peace* 20). For Bell, the greatest casualty of war was individual liberty: in the late 1930s, he would claim in *Warmongers* (1938) that any war was indistinguishable from, or even worse than, tyranny.

Nicoletta Gullace has argued that 'the denigration of the unenlisted man, the pacifist, and the conscientious objector was central to disrupting a notion of citizenship based on manhood alone' (6). Soon after the introduction of conscription, 'a broad array of commentators began to cry for the disenfranchisement of conscientious objectors, whose ability to vote was an insult to the logic that grounded citizenship in military service' (8). Bell points out in *Peace at Once* that treaties had often been violated in the past without nations going to war, and so the political reasons offered for the conflict were disingenuous. The political rationalisations for war in 1914 had very early on begun to merge with a discourse that emphasised the need to protect women and children, to preserve a notion of 'the home' that had its roots in the Victorian ideology of separate spheres. As Gullace explains, 'In the press and in popular imagination, the invasion of Belgium was transformed into the rape of Belgium, an image that informed the entire iconography of the war' (24). Propaganda had 'summoned up the specter of ruined Belgium and hinted darkly at the possibility of invasion – an invasion that would mean the rape and mutilation of British women and children' (Gullace 37). Therefore, there should be no need for compulsory military service because British men would volunteer to do their duty *as men* and defend women and children: 'the mere specter of an attack upon the family seemed to justify the abandonment of free choice and to render incontestable the claim upon men of military age' (Gullace 108).

In November 1917 COs were stripped of the franchise (Gullace 180) and in the context of the debate that followed, the gendered binary that had simply separated men from women was disrupted by what Gullace calls 'the "other" within a new binarism, based not upon sexual difference but upon differential service' (181). Conscientious objectors came to replace 'defenseless women' 'as the symbolic and literal embodiment of the non-citizen' (Gullace 182). The idealised patriarchal family seems, therefore, to be a necessary concomitant to war-making, and if men do not 'do their duty', if they even resist compulsion, then such men must be placed beyond the boundary of the masculine so as to preserve the family structure upon which the rationale for war depends. Judith Butler's commentary on Hegel's reading of *Antigone* demonstrates this structure's deep-rootedness in western culture:

> [Hegel] argues that the ideal is for the family to furnish young men for war, those who come to defend the boundaries of the nation, who come to confront one another in the life and death struggle of nations, and who ideally come to reside under a legal regime in which they are to some degree abstracted from the national *Sittlichkeit* that structures their participation. (Butler 12)

But Antigone disrupts this mechanism by putting family before the interests of the state, and thus is guilty of 'a criminal individualism' (Butler 36) that must be punished.

> The effort to pervert by feminine means the universality for which the
> state stands is thus crushed by a countermovement of the state, one
> that not only interferes with the happiness of the family but enlists the
> family in the service of its own militarization. The state receives its
> army from the family, and the family meets its dissolution in the state.
> (Butler 36)

Hegel, however, shifts his attention from Antigone herself to a generalised notion of womankind and by doing so he 'performs the very generalization that Antigone resists, a generalization according to which Antigone can only be held criminal and that, consequently, effaces her from Hegel's text' (Butler 36).

Butler's argument primarily concerns the implications of *Antigone* for family structure and kinship, rather than being concerned with war, though it does demonstrate how they are imbricated. It is illuminating to see how the *Antigone* is more than a story of individual resistance to state power, but lays bare also the gendered nature of that power. The war resisters in whose name Bell spoke throughout the First World War confronted a logic that excluded them *as men* from a family structure that required them to offer themselves as sacrifice or avenger in a conflict that necessarily removed them from the very structure their presence in it would seem to have been necessary to sustain.

By mid-1916, two Military Service Acts had been passed, and the hastily established system of local tribunals was hearing the applications of anyone claiming an exemption from the required call-up. Bell threw himself into this debate with vigour. He asked for Vanessa Bell's opinion of a memorandum he had written for Asquith on the treatment of conscientious objectors, and met with Lloyd George and other members of the Cabinet to give his opinion on the matter (Atkin 49n69). To Vanessa, he acknowledged that his views might not be popular among the more ardent pacifists, but as he had conferred with both Clifford Allen and Bertrand Russell he believed his position was sound. Lytton Strachey rather snootily wrote to his brother James in May 1916 that although Russell and Allen did support Bell, 'they did not want it supposed that he represented anything' (qtd. in Atkin 49–50n69). Such disparagement of Bell by his Bloomsbury contemporaries was not unusual. In 1905, for example, Strachey had described Bell as follows:

> His character has several layers, but it is difficult to say which is the *fond*. There is the country gentleman layer, which makes him retire into the depths of Wiltshire to shoot partridges. There is the Paris decadent layer, which takes him to the quartier latin where he discusses painting and vice with American artists and French models. There is the eighteenth-century layer, which adores Thoby Stephen. There is the layer of innocence which adores Thoby's sister. There is the layer

of prostitution, which shows itself in an amazing head of crimped straw-coloured hair. And there is the layer of stupidity, which runs transversely through all the other layers. (Holroyd, *Strachey* 59)

In the spring of 1916, Bell wrote frankly to his wife about what she should do to maintain her household if he were sent to prison. Despite an 'unhealed rupture' preventing him from being called to active duty, Bell was still required by the Military Service Act to render his services to the nation. Shaw, whose 'Common Sense About the War' had elicited widespread vituperation (Holroyd, *Shaw* 354f), recommended to Bell that he 'yield to the conscience of the community and see the military business through from the inside' (Holroyd, *Shaw* 365) after Bell had written to ask if he would write a letter to the tribunal on his behalf.[8] In May 1916, after initially being denied by the tribunal at Blything, Duncan Grant and David Garnett were granted the exemption that allowed them to apply to the Central Tribunal for alternative employment. In September 1916, the Central Tribunal granted them non-combatant status but the Pelham Committee, which had been set up to advise the Central Tribunal on alternative employment for COs, did not approve their farm work at Wissett Lodge, the property that had been provided by the bequest of a deceased aunt of Grant's (Spalding, *Bell* 149). This turn of events led to Vanessa Bell taking the lease on Charleston so that Grant and Garnett would be able to fulfil their required non-combatant work (Spalding, *Grant* 188f). Vanessa visited the leaseholder, a Mr Stacey, in September 1916, reporting to Duncan that 'Mrs. Stacey and I hated each other instinctively and she revealed to me the present state of mind of the British nation and why we want to go on with the war and why mothers like their sons to be killed' (Spalding, *Grant* 191).

Eight members of the No Conscription Fellowship's executive were convicted on 17 May 1916. In that day's *Daily News* appeared a letter from Clive Bell stating that he had been 'negotiating incessantly for a modus vivendi', and that shortly before Easter his recommendations had received sympathetic attention from 'some of the leading members of the Cabinet' (Bell, *Daily News* 17 May 1916). The following week, he wrote again to explain in more detail his idea that a committee 'composed of men who are in general sympathy with the war policy of the Government, but who understand the nature of a conscientious objection' should advise the Central Tribunal (Bell, *Daily News* 22 May 1916). Clive explained to Vanessa that much of his time was taken up meeting with anti-conscriptionists and in writing letters, because he believed in the importance of keeping the issue in the forefront of the public mind and in not letting it disappear from the government's attention. At the same time, he was acutely aware that his stance as a CO threatened his relations with his family. The Bell millions derived from their ownership of Welsh coal mines – mines that produced the slow-burning anthracite that powered the engines of Britain's navy (Strachan 76). Already, his allowance had been temporarily suspended in 1915 following the publication of *Peace at Once*.

The conscientious objector's appeal against being compelled to fight, or, in the case of absolutists, against being made to take any role whatsoever in the prosecution of the war, was often treated by both the tribunals and in the press as casting doubt upon the applicant's proper masculinity. Norman Angell, in January 1917, noted that on any given day at any of the many tribunals throughout England could be heard some variation of the question 'If a German attacked your mother – ... would you not defend her?' (261). The question has become infamous largely thanks to the anecdote about Lytton Strachey's camp response when his tribunal asked what he would do were a German trying to rape his sister ('I should try to come between them', he responded [Holroyd, *Strachey* 349]). Strachey's appearance at the Hampstead Tribunal in spring 1916 had been a carefully managed performance (Philip Morrell, MP, ceremoniously handing Strachey a blue cushion that Strachey then inflated and slowly lowered himself upon). For the COs who went to jail, the masculinist menace behind the question that typified the tribunal system's attitude toward COs was not always so much a matter of fun.

Philip Morrell, tirelessly arguing the case of the CO in Parliament throughout 1915 and 1916, had on 26 July 1916 (*Hansard*) mentioned two men in remarks addressed to Lloyd George, by this time Secretary of State for War. One of them was Ernest Everett, whose cause had been taken up by Bertrand Russell, with the result that Russell was fined £100.[9] The other was Eric Chappelow, who, Morrell said, 'has suffered immensely in prison' (*Hansard*) and had that day been released, but would certainly again be court-martialled and sent back to prison. When the No Conscription Fellowship convention was held in London in April 1916, the pro-war press (e.g. *Daily Express*, *Daily Sketch*) encouraged 'efforts which are being secretly made to arrange for "hospitality" in London' for its delegates (Bibbings, *Telling* 87n134), a coded encouragement of violence against them. Chappelow was portrayed in a series titled 'Conscientious Percy's Progress' in the *Daily Sketch* that month, where he appeared 'grinning maniacally and wrapped in an army blanket' (Bibbings, *Telling* 65) because he had on principle refused to don the khaki uniform for which he had been fitted.[10] Alongside the narrative of unmanliness was also deployed another, in which the COs were portrayed as lunatics and madmen, echoing the reception by the English establishment of the post-impressionist painters with whom Bell was so closely identified.[11]

For Clive Bell, British society before the war had afforded 'a certain receptivity to new ways of thinking and feeling, a mind at least ajar' ('Before'

581). '*Punch* was rarely seen in the best houses' and 'for a few dizzy years it was wildly surmised that to found a civilisation might be as thrilling as to found a family' (581). That moment of possibility seemed to Bell irretrievably lost by the end of the war as nationalist and homophobic rhetoric converged (Cohler 83). The unsuccessful libel suit brought by the dancer Maud Allan against Member of Parliament Pemberton Billing – 'perhaps the most sensational scandal in Britain during World War I' (Medd 21) – represented for Bell the worst social effects of the war, confirming, as he wrote to Vanessa from Garsington in 1918, his worst opinion of the English. In an article titled 'Cult of the Clitoris', published in his *Vigilante* newsletter, Billing had linked Allan's private performance of Oscar Wilde's *Salomé* to his earlier claim that a 'Black Book' had been discovered in Berlin that listed the intimate 'debauched' secrets of 47,000 British subjects (Cohler 84–5). The libel case brought Wilde and his circle back into public consciousness in association with a decadence that since 1916 also had been associated with resistance to military service (see Hoare).

That civilisation had plunged into what Virginia Woolf described in 'The Leaning Tower' as a 'chasm in a smooth road' became a refrain in Bell's post-war writings (Woolf 264). In later editions of *Art*, for example, he explained that part of the reason he had not revised his rather wild claims was that he wanted to preserve 'a record of what people like myself were thinking and feeling in the years before the first War' (10), as if such thought could now be only an historical artefact. In a 1921 article on 'Criticism', Bell wrote sarcastically that sincerity was the most one could ask of a critic, and that 'divine certitude' was better left to 'superior beings – magistrates, for instance, and curates, and fathers of large families, and Mr. Bernard Shaw' (171).

In *On British Freedom*, Bell deplored the lasting effects on British society of the government's suppression of thought and expression during the war. The solid citizens who had sat on the local tribunals and pronounced upon the conscience of their peers had been but the forerunners of the institutionalising of 'a peculiar brand of genteel servitude which passes under the name of Anglo-Saxon civilization' (*British* 2). An Englishman in the decade after the war, 'saddled in addition with certain surviving bastards from D.O.R.A., is at least as much a slave as he was under Cromwell and his colonels' (1).[12] Citing cases of imprisonment for blasphemy, censorship that inhibited free expression and decrying a situation in which 'you are expected to earn your own living, support your own family, and pay your own taxes; but you cannot be trusted to choose your own books and plays: some one must do that for you' (19), Bell made the arguments for liberation of personal freedom and expression that would have to wait until the 1960s to be realised.[13] In a chapter of *On British Freedom* titled 'Self-Regarding Vices', Bell makes an amusing yet eloquent analogy. He cannot abide cheese, and yet he understands that other people enjoy it: why should one person's disgust be the reason to criminalise another's enjoyment? Making clear that he is referring to the 'vice' of homosexuality, Bell points out that 'in a truly free country people would be allowed not only to read what books they pleased, see what plays they pleased, and take a drink or play a game of cards when they pleased, but to make love as they pleased – always provided that they injured no unwilling victim in the process' (*British* 41). The modern tyrant looks like a middle-class man or woman, sitting on committees, 'brooding over human wrongs and miseries and the odious frivolity and wickedness of those who are in any way unlike themselves' (53). Against the tyranny of the average, Bell opposed a vision of 'a great civilized capital … full of queer contrasts and odd professions, anomalies and eccentricities' (25) – the philosophy of a voluptuary.

Notes

1. Brockington describes British pacifist modernists as 'cultural descendants of Oscar Wilde' (7) and notes several examples of opprobrium directed at proponents of aestheticism during the First World War period (4–5).
2. Atkin leaves vague which Strachey he refers to here, but it must be James, who answered Bell's letter enquiring about possible service.
3. Hills in fact volunteered and in October 1914 was made a captain in the Durham Light Infantry; he was severely wounded at the Somme in July 1916.
4. 'In 1900 boys at Marlborough decided by 20 votes to 6 that the safety of the Empire was assured without the necessity of resorting to conscription. Ten years later, in the shadow of the growing German aggression frequently condemned in the press, the motion that "conscription is necessary to the welfare of this country" was carried in the house by "a considerable majority"' (Parker 62).
5. Elaine Scarry makes a similar point in *The Body in Pain*: 'In the course of war at least one side must undergo a perceptual reversal … in which claims or issues or elements of self-understanding that had previously seemed integral and essential to national identity will gradually come to seem dispensable or alterable, without seeming (as it once would have) to cancel out, dissolve, or irreparably compromise the national identity' (92).
6. The following year, Haynes published *The Decline of Liberty in England* (Atkin 215–16).
7. As Elaine Scarry would later write, 'it is when a country has become to its population a fiction that wars begin' (131).
8. Holroyd explains Shaw's advocacy for compulsory national service as 'calculated to strengthen his arguments for a fairer law and better treatment of individuals' (*Shaw* 365). Such pragmatism would have appeared to Bell as capitulation.
9. Everett had been described by the St Helen's Tribunal as a man who 'would see his sisters ravished or the war lost rather than do anything to help' (Graham 194).

10. According to Harold Bing, when the sergeant greeted Chappelow at the prison by saying 'We tame lions here', Chappelow replied 'But you cannot make a lamb fierce'.
11. The press response to the 1910 exhibition 'Manet and the Post-Impressionists' employed the discourse of insanity in mocking the paintings. The eminent 'nerve specialist' T. B. Hyslop gave a lecture – subsequently published as 'Post-Illusionism and the Art of the Insane' – in 1911 in which he compared an exhibition of patients' work at the Bethlem asylum with that exhibited by Roger Fry at the Grafton Galleries. This was a strategy Hitler's propagandists would employ again in 1937 for the infamous exhibit of 'Degenerate Art' (*Entarte Kunst*) in Munich.
12. The Defence of the Realm Act (DORA) was passed on 8 August 1914 to give the British government sweeping powers of social control, including censorship. The Act was extended several times during the war.
13. 'I doubt whether Roy Jenkins or any of the other legislators who introduced those measures which have put an end to the persecution of homosexuals, have liberated the stage and remedied all the ills which Clive deplored in the 1920s, ever read *On British Freedom*, but it played I think a useful part in a gradual change in the moral climate of the British nation' (Q. Bell, *Elders* 33).

Works Cited

Angell, Norman. 'If a German Attacked Your Wife – '. *New Republic* 6 Jan. 1917: 261–3.
Asquith, H. H. *Letters to Venetia Stanley*. Sel. and ed. Michael Brock and Eleanor Brock. Oxford: Oxford University Press, 1982.
Atkin, Jonathan. *A War of Individuals: Bloomsbury Attitudes to the Great War*. Manchester: Manchester University Press, 2002.
Beechey, James. 'Clive Bell: Pacifism and Politics'. *Charleston Magazine* 14 (1996): 5–13.
Bell, Clive. *Art*. 1914. New York: Perigee, 1981.
—. 'Before the War'. *Cambridge Magazine* 12 May 1917: 581–2.
—. 'The Creed of an Aesthete'. *New Republic* 25 Jan. 1922: 241–2.
—. 'Criticism'. *Since Cézanne*. London: Chatto, 1922. 154–79.
—. Letter. ['Conscription'] *Nation* 16 Jan. 1915: 500–1.
—. Letter. ['Conscription'] *Nation* 26 June 1915: 419–20.
—. Letter. ['Mr. Clive Bell's Pamphlet'] *Nation* 4 Sept. 1915: 737–8.
—. Letter. ['The Destruction of a Pamphlet'] *New Statesman* 4 Sept. 1915: 515–16.
—. Letter. ['"A Grave Issue" and a Way Out'] *Daily News* 17 May 1916: 4.
—. Letter. ['The Conscientious Objector'] *Daily News* 22 May 1916.
—. *On British Freedom*. New York: Harcourt, 1923.
—. 'Order and Authority II'. *Athenaeum* 14 Nov. 1919. Rpt. in *Since Cézanne*. London: Chatto, 1922. 129–38.
—. *Peace At Once*. Manchester: National Labour, 1915.

Bell, Quentin. *Elders and Betters*. London: Murray, 1995.

—. *Virginia Woolf: A Biography. Vol. 2: Mrs. Woolf 1912–1941*. London: Hogarth, 1973.

Berman, Jessica. *Modernist Fiction, Cosmopolitanism and the Politics of Community*. New York: Cambridge University Press, 2001.

Bibbings, Lois. 'Images of Manliness: The Portrayal of Soldiers and Conscientious Objectors in the Great War'. *Social and Legal Studies* 122.3 (2003): 335–58. Web. 10 Nov. 2014.

—. *Telling Tales About Men: Conceptions of Conscientious Objectors to Military Service During the First World War*. Manchester: Manchester University Press, 2009.

Bing, Harold Frederick. Imperial War Museum interview conducted 5 June 1974. Cat. 358. Web. 7 Nov. 2014.

Bracher, S. V. Letter. ['The Suppression of a Pamphlet'] *New Statesman* 11 Sept. 1915: 540.

Brockington, Grace. *Above the Battlefield: Modernism and the Peace Movement in Britain, 1900 – 1918*. New Haven: Yale University Press, 2010.

Butler, Judith. *Antigone's Claim*. New York: Columbia University Press, 2000.

Chesterton, G. K. Letter. ['Mr. Bernard Shaw and Mr. Bell'] *Nation* 18 Sept. 1915: 801.

Clark, Christopher. *The Sleepwalkers: How Europe Went to War in 1914*. New York: HarperCollins, 2012.

Cohler, Deborah. 'Sapphism and Sedition: Homosexuality in Great War Britain'. *Journal of the History of Sexuality* 16.1 (2007): 68–94.

Graham, John W. *Conscription and Conscience: A History 1916–1919*. London: Allen, 1922.

Gullace, Nicoletta F. *'The Blood of Our Sons': Men, Women, and the Renegotiation of British Citizenship During the Great War*. New York: Palgrave, 2002.

Hansard. Parliamentary Debates 1803–2005. Web. 22 Nov. 2014.

Haynes, E. S. P. Letter. ['The Suppression of a Pamphlet'] *New Statesman* 11 Sept. 1915: 540.

Hills, John Waller. Letter to Clive Bell. 15 Sept. 1914. MS. The Keep, Sussex.

Hoare, Philip. *Oscar Wilde's Last Stand: Decadence, Conspiracy, and the Most Outrageous Trial of the Century*. New York: Arcade, 1998.

Holland, Merlin. *The Real Trial of Oscar Wilde: The First Uncensored Transcript of the Trial of Oscar Wilde vs. John Douglas (Marquess of Queensberry), 1895*. New York: HarperCollins, 2003.

Holroyd, Michael. *Bernard Shaw. A Biography. Vol. 2: 1898–1918. The Pursuit of Power*. New York: Random, 1989.

—. *Lytton Strachey: The New Biography*. New York: Farrar, 1994.

Hussey, Mark. 'Virginia Woolf: After Lives'. Ed. Bryony Randall and Jane Goldman. *Virginia Woolf in Context*. Cambridge: Cambridge University Press, 2012. 13–27.

Lambert, Richard C. *The Parliamentary History of Conscription in Great Britain, Being a Summary of the Parliamentary Debates &c., with an Index and Text of the Military Service Acts*. London: Allen, 1917.

Medd, Jodie. '"The Cult of the Clitoris": Anatomy of a National Scandal'. *Modernism/modernity* 9.1 (2002): 21–49.

Millman, Brock. *Managing Domestic Dissent in First World War Britain*. New York: Routledge, 2013.
Newman, John Henry. *The Idea of a University Defined and Illustrated*. London: Longmans, 1905.
Parker, Peter. *The Old Lie: The Great War and the Public-School Ethos*. London: Constable, 1987.
Roper, Michael, and John Tosh, eds. *Manful Assertions: Masculinities in Britain Since 1800*. London: Routledge, 1991.
Scarry, Elaine. *The Body in Pain: The Making and Unmaking of the World*. New York: Oxford University Press, 1985.
Seymour, Miranda. *Ottoline Morrell: Life on the Grand Scale*. London: Hodder, 1992.
Shaw, Bernard. Letter. ['In Defence of Mr. Clive Bell'] *Nation* 11 Sept. 1915: 769–70.
—. Letter. ['On Sin and Death'] *Nation* 25 Sept. 1915: 833–4.
—. 'Shaw's Comment on Clive Bell's Article'. *New Republic* 22 Feb. 1922: 361–2.
Sherbo, Arthur. 'On John Maynard Keynes'. *Notes and Queries* 38.3 (1991): 337–9.
Skidelsky, Robert. *John Maynard Keynes. Vol. 1: Hopes Betrayed, 1883–1920*. New York: Viking, 1983.
Spalding, Frances. *Vanessa Bell*. New Haven: Ticknor, 1983.
—. *Duncan Grant*. London: Chatto, 1997.
Strachan, Hew. *The First World War*. New York: Viking, 2004.
Strachey, James. Letter to Clive Bell. 23 Sept. 1914. MS. The Keep, Sussex.
Strachey, Lytton. *The Really Interesting Question and Other Papers*. Ed. Paul Levy. New York: Capricorn, 1974.
Woolf, Virginia. 'The Leaning Tower'. *The Essays of Virginia Woolf*. Ed. Stuart N. Clarke. Vol. 6: 1933–1941. 259–83.

'I didn't know there could be such writing': The Aesthetic Intimacy of E. M. Forster and T. E. Lawrence

Jodie Medd

As 1927 drew to a close, E. M. Forster prepared to publish his last book of fiction, *The Eternal Moment and Other Stories*, with the dedication:

To
T. E.
IN THE ABSENCE
OF ANYTHING ELSE

The dedicatee is T. E. Lawrence, although he had tried to dodge his 'Lawrence of Arabia' fame by changing his last name in 1923. Indeed, omitting the surname both signals an intimacy with 'T. E'. and grants him a degree of anonymity. The subsequent prepositional phrases constitute a bit of a queer tease. As Forster writes flirtatiously to Lawrence, 'The dedication can be given a wrong meaning, which you will enjoy doing, and I shall like to think of you doing it' (*Letters* 99).[1] One such 'wrong meaning' might be that in the absence of an explicit or embodied gesture of affection, Forster can only offer this literary dedication; both public and private constraints forbid 'anything else' between them. Further, since Forster expects this book 'to be the last created word that will ever find public utterances', there will be nothing else that he *could* dedicate to Lawrence (*Letters* 100). Here, Forster's claim that his 'weariness of' the conventional subject of 'the love of men for women' (qtd. in Moffat 6) prompted this early retirement from literary publication opens another meaning, for he still continued writing 'unpublishable' male homoerotic stories, which he circulated to a counterpublic of select friends. In fact, he wrote the dedication just after Lawrence had superlatively pronounced one such story, 'Dr Woolacott', 'the most powerful thing I ever read' (*Letters* 97). Accordingly, Forster notes that *The Eternal Moment* includes a story that 'is a feeble timid premonition of the one which is with you now

["Dr Woolacott"] and which is yours really, and that is what the dedication really means' (99). In his beautifully layered and coyly phrased dedication about absence, then, Forster presents us not only with the question of his relationship with Lawrence, but also with many of the questions that crowd around the idea of queer Bloomsbury and its relation to cultural production.

Given the ostensible contrast between Forster's literary prominence and his private queer life, Forster's truncated career writing publishable fiction may seem a casualty of heteronormativity, in which closeted queer writing and lives become public only in a posthumous future. This model of queer Bloomsbury is constituted by what was lost – a novelist's career – and what has been buried – the 'great unrecorded history' of male homosexuality, a history that Forster's own archive preserved, simultaneously remembering and anticipating 'a happier year'.[2] In such absences, however, we may find something else. Forster's archive evidences a different kind of queer intervention, one in which the creation, appreciation and exchange of art between friends generate new possibilities of interpersonal intimacy, individual transformation and aesthetic experience, all central components of Bloomsbury's ethos.

As champions of good friends and good art, the Bloomsbury Group exemplified G. E. Moore's philosophy that 'personal affections and aesthetic enjoyments include *all* the greatest, and *by far* the greatest, goods' (189, original emphasis). For Moore, these two 'ideals' overlap insofar as the 'most valuable' personal affection combines an appreciation of both 'mental qualities' and their outward 'corporeal expression' (203). Bloomsbury, however, more deeply united these ideals by forging and maintaining personal affection through the mutual creation, exchange and appreciation of aesthetic objects. This interplay of art and affection constitutes an *aesthetic intimacy*, in which aesthetic production and circulation enable new forms of intimacy, while, reciprocally, interpersonal intimacy inspires new aesthetic possibilities and productions. Conventionally denoting a relationship that is 'close in acquaintance or association' or referencing an individual's 'inmost self', 'intimacy' is also a well-known euphemism for sexual relations. In unfurling intimacy's erotic potentialities, I mean to explore the queer capacities of aesthetic intimacy. Particularly among the Bloomsberries, queerly eroticised sociality and artistic practices mutually facilitated one another, often in complex ways that not only fostered alternative intimacies, but also transformed traditional artistic production, circulation, appreciation and consumption. Furthermore, aesthetic intimacy often transforms the 'inmost self' of those involved. Indeed, the positing of an intimate 'inmost self' that risks exposure through a close encounter with another invokes the familiar interplay of inside/outside and private/public that subtends both queer identities and what Eve Sedgwick has described as the 'epistemology of the closet'.[3]

Aesthetic intimacy animates literary networks when relationships are facilitated through sharing books; exchanging manuscripts or works in progress for comment; literary mentorship or collaboration; literary labour on behalf of a friend; writing about an intimate in a literary or critical work; and, of course, literary dedications. It also dwells in the intimate personal and relational effects of exchanging reading and writing. Needless to say, practices of aesthetic intimacy, literary and otherwise, abound in the Bloomsbury Group: Virginia Woolf's *Orlando*; Virginia and Leonard Woolf's collaboration on the Hogarth Press; memoirs, reviews, biographies, and literary and visual portraits of Bloomsbury members by their friends; Vanessa Bell's cover illustrations for her sister's novels, to name just a few.

Certainly, aesthetic intimacy governs Wendy Moffat's biography of Forster, which places his networks of gay male friendship at the centre of his writing life and posthumous legacy. Moffat emphasises how such friendships involved a 'dance toward intimacy' (193) whose first tentative steps were often choreographed through the exchange of art and literature, with Forster then sharing his own 'unpublishable' fiction in what became a recurrent 'ritual of intimacy' (15). For example, Moffat notes that when Christopher Isherwood first visited Forster, his London *pied-à-terre* displayed a portrait of an Arab boy, an original illustration from *Seven Pillars of Wisdom*, T. E. Lawrence's account of his experience in the Middle East during the Arab Revolt. Furthermore, 'In a special token of intimacy, Forster lent Isherwood the precious copy of *Seven Pillars of Wisdom* given to him by Lawrence himself' (Moffat 14). The anecdote exemplifies Forster's practice of forging queer attachments through literary exchange; however, this 'precious' book was itself a 'special token of intimacy' exchanged between Forster and Lawrence in the literary circuitry of *their* friendship. In fact, Forster and Lawrence's own intriguing relationship grew from an epistolary dialogue over *Seven Pillars* into a rich, subtle and multifaceted aesthetic intimacy.

Isherwood's encounter with Forster also queerly inflects 'Lawrence of Arabia's' heroic masculinity. The displayed portrait invokes not only Forster's relationship with Mohammed el Adl, a young Arab tram conductor with whom he fell in love in Egypt, but also Lawrence's own formative intimacy with an Arab youth during his early travels in Syria.[4] Indeed, although Forster and Lawrence seem worlds apart in their public image and life experiences, the parallels between them are remarkable, not least in their queer relation to the sexual. Biographies debate the facts and fictions of Lawrence's life, but all agree that his sexuality defies easy categorisation. Far from (hetero)normative, it encompassed asexuality, celibacy, suffering sexual assault and torture, masochism, flagellation, a thoroughgoing sexual disinterest in women, a distinctly non-homophobic regard for homosexuality in others, and a range of same-sex experiences, appreciations, intimacies, fantasies, identifications, repressions and shame.[5] Within this history, his literary friendship with Forster deeply affected Lawrence's own sexual attitudes and self-understanding.

Accordingly, the balance of my essay examines Forster and Lawrence's correspondence to propose that their aesthetic intimacy constitutes models of reading, friendship, self-understanding and literary transmission that creatively reconfigure conventional literary and affective relations. Attending patiently, even intimately, to this correspondence, we find Forster and Lawrence shape their friendship through a self-reflective and self-revealing process of literary exchange. These encounters negotiate the tricky landscape of male intimacy and homoerotic im/possibilities, while transforming modes of sexual and literary identity and inter-relationality. Together, Forster and Lawrence both enact and enrich Michel Foucault's notion of 'friendship as a way of life', which posits (male) homosexuality as 'a historic occasion to reopen affective and relational virtualities' given 'the "slantwise" position of the [homosexual], as it were, the diagonal lines he can lay out in the social fabric allow these virtualities to come to light' (138). Similarly, the editors of *GLQ*'s special issue on 'Queer Bonds' note how 'an askew relation to the normative terms of sexuality' not only 'occasions a certain negative relation to the social' but 'also precipitates a certain reinvention of the social, of the nature of "bonds"' (Weiner and Young 226). This simultaneously 'disabled and inventive sociality' is exactly what Forster and Lawrence's aesthetic intimacy constitutes and negotiates (226).

Forster first met Lawrence at a 1921 luncheon. Afterward, he sent a note expressing 'how glad, how proud' he had been to meet the celebrated colonel, but received 'no reply' (Forster, 'T. E. Lawrence' 282). Although Lawrence shrugged off this fan mail, he did respond later, when Forster appealed to his literary aspirations. In December 1923, as Forster struggled to complete *A Passage to India*, Siegfried Sassoon lent him a copy of the privately printed *Seven Pillars of Wisdom*. Reading it, Forster tells Sassoon, 'moves me so deeply that I nearly cry', particularly given his shared 'romantic passion for the East', an 'intensity' of feeling about 'foreign climes', known only by those who have 'slept in the body or the spirit with some of their inhabitants' (qtd. in *Letters* 3). Inspired to complete his own novel, Forster wrote Lawrence a detailed letter of praise and constructive criticism, concluding,

> By the way your book helped me to finish a book of my own. Seemed to pull me together. [...] You will never show it to any one who will like it more than I do: its subject and incidentals suit me: also my critical sense never stops telling me it's fine. (*Letters* 9)

Lawrence was 'giddy' from such attention from a writer he considered 'among the elect' (*Letters* 15, 12). As Forster recounts, 'T. E. Lawrence liked to meet people upon a platform of his own designing. In my own case it was the platform of aesthetic creation, where I had to figure as a great artist and he was a bungling amateur' ('T. E. Lawrence' 282). Responding to Forster's letter in candid detail, Lawrence paused to reflect, 'I wonder why I'm writing all this to you. I think perhaps because you are a stranger, and have been interested in my addled egg. It was an extraordinary experience for me, the reading of your letter' (*Letters* 14). Forster agrees, 'Yes, it is easier to write to strangers, and that is the objection against meeting: the illusion of social intimacy starts, and spoils the other thing' (*Letters* 16). This 'other thing' may well be the queer sanctuary of epistolary aesthetic intimacy, distinct from 'the illusion of social intimacy'. Or, to cite Lauren Berlant: 'Reading is one place where the impersonality of intimacy can be transacted without harm to anyone' (126). Yet, Forster also encourages Lawrence's shy invitation to collaborate over his book's revisions: 'But I should enjoy seeing you and think there is a practical reason for it, since you are revising the book again, and I might just possibly be of help' (*Letters* 16).

This initial epistolary encounter established the key dynamics of a delicate literary friendship that would explore the terms, possibilities and limitations of male friendship, sexual self-understanding and authorial identity, through the exchange of the written word. Drawn together as intimate strangers through literature's allure, they proclaimed the transformative impact of the other's writing and reading. Agreeing that avoiding social intimacy facilitates expressive candour, while paradoxically planning further literary collaboration in person, they embarked on a friendship that lasted until Lawrence's untimely death in 1935.

Within a few months, Forster fulfilled the promise of a visit. By this time, Lawrence had withdrawn from the public eye, taken a pseudonym and enlisted in the ranks of the Royal Air Force (RAF), later transferring to the Tank Corps. A private at a Dorset training camp, he took refuge in a nearby rustic cottage, Clouds Hill. After their meeting Lawrence wrote, 'Your coming here was a very great pleasure to myself: and a very great profit, I hope, to that difficult book I'm engaged in' (*Letters* 20), a telling structural parallel that binds together personal pleasure and literary production. Forster confides to Sassoon *his* pleasure in the visit: 'I like him. In fact I have to stop myself from going to pieces before him. I have no right to go to pieces, not enough beauty' (qtd. in *Letters* 20). In lieu of corporeal beauty, Forster offered the aesthetic and intimate appeal of his 'unpublishable' homoerotic fiction, sending Lawrence 'The Life to Come', about the sexual relationship between a missionary priest and the chief of a colonised village.

Lawrence's initial response indicates little appreciation of the story; both Moffat and P. N. Furbank note his risible description of it as 'one of the funniest things I'd ever come across' (*Letters* 22; Moffat 193; Furbank 121). Such a reaction may seem dismissive – even socially disabling to a burgeoning intimacy – but there is more to it. Although admitting that he 'laughed and laughed' after his first 'avid reading' of the story, Lawrence also seriously engages with its literary qualities and adds a curious identification:

> Contrary to your opinion I incline to consider it quite fit to publish. Perhaps other people's improprieties come a little less sharply upon one? It doesn't feel to me nearly so bad as my true story.
>
> Incidentally we're different, aren't we? I make an awful fuss about what happened to me: and you invent a voluntary parallel, about which the two victims make no bones at all. Funny the way people work. (*Letters* 23)

Here Lawrence alludes to the sexual assault and torture he experienced when held captive by the Turkish Bey in Deraa during the Middle Eastern campaign for Arab independence. *Seven Pillars*' description of this event is as elusive as it is graphic, implying without stating that Lawrence was forcibly sodomised or narrowly escaped being sodomised. Extra-textual evidence suggests Lawrence was raped, instilling in him a lifelong sense of shame – not least from the masochistic pleasure he may have experienced in the ordeal – and perhaps infecting him with venereal disease. This trauma profoundly affected his attitudes toward corporeality, sexuality and physical intimacy, including contributing to the flagellation fantasies that he played out throughout his life.[6] Although Lawrence undercuts his identification with Forster's story with the banal, 'Funny the way people work', he conveys the shame that haunts and constitutes his sexuality, while demonstrating a disturbing inability to distinguish between his history of sexual violation and the 'victims' of a 'voluntary' homosexual encounter.[7] Addressing the story's literary qualities while candidly identifying with its plot, Lawrence does not simply laugh off Forster's gesture of queer aesthetic intimacy, but rather reciprocates and extends it.

'Yes, we're different all right', Forster replies cagily, noting that Lawrence's laughter over the story 'makes me laugh and laugh'. Challenging some of Lawrence's criticisms as misreadings, he also confesses, 'I am glad you wrote, as I had assumed you were disgusted, and was sorry, though I knew that in such a contretemps neither the disgusted nor the disgustery [*sic*] party would be the least to blame' (*Letters* 24). Admitting the risk of sharing this story, Forster nonetheless refuses to accept or apportion blame for any homosexual panic it might incite; his rhetorical subtlety continues the 'dance toward intimacy'. Personal pronouns and emotional directness characterise the first clauses ('I am glad you wrote, as I had assumed you were disgusted, and was sorry') only to shift into an ambiguous impersonal mode ('in such a contretemps neither the disgusted nor the disgustery party would be the least to blame'), thereby consolidating intimacy while withdrawing just enough to protect against potential queer discomfort. Defending the story, Forster also places Lawrence among its select queer readers: 'I think the story as good as any I've written, so does Siegfried [Sassoon]. Lowes Dickinson doesn't like it. Scarcely anyone else has seen it' (*Letters* 24).

Moffat characterises this exchange over 'The Life to Come' as a failed 'billet-doux', after which 'the friendship rested delicately, for the moment' (193). In fact, however, Lawrence immediately replied:

> I don't seem to have put my remarks on your story very well. That's good, because my mind has never cleared upon it. I agree with S.S. [Siegfried Sassoon] as to its excellence: my memory is still concerned, not with its parts, but with its general impression. (*Letters* 26)

Far from dismissive of the story, Lawrence discloses that 'this preoccupation is a daily one, almost', while still challenging Forster's technical choices: 'Why make it over-ripe? or cynical? That seems to me grievous; the thing is so healthy as it stands, in its meaning, that it seems a pity to taint any detail of it' (26).

This 'so healthy' diagnosis recalls how Lawrence, unlike Forster, considered it 'quite fit to publish', and 'not nearly as bad as my true story'. Indeed, the friends recurrently bond over the unpublishability of their writing. '"Unpublishable" is a relative, even a passing qualification', Lawrence remarks, 'The *Seven Pillars* earned it two or three years ago: and have lost it in that little time' (*Letters* 21).[8] Addressing Forster's concern about sending the story, Lawrence reassures him,

> the writing which disgusts me is stuff aimed deliberately below the belt [...]. Your efforts are always so patent, that no one could ever be troubled by them. It isn't a subject which can give offence, but its treatment. (26)

Here again the correspondence simultaneously acknowledges and deflects the story's queerness, by (re)focusing on literary style. Ultimately, whether or not Forster's literary allure may have failed as a mode of cruising or seduction, it successfully enabled and developed his aesthetic intimacy with Lawrence.

Realising Lawrence's physical and emotional inhibitions, Forster himself divined it best to confine the relationship to literature. After visiting Clouds Hill again, he reports to Sassoon:

> He is a rare remote creature, uncanny, yet attractive. I suspect him of 'practices' – i.e. of some equivalent of yoga, otherwise I cannot

understand his attitude towards the body – his own and other people's. He thinks the body dirty, and so disapproves of all voluntary physical contact with the bodies of others. Hence the flabby handshake, no doubt. I should like to know whether he held that view <u>before</u> he was tortured at Deraa. (*Letters* 28)

Forster's observations are characteristically astute, although Lawrence's 'practices' were masochistic, not yogic. He not only hired a young man to flagellate him, recalling his experience at Deraa but, as we will see, he eventually confesses his dissociation from embodiment and physical intimacy after reading another 'unpublishable' story by Forster. In a memoir, Forster similarly and poignantly associates Lawrence's 'bad handshake' with the fact that 'he did not like being touched (by me anyhow); in later years I realized this, and touched him as seldom as possible' ('T. E. Lawrence' 283).

Acknowledging the necessary distance in their relationship, Forster savoured the moments when Lawrence edged closer through literature, touching feeling without touching. At the end of 1926 Lawrence was posted overseas and Forster gently boasted to a confidante:

> T. E. Lawrence did me proud, devoted a whole day to catching hold of me before his departure to India, and gave me a gorgeous copy of the private edition of the *Seven Pillars of Wisdom* with practically all the illustrations. [...] I hoped I should get some sort of copy, but that he should do me so regally was a very great pleasure and surprise. [...] I used to think him incapable of affection, but have changed my opinion, and think he has some for me. To be with him, or read him, is a great experience, as he has the power of making one feel one could do all he has done. (Qtd. in *Letters* 49)

The queer dynamics of aesthetic intimacy abound here. Lawrence's effort to deliver his 'gorgeous' literary gift demonstrates an affection of which Forster had thought him incapable. Forster's parallel between being with Lawrence and reading him as both 'a great experience' recalls Lawrence's earlier equation of the personal pleasure and literary profit gained from Forster's first visit, and anticipates Lawrence's subsequent equation between reading Forster's books and knowing him personally. For, while in India, Lawrence expressed to a mutual friend his desire to write about Forster as a literary figure:

> Do you know, he is the most civilised person I've ever met? I dally continually with my memory of him and of his books, trying to find out for myself something of their secrets. There was never anything so elusive, so subtle, so delicate, so robust, so unusual, as his way of

> thinking. It baffles me: as yet. But I'll get at the business again and again. This place gives me excessive leisure, and quite a regular event is a meditation upon E.M.F. (Qtd. in *Letters* 54)

Here geographic and temporal distance draws Lawrence closer to Forster, as he leisurely dallies with the 'memory of him and of his books', seeking the 'elusive' 'secrets' held in both.

Consequently, Lawrence tells Forster that he has been avidly re-reading his books. 'They beat me', Lawrence declares,

> All over them are sayings (genuinely terrible) which I feel are bursting out from your heart, and represent yourself: but when I put together a sheet of these, the portrait they make is not the least like you, as I've sat at tea with you. (*Letters* 70)

In response, Forster offered to send both 'Dr Woolacott' – a short story that 'is closely woven and distinguished, but it will not ever be published, as it belongs to the same class as the story which made you laugh' – and *Maurice*: 'Do you remember, too, a novel I mentioned to you? I offered you the reading of it when you were in England, but you did not seem keen. I did not understand why'. These unpublishable works, Forster contends,

> are items which you must have in your mind if you want to sum me up. […] I suppose I am elusive and difficult, but there are one or two people (and you're one of them) to whom I'd like to be clear. I haven't any secrets from you – that is to say there's no question you asked which I wouldn't answer. But this again is not what you want, not what you want, alas.

Assessing Lawrence's interpretative dilemma, he advises, 'Don't bother about reconciling the statements in my books with my conduct at the tea table. See whether you can reconcile the statements with each other, and you will find that you cannot, alas that you cannot' (*Letters* 73–4).

Ostensibly resisting Lawrence's impulse to 'reconcile' Forster's published writing with his private 'conduct at the tea table', this letter in fact sutures the literary to the intimate, while acknowledging intimacy's limitations. Forster's offer of uninhibited self-disclosure presumes Lawrence's refusal: 'this again is not what you want, not what you want, alas'. As much as Lawrence might want to '[try] to find out for [himself]' the 'secrets' of Forster and his books, he does not want Forster to be the one to lay them bare. Challenging Lawrence's impulse to reconcile published writing with private persona, Forster refocuses on the literary realm even as he longs for more. Insisting that his writing is simply inconsistent, Forster's phrasing matches his previous lament about Lawrence's emotional evasiveness, in which greater intimacy is 'not what you want alas, not what you want'. Now, however, he playfully laments his own literary evasiveness, warning that as much as Lawrence may try to impose coherence on Forster's *oeuvre*, he will find 'you cannot, alas, that you cannot'. This forms a revealing parallel between what Forster wants in his friendship with Lawrence but cannot have, and what Lawrence wants in his reading of Forster but cannot have.

Continually traversing questions of reading, being with, 'dallying' with, and knowing (or not) the other as and through writing, Forster and Lawrence's negotiations of aesthetic intimacy travel along queer lines. Accordingly, as Lawrence struggles to explain why he 'did not seem keen' about reading *Maurice*, he extends the discussion of intimacy, secrecy, exposure and (homo)sexuality:

> I wanted to read your long novel [*Maurice*], & was afraid to. It was like your last keep, I felt: and if I read it I had you: and supposing I hadn't liked it? I'm so funnily made up, sexually.[9] (*The Letters*, Ed. Brown 347)

Lawrence's potential discomfort with such intimate possession is not only laced with erotic implications ('if I read it I had you'), but also recalls their initial correspondence in which frank exchange is predicated on the foreclosure of interpersonal intimacy; it also confirms Forster's expectation that Lawrence wants Forster to keep his secrets to himself. Concomitantly, Lawrence conveys that his fear of not liking the novel, which might lead to not liking Forster, is in fact a projection – he is less concerned with reading what he already knows about Forster than with facing what Forster might already know about *him*:

> At present you are in all respects right, in my eyes: that's because you reserve so very much, as I do. If you knew all about me (perhaps you do: your subtlety is very great: shall I put it 'if I knew that you knew...'?) you'd think very little of me. And I wouldn't like to feel that I was on the way to being able to know about you. (*Letters* 77)

Negotiating the terms of their aesthetic intimacy, Lawrence wants to protect their secrets, or at least the outward appearance of them. Left unread, *Maurice* represents the impasse of (sexual) knowledge, intimacy and disclosure necessary to Lawrence's friendship with Forster. Forster responds reassuringly to these verbal contortions, 'I was very pleased to get your letter. I like your reasons for not wanting to read my unpublished novel, and you shall never read it' (*Letters* 79).

Forster did, however, send 'Dr Woolacott', the story of a young wealthy 'chronic invalid', Clesant, visited by an attractive farmhand. Evasively describing his disease as 'functional', 'not organic', and even as being sick 'of being myself perhaps!', Clesant abides the orders of the eponymous Dr Woolacott to 'avoid all excitement', not play his violin and not tire himself; Clesant hesitates to add that he also 'mustn't be intimate with people' ('Dr Woolacott' 114).[10] His illness, in this way, is shaded with the pathological constructions of deviant sexuality; meanwhile, the labourer conveys his prior knowledge – and distinct distrust – of Woolacott. Awakening Clesant's vitality and seducing him into 'intimacy' (124) and 'love' (125) this mysterious stranger proves to be the spectre of a soldier who succumbed to his injuries after he 'refused' Woolacott's inept medical care at a frontline hospital (121). Clesant himself dies in a passionate kiss with the farmhand, just as Woolacott arrives on the scene. Shortly after receiving 'Dr Woolacott', Lawrence writes,

> It's the most powerful thing I ever read. Nearly made me ill: and I haven't yet summoned up the courage to read it again. [...] A great privilege, it is, to get a thing like that. [...] I hope you know what a wonderful thing Dr. Woolacott is. It is more charged with the real high explosive than anything I've ever met yet. [...] It is also very beautiful. I nearly cried, too. (*Letters* 97)

Heartily agreeing that 'Doctor Woolacott is the best thing I've done and also unlike anyone else's work', Forster's pleasure in his story is reinforced by Lawrence's enthusiasm:

> The story makes me happy. It gives bodily ecstasy outside time and place. I shall never be able to give it again, but once is something.
> Odd that in my daily life I should be so timid and ingratiating and consequently so subject to pain. Your letter helps me a lot. I have gone through the story today in my mind, with the knowledge you have read it, and this ~~comforts me strengthens~~ hardens (got it!) me. (*Letters* 98–9)

Self-cast as weak, 'timid and ingratiating', much like the convalescent Clesant, Forster finds 'bodily ecstasy' – perhaps a *jouissance* – through his writing, which further, suggestively, 'hardens' with the conjured presence of Lawrence, who, like the farmhand, is an uncannily attractive veteran with a heroic and traumatic history. Forster closes with the injunction, 'Write again about Doctor Woolacott' (99).

Replying with an extended commentary, Lawrence concludes, 'The rest is marvellous. There is no other word for it. It bruises my spirit. I did not know there could be such writing' (107). It even prompts his dramatic reconsideration of (homo)sexuality and physical intimacy:

> There is a strange cleansing beauty about the whole piece of writing. So passionate, of course: so indecent, some people might say: but I must confess that it has made me change my point of view. I had not before believed that such a thing could be so presented – and so credited. I suppose you will not print it? Not that it anywhere says too much: but it shows far more than it says: and these things are mysteries. The Turks, as you probably know (or have guessed, through the reticences of the *Seven Pillars*) did it to me, by force: and since then I have gone about whispering to myself unclean, unclean. Now I do not know. Perhaps there is another side, your side, to the story. I couldn't ever do it, I believe: the impulse strong enough to make me touch another creature has not yet been born in me: but perhaps in surrender to such a figure as your Death there might be a greater realisation – and thereby a more final destruction – of the body than any loneliness can reach. (107)

Through this transformative therapeutic reading, Lawrence revisits and cleanses the shame of his past and his own vexed sexuality by conceding the attraction of 'surrendering' to a self-annihilating homosexual pleasure. By 'show[ing] far more than it says', the story does not necessarily reveal Forster to Lawrence, but in revealing Lawrence *to himself* makes the 'last keep' of Forster far less threatening. This queerly enabling remediation, initiated by an unpublishable story about the ecstatic possibilities of male same-sex love, indicates the radical potential of aesthetic intimacy to transform individuals, interpersonal understandings and circuits of reading.

As much as this literary encounter intensifies Forster and Lawrence's intimacy, however, it also requires that intimacy's ongoing management. Lawrence concludes:

> Meanwhile I am in your debt for an experience of such strength and sweetness and bitterness and hope as seldom comes to anyone. I wish my account of it were not so vaguely inadequate: and I cannot suggest 'more when we meet' for it will be hard to speak of these things without dragging our own conduct and bodies into the argument: and that's too late, in my case. (*Letters* 108)

Here epistolary exchange remodels both conventional literary relations and embodied conversation. Author and reader directly negotiate their literary interaction and even alter the text between them – Forster amended his story based on Lawrence's suggestions; meanwhile, their erotically incorporeal intimacy is mediated through scenes of reading that both reveal and protect 'a greater realisation [...] of the body'. We see this in Forster's response:

> I shall respect what you say about 'not more when we meet'. It is natural for me to drag my own body and conduct into an argument (should be dotty and sterile but for these and other outlets), so you may every now and then have to fend me off, but I shall never feel snubbed when you do. (108)

Forster further registers the personal impact of Lawrence's literary appreciation:

> No one will ever write to me as you wrote about Doctor Woolacott. It is the experience of a life time to get such praise and I don't think of it as praise. I mean never to send you anything of mine again (unless you should ask me to do so). What you have written has the effect of something absolute on me. (113)

If for both friends 'Dr Woolacott' is the superlative moment of literary exchange, then Forster proposes protecting its perfection. He vows to withhold future work, not because it might fail to move Lawrence to the same degree, but because Lawrence may fail to move *him* again with such effusive appreciation. Not only does Forster's unpublishable fiction radicalise the subject matter of fiction, then, its transmission between friends also fosters an emotional circuit that both reconfigures Lawrence's wounded past and reinvents modes of literary interaction. This exchange of 'absolutes' between reader and writer even mimics the story's climax, where the ailing young man's ultimate experience of homoerotic intimacy marks his final apotheosis. Such a mutually transformative circuit recurs a few months later, when Forster responds to an unpublishable manuscript by Lawrence.

Lawrence began *The Mint* as a series of notes for a book he claimed 'mustn't be published till after 1950' given its criticism of the RAF and candid depiction of Lawrence's fellow servicemen (*Letters* 130). Forster declares it 'more new, more startling and more heartening than either the [*Seven Pillars*] or anything else I've read. [...] There seems to me now no reason why you shouldn't write all sorts of books'; testifying to Lawrence's literary potential, he tellingly cites their shared sexual disinterest in women: 'I rather wish you would make yourself examine and describe women: many of them are about, and reluctance can lead us to profitable discoveries' (124). A subsequent letter reiterates: '*The Mint* proves to me that you can write creatively about anything that happens to you', whether 'ladies or fairy tales or even some subject of your own selection: I have the feeling that after this great success you can write what you like' (131–2). As 'Dr Woolacott' transformed Lawrence's 'point of view' regarding sexuality, including Forster's sexual identity, here *The Mint* expands Forster's opinion of Lawrence's authorial identity and abilities.

Flattered that Forster addressed him 'from the point of view of a fellow-writer' (Lawrence to Charlotte Shaw, qtd. in *Letters* 125), Lawrence enthuses:

> Your wonderful letter about *The Mint* has given me about eight readings of unalloyed pleasure, so far. [...] It is just like the letter of one writer to another. Marvellous, that you and I should be on such apparent terms. I looked up to you for years as a distant but impeccable star. Now you are no further from me than the thickness of this sheet of notepaper, and my reluctance to cover it with black marks ... and not impeccable, since I have found your critical judgement partial to my imperfections. However, perhaps I am your blind spot. (126)

Figuring their literary affinity and intimacy through the metaphorics and materiality of writing, Lawrence conveys how their literary correspondence both draws them together and maintains a productively safe space between them – much like the dynamic gravitational tension that keeps a celestial body orbiting a star. As both the means and measure of their friendship, 'the thickness of this sheet of notepaper' calibrates the exact margin of intimacy and distance afforded by their literary exchange. Passing between their hands and inscribed with their thoughts about writing, corporeality and intimacy, the notepaper is literally the medium of their friendship, allowing them to be queerly and intimately in touch, without being touched.[11] And yet, Lawrence's 'reluctance to cover it with black marks' implies that as much as writing figures and mediates their friendship, it also disfigures the fantasy of a pure, unmediated and discarnate intimacy, just as writing's 'black marks' inevitably disfigure the notepaper exchanged between them. Even Forster's impeccability is blemished by his partiality to Lawrence's 'imperfections'.

This aesthetic intimacy established through private exchanges of unpublishable work is publically glimpsed in Forster's dedication of *The Eternal Moment and Other Stories*. Forster first suggests a dedication in the same 1927 letter responding to Lawrence's interest in writing a critical piece about him:

> If ever I ~~write~~ & publish a book again, a real one, it will be dedicated to you. Do not bother to refuse permission. I am bringing out some old short stories next spring. I like them. They will not however be dedicated to any one. (*Selected* 80)[12]

Included in a letter offering access to Forster's queer fiction and personal secrets, this promise of a dedication compounds their aesthetic intimacy while anticipating the end of Forster's career as a publishable fiction writer. Once he decides the stories will be the last he publishes, Forster tells Lawrence, 'they seem all that I am likely to have to give you and I should like to give you something. You should have become more intimate with me in my prime' (*Letters* 80).

Although ostensibly referring to his 'prime' as a writer, Forster's *double-entendre* sexual flirtation characteristically melts together writing, intimacy and queer sexuality. His choice to dedicate his last publishable book of fiction to Lawrence, with a self-consciously cheeky and prismatic inscription attests to an aesthetic intimacy that is both momentous and evasive. 'In the absence of anything else', as previously noted, carries multiple references: in the absence of any other future public work; in the absence of an explicit or embodied affective display – since this is not what Lawrence wants, alas; and in the absence of dedicating a more meaningful work such as the unpublishable 'Dr Woolacott'. Instead, this collection publishes that story's 'feeble timid premonition' (*Letters* 99), entitled 'The Point of It', in which a young man's brief friendship with an invalid who dies suddenly in an ecstatic moment of passionate and rebellious exertion in a rowboat becomes his final salvation in the afterlife. After his progressive 'decomposition' into a conventionally respectable, 'soft' and 'conciliated soul', the man, in death, is poised on the edge of a placid Hell (disguised as Heaven), only to be rescued by desire, truth and love – 'the point of it' – voiced by his friend rowing heroically toward him (Forster, 'The Point' 118, 105, 124–5). Forster's dedication, then, is a lightly coded queer flirtation that can pass in public view, while the collection includes a lightly coded story in which male friendship passes as the symbol of the meaning of life and the afterlife.

Lawrence joked that Forster's dedication would enhance the prospects of his own afterlife: 'if you dedicate anything to me I'll wear the first page of it as an identity disc. So that when I die the chaplains will know what sort of burial service to give the body' (*Letters* 77). The archive of their intimacy might indeed serve as a kind of posthumous 'identity disc' of a friendship that baffles precise identification. Their writing and reading to, of, and about one another and their work charts the discarnate but intimate embrace of aesthetic creation, critical appreciation and personal affection. Here, intimacy contracts and expands, fails and revives, is disabled and reinvented, through a literary exchange that reconfigures modes of literary transmission and personal relations.

In fact, Forster even enjoined Lawrence to write a 'new' kind of novel about human relationships. Commenting in December 1929, 'I have been thinking a bit about you and writing lately', Forster recalls:

> a remark of mine which you once approved and which has become yours in my mind. It was about love, how over-rated and over-written

it is, and how the relation one would like between people is a mixture of friendliness and lust. [...] There's so much new to be said about human relationships now that the sac of lust has been dissected and been discovered to be such a small and innocuous reservoir. [...] What I want from you is something about the feelings that occur between people: a novel perhaps. [...] I see no reason you shouldn't do a novel. It would go queer and poetic all right. (149)

Lawrence had never written a novel; Forster planned never to publish another one. Did Forster task Lawrence with the kind of novel he felt had eluded his own career? Perhaps, now, 'in the absence of anything else', it is Forster and Lawrence's own correspondence that composes an inventive collaborative epistolary novel of and about aesthetic intimacy, to say something new 'about the feelings that occur between people', about the 'mixture of friendliness and lust' – and writing and reading – between people: one that certainly goes 'queer and poetic all right'.

Notes

My sincere thanks to Alicha Keddy, Stecha Dehghani, Nicholas Taft and Audrey Medd who, each in their own way, provided the practical and personal resources I needed for this essay.

1. Quotations from Forster and Lawrence's correspondence are from Lawrence, *Letters: Correspondence with E. M. Forster and F. L. Lucas*, ed. Jeremy Wilson and Nicole Wilson. Subsequent quotations are referenced as '*Letters*' in parenthetical citation. Where other published versions and/or my own transcription of the original letters differ significantly from Wilson and Wilson, I have noted it.
2. The American title of Wendy Moffat's biography of Forster, *A Great Unrecorded History*, is Forster's own term for the suppressed history of gay male experience. Forster's posthumously published gay novel, *Maurice*, is dedicated to 'a happier year'.
3. Eve Sedgwick's *Epistemology of the Closet* influentially argues that the 'modern crisis of homo/heterosexual definition' has profoundly shaped western categorisations of 'secrecy/disclosure, knowledge/ignorance, private/public' and 'in/out' (11).
4. Lawrence met fifteen-year-old Dahoum in 1911, while on an archaeological dig, and formed a great affection for him. Dahoum died in the Great War, but continued to function as a romantic figure of the Arab 'native' in Lawrence's later political views, and most likely was the dedicatee of *Seven Pillars of Wisdom*. Harold Orlans's 2002 biography of Lawrence concludes that 'Lawrence was in love or came closer to love with Dahoum than with anyone ever again' (224).

5. For a helpful compilation of sources and claims regarding Lawrence's sexuality, see Bray. For a theorised account of Lawrence's 'masochistic homosexuality', see Silverman's chapter on Lawrence.
6. See chapter 80 of *Seven Pillars of Wisdom*.
7. The orientalising political dynamics are also virtually reversed in the two situations: in Lawrence's account, the 'savagery' of the Turks is represented through their homosexuality; whereas in 'The Life to Come', it is the priest who first seduces the village chief in order to convert him to Christianity, and once homosexuality has served the colonising and missionary project, the ashamed priest denies the relationship. Lawrence's identification with and differentiation from the story indicate how both he and Forster were writing through homosexuality and imperialism. Lawrence seems to be working through his shame and, by some accounts, his masochism, while Forster's story refuses the social demand for homosexual shame.
8. See also *Letters* 76, on the question of unpublishability in relation to 'Dr Woolacott' and Lawrence's *Revolt in the Desert*.
9. Wilson and Wilson transcribe this word as 'sensually', but Malcolm Brown transcribes it as 'sexually' (347), which accords with my transcription from the letter held at King's College Cambridge Modern Archives.
10. The quotations are cited from the posthumously published version of 'Dr Woolacott' and accord with the draft version of the story that Forster sent Lawrence, reprinted in *Letters*.
11. See Kate Thomas's queer readings of the postal system and communication networks, referenced in 'Post Sex'.
12. This citation is from *Selected Letters of E. M. Forster* (vol. 2, ed. Lago and Furbank, 80) and accords with my own transcription of the letter. Wilson and Wilson's *Letters* does not include the strike-out.

Works Cited

Berlant, Lauren. *Cruel Optimism*. Durham: Duke University Press, 2011.
Bray, Tim. *Sex and T. E. Lawrence*. N.p. 20 Dec. 2009. Web. 17 Jul. 2015.
Forster, E. M. 'Dr Woolacott'. *The Life to Come and Other Stories*. London: Penguin, 1989.
—. 'T. E. Lawrence'. *T. E. Lawrence: By His Friends*. Ed. A.W. Lawrence. London: Cape, 1937.
—. 'The Point of It'. *The Eternal Moment and Other Stories*. New York: Harcourt, 1928. 89–125.
—. *Selected Letters of E. M. Forster*. Vol. 2. Ed. Mary Lago and P. N. Furbank. London: Collins, 1985.
Foucault, Michel. 'Friendship as a Way of Life'. *Michel Foucault: Ethics, Subjectivity, and Truth*. Ed. Paul Rabinow. Trans. Faubion, Hurley, et al. New York: New Press, 1994. 135–40.

Furbank, P. N. *E. M. Forster: A Life*. 1977. San Diego: Harvest-Harcourt, 1981.
Lawrence, T. E. *Letters: Correspondence with E. M. Forster and F. L. Lucas*. Vol. 5 of *T. E. Lawrence Letters*. Ed. Jeremy Wilson and Nicole Wilson. Salisbury: Castle Hill, 2010.
—. *The Letters of T. E. Lawrence*. Ed. Malcolm Brown. London: Dent, 1988.
—. *Seven Pillars of Wisdom*. 1935. London: Vintage, 2008.
Moffat, Wendy. *A Great Unrecorded History: A New Life of E. M. Forster*. New York: Farrar, 2010.
Moore, G. E. *Principia Ethica*. Cambridge: Cambridge University Press, 1903.
Orlans, Harold. *T. E. Lawrence: Biography of a Broken Hero*. Jefferson: McFarland, 2002.
Sedgwick, Eve Kosofsky. *Epistemology of the Closet*. Berkeley: University of California Press, 1990.
Silverman, Kaja. *Male Subjectivity at the Margins*. New York: Routledge, 1992.
Thomas, Kate. 'Post Sex'. *After Sex? On Writing Since Queer Theory*. Ed. Janet Halley and Andrew Parker. Durham: Duke University Press, 2011. 66–75.
Weiner, Joshua J., and Damon Young. 'Queer Bonds'. *GLQ* 17.2–3 (2011): 223–41.

Virginia Woolf's Queer Time and Place: Wartime London and a World Aslant

Kimberly Engdahl Coates

The letters Virginia Woolf writes beginning in 1939 describing her gradual severance from the 'passion of [her] life – the City of London' and her final retreat to Monk's House in the autumn of 1940 chronicle what a queer and disorienting time and place wartime London had become (*Letters* 6: 431). 'You can't think', she writes to her niece Angelica Bell in October 1939, 'how difficult it is to write a letter in this doomed and devastated but at the same time morbidly fascinating town.... [Y]ou don't know what a queer place London is' (6: 363–4). Later, in a January 1941 letter written to Lady Shena Simon, she exclaims:

> No, I don't see what's to be done about war. It's manliness; and manliness breeds womanliness – both so hateful. [...] They said if women had as much money as men, they'd enjoy themselves: and then what about the children? So they have more children; more wars; and so on. (6: 464)

Woolf's comments not only acknowledge the patriarchy's inability to recognise women's labour and socioeconomic status outside of a gendered economic system, but like *Three Guineas*, they also link war with patriarchy, heteronormativity and the temporal frames of bourgeois reproduction and family that each of these supports.

And yet, if it is heteronormativity in part that fuels history's insufferable repetition of war, it is also, as Woolf's letters make evident, war's destruction that exposes London as such a 'queer' and 'morbidly fascinating' place. This essay attempts to reconcile precisely this paradox. In novels like *Jacob's Room*, *Mrs Dalloway*, *The Waves* and *The Years*, Woolf depicts a London irrevocably queered by war or its anticipation. Rendering familiar temporal and spatial frames suddenly askew, wartime London and Woolf's queer analysis thereof call us to heed the destructive consequences of a militancy facilitated by patriarchy and heteronormativity, while simultaneously inviting us to inhabit a city capable of offering radically alternative modes of social gathering.

Judith Halberstam has argued that 'queer time' and 'queer space' develop in 'opposition to the institutions of family, heterosexuality, and reproduction' and 'according to other logics of location, movement, and identification' (1). Such 'strange temporalities', she insists, may help us to rethink queerness as relevant not only in terms of sexual identity, but also more broadly and philosophically as a way of being in the world (1). Similarly, Sara Ahmed has examined the way in which spaces impress themselves upon, and in turn take shape within, bodies whose orientation disorients hegemonic assumptions about the experience of temporality and space. In its most general sense, notes Ahmed, phenomenology reminds us that spaces are not exterior to bodies; instead, spaces are like a second skin that 'unfolds in the folds of the body' (9). A queer phenomenology, then, might begin by redirecting or reorienting our attention toward queer moments, moments at which the world appears 'slantwise' (65). Accordingly, to become vertical, to pull one's self 'upright', would mean that the queer effect is being overcome and objects in the world no longer appear off-centre or slantwise. Ahmed asks her readers to consider what it might mean to live out a politics of disorientation, one that would insist we not straighten up, but rather continue to see slantwise:

> If we think with and through orientation, we might allow the moments of disorientation to gather, almost as if they are bodies around a different table. We might in gathering, face a different way.... Indeed, to live out a politics of disorientation might be to sustain wonder about the very forms of social gathering. (24)

Disorienting our relationship to the power dynamics and hierarchies inherent in London's normative logic and reorienting us through the perceptual angles of subjects who struggle with 'seeing straight', Woolf's novels move us toward a broader politics of perception, laying bare the gendered and sexualised hegemonic space that is urban London in the early and mid-twentieth century while also offering alternative and queer phenomenological encounters premised on contingency and flux. Keeping in mind Halberstam's and Ahmed's queer phenomenology, this essay will traverse the urban space of London as it is perceived and embodied in Virginia Woolf's war novels – most specifically *Jacob's Room*, *Mrs Dalloway*, *The Waves* and *The Years* – so as to elucidate what new narratives and alternative relations to time and space are opened up by the queer angles from which Woolf asks her readers to see London, a city where, as she writes in *The Voyage Out*, 'eccentricity must pay the penalty' (1). Woolf's work is, I argue, foundational to our understanding of how, as subjects, we are continually oriented, discursively and visually, toward lines of thought and action that encourage the repetition of gendered and sexualised hegemonic constructions. Orienting us toward an awareness of these hegemonic straightening devices, Woolf's war novels reorient readers perceptually by insisting that we follow lines of deviation, lines that encourage perpetual reorientation and refuse any easy return to history's seemingly irrevocable and upright march toward a repetition of the same.

'Eccentricity must pay the penalty': London's Normative Logic

Rendered temporally exact by the chimes of its many clocks, Woolf's London is an urban space that excels at coercing its inhabitants to remain vertical in stance and upright in carriage. However, while it spatially and temporally orients its dwellers away from more 'obscure angles and relationships', London, as Woolf's essay 'Street Haunting' testifies, can also reveal them (483). The aesthetic disorientations of Woolf's first experimental novel, *Jacob's Room* (1922), were inspired by this tension between what she refers to as London's 'queer, incongruous voices' (47) and Britain's institutions, practices and ideologies, all of which she felt bore responsibility for the 'preposterous masculine fiction' that became World War I (*Letters* 5: 76).

The roving narrative eye and voice of *Jacob's Room*, itself disoriented by the futile attempt to capture Jacob Flanders in any definitive terms, never takes us directly to the theatre of war but is instead concerned with what *will be* as a result of *what is*. Hence, Woolf exposes how Britain's greatest city temporally and spatially disciplines bodies to straighten up, and through its institutions – for example, Cambridge and the Church – shapes the ideal masculine subject, a man in military uniform. Pointing to a war that will emerge from and be sustained by disciplinary structures and rituals that reflect and dictate London's normative logic, Woolf requires that we entertain the narrator's attention to the queer and incongruous facets of such logic. It is the queer meanderings of Woolf's narrator that direct us, for example, away from Jacob into the lives of a Mrs Jarvis, Mrs Pascoe, or Florinda – women for whom time is a material abstraction, one that regiments their lives according to patriarchal temporal frames grossly out of sync with their own experiences.[1] Or again that we see Jacob striding freely and confidently through deserted streets, but are quickly reoriented to look towards the poor, who can be seen in 'hordes crossing Waterloo bridge', or to a young woman of twenty-two whose gaze is 'bright and vague' and whose attire is 'shabby' as she makes her way hesitantly across the road (117, 119). Not only does Woolf make it clear that to walk with Jacob's ease and confidence remains a privilege available to his gender and class alone, she also exposes 'the hoary city, old, sinful, and majestic' and its masculine privileges as funded by young women's bodies (68). Such queer narrative meanderings introduce a disorienting array of personal histories that force us to confront the gendered social and ethical implications of normative temporalities and their spatial equivalents.

If *Jacob's Room* makes London's normative logic abundantly clear and reveals how its hegemonic structures, temporal and spatial, are gendered and sexualised, it also acknowledges the heteronormative imperative behind reproducing such structures. Hence, as I discuss below, if as a young British man Jacob is rewarded by a city whose privileges are inherently masculine, he nevertheless struggles to remain vertical and to direct his passions along a straight line. Jacob's efforts to straighten up, as will Septimus Smith's failed efforts to do the same in *Mrs Dalloway*, serve as testimony to Woolf's assertion that while 'the streets of London have their map', nevertheless 'our passions are uncharted' (*Jacob's Room* 99).

Struggling to See Straight: Uncharted Passions in *Jacob's Room* and *Mrs Dalloway*

If, according to Sara Ahmed, a queer phenomenology redirects our attention toward queer moments, a world seen slantwise, then becoming vertical means overcoming the queer effect. How then, asks Ahmed, do individuals go about straightening queer effects? In both *Jacob's Room* and *Mrs Dalloway*, we witness characters succumb to, or, in the case of Septimus Smith, resist the imperative to straighten up. While in *Jacob's Room* the effects of World War I do not register as anything other than ominous shadows and whispers until the final chapter, which leaves us in Jacob's room with his mother and would-be lover after Jacob has died on the battlefield, in *Mrs Dalloway* post-war London is a city where queer moments increasingly take precedence over the mundane and the ordinary. Eve Sedgwick contends that counter to our understanding of a moment as a passing instant, irretrievable in its transience, a 'queer moment' is 'inextinguishable' and 'recurrent' (xii). Furthermore, as Sedgwick defines them, such moments are '*troublant*' or troubling: they disturb the natural order of things. As such, queer moments can be particularly troubling due to their nature as 'multiply transitive', implying that multiple objects and/or persons of desire can be taken into their 'strange' and 'relational' orbit (xii). Transcending the spatial confines of both genre and domesticity and troubling the linear and heteronormative temporality of the marriage plot, Woolf's queer moments anticipate Sedgwick's definition. As we find them in the novels, such moments are indeed 'inextinguishable' (Sedgwick xii). They return, they haunt and they continually reverberate across the lives of Woolf's characters.

In *Jacob's Room*, queer is rendered conventional as long as it stays within the safe confines of the halls and dormitories of Cambridge: 'It was the intimacy, a sort of spiritual suppleness, when mind prints upon mind indelibly' (45). When this 'spiritual suppleness', which our narrator tells us leads Jacob to feel 'extraordinarily happy', shades into a deeper, more forbidden desire, that happiness shifts into avoidance: 'Simeon said nothing. Jacob remained standing. But intimacy – the room was full of it, still, deep, like a pool. Without need of movement or speech it rose softly and washed over everything.... But Jacob moved' (45). While Richard Bonamy, Jacob's closest friend at Cambridge and would-be lover, is clearly marked by others in the text as queer – he is rumoured to have a 'peculiar disposition', for example (163) – Jacob, as we see him through Bonamy's eyes, is resolutely straight:

> But then Jacob Flanders was not at all of his own way of thinking – far from it. [...] The trouble was this romantic vein in him. [...] 'there is something – something' – [Bonamy] sighed, for he was fonder of Jacob than of any one in the world. (148)

Although Bonamy tends to dismiss this 'something' as wishful thinking, several moments in the novel lend it credence. It is very clear, for example, at the Durrant's dinner party, that Jacob finds the heteronormative bourgeoisie world represented by such social gatherings more than a little distressing. Having just returned from an idyllic sailing trip with Timmy Durrant to the Scilly Isles, Jacob goes through the motions of straightening himself up by donning a 'dinner jacket', which, as our narrator humorously notes, is the only thing that 'preserved him' and rendered the world 'stable', a fact for which '[h]e could not be sufficiently thankful' (57). While Jacob's efforts to 'straighten' himself here likely have much to do with the sea legs he developed on the sailboat with Durrant, in the context of the dinner party, the ulterior motives of which are clearly to encourage his relationship with Timothy's sister, Clara, Jacob's queer relationship to and feelings about the dinner's coercive normativity are worth noting. For Jacob participates in the meal feeling simultaneously detached and 'exposed without cover' (57). The bones of the cutlets dressed with 'pink frills' contrast objectionably with his memory of gnawing 'ham from the bone' only yesterday with Timmy Durrant, and the figures and objects around him appear like 'hazy, semi-transparent shapes of yellow and blue' (57). Mrs Durrant, holding herself 'very straight', gazes at 'the extraordinarily awkward' Jacob interacting with her daughter Clara – '"Shall I hold your wool?" Jacob asked stiffly' (61–2).

That Jacob's struggle to straighten up even when well suited belies the 'something else' that Bonamy senses in him becomes apparent in Jacob's queerest moment, a moment which, if quickly repressed and checked by his supposed love for the unavailable, because married, Sandra Wentworth Williams, eddies and returns in the novel's final moments. While sight-seeing in Greece, Jacob finds himself overcome with a desire to see Bonamy and writes a telegram telling him to 'come at once', which he then immediately 'crumpl[es] in his hand and [throws] in the gutter' (157). Having heeded his desire, Jacob quickly rationalises why he is unable to follow through:

> 'For one thing he wouldn't come', he thought. 'And then I daresay this sort of thing wears off.' 'This sort of thing' being that uneasy, painful feeling, something like selfishness – one wishes almost that the thing would stop – it is getting more and more beyond what is possible. (157)

Delightfully vague while at the same time deliciously obvious, Woolf's use of unclear pronoun referents and innocuous nouns – the 'thing' that is 'beyond what is possible' – reveals, in a rare moment, Jacob's love for Bonamy. While he works hard to straighten that love, here it overwhelms him to the extent that 'if *it* goes on much longer', he may find himself 'unable to cope with it' (157, emphasis added).

Back in London, while paying a visit to Clara, Bonamy is feeling the same suffocating effects induced by conventional domesticity that Jacob had experienced at the Durrant's dinner: 'Bonamy kept on gently returning quiet answers and accumulating amazement at an existence squeezed and emasculated within a white satin shoe' (160). Disoriented by the experience of speaking to Clara, who unintentionally refuses him the opportunity to share his feelings for Jacob and instead brutally reminds him of the temporal frameworks induced by heteronormativity, Bonamy finds his world aslant suddenly forced straight:

> For a man of his temperament, [he] got a very queer feeling, as he walked through the park, of carriages irresistibly driven; of flower beds uncompromisingly geometrical; of force rushing round geometrical patterns in the most senseless way in the world. (160)

As Bonamy himself recognises, this 'very queer feeling' has nothing to do with his own 'temperament', but is induced instead by the 'senseless' rush of 'geometrical patterns' he sees before him in the London square and the drive to be straight that such patterns demand. Patterns, which Bonamy also knows, at the level of society, orient Jacob's desire away from him toward what will always be the 'silent woman' between them.

In the end, *Jacob's Room* confirms that it is precisely this senseless rush of patterns that needs to be done away with, for the price of submission is, quite literally, Jacob himself. We are left in Jacob's room with his mother Betty, whose vision we know from the novel's first pages has been slanted by grief. With Betty is not Clara Durrant but Richard Bonamy. As Jacob's mother and Bonamy survey the room and go through Jacob's things, Woolf's narrator calls our attention, as she had when first describing his room, to the 'distinction' of the eighteenth-century building and the room within; a room which, in its architectural shapelessness, gestures toward the order of its day but whose lines and décor, however predictable, however representative, could not prevent his death any more than they can contain his absence or the confusion it has caused. The novel ends with a recognition of that confusion – '"Such confusion everywhere!" exclaimed Betty Flanders' – and offers readers a sign that the old order may yield to a world seen aslant as Bonamy's cry of 'Jacob! Jacob!' meets with Betty Flander's plaintive query as she holds up a pair of Jacob's old shoes, 'What am I to do with these, Mr. Bonamy?' (187). Significantly, Woolf's first experimental novel, as Vara Neverow has stated, offers us a 'bitterly caustic and yet elegiac inversion of the traditional marriage plot', thereby leaving suspended the possibility of a future where new relations and alternative plots might be available (lxxvii).

Woolf's second radical departure from conventional forms of the novel, *Mrs Dalloway*, takes us into that future – post-war London – where, as the queer moment of a long ago kiss eddies around the quotidian, the otherwise conventional Clarissa Dalloway struggles to remain within the narrow confines of her role as hostess, mother and wife, and where Septimus Smith, his mind ravaged by the war, remains increasingly unable to overcome the queer effects induced by combat and his love for another soldier. Conveying queer affinities with much more subjective intensity than had *Jacob's Room*, *Mrs Dalloway* accounts for how, with varying degrees of success, such affinities are brought back into 'proportion' or made to line up with London's hegemonic and heteronormative cartographies. Nevertheless, the novel begins to elucidate what new narratives and alternative relations to time and space might be opened up if we see London from the queer angles of a Clarissa Dalloway or Septimus Smith.

Clarissa Dalloway, seemingly 'light, tall, very upright' (12) and, according to Peter Walsh, 'straight as a dart' (76), plunges readers into inhabiting two temporal zones simultaneously: in the first – the present moment – Clarissa walks the streets of London, which, though intimately familiar, have been rendered strange by a war whose dead haunt every corner, and by an illness, which, having removed her temporarily from the 'army of the upright',[2] has left her seeing aslant. In the second temporal zone, the arc of time is bent backwards toward her young life in Bourton and toward the most 'exquisite moment of her whole life', Sally Seton's kiss (35). While Clarissa is unlikely to move beyond the confines of her 'narrow bed', her perceptual ecstasies and their queer ripples inform a larger politics of perception that Woolf's novel in its entirety is intent on conveying. For pushing against the sensible sounds of Big Ben 'laying down the law, so solemn, so just' and against the supposedly progressive march forward of historical time, Clarissa's queer revelations amount to a theory of being in the world that marks the human as that which is most contingent, most transient and therefore most astonishing (128). Thus, the 'supreme mystery' is the old lady seen but not heard across the way: 'How extraordinary it was, strange, yes, touching to see the old lady [...]. [I]t had something to do with her' (127). This sudden and deeply felt affinity Clarissa finds herself having with others in post-war London – at this particular moment an affinity with an old lady who is not but indeed someday will be herself – renders her world indelibly queer.

Nevertheless, in order to move through a world that is oriented vertically, Clarissa understands, despite the effort it takes, that she must 'give her face point' and pull herself upright in order to extend her body into space (36). Sara Ahmed notes that

> the queer moment, in which objects appear slantwise and the vertical and horizontal axes appear 'out of line', must be overcome not because such moments contradict laws that govern objective space, but because they block bodily action: they inhibit the body such that it ceases to extend into phenomenal space. (66)

Unlike Clarissa, Septimus, her alter ego, fails to straighten himself up. He ultimately chooses death as preferable to Holmes and Bradshaw's prescriptions for returning him to his position as a 'soldier in the army of the upright',[3] or to health and thus 'proportion'. Like Clarissa, Septimus glides on the surface of the present and sinks into the depths of the past. As Clarissa's memory bends her back toward Sally's kiss, so too does Septimus's memory throw him back on to his passion for Evans, who was killed 'just before the Armistice in Italy' (86). Although Woolf provides us with no explicit evidence for a homosexual relationship between Septimus and Evans beyond the homosocial bonds forged in combat, we do learn that prior to Septimus's enlistment, his employer, Mr Brewer, worries that 'something [is] up [...] he looked weakly; advised football' (85). Mr Brewer's need to bring Septimus back into line with a heteronormative British masculinity is met, as Woolf's narrator tells us, by 'the prying and insidious [...] fingers of the European War': 'There in the trenches the change which Mr. Brewer desired when he advised football was produced instantly; he developed manliness' (85–6). The final proof of what the war had taught him, Septimus realises, is that he is able to congratulate himself upon Evans's death for 'feeling very little and very reasonably' (86). Any abiding affection Septimus had for Evans, who, as we learn from Lucrezia, was 'a quiet man [...] undemonstrative in the company of women', is lost in the defensive indifference with which he watches the war's last shells explode (86). Until, that is, having returned to Milan, he finds himself seized by the panic that he cannot feel and promptly becomes engaged to Lucrezia.

However, this attempt to pull himself upright, to move through the world as a 'normal' British male is wont to do, fails miserably. As Septimus sits on a bench in Regent's Park being beckoned by trees whose leaves seem to be 'connected by millions of fibres with his own body' and listening to the queer 'harmonies' echoing in the spaces between the sounds of 'sparrows fluttering, rising', Lucrezia tries desperately to pull him from the queer temporality the war has locked both of them into: '"Look", she implored him, for Dr. Holmes had told her to make him notice real things, go to a music hall, play cricket' (22, 25). However, her continued cries of 'look' cannot overwhelm the other voice Septimus hears: 'Look the unseen bade him, the voice which now communicated with him who was the greatest of mankind' (25). To emphasise the temporal disjunction being experienced by this husband and wife, Woolf abruptly switches readers to seeing them through the eyes of Maisie Johnson, a young Scottish woman, who is in London for the first time:

> Both seemed queer, Maisie Johnson thought. Everything seemed very queer. [...] this couple on the chairs gave her quite a turn; the young woman seeming foreign, the man looking queer [...] how queer it was, this couple she had asked the way of [...] all seemed, after Edinburgh, so queer. (25–6)

By spinning readers outside of Septimus's and Lucrezia's perceptual field and into that of a London outsider, who somehow equates the city with the 'queer' couple she sees before her, Woolf implies that despite Big Ben's 'sensible sound', the war indeed has turned London and its inhabitants upside down (150).

Unable to disarticulate his past from his present, Septimus finds himself facing the ultimate straightening device: Sir William Bradshaw and his 'divine proportion' (99). Normative time takes hold with a vengeance in the pages of *Mrs Dalloway* dedicated to an account of William Bradshaw and his more benign compatriot Hugh Whitbread: 'Shredding and slicing, dividing and subdividing, the clocks of Harley Street nibbled at the June day, counselled submission, upheld authority, and pointed out in chorus the supreme advantages of a sense of proportion' (100). Laying, 'very high, on the back of the world' his mind's eye slanted toward the 'queer harmony' he hears coming from London's streets, Septimus sees beauty 'made out of ordinary things […] beauty, that was the truth now. Beauty was everywhere' (68, 69). As the trees wave and brandish their branches, Septimus's strange temporality clashes irrevocably with the time of Bradshaw's arrival: '"It is time", said Rezia. The word "time" split its husk; poured its riches over him' (69). From behind the branches, Evans appears, 'without mud, without wounds', leading Septimus to believe that his own time is 'real' time (70). Hence, to Lucrezia's continued query of '"The time Septimus […] What is the time?"' comes the response: '"I will tell you the time," said Septimus, very slowly, very drowsily, smiling mysteriously. As he sat smiling at the dead man in the grey suit the quarter struck' (70). And, although he waits until the 'very last moment', he ultimately chooses his own queer time (149).

'Queer', Eve Sedgwick tells us in *Tendencies*, is 'relational and strange' (xii). If Woolf finds herself unable to actualise her queer moments in the larger social fabric, she nevertheless provides readers in *Mrs Dalloway* with a politics of perception that privileges disorientation and seeing 'slantwise'. Like Clarissa, Woolf asks us to inhabit 'queer little scenes' and to feel ourselves everywhere, not 'here, here, here' but 'everywhere' (*Mrs Dalloway* 51). It is the 'odd affinities', the relations Clarissa had with people to whom she had 'never spoken, to some woman in the street, some man behind a counter – even trees, or barns' that Peter Walsh remembers as he walks to her party at the end of the novel (153). Such 'odd affinities' ask us as readers also to 'face a different way' and thus offer what Ahmed contends are possibilities for creating new forms of social gathering (24).

Seeing Slantwise: Alternative Forms of Social Being and Organisation in *The Waves* and *The Years*

New forms of social gathering born of temporal and spatial disorder are very much at the heart of Woolf's most highly experimental novel, *The Waves*, as well as *The Years*, the latter of which is perhaps most surprising in this regard, given its apparent return to the more conventional form of the Victorian novel.[4] More intensely than in either *Jacob's Room* or *Mrs Dalloway*, time is perceived in Woolf's later novels as constituting space too often shaped by the tyranny of the same. Both texts reveal the ultimate futility of hegemonic efforts to order and control lived experiences as well as the danger such efforts pose. Thus, Bernard thinks towards the end of *The Waves*,

> [I]t is a mistake, this extreme precision, this orderly and military progress; a convenience, a lie. There is always deep below it, even

when we arrive punctually at the appointed time with our white waistcoats and polite formalities, a rushing stream of broken dreams. (189)

The invisible realities running beneath the ostensibly placid veneer of civilisation and the alternative temporal and spatial dimensions those invisible realities open up are precisely what Woolf folds into her 'play poem', *The Waves*; they brew as well beneath the ostensibly logical temporal divisions of *The Years*, where characters find themselves continually disoriented despite, and perhaps because of, temporal and spatial divides.

Woolf's struggle with what kind of aesthetic form *The Waves* should take illustrates this tension between precision and flux: 'I shall have two different currents – the moths flying along; the flower upright in the centre; a perpetual crumbling and renewing of the plant' (*A Writer's Diary* 140). She knew that this form must 'eliminate all waste, deadness, superfluity' and also show 'the light through' (136, 138). But what, she asks herself as she struggles with the 'great pressure of difficulty' felt in writing the novel, 'is the light? I am impressed by the transitoriness of human life', and 'I am bored by narrative' (138). Ultimately, Woolf's 'play poem' emerges organically from the voices she creates and is less of a definitive form than it is a moving orchestration of sensate beings whose proximity to and impingement upon one another connect them until they are like the tissues of one body. 'The skin of the social', writes Ahmed, 'might be affected by the comings and goings of different bodies, creating new lines and new textures in the ways in which things are arranged' (9). In *The Waves*, Percival stands for – however ironically, given his fatal fall from a 'flea-bitten mare' – Britain's propensity for precision, order and progress; his death then 'abolishes the ticking of time's clock with one blow', leaving those left behind to trace new lines and discover new textures in the chaos of London's modernity (131).

Following the news of Percival's death, as Bernard notes, they all 'see' a world that 'Percival sees no longer' (110). However, of the six 'states of soul', words I borrow from Woolf in lieu of the more conventional notion of 'characters' – Bernard, Neville, Louis, Susan, Jinny, Rhoda – it is Rhoda who sees the world most consistently aslant.[5] As Rhoda walks through London and down Oxford Street she envisages 'a world rent by lightning' (115). According to Sara Ahmed, the work of inhabiting space involves a dynamic negotiation between what is familiar and unfamiliar: 'Familiarity is shaped by the "feel" of space or by how spaces "impress" upon bodies. This familiarity is not, then, "in" the world as that which is already given. The familiar is an effect of inhabitance' (7). Rhoda's walk down Oxford Street and her vision of 'a world rent by lightning' highlight precisely this 'effect of inhabitance' by disorienting us away from an ontological security based on the assumed stability of a civilised world and its material structures toward what Bernard refers to as a 'queer territory': 'London has also crumbled. [...] Could I prolong this sense another six inches I have a forboding that I should touch some queer territory' (134–5). Without clear dimensions either spatial or temporal, this 'queer territory' allows for uncertainty and indeterminacy, thereby contrasting markedly with the pageantry – the 'extreme precision, [the] orderly and military progress' embodied by Percival. While writing *The Waves*, Woolf feared that this 'extreme precision' and military orderliness would find its fullest expression in fascism. If, however, the 'iron black boot' of fascism casts its dark shadow ominously across the pages of *The Waves*, the hope for 'some sort of renewal' (220) is invoked by the 'abysses of space' opening up beyond the canopy of a 'burnt out' civilisation and by the 'queer territory' Bernard senses he might touch as he sees London crumble before him. Such renewal is not redemptive in the definitive sense of the word, for Bernard's final meditations on time and space, like the novel in its entirety, speak instead to an 'eternal renewal' elaborated as an 'incessant rise and fall and fall and rise again' (220). As *The Waves* makes clear, such ebbs and flows do not come to a final still point but instead leave us like Bernard – 'looking up rather dizzily at the sky' – thereby inviting us to slant our vision toward an uncertain future (220).

If Percival's life and death initiate the journey into a 'queer territory' rife with ontological uncertainty, Rhoda, for one, recognises that the move into such a territory is enabled by her relations with the others: 'But these pilgrimages, these moments of departure, start always in your presence, from this table, these lights, from Percival and Susan, here and now' (101). *The Years*, frequently referred to as Woolf's 'London novel', is, like *The Waves*, vexed by ontological uncertainty. Taking us back to a war that for Woolf was well in the past, perhaps in an effort to grasp the war that she feared was to come, *The Years*' clear temporal divides would seem to refute such uncertainty with a faith in chronology and linear progress; however, such clear divisions belie the anxiety of the characters, within whom the refrain 'Where am I?' continually resounds. This sense of disorientation only intensifies in the '1914' and '1917' sections of the novel where the war slants the world away from its normative temporal and spatial dimensions and toward a queer relationality.

In the '1914' section of *The Years*, the queer visionary Sara Pargiter and her cousin Martin, a presumably straight – though increasingly doubtful – military man, meet on the steps of London's St Paul's Cathedral and proceed to journey across the city from a chophouse, down Fleet Street, along the Strand to Charing Cross, there boarding a bus to Hyde Park Corner and walking to Kensington Gardens, where they come upon Martin's sister and Sara's cousin, Maggie, with her baby. As Eleanor McNees observes,

> their journey is significant, as it allows for a final pre-World War I summary both of the characters' movements within London from 1880–1914 and the various religious, commercial, monarchical, legal, and civilian aspects of a city on the brink of a war that would alter if not the landscape (as would World War II), then the consciousness of the people. (lxvii)

Indeed, while our attention is called to what is most familiar about London as a centre of historical tradition and commercial power, the chapter is most preoccupied with how we see those familiar landmarks through the disoriented visual consciousness of the ostensibly straight man, Martin. Unlike previous novels where the clock as a temporal marker predictably regulates the hours in the day, whether or not individuals agree to march accordingly, in *The Years* these clocks are ominously either malfunctioning or out of sync: 'In the country old church clocks rasped out the hour' and '[t]he air over London seemed a rough sea of sound through which circles travelled. But the clocks were irregular, as if the saints themselves were divided' (212). Time indeed seems to have been abolished: '[Martin] looked up. "The station clock's always fast", he assured a man who was hurrying to catch a train. Always fast, he said to himself as he opened the paper. But there was no clock' (223).

If Sara, who consistently orients others toward rather than away from queer moments, remains unperturbed, Martin finds himself temporally out of sorts and feels increasingly dislocated by what should be London's familiar sights and sounds. As if to affirm the invisible forces rumbling beneath the city's ostensibly firm foundation, the narrative voice emphasises that those familiar sights and sounds only 'seem' to be what they are:

> The omnibuses swirled and circled in a perpetual current round the steps of St Paul's. The statue of Queen Anne *seemed* to preside over the chaos and to supply it with a centre, like the hub of a wheel. It *seemed* as if the white lady ruled the traffic with her scepter [...]. The great clock, all the clocks of the city, *seemed* to be gathering their forces together; they *seemed* to be whirring a preliminary warning. (214–15, emphasis added)

As Sara and Martin move on down Fleet Street, the 'queer thrill' of the correspondence Martin had often felt in the past when encountering sites like St Paul's comes under further assault:

> They began to walk along Fleet Street. Conversation was impossible. The pavement was so narrow that he had to step on and off in order to keep beside her. [...] People pressing against him made him step off the pavement. (221)

If keeping himself on the straight and narrow path were not hard enough, Martin finds himself in the position of having to steer Sara, whose 'queer little shuffle' reminds him of a 'somewhat dishevelled fowl', back on to their designated path as she continually pulls him off line, skipping perversely wherever she pleases (216). Entirely disoriented by having to follow Sara's unpredictable movements as well as her odd exclamations and strange beholdings, Martin suddenly realises they have been walking in the wrong direction.

'Getting lost', writes Sara Ahmed, 'takes us somewhere; and being lost is a way of inhabiting space by registering what is not familiar: being lost can in its turn become a familiar feeling' (7). But, for Ahmed, as I mentioned earlier, this 'familiar feeling' is not a familiarity that is already a given:

> The work of inhabiting space involves a dynamic negotiation between what is familiar and unfamiliar, such that it is still possible for the world to create new impressions, depending on which way we turn, which affects what is within reach. (7–8)

Woolf leaves us, at the end of Martin and Sara's long walk through the city, in a moment of 'primal innocence', a moment that suggests the impressions Martin is registering as a result of his queer time with Sara may have the potential to open out into a more ethical way of seeing and being in the world.

Woolf's odd couplings, Sara and Martin, and, as we are about to see, Eleanor and Nicholas, are absolutely central to this new ethics. Speaking to these affinities and relations, Stephen Barber writes, 'Woolf represents queer novelistic subjectivities in the defamiliarizing light of conspiratorial relationships between women and gay men' (403). In the '1917' section, the 'novel ethical possibilities', which Barber argues are inherent to 'Woolf's inscription of queer relationality' (405, 404), find explicit expression in the relationship that forms between Eleanor and Nicholas, the latter of whom, as Sara informs Eleanor, 'loves the other sex, you see' (282). On a frigid winter evening three years into World War II, Eleanor, Sara and Maggie Pargiter begin by dining in a basement with Maggie's French husband Renny and his queer Polish friend, Nicholas, and finish pressed against each other in a cellar as air raid sirens wail overhead. Prior to the air raid, the conversation had circled tensely around issues concerning nationality, religion, the law and identity, and those tensions only intensify in the close quarters of the cellar. The dissension in the room is palpable, but the honesty, as Eleanor finds it, is also invigorating and yields a new way of seeing the world. Whether blurred by wine or war, Eleanor's vision extinguishes the bodily boundaries between self and other – 'things seemed to have lost their skins' – replacing the usual 'surface hardness' with a new 'porousness' (272).

Upon re-entering the drawing room, Eleanor feels a sense of expansion and 'great calm' as if a 'New World' were opening before her: 'It was as if another space of time had been issued to her' (278). Turning to the sage-like Nicholas, Eleanor asks, '"how can we improve ourselves, live more naturally … better?"' (280). As he speaks in hushed tones about the way they live their lives in tight little knots and argues for the need to embrace the 'whole being', for it 'wishes to expand; to adventure; to form – new combinations', Eleanor feels as if Nicholas has released in her 'new powers, something unknown within her' (281). However, Eleanor's synchronic willingness to be captivated by the revelations of a moment, the here and the now, is interrupted by Renny's diachronic awareness that history has always allocated violence in a non-democratic fashion and will inevitably continue to do so – '"I have spent the evening sitting in a coal cellar while other people try to kill each other above my head"' (279). Aesthetically and philosophically speaking, it is this struggle between the diachronic and the synchronic that preoccupies Woolf in much of *The Years*.

As suggested by the searchlights fanning ominously across the novel's final pages, new relations and 'new combinations' will take heroic efforts to sustain beyond the small moments that reveal them. Bringing our attention back, as Renny had also, to the war and its violence, the searchlights leave us with a sense that Nicholas and Eleanor's vision of a new world born of a queer moment in an air raid shelter will remain vulnerable as history grinds tragically forward. Thus, as Eleanor's last words in the novel indicate – '"There?" […] "And now?"' – new worlds and their new combinations are best borne out moment by moment, a temporal unfolding with endless potential if it is continually and self-reflexively phrased as a question: 'We have been there, and now?'

Woolf's Politics of Disorientation

It is toward the possibilities inherent in the 'now' that Woolf's aesthetic disorientations in the novels are wont to move us. The temporal space of 'now', as queer scholar Carolyn Dinshaw observes, has no duration:

> As soon as you fix on it, it's gone, it's a has-been, and we're on to the next now. In fact, now is never purely there at all: it is a transition, always divided between no longer and not yet; each present now is stretched and spanned by a past now and a future now. […] And because the present moment never comes – never is – longing in or for the present never can be fulfilled. […] Now cannot specify a determinate moment after all. (2)

Undoing, unsettling and recursively moving between more fixed ideological and material structures, this 'now', which is where Woolf's most chronologically conscious novel *The Years* wants to leave us, necessitates a politics of disorientation. Aesthetically speaking, in the novels I have examined here, such disorientation is prompted by failed orientations induced by either the anticipation of a war to come or the memory of a war that has been. Losing their place in what should be a familiar world, they – Woolf's characters – and we – Woolf's readers – must continually register somatically and psychically a 'becoming oblique of the world, a becoming that is at once interior and exterior, as that which is given, or as that which gives what is given in its new angle' (Ahmed 162).

In inviting us to imagine what might be if we continually ask questions about what is, Woolf's work models for us the critical force of queer and of a queer critical history and politics that does not naively idealise a 'now' as positing some sort of redemptive utopia, but instead mines that temporal moment for its constant unfolding of yet another possibility. 'We look back', writes Ahmed, 'as a refusal to inherit, as a refusal that is a condition for the arrival of the queer' (178). If the ordinary work of perception straightens the queer effect (in a blink, the slant of a kiss between women is straightened up), then Woolf's work is bent on disturbing that ordinary work of perception and staying with the queer effects that follow such a disturbance. Thus, as we traverse the urban landscape that is Woolf's London before, during or after a war, we are disoriented so as to be reoriented toward a more radical future. A future where sexuality is determined, as Ahmed has suggested, not only by object choice, 'but as involving differences in one's very relationship to the world – that is in how one "faces" the world or is directed toward it' (68). Rejecting any and all totalitarian truths, Woolf's 'Outsider's Society', to which 'elasticity is essential' (*Three Guineas* 134) and to which many of her characters no doubt belong, invites us into a queer territory where the time of 'now' – infinitely expansive, impossible to pin down – creates an awareness of space as that which shapes us and is shaped by us, but also space as that which can emerge from us. With this queer phenomenological awareness facilitated by Woolf in hand, we might, like Eleanor, look 'there' – always refusing any gestures of return – and move into the 'now' aware that, if we let it, that 'now' has the capacity to endlessly confound and lead us astray, but also to reorient us toward new and better worlds, moment by moment.

Notes

1. Here I invoke Sedgwick's emphasis on the etymological origins of the word 'queer': 'to transverse, to twist, to move across' (xii).
2. Woolf, 'On Being Ill' 321.
3. 'On Being Ill' 12.
4. Eleanor McNees reminds readers of *The Years* that Woolf saw her form as anything but conventional. She cites Pamela Caughie, who sees the novel 'as postmodern in its emphasis on relations instead of representation' (lvi).
5. In response to *The Times*' review of *The Waves*, Woolf writes on 5 October 1931, 'I wonder if it is good to feel this remoteness – that is, that *The Waves* is not what they say. Odd, that they (*The Times*) should praise my characters when I meant to have none' (*A Writer's Diary* 170). I take the phrase 'states of soul' from her observation that same year on 10 September: 'Really these premonitions of a book – states of soul in creating – are very queer and little apprehended' (*A Writer's Diary* 142).

Works Cited

Ahmed, Sara. *Queer Phenomenology: Orientations, Objects, Others*. Durham: Duke University Press, 2006.

Barber, Stephen. 'Lip-Reading: Woolf's Secret Encounters'. *Novel Gazing: Queer Readings in Fiction*. Ed. Eve Kosofsky Sedgwick. Durham: Duke University Press, 1997. 401–43.

Dinshaw, Carolyn. 'How Soon Is Now?' *How Soon Is Now? Medieval Texts, Amateur Readers, and the Queerness of Time*. Durham: Duke University Press, 2012. 1–39.

Halberstam, Judith. *In a Queer Time and Place: Transgender Bodies, Subcultural Lives*. New York: New York University Press, 2005.

McNees, Eleanor. Introduction. *The Years*. By Virginia Woolf. New York: Harcourt, 2008. lvi–lxxxiii.

Neverow, Vara. Introduction. *Jacob's Room*. By Virginia Woolf. New York: Harcourt, 2008. xxxvii–xciv.

Sedgwick, Eve Kosofsky. *Tendencies*. Durham: Duke University Press, 1993.

Woolf, Virginia. *The Diary of Virginia Woolf*. Vol. 2. Ed. Anne Olivier Bell. New York: Harcourt, 1978.

—. *Jacob's Room*. 1922. Ed. Vara Neverow. New York: Harcourt, 2008.

—. *The Letters of Virginia Woolf*. Ed. Nigel Nicolson and Joanne Trautmann. 6 vols. New York: Harcourt, 1975–80.

—. *Mrs Dalloway*. 1925. Ed. Bonnie Kime Scott. New York: Harcourt, 2005.

—. 'On Being Ill'. 1926. *The Essays of Virginia Woolf*. Ed. Andrew McNeillie. Vol. 4. New York: Harcourt, 1994. 317–29.

—. 'Street Haunting: A London Adventure'. 1927. *The Essays of Virginia Woolf*. Ed. Andrew McNeillie. Vol. 4. New York: Harcourt, 1994. 480–91.

—. *Three Guineas*. 1938. Ed. Jane Marcus. New York: Harcourt, 2006.
—. *The Voyage Out*. 1915. Ed. Elizabeth Heine. New York: Vintage, 1992.
—. *The Waves*. 1931. Ed. Molly Hite. New York: Harcourt, 2006.
—. *A Writer's Diary*. 1953. Ed. Leonard Woolf. New York: Harcourt, 1982.
—. *The Years*. 1931. Ed. Eleanor McNees. New York: Harcourt, 2008.

Index

Ahmed, Sara, 10, 277, 279, 283, 285, 286, 289, 291
Allan, Maude, 253
Allen, Clifford, 245, 250
Allen, Dennis, 5
Angell, Norman, 252
Annan, Noel, 28
Anrep, Boris, 142
Anrep, Helen, 142
Anscombe, G. E. M., 212–14, 216
Appignanesi, Lisa, 136
Ashbee, C. R. (Charles Robert), 43
Asquith, H. H. (Herbert Henry), 245, 250
Atkin, Jonathan, 243, 246, 250
Auden, W. H. (Wystan Hugh), 31–3

Bagenal, Barbara (Hiles), 139, 143, 193, 201
Banfield, Ann, 211, 215
Barber, Stephen, 289
Barbican Art Gallery, 189
Bartley, W. W. (William Warren), 212–14
Bar-Yosef, Eitan, 226
Beja, Morris, 20, 21
Bell, Clive, 1, 3, 8, 9, 27, 29, 30–5, 40, 42, 44–6, 64, 67, 138–40, 143, 156, 157, 176, 186, 194, 203, 240–54
Bell, Julian, 29, 30, 211, 240
Bell, Quentin, 3, 4, 21, 24–6, 35, 40, 66, 138, 156, 157, 162, 166
  On British Freedom, 253
  Peace at Once, 246–9, 252

Bell, Vanessa (Stephen), 1, 3, 16, 25, 26, 28, 34, 37, 39, 43, 44, 48, 51, 53, 56–8, 66, 96, 97, 135, 137, 138, 140, 143, 147, 148, 152–5, 157–64, 167, 193, 194, 251, 253, 260
Bergman, David, 72
Bibbings, Lois, 241, 242, 244, 245, 252
Bingham, Emily, 189, 200–4, 209
Bingham, Henrietta, 9, 189, 200–4, 209
Birrell, Francis, 200
Boyarin, Daniel, 229, 230
Brenan, Gerald, 35, 141, 148, 198–205, 208
Bretton Woods, 89, 91–3, 106–8, 111
Brooke, Rupert, 27
Brown, Gavin, 2
Brown, Wendy, 5
Browne, Kath, 2
Broyard, Anatole, 18
Buckingham, Bob, 142
Buckingham, May, 142
Burgess, Anthony, 27
Butler, Judith, 2, 68, 69, 216, 217, 249, 250

Cambridge Apostles, 9, 23, 54, 140, 141, 174, 176, 177, 182, 186, 194, 211
Cambridge University, 3, 9, 23, 26, 27, 35, 54, 67, 77–9, 82, 93, 116, 117, 125, 140, 141, 173, 174, 176, 178, 179, 181, 194, 211–14, 220, 223–6, 231, 233–6, 278, 280

Camp, 8, 51, 64–83, 85, 172, 173, 175, 177–9, 185, 187, 195, 208, 223
Carpenter, Edward, 70, 117, 141
Carrington, Dora, 9, 28, 139, 141, 144, 145, 147, 148, 182, 189–209
Carrington, Noel, 190, 191, 196, 197, 199
Caserio, Robert, 175, 176
Ceylon (Sri Lanka), 137, 224, 225, 236
Charleston Farmhouse, 3, 9, 10, 29, 33, 39, 41, 42, 59, 61–3, 96, 97, 102, 110, 144, 145, 152–71, 205, 220, 251
Chauncey, George, 152
Chesterton, G. K. (Gilbert Keith), 248
Chisholm, Anne, 148, 189, 197, 199
Clark, Christopher, 242
Compton-Burnett, Ivy, 27
Condo, George, 185
Cook, Matt, 162, 166
Cubism, 49

Davidson, Angus, 155
DeSalvo, Louise, 56–8
Dickinson, Goldsworthy Lowes, 28, 82, 264
Dinshaw, Carolyn, 290
Doan, Laura, 118
Dreadnought Hoax, The, 30, 76, 77
Dreyfus, Alfred, 229, 230
Du Bois, W. E. B. (William Edward Burghardt), 126

Eagleton, Terry, 68–70
Edelman, Lee, 68, 69
Eliot, T. S. (Thomas Stearns), 31, 67, 68
Ellis, Havelock, 67, 116, 141

Ferrante, Joan, 20
Fitzroy Square, 3, 141
Fordism, 91, 92
Forster, E. M. (Edward Morgan), 1, 8, 9, 28, 30, 34, 38, 39, 47, 48, 53, 54, 64–88, 117, 142, 155, 179, 223, 224, 238, 258–75
  Abinger Harvest, 81
  Eternal Moment and Other Stories, The, 258, 271
  Howards End, 28
  Marianne Thornton, 8, 64, 82, 83
  Maurice, 53, 54, 117, 266, 267
  Passage to India, A, 71, 76, 79, 261
  Pharos and Pharillon, 71, 81
Foucault, Michel, 38, 39, 217, 218, 261
Freud, Sigmund, 28, 33, 75, 115, 116, 122, 123, 129, 130, 137
  Three Essays on the Theory of Sexuality, 123
Fry, Helen (Combes), 142
Fry, Roger, 1, 29, 34, 40–5, 49, 55, 56, 57, 82, 141–3, 146, 155, 158
Fryern Court, 205, 208
Furbank, P. N. (Philip Nicholas), 71, 262, 263

Gallop, Jane, 68, 69
Garnett, Angelica (Bell), 3, 16, 96, 139, 142, 143, 145–7, 276
  Deceived with Kindness, 145
  Unspoken Truth, The, 145
Garnett, David, 3, 16, 20, 21, 33, 96, 135, 140, 143, 145, 146, 152, 153, 157, 158, 159, 192, 195, 196, 200, 201, 203, 251
  Aspects of Love, 145
Garsington Manor, 193, 253
Gautier, Théophile, 116
Gertler, Mark, 189, 191–3, 195, 196, 198, 199, 208
Gerzina, Gretchen Holbrook, 139, 194, 195, 196
Gibson-Graham, J. K. (Julie Graham and Katherine Gibson), 90, 93, 111
Gilbert, Sandra, 67
Gilroy, Paul, 1, 11
Goldsworthy Lowes Dickinson, 8, 28, 82, 87
Gordon Square, 3, 27, 35, 37, 160, 175, 176, 220
Grant, Duncan, 1, 3, 4, 8, 9, 17, 27, 29, 34, 39, 42–8, 51, 53–7, 89–111, 135, 138–40, 143, 145, 152–69, 193, 194, 201, 224, 225, 247, 251
Greer, Germaine, 51, 52
Gubar, Susan, 67
Gullace, Nicoletta, 245, 248, 249

Halberstam, Judith (Jack), 10, 277
Hall, Radclyffe, 117–19

INDEX

Ham Spray House, 144, 145, 148, 202, 204, 205, 208
Hamnett, Nina, 192
Hampton, Christopher, 139
Hancock, David Boyd, 189, 191, 192
Harrison, Charles, 42–6, 51, 58
Heilbrun, Carolyn, 4, 7, 15–21, 23–35, 36, 41, 67, 136
Herz, Judith Scherer, 65, 71, 77, 80
Hill, Jane, 189
Hills, John (Jack) Waller, 141, 243
Himmelfarb, Gertrude, 39, 46–9, 53, 58
Hirschfeld, Magnus, 116
Hogarth Press, The, 32, 34, 220, 260
Holroyd, Michael, 15, 17, 24, 28, 29, 33, 50, 75, 76, 135, 136, 139–42, 156, 172, 176, 182, 184, 204, 225, 251, 252
Howard, Jean, 20
Hussey, Mark, 4, 11n4, 19, 153, 248
Hutcheon, Linda, 65, 71
Hutchinson, Mary, 147, 193

Independent Review, 79, 80
Isherwood, Christopher, 260

Januszczak, Waldemar, 42
Jebb, R. C. (Richard Claverhouse), 77–9
John, Augustus, 142, 191, 205
John, Dorelia, 205
John, Poppet, 191, 205–8
John Bull, 240, 241, 244
Jones, Ernest, 203
Jowett, Benjamin, 183
Joyce, James, 20, 26, 40, 67, 68
  Ulysses, 24, 67

Kenner, Hugh, 67, 69, 139
Keynes, John Maynard, 1, 3, 8, 9, 24, 25, 28, 29, 34, 35, 46–8, 53, 54, 63, 64, 89–113, 138, 140, 145, 147, 152, 155, 157, 158, 163–5, 167, 180–2, 194, 196, 210–12, 223, 224, 247
  Economic Consequences of the Peace, The, 29, 84
  General Theory of Employment, Interest, and Money, 91
  Indian Currency and Finance, 108
  Tract on Monetary Reform, 105
  Treatise on Probability, 97–9, 101, 105
Keynesianism, 92, 93, 111
King, James, 71, 76
Kinsey Report, 47
Kirstein, Mina, 200, 203
Kramer, Hilton, 48–51, 58
Kress, Susan, 16, 19

Labouchère Amendment, 169, 186
Lacan, Jacques, 68, 69
Lamb, Henry, 142
Lamb, Mary, 205
Lamb, Pansy, 205
Lawrence, D. H., 4, 18, 23, 25, 26, 68, 71, 117, 224
  Fox, The, 117
  Rainbow, The, 117
Lawrence, T. E. (Thomas Edward), 9, 258–75
  Mint, The, 270, 271
  Seven Pillars of Wisdom, 260, 261, 265
Le Corbusier, 96
Leavis, F. R. (Frank Raymond), 4, 11, 25, 30, 33
Leavis, Q. D. (Queenie Dorothy), 4, 54
Lee, Hermione, 143, 144, 225, 226
Lehmann, John, 21, 29
Lehmann, Rosamond, 117
Lewis, Wyndham, 4, 45, 67, 68, 70
Lim, Jason, 2
Lopokova, Lydia, 147, 157, 163, 212

MacCarthy, Desmond, 1, 32, 140, 142
MacCarthy, Molly (Mary), 140, 142, 143, 148
McNees, Eleanor, 287
Marcus, Jane, 38, 54–8, 70
Marler, Regina, 11n4, 17, 136, 149n3, 170n1
Marsh, Eddie, 243
Maurer, Bill, 8, 89–113, 219
Medd, Jodie, 253
Meisel, Perry, 65
Memoir Club, The, 17, 38
Meyer, Moe, 72
Miller, Nancy K., 19
Moffat, Wendy, 258, 260, 262–4

Monk, Ray, 211, 212
Moore, G. E. (George Edward), 1, 25, 26, 31, 35, 91, 93, 94, 98, 141, 180, 181, 211, 231, 259
  Principia Ethica, 25, 35, 91, 93, 141
Morrell, Lady Ottoline, 142, 192, 193, 198, 243
Morrell, Philip, 142, 193, 252
Morris, William, 42–4, 51
Mortimer, Raymond, 96, 138, 155

Naremore, James, 20
Nevinson, C. R. W. (Richard), 189–92
New Criterion, The, 48–50
New Republic, 241
Nicolson, Harold, 138
Nicolson, Nigel, 21, 32, 129n2, 138
No Conscription Fellowship, 251, 252

Oates, Joyce Carol, 18
Omega Workshops, 29, 43, 44, 49, 155, 215

Parsons, Trekkie, 143
Partridge, Frances (Marshall), 137, 140, 141, 146–8, 189, 198, 199, 201, 204
Partridge, Ralph, 139, 141, 145, 182, 197, 198, 204, 208
Pater, Clara, 32
Pater, Walter, 70, 177, 178
Piggford, George, 64–5, 86n15, 179, 223
Pinsent, David, 212, 214
Plato, 141, 174, 176
Plomer, William, 32
Pound, Ezra, 4, 67–9
Price, Richard N., 243
Proust, Marcel, 55
Punch, 240, 241, 253

Ramsey, Frank, 211
Reed, Christopher, 4, 7, 17, 36–9, 59n5, 65, 70, 85n10, 85n13, 96, 155, 162, 165, 168, 169, 189, 190, 194, 195, 208, 231
Robinson, Joan, 99
Roche, Paul, 153, 155, 158–60, 165, 167
Rodmell, 3, 32
Rolls, Jans Ondaatje, 2

Roper, Michael, 243
Rose, Phyllis, 32, 52, 53, 56, 58–60, 63
Rosenbaum, S. P. (Stanford Patrick), 65, 77, 79, 186
Rosenfeld, Natania, 235
Rosner, Victoria, 1, 19, 62
Ross, Andrew, 72
Rotheim, Roy, 99, 100
Runciman, Leslie, 116, 117
Ruskin, John, 42, 43, 51
Russell, Bertrand, 23, 98, 136, 141, 142, 211, 250, 252

Sackville-West, Eddy, 117, 118
Sackville-West, Vita, 8, 32, 76, 88, 118, 120–3, 125, 138, 139, 143, 147, 157
Sassoon, Siegfried, 261, 262, 264
Scrutiny, 28
Sedgwick, Eve Kosofsky, 2, 5, 6, 144, 212, 213, 259, 279, 280, 285
Senhouse, Roger, 9, 76, 183–6
Shaw, George Bernard, 232, 241, 247, 248, 251, 253
Sickert, Walter, 43–5
Slade School of Fine Art, 189, 190, 191, 201
Smyth, Ethel, 118, 119, 128
Socrates, 176, 184, 229
Sontag, Susan, 71, 178
Spalding, Frances, 139, 140, 147, 157, 160, 161, 167, 251
Spencer, Stanley, 189
Spender, Stephen, 32, 34
Spurr, Barry, 72, 73, 179
Stephen, Adrian, 1, 3, 37, 137, 140, 152, 194
Stephen, Leslie, 16, 25, 64, 75, 137
Stephen, Thoby, 1, 3, 25, 26, 37, 137, 146
Strachey, James, 243, 247
Strachey, Lytton, 1, 6, 9, 15, 17, 23–31, 33–5, 37, 46, 49–55, 64–6, 71–7, 80–4, 115, 117, 135, 136, 139, 140–2, 145, 152, 155–7, 167, 172–88, 193–5, 197, 198, 200, 223–6, 228–31, 233, 236, 240, 243, 246, 250–2, 257
  Elizabeth and Essex, 76
  Eminent Victorians, 73, 75, 83, 177, 196
  Queen Victoria, 88

Strachey, Margery, 160
Strachey, Pippa, 55,
Stracheyism, 65, 71, 83, 85, 179
Sydney-Turner, Saxon, 1, 139, 143
Symonds, John Addington, 67, 70, 162

Thackeray, William Makepeace, 43
Thatcher, Margaret, 4, 5
Tidmarsh Mill House, 196, 197, 200–2
Times Literary Supplement, 212
Tomlin, Stephen, 201
Tosh, John, 243
Toynbee Hall, 44
Trilling, Lionel, 25, 34, 39, 47

Valman, Nadia, 226
Vandenburg, Margaret, 19

Warner, Michael, 37, 175
Waters, Sarah, 167
Watney, Simon, 42, 59, 60, 63, 96, 97, 113, 159, 162, 169, 171
Weininger, Otto, 115, 118, 212
Wilde, Oscar, 31, 47, 70, 118, 141, 185, 194, 229, 241, 243, 246, 253
   Picture of Dorian Gray, The, 241
Williams, Raymond, 38
Wittgenstein, Ludwig, 9, 210–20
   Philosophical Investigations, 212, 215, 216
Woolf, Leonard, 1, 3, 6, 9, 28, 30, 34, 38, 42, 66, 128, 137, 139–43, 176–8, 181, 184, 193, 194, 211, 212, 223–39
   Sowing, 188, 226, 229, 231, 233, 234, 239
   Wise Virgins, The, 9, 223, 227, 228, 231, 232, 236, 239

Woolf, Virginia (Stephen), 1, 3, 4, 6, 8, 9, 10, 16–20, 25–35, 36–8, 40–4, 50, 52–6, 64–7, 70–2, 74–7, 80–3, 109, 114, 115, 117–29, 137–9, 141–3, 148, 156, 157, 175, 176, 190, 193, 194, 210–12, 215, 218–20, 224, 226, 229, 231, 236, 240, 248, 253, 260, 276–93
Between the Acts, 52, 215
Flush, 8, 74
Freshwater, 109
Mrs Dalloway, 122, 123, 124, 128, 129, 130, 276, 277, 279–85
Orlando, 8, 36, 71, 74–6, 82, 83, 115, 118, 120–4, 126–9, 260
Room of One's Own, A, 18, 115, 119, 124, 215
Three Guineas, 1, 54, 55, 276, 291
To the Lighthouse, 33, 122, 124
Voyage Out, The, 124, 277
Waves, The, 33, 215, 276, 277, 285–7
Years, The, 276, 277, 285–8, 290, 291
World Bank, 91, 107
World War I, 9, 17, 23, 46, 76, 93, 110, 136, 143, 153, 240, 241, 191, 209, 211, 215, 244, 250, 253, 278, 279, 288, 289
World War II, 110, 153, 159, 167, 241, 288, 289